The Small Freezer C

Caroline Rennie was bor … although she has lived in … regards Scotland as her home.

Her varied career has included college lecturing in Aberdeen, services club management, public relations, cooking for television commercials, hotel staff training consultancy, teaching in a London comprehensive, lecturing on food and fabrics throughout the UK and even a spell of dressmaking for Thea Porter. The momentum and variety of her life are reflected in her recipes which aim for maximum effect with minimum time and effort.

Caroline spends her money on travel, expensive shoes, entertaining (which is how her recipes are tested), and her telephone bill. She hates women's lib, the idea of Scottish devolution, getting up in the morning, the tube at rush hour, oxtail, and men who can cook better than she can. She loves her dog, her god-daughter, roast beef, Chanel Number 5 and, of course, Scotland.

The Small Freezer Cookbook

Caroline Rennie

Fontana/Collins

First published in Fontana 1977
Made and printed in
Great Britain by
William Collins Sons and Co. Ltd,
Glasgow

Contents

Acknowledgements

For help and advice of a professional nature I would like to thank Professor Bender of the Department of Nutrition, Queen Elizabeth College; Jill MacWilliam of Bejam; June Copeland of the Metrication Board; Joan Peters of Metal Box; Lillianne Ransom of the Dairy Trades Federation; and the Home Economics Department of the Flour Advisory Bureau.

My thanks are also due to all my family and friends who suffered my various moods during the writing of this book, but most particularly to Jean for her generosity and work in deciphering my handwriting and typing all the recipes.

Introduction

Did you know that nearly 25 per cent of homes in Britain now have a freezer of some sort and that of those 25 per cent nearly half have fridge/freezers or small freezers of less than six cubic feet (170 litre)? That's an awful lot of small freezers – over a million.

It was this fact, together with pleas from friends both young and old, that made me realize that a whole 'new think' on this business of freezers was required. Most owners of small freezers are not concerned with catering for large families; what they want from their freezer is speed and ease first, with low cost a close second. Space is limited so the sides of beef and endless 'freeze-ups' of fresh garden produce are simply not relevant. Few working women relish spending weekends messing about in the kitchen being a slave to that 16 cubic feet (480 litre) effort in the garage; nor do they fancy living on omelets when they've got held up at work until all the shops are closed. Equally, the retired householder can often find the freezer 'an awful lot of work, dear'.

So I have put this book together to show how to make the small freezer *your* slave. It is specifically geared to working single people or couples, and to retired folk; in other words those who normally cook for one or two. But that is not to say that everything in the book cannot, with adaptation, be of equal use to the family freezer owner.

I have concentrated on recipes for high-class food which can be prepared with ease and speed. Although the recipes are written out using the conventional measures, I have included a section on handy measures which, when memorized, speed up food preparation. There's also information on packaging using the 'proper' materials, as well as improvisations; there's a calendar so you know when to pop into the freezer a little of your favourite fruit before it disappears off the market stall; for the novice cook, there's an explanation of general food and cookery terms; some advice on how to make dishes not only taste nice but look good, too; a guide to the value of foods; and, of course, there are recipes – 200 in all.

Many of these recipes are fairly sophisticated because I believe that, young executive or retired, this is often the sort of food you eat when you're out and long to be able to create at home. But such sophistication, as you will see, requires neither special cooking expertise nor hours of preparation. The recipes are divided into sections applicable to attitudes of mind or particular circumstances because eating is very often dictated by the prevailing mood – especially when the cook doesn't have a whole family to consider. There are times, however, when visitors arrive or nieces and nephews or grandchildren come to stay; hence the inclusion of 'People to Dinner', 'Instant Parties' and 'Children's Hour'.

Made-up dishes take up valuable space in the freezer so, although there are some of these, I have mainly concentrated on stocking the freezer with easily prepared basics which make assembly of a super meal both quick and easy.

For those who already have a small freezer, I hope that the following pages will help you make it earn its keep in sheer time-saving and, for those who think perhaps it isn't worth having a freezer, I hope it will encourage you to think again. Perhaps even the 20 cubic footers (600 litre) will learn a thing or two!

Part 1

CHAPTER 1

Healthy Eating

Good sleep and healthy eating combine to make a strong weapon against pressure, whatever your life-style. I can't do anything about your sleep, but I can give some pointers to healthy eating.

Personally, I believe that the key to good eating lies in its visual effect. If a meal is colour-balanced, and therefore looks appetizing, your digestion is well on the way to receiving that food willingly and will therefore make best use of it. The variety of texture is also very important, to say nothing of the quality of the cooking and the actual arrangement of it on the platter. In a later chapter I give some hints on the presentation of food. Sufficient to say at this stage that as far as food is concerned, eye-appeal is digestion-appeal. Long before the science of nutrition became such a talking-point, nature looked after itself: we thought mainly about the colours and textures of a dish and we've survived well enough. That said, let's be more specific.

Daily Dietary Requirements

We all know that calories are the units in which the energy value of food is measured, and that we need a certain number each day. But the straight calorie-counting that so many of us make a 'thing' about can be decidedly detrimental to health. For example, I could make up my calorie requirements of 2200 a day simply by eating just over half a small loaf of bread spread with just over half a standard block of butter. In the short-term I should have a good clear skin and a happy disposition because of the riboflavin and thiamin content, but overweight and internal digestive problems due to lack of other necessary nutrients would soon destroy the clear happy face. So don't be tempted to live on a very limited range of foods even if they do appear to satisfy your calorie or nutrient requirements. Eggs, for example, if eaten in excess, do more harm than good because the benefit gained from their cheap, high-protein content can be cancelled out by an over-sufficiency of fat and cholesterol which can, in extreme cases, lead to heart, liver and gall bladder troubles.

But few people would want to live on such a narrow diet, and on the whole you can eat what your 'fancy' dictates so long as you temper it with good sense.

Calorific intake

As far as calorific intake is concerned, rely on your appetite unless you are getting fat – then your appetite must be curbed. But as a general guide, men doing light manual work require 3000 calories a day, women in office jobs require 2200, and retired men and women need rather less. But don't forget that energy is used up rapidly in physical strain.

The provision of calories each day should come from each of the following:

milk
butter (*or, even better, margarine*)
bread (*wholemeal is best*)
an orange (*this gives your total vitamin C requirement*)
vegetables (*fresh or frozen; some green, some root*)
fruit
meat (4 *oz* (100 *gm*) *lean meat is sufficient, with fish, cheese or eggs as an alternative*)

Bear in mind that for variety some food should be hot and some cold. And include a beverage: four glasses of water a day, if you can manage it, makes sure your fluid needs are satisfied.

Nutrients, their Properties and Sources

Besides calories – or 'joules' in some EEC countries – what does food contain in the way of nutrients and what do they do?

Protein is used to build and repair worn-out body tissue and any excess is used for warmth and energy. If not enough energy-giving foods are taken, protein will first be used for warmth at the expense of its repair faculty. It is the only nutrient that can repair tissue, but it is not stored in the body so must be taken daily. No one in Britain is likely to be short of protein. *Some sources:* beef, chicken, pork, tuna fish, cheese, nuts, pulses.

Carbohydrates are sugars and starches which oxidize in the body and release energy for warmth, for work and to aid digestion and tissue building. Their energy value is reckoned in calories. *Some sources:* jams, jellies, cakes, pastries, bread, pasta, cereals.

Fats come in two categories – vegetable and animal, vegetable generally being lower in cholesterol. Fats are required for warmth. They give out more warmth than the corresponding amount of carbohydrate but take longer to release it. *Some sources:* butter, lard, margarine, nuts, egg yolk, pork, cheese.

Vitamins

A aids growth and fights colds, bronchitis and disease of the eyes, ears and nose. *Some sources:* spinach, liver, broccoli, apricots.

B_1 (***thiamin***) helps make carbohydrate available to the body and is necessary for the good condition of the nervous system. *Some sources:* wheatgerm, yeast.

B_2 (***riboflavin***) is similar to B_1 but deals with stimulating the appetite and keeping skin, mouth and nose free of rashes. *Some sources:* yeast, liver, wholemeal bread.

C (***ascorbic acid***) keeps gums in good order and teeth and bones strong. *Some sources:* green vegetables and fruit, especially oranges and lemons.

D (***the anti-rachitic factor***) works in conjunction with calcium to strengthen bones, teeth and nails. *Some sources:* oily fish and cheese (and sunshine and fresh air).

Minerals

Calcium works with vitamin D and is also needed for good muscle tone, coagulating blood and strong walls to blood vessels. *Some sources:* cheese, turnips, almonds.

Phosphorus also works with vitamin D to promote good muscle tone and strong bones. *Some sources:* cocoa, eggs, liver.

Sodium keeps blood in good condition. It is lost through sweating. *Main source:* the salt in your cooking.
Iron keeps the red corpuscles in the correct ratio in the blood stream and helps prevent anaemia. *Some sources:* liver, kidney, eggs, pulses.
Iodine is closely connected with the working of the thyroid gland which helps control the ratio of intake of food to output of energy. *Some sources:* sea foods, pulses and watercress (and sea bathing and sea air).

Those are the main nutrients and, contrary to some rumours, it has not been proved that freezing in any way alters the nutrients in food. In fact, bad or prolonged storage or transport time of 'fresh' food can destroy far more of the nutritional content than freezing ever did.

CHAPTER 2

Look, No Scales!

Accurate measurement of ingredients is essential for consistently good results. But some cooks don't own scales – an expensive and space-consuming piece of equipment – or can't be bothered to get them out each time. Some people reckon they have the knack of 'just knowing' what, say, 4 oz sugar looks like; others simply guess and are disappointed when recipes go wrong. So here is a guide to quick and easy measuring without using scales. All you need is a set of standard measuring spoons, a 5 fl. oz yogurt or cream pot and a pint milk bottle or carton.

Measuring without Scales

The comparative weights table that follows takes the guesswork out of your cooking – look, no scales!

Commodity	*Imperial*	*Metric*	*American*	*Handy*
Sugar, dried fruit and jam	4 oz	100 gm	½ cup	2 tblsps.
Flour, cornflour, icing sugar, oatmeal, suet, gelatine, cocoa and raw rice	4 oz	100 gm	½ cup	4 tblsps.
Grated cheese and ground almonds	4 oz	100 gm	½ cup	8 tblsps.
Fresh breadcrumbs	4 oz	100 gm	1 cup	16 tblsps.
Melted fats	4 oz	100 gm	½ cup	8 tblsps.
Liquids – ⅛ pt	2½ fl. oz	63 ml.	—	4 tblsps.
¼ pt	5 fl. oz	125 ml.	—	8 tblsps.
	8 fl. oz	190 ml.	1 cup (½ pt)	12 tblsps.
½ pt	10 fl. oz	250 ml.	—	16 tblsps.
	16 fl. oz	400 ml.	2 cups (1 pt)	24 tblsps.
1 pt	20 fl. oz	500 ml.	—	32 tblsps.

Spoonfuls: In this table and throughout the book, when reference is made to a spoon of something, it presumes a rounded spoonful unless a level or heaped spoonful is specifically stated – except, obviously, in the case of liquids. Although the standard spoon-set includes quarter- and half-teaspoons, these diagrams may be helpful.

Half Quarter *Level* *Rounded* *Heaped*

To measure ½ pint (250 ml.) using a milk bottle, fill the bottle to the top and then tip it until it is exactly horizontal and the liquid is only half way up the base. If using a carton, make a mark exactly half way up the side between the base and where it begins to slope inwards for the closure. Fill the carton up to the mark, holding it up to a strong light to check the level. Or, even more simply, use a 5 fl. oz (125 ml.) yogurt carton filled up twice.

Eggs weigh an average of 2 oz (50 gm) each for the standard size which is used in recipes unless expressly stated otherwise.

Usual Weights

Packs

Although the trend in packaging is towards metrication and standardization with EEC member countries, the change-over is very gradual and the standard metricated pack is still some way off.

Cans come in many sizes but, generally, the various commodities are packed as follows:

4½ oz	127 gm	Fish, vegetables, fruit and purée
5 oz	142 gm	Peas and beans
7 oz	199 gm	Meat and fish
8 oz	227 gm	Fish, meat, pies, beans, spaghetti and fruit
10 oz	284 gm	Soup, fish, meat, vegetables and fruit
11½ fl. oz	320 gm	Beverages
12 oz	341 gm	Meat
14 oz	397 gm	Fish, meat, vegetables and fruit
15 fl. oz	440 gm	Beverages
16 oz	454 gm	Soup, fish, meat, pies, vegetables, spaghetti, fruit and puddings

Bread usually comes in 14 oz (400 gm) or 28 oz (800 gm) loaves, though a variety of smaller weights are available. However, loaves over 14 oz (400 gm) have to be a multiple of that weight. There are 12 sandwich slices (or 10 toast slices) to the 14 oz loaf and 24 (20 toast) to the 28 oz one. But a change-over to show only metric weights on the wrapper is in process.

Fats are usually sold in 8 oz (227 gm) packs.

Ketchups come in 12 oz (340 gm), 15 oz (425 gm) and 1 lb 4 oz (567 gm) bottles or jars.

Sausages of the standard size are 8 to the lb (400 gm); the thin chipolatas are 16 to the lb (400 gm); and there is also a recent innovation of 10 to the lb (400 gm).

Rice and dried fruits have to be watched, for besides the 5 lb (2¼ kilo) bags now available in supermarkets, sometimes the pack may be a 1 lb (454 gm) size and sometimes only a 12 oz (340 gm) size.

Flour is now sold in metric packs of 500 gm (approx. 1 lb) and 1500 gm (approx. 3 lb).

Cream is another variable because producers of cream and yogurt are free to pack their product in whatever size of cartons they wish. As a result it is available in cartons of 2½ fl. oz (⅛ pt) (63 ml.), 5 fl. oz (¼ pt) (142 ml.), 8 fl. oz (227 ml.), 10 fl. oz (½ pt) (284 ml.), 16 fl. oz (448 ml.) and 20 fl. oz (1 pt) (568 ml.).

Yogurt is generally in either 5 fl. oz (¼ pt) (142 ml.) or 16 fl. oz (448 ml.) containers.

Sugar has gone metric. The old 2 lb bag now weighs 2.2 lb (1 kilo) and the 1 lb size is 1.1 lb (½ kilo).

Chocolate is also deceptive, so be careful. What looks like the old 2 oz bar now weighs 1.8 oz (50 gm) and the larger one is 3.5 oz (100 gm). Therefore recipes calling for 4 oz require more than one bar.

Note on Metrication: Throughout this book, metric equivalents of imperial measurements have been taken as 25 gm being a workable equivalent of 1 oz; 500 ml. to 1 pt; and 200°C for 400°F, Gas 6, as recommended by the Metrication Board. However, it should be noted that 1 oz is in fact 28.35 gm and 1 pint is really 568 ml. Quantities, therefore, will become progressively more inaccurate as the bulk increases. But don't worry too much because the Metrication Board, in collaboration with a working party of professional home economists, concluded that the 1 oz↔25 gm and the 1 pt↔500 ml. norm would be most easily understood and applied whilst still keeping the ratio of 'dry' to 'liquid' correct.

CHAPTER 3

In a Word

Many would-be cooks complain that it isn't that they wouldn't like to learn to cook or that they don't want to cook, it's merely that, fired with the enthusiasm of a newcomer they went out and bought a book that professed to be 'Easy Whatever', opened it up and it began 'take the basic roux . . .'! Exit one more potential Escoffier!

In this book I have tried to keep jargon to a minimum but for your own general information, here is a list of some of the more commonly used words and phrases and their meanings, plus a few snippets of information:

aigrette of an acid or sour character.
à la in the style of.
à la carte foods cooked to order.
Alderman's Walk the fillet on a sirloin of beef, so named because the City of London Aldermen used to walk up to the carving table to check that their delicious fillet was cut to their liking.
allspice dried unripe berry of the pimento, sometimes called Jamaica Pepper. It is hot and not at all like the mixed spice with which it is often confused.

almond paste more usually called marzipan.
aspic jelly a clear or slightly brown savoury jelly used to coat cold meat dishes or as a setting agent in place of gelatine for added flavour in a savoury dish.
au beurre with butter poured over, or cooked in butter.
au gratin cooked food coated in a sauce and then sprinkled with grated cheese and/or breadcrumbs and crisped and browned under a high grill or in a hot oven.
au naturel plainly or simply cooked with no added flavours or presentation.

bain marie a container of hot water into which is put a dish of food either to cook very slowly or to keep warm. It helps prevent drying out of food.
bake cook in the dry heat of an oven.
baking powder helps scones and cakes to rise. It will start reacting when liquid is added and continue during baking until exhausted or killed off by heat. It is added to flour and is normally a commercial preparation being a mixture of two parts of cream of tartar to one part of bicarbonate of soda with a small amount of rice flour mixed in to make it less prone to lumping.
baking soda bicarbonate of soda used to soften dried peas during soaking, to preserve colour in green vegetables during cooking and as a raising agent. It is also useful mixed with water for cleaning ovens – and, of course, your freezer.
Baron of beef the cut of beef consisting of two sirloins not cut apart. It is said that Henry VIII so loved his meat that he knighted 'Sir Loin' and elevated the 'Baron' to even higher noble status.
baste to pour hot fat or liquid over the top of food – usually meat – during cooking to keep it moist.
batter a beaten mixture of flour, eggs and milk or water used to make pancakes or to coat sweet or savoury food before frying or baking.
béchamel a basic, flavoured, white roux sauce. See recipe p. 47.
beestings the first milk given by cows after calving. Sometimes found in old recipes.
beignets the *haute cuisine* word for fritters.

beurre manie little pieces of roux (see p. 25) dropped into soups or stews to thicken.
blanche a method of facilitating the removal of skins from such things as nuts and tomatoes by dipping into boiling water and then plunging into cold water. The skins then slide off easily. Vegetables or fruit may be blanched to set the colour and/or par-cook (particularly for the freezer) by plunging them into already boiling water, boiling for a stated length of time, draining them and then immediately plunging them into ice-cold water to cool rapidly and stop further cooking.
blend mix to a smooth paste in the case of flour and water or merely to mix thoroughly and possibly gradually as in the case of the oil used in making of hollandaise or Malta sauce or a mayonnaise. It implies constant stirring.
boil cook in rapidly bubbling hot liquid.
bouillon good flavoured stock.
bouquet garni a bunch of mixed herbs and spices tied in a muslin bag and used for flavouring food during cooking. It is removed before serving the food. A basic bouquet garni consists of a bayleaf, six peppercorns, a blade of mace and a teaspoon of mixed herbs.
brace the word used to describe a pair of game birds. Thus, in old recipes, six game birds would be referred to as three brace.
braise to cook slowly in an enclosed pot, usually in the oven. The food is placed on a bed of mixed vegetables for moisture and flavour and the food is browned towards the end of the cooking-time by removing the lid and turning up the oven heat. It is a cross between roasting and stewing.
brine strongly salted water used for pickling, preserving colour or cleaning (shellfish). Sometimes sea fish is cooked in a brine.
broil to grill or spit roast. It is an American cooking term but is increasingly in use in the UK.
broiler usually refers to a young oven-ready chicken implying that it is tender enough for grilling or spit roasting.
brown butter butter that has been carefully heated until it is lightly browned. Used as a sauce.

candied peel sugared, dried, preserved rind of oranges, lemons and limes.

caramel sugar heated until almost black and toffee crisp when cold. Gravy browning is basically caramel dissolved in water and has virtually no flavour so may be used for sweet or savoury dish colouring.

casserole fireproof dish with a tight-fitting lid in which food is both cooked and served. It can also refer to the method of slow cooking in such a dish.

catsup the American word for ketchup.

chafe literally, to warm by friction but more usually used in the context of 'chafing-dish' which is a dish or small pan in which already cooked foods are gently reheated by shaking over a flame such as in flambé work in a high-class restaurant.

charcuterie cooked cold meats. The word is usually used in referring to the selection of cold meats on a buffet table.

chilled made cold in a refrigerator but not frozen as in a freezer.

chilli a very hot tropical vegetable used in minute quantity for flavouring.

choux a type of soft pastry which puffs up on cooking. See recipe for White Swans p. 201.

citrus fruits acidic fruits such as oranges, lemons, limes and grapefruit.

clarify means clear as in the case of consommé or butter by heating and then skimming off impurities.

cocotte a small fireproof dish used for cooking and serving an individual portion of such things as eggs, custards, creams and shellfish.

concassé chopped roughly, usually fruit or vegetables, particularly tomatoes.

conserve a rather posh word for jam.

consommé a clear soup.

corn starch the American word for cornflour.

cream the method of combining sugar and fat (usually butter or margarine) by beating them together in a basin until the mixture is paler in colour, light and fluffy and the texture of lightly whipped cream. The term can also refer to the blending together of yeast and sugar until liquid, as required in yeast cookery.

croûte a thick piece of fried bread used as a base on which to serve game, meat or fish.
croûtons small cubes or fancy shapes of fried bread or toast, used as garnish with puréed soups or meats such as mince.
curd the coagulated part of milk formed after the addition of acid or rennet.

dariole a small, usually cylindrical mould in which food is cooked and then turned out to serve. Caramel custards are often cooked in these.
devilled meat grilled with hot spices and usually served with a hot spiced sauce.
dice to cut into small cubes. Usually refers to bread, vegetables or meat.
dot to put small pieces of butter or another fat over the top of a dish before baking or grilling.
dredge to sprinkle liberally and usually refers to flour, seasoning or sugar.
dress to make look attractive; can refer to cooked (dressed salmon) or uncooked (dressed chicken) food.

échalote shallot, a small type of onion with a more penetrating but fine flavour.
éclair choux pastry piped into finger shapes before baking.
endive either chicory, or curly endive which is more like a slightly bitter tasting curly lettuce.
entrée a savoury dish served with a sauce and accompaniments. Nowadays, virtually the main course to a meal.
espagnol a basic flavoured brown roux sauce. See recipe, p. 50.
essence concentrated flavour extracted from a particular commodity, e.g. vanilla.

farce the old-fashioned word for stuffing, implying a meat content.
filbert a nut, very similar in every way to the hazelnut.
fillet the tenderest, leanest and most expensive cut of meat, e.g. fillet of pork, veal, beef or lamb. When applied to fish, it means a side of fish from which the bone has been removed.

fines herbes a mixture of chopped fresh (or frozen) herbs. The flavour is very delicate and is used with delicately flavoured foods such as eggs, veal and sole.

flake to break up cooked fish into its natural small pieces or 'flakes'.

flame, flambé to burn off hairs from poultry; or, more usually, to set a pan of sweet or savoury food alight by adding alcohol and heating quickly. This process is partly showmanship, but burning off the alcohol content of a liqueur added to a dish also results in a more subtle flavour and food that is less heavy on the digestion.

flavouring strictly speaking, a cheaper, chemically-made alternative to essence. In freezing, essences are preferable because they retain their true taste better than flavourings.

flour when a recipe calls for 'flour' it usually presumes plain flour. Otherwise, self-raising flour which already contains a raising agent is stated.

fold to mix in delicately, using a metal spoon.

forcemeat stuffing.

fricassé a white stew. Now more often used to describe cooked white meat in a well-flavoured béchamel sauce.

frosting a particular type of meringue cake icing; but in America it refers to any cake icing.

frothing a traditional method of giving roasted game and poultry a nice crispy, 'frothy' skin. Just before the end of cooking time, sprinkle the breast liberally with flour and turn up the oven heat.

galantine a cold pressed meat or meat loaf usually decorated in a very elaborate fashion.

game the name given to all edible wild animals and birds.

garni garnished or decorated.

glace ice.

glacé frozen, candied or covered with an aspic or jelly glaze.

glaze to make food shine, either by brushing pastry with egg or milk before baking or, in the case of cold dishes, by covering with a thin coating of jelly, aspic or gelatine.

griddle, girdle a flat, smooth metal plate used for cooking scones.

grilse a young salmon.

jugged casserole-cooked meat, poultry or game.
junket milk that is flavoured, sweetened and thickened with rennet.

knead the method of lightly working pastry with the fingertips (or fists in the case of yeast dough) on a floured board until the pastry is smooth.

larding strictly speaking, a method of keeping roasting meat moist by 'sewing' thin strips of fat bacon into the breast of rather dry poultry or game or very lean meat before roasting. Special larding needles are used. Often the word 'larding' is used instead of the correct 'barding' which actually means simply laying strips of fat bacon over such meats before roasting.
love apple the old name for a tomato.

macédoine a mixture of diced vegetables or fruit.
marinade either the practice of soaking uncooked fish, meat or poultry in vinegar with oil, various herbs, spices and flavourings added; or the mixture itself. It is done to tenderize as well as to flavour.
mask to cover completely, usually with a sauce or mayonnaise.
mirepoix the bed of vegetables on which food is braised.
mornay in a cheese sauce.

panada a very thick roux sauce used as a base for choux pastry, croquettes, etc.
parboil to half-cook by boiling.
pikelet the North of England name for the English crumpet.
pinch the amount that can be lifted between the first finger and the thumb. More accurately, it is reckoned to be ¼ teaspoon.
piquant tastes pleasantly sharp.
pluck either, to remove the feathers of poultry or game birds; or, the composite name of the liver, heart and lights (lungs) of animals.
purée a smooth pulp of fruit or vegetables that have been rubbed through a sieve or liquidized.

receipt the old-fashioned word for recipe.

réchauffé a reheated dish, e.g. shepherds' pie, in which previously cooked food is made up into another dish and made hot a second time.

roux a paste made from equal quantities of fat and flour, heated, well beaten together and cooked until very thick. This is used as a basis for various sauces made by gradually beating in liquid.

rub in the method by which fat is combined with flour in cake- or pastry-making. The fat and flour is gently rubbed together with the fingertips while lifting the hands about 8 inches (20 cm.) above the basin and allowing the mixture to fall through the fingers and back into the basin. This allows air to add to the lightness of the end product. When properly rubbed in, the fat and flour mixture should look like fine white breadcrumbs.

sauté tossed in fat or butter in a pan over a quick heat.

score to make several close cuts, usually across the skin of meat or fish, before cooking.

seal, sear to brown the surface of meat quickly, either under or over a quick heat.

seasoned flour flour with salt and pepper added.

seasoning usually simply means salt and pepper but can also include herbs and spices.

separate with reference to eggs means to break open the raw egg and divide the yolk from the white by holding the yolk in the half shell and letting the white drop into a basin.

shaddock another name for grapefruit.

shortening any edible fat used in pastry making. This is the word usually used in America.

shred to slice in fine pieces.

simmer to cook over a low heat so that the cooking liquid is just below boiling point and the air bubbles are only occasionally breaking the surface.

sippets another word for croûtons.

skillet is an American word meaning a cooking pot but in UK it presumes a small, shallow, two-handled frying pan with a lid.

syrup a mixture of sugar and water or of sugar and fruit juice that is boiled to obtain the required degree of stickiness.

tepid lukewarm or blood heat.
truss to fasten with string the legs and wings of poultry and game to make ready for cooking.

zest the outer, coloured part of the skin of citrus fruits. This is the part that has all the flavour. The pith, or white bit of the skin, is bitter and if used will damage flavour. When grated rind or zest is required, grate gently and use only this coloured part. Sometimes, for sweet dishes, the zest is rubbed off the fruit with a sugar lump.

CHAPTER 4

What About the Small Freezer?

All the advice says 'buy the biggest freezer you can afford and have room for'. But it may well be just that latter point that is the restricter. Perhaps you live in a city flat where space is at a premium and garages are almost unheard of, or perhaps you are a working couple, who, for all sorts of reasons, have only a small house. At the other end of the age scale, you may have retired to that cottage in the country now the family have all left home and feel you would simply have no use for a massive 16 cubic feet (480 litre) freezer besides not wanting the work involved. Whatever your reason, you have decided on a small freezer.

To get real value from a small freezer, much careful planning is necessary. The planning starts with the type of freezer. By a small freezer, one must understand anything from 1.5 cubic feet (40 litre) to 6 cubic feet (170 litre) and all but the very smallest may be obtained in the guise of chest, upright or combination. Thus, the first thing to determine is what size and shape you can best accommodate.

If you do not already have a fridge and you intend siting your freezer in the kitchen, then possibly the combination type (also known as a fridge/freezer) is your answer. The floor space used is then only such as a fridge would use. On the market there are three types of combination freezer – **1** those where the two units are of the same capacity with either the freezer standing on top of the fridge or vice versa (the fridge on top means less bending), **2** those where a small freezer tops a much larger fridge (here it is as well to check that the unit really is a freezer and not merely a conservator) and **3** a relatively new innovation where the fridge is sensibly about one third the size of the freezer.

Should you already have a fridge, you will probably want to choose an entirely separate freezer unit. The main consideration is whether you prefer opening a door or lifting a lid. As the unit is a small one, the disadvantage of cold loss in the upright, and of acrobatics required to reach the bottom of the chest varieties hardly pertain. It may also be worth noting that if you are going to incorporate the freezer in a fitted kitchen, the necessity of lifting a lid can be most inconvenient at times. On the other hand, chest freezers in a wood grain finish can unobtrusively become part of the furniture in a sitting-room, bedroom or hall if lack of space necessitates such a measure. In fact, cabinets are now made in a variety of colours to suit your décor.

Each type is obtainable with any one of three different condensers – that's the working part. There is the *skin* model where the condenser is fitted inside the outer casing of the freezer so that there is no projection. If space, particularly depth, is very limited, it's a skin model for you. The more conventional type – the one that protrudes at the back – is called a *static* condenser. Should any repair be necessary (and it seldom is), it is marginally more simple to carry out on this type. The third type, designed for freezers that have to be kept in a place where there is limited air circulation or where the temperature is high such as in hot countries, centrally heated rooms or warm kitchens, is *fan-assisted.* This type is also said to lower the temperature in the fast-freeze section even below the normal —23°C. Again, there is little to set any one condenser above the other – it may simply be a case of what's available. But a word of warning: do find out if the condenser makes a noise and what sort of noise! I stayed in a house recently where I nearly jumped out of my skin when the freezer suddenly came to life in the middle of the night – and it was two rooms away!

All the freezers are provided with racks or baskets and all have a special fast-freeze or super-freeze compartment in which to freeze down fresh food. Some have locks – useful if the freezer is going to have to sit on a communal landing.

The most usual capacities for small freezers are 1.5 cubic feet (45 litre), 2.3 cubic feet (65 litre), 3.5 cubic feet (100 litre), 4.1 cubic feet (120 litre), 5.4 cubic feet (150 litre), 5.8 cubic feet (165 litre) and 6.7 cubic feet (180 litre) and most of those available in the UK are made in Denmark, Sweden, Italy, France or Eire, though a few are indeed manufactured in Britain. But whatever the country of origin, if you buy from a reputable dealer, spares (if ever necessary) will be no problem.

Before finally deciding, do remember that 1 cubic foot (30 litre) of freezer space will accommodate about 20 lb (10 kilo) of frozen food depending on the shape and density of the commodities and your packing skill. This is an awful lot of food that can cost a deal of money so note that most freezer centres, besides having a range of freezers and bulk food packs to tempt you, also run purchase schemes to cover the massive initial cost of both freezer and food.

CHAPTER 5

Wrap It Up

A great deal of unjustified mystery and expense is sometimes attached to the packaging of frozen food. It's easy and definitely need not be expensive. The main thing is to use a moistureproof and vapourproof wrapping; to exclude as much air as possible from the pack, so minimizing food texture spoilage through freeze drying; and to label things carefully for your own convenience.

Most stationery departments in large stores and, of course, freezer centres stock a range of 'purpose-built' frozen food wrappings. Buy carefully, otherwise you will find you have an unnecessarily enormous bill when you get to the checkout. A good basic stock for a small freezer may even be limited to a good selection of freezer bags with twist ties, a roll of aluminium freezer foil, several rigid containers either of plastic or the less-expensive waxed cardboard – and, of course, a roll of tape and a few labels. However, the choice is ultimately yours – you know what commodities you are going to put in the freezer. So, what's available?

Commercial Packing Materials

Polythene bags for the freezer must be of good quality (120–150 gauge) otherwise they become brittle and tear easily at freezing temperatures. You can buy suitable polythene freezer bags by the roll or in packets of uniform or varied sizes. Some have a 'label' printed on them and there are even coloured bags on the market which could be of use for a colour coding system. All packs include wire twist closures. Polythene bags may be used for any commodity at all and, providing they are cleaned thoroughly, dried well and not damaged, can be used several times. A recent addition to the range of polythene bags is the *boil-in-the-bag* which is excellent for cutting down the washing-up. However, these cost rather more than the ordinary variety and can be used only once. For real space saving, buy the bags with gussets in them.

Polythene film or layering tissue is a more specialized item of freezer packaging and, unless you are making hamburgers or pancakes by the hundred, I would think it hardly a justifiable expense. It usually comes in boxes of 50 sheets and is used to separate the individual items in packs of hamburgers, pancakes, chops, steaks or slices of cake. Frankly, oiled greaseproof paper or butcher's paper works just as well.

Foil is another item of wrapping that can be used for anything except liquids and is particularly useful for wrapping irregularly shaped things such as poultry as it will fit close to exclude air. Foil packs ought to be sealed with freezer tape and it is important that the heavy freezer quality be used otherwise it will puncture easily. The advantage of foil over bags is that it fits more closely; the disadvantages are that it can't really be re-used, nor can one easily identify the contents of a foil-wrapped pack. Labelling has to be clear and secure. For economy, buy the biggest and widest roll you can find. Also under the heading of foil comes *foil containers.* All sorts of shapes and sizes are available and are useful for stews, pies and non-acidic liquids. Some packs include lids; don't bother with these. Save yourself some money and use foil to cover the dishes because the lids can be used only once anyway. Cheaper than waxed cartons, stronger than polythene bags and less prone to discoloration than plastic are *polythene-lined foil bags.* These are usually available in packs of six and may be re-used several times.

Cling film is now available in rolls of heavier weight than formerly so it is less liable to splitting and puncturing at low temperatures. It has the same uses as foil but has the added advantage of being transparent.

Waxed cartons are cheaper than plastic containers but, despite having several lives, are not quite as longlasting. Waxed cartons hold a rigid shape which, besides looking neater in the freezer than misshapen bags of frozen liquids or fruits, actually save space because of their packability. They are useful for soups, fruit or vegetable purée, sauces and easily damaged fruits. However, do make a habit of lining them with a polythene bag – it makes cleaning for re-use easier and prevents staining from strongly coloured contents. The closures on waxed cartons should be taped.

Plastic boxes look all very pristine and professional but they are expensive. So what price glamour? Do not be persuaded that you must have lots of lovely Tupperware. Unnecessary. But if you do decide to invest, even very gradually, do buy a good quality – slightly pliable as rigid plastic is prone to splitting if subjected to extremes of temperature – and with very-well-fitting lids. The sizes you choose should be appropriate to your needs but remember that square and oblong boxes take up less space than round ones. I will concede, however, that plastic boxes are best for packing cream, whirls, meringues, biscuits and fancy gâteaux which are so fragile when frozen crisp.

Improvised Packing Materials

So, there are plenty of freezer packaging items that you can go out and spend your money on. But what is there around the kitchen that could be used just as well and might otherwise simply find itself in the bin?

Yogurt and cream pots of various sizes – wash well and seal with foil or cling film. Use for sauces, soups, purées, chocolate curls, etc.

Margarine cartons with well-fitting lids – wash them and use for the same sort of items as above as well as for icecream.

Plastic pots with lids in which you buy local cream cheese or the taramosalata or bean salad from the 'deli.'. Great for small quantities of sauce, grated chocolate, nuts, herbs, etc.

Waxed milk cartons washed well and lined with a polythene bag are every bit as good and as useful as the specially bought variety. Use for sauces, soups, etc.

Waxed paper or polystyrene cups – for hygiene's sake, do not use cups that have been drunk out of; but those previously used for freezing food may safely be re-used. Cover with foil or cling film and seal well. It's a good idea to line them with a small polythene bag to prevent discoloration. Use for grated cheese, breadcrumbs, sauces and small quantities of soup.

Plastic egg cartons are actually quite useful for freezing cubes of concentrated stock or flavoured ice or icecream for drinks, but do make sure that the boxes are not split and that they are sealed carefully. In case of accidents, I would overwrap such items in a polythene bag.

Foil dishes from the Chinese take-away or from commercially frozen foods. Wash well and use for the same things as the specially bought variety. Seal with foil or cling film.

Sugar boxes are useful for shaping liquids in the freezer so that they pack better. Line the box with a polythene bag, pour in the liquid, seal the bag and freeze. When frozen, remove the outer box and you will be left with a neat oblong or square shape. These boxes (lined, of course) make an economical protection for fragile items.

Cooking or serving dishes themselves are of use, not to leave in the freezer for any length of time, but merely to shape the food. Line the container with foil, pour in the soup, stew or whatever and freeze it. Then remove the food and foil from the dish and overwrap the food before returning it to the freezer. When required, merely unwrap the food and place the frozen block in the original dish.

Sponge sandwich tins are useful for shaping such items as icecream that I want eventually to decorate and serve like a cake or that I know I am going to use on top of a pavlova or sponge base. Line the tin with foil, pour in the food, freeze it and then remove the tin and rewrap the item before returning it to the freezer.

Labelling

Whether you choose to use 'purpose-built' or 'instant-to-hand' items for packing food for the freezer, labelling is of great importance. You can buy packs of coloured tie-on or special sticky labels (ordinary gummed labels won't stay on). Do use a felt pen or a chinagraph pencil as ordinary ink or lead fades to invisibility at freezing temperatures. The essentials to put on the label of each item are commodity, quantity and date but on some items of prepared foods I also like to note reheating instructions.

Finally, if you pack carefully and try to group like items together, it will save a great deal of time otherwise spent rummaging around hunting for the one ingredient you then discover you've run out of after all!

CHAPTER 6

Good Results

A freezer will preserve miracles but it will not create them. You will get out of it exactly what you put in. So make sure that you put good quality food, properly prepared, into a correctly functioning freezer and keep it no longer than the advised time.

Freezer Care

The first essential for good results is care and maintenance of the freezer:

1 Try to site the freezer in the coolest place possible – certainly not next to the cooker.
2 Keep racks and baskets in good condition so they do not damage food packs.
3 Make sure the electricity is not accidentally switched off. Tape the switch down if necessary, or have it on an independent circuit.
4 When you go on holiday, be sure to leave the freezer on.
5 Do not put hot food into the freezer.
6 Do not put more than 10 per cent of the freezer's total capacity of fresh food into the freezer for freezing down every 24 hours.
7 Check every couple of months or so that the temperature is correct. It should be at most —18°C in the main section and —23°C for fast-freeze.
8 Do not open the freezer any more frequently than is absolutely necessary.
9 See that the lid or door is firmly shut and that the seal is in good condition.
10 Do not keep glass bottles of liquid, especially fizzy liquids, or cans of beer in the freezer. They can easily blow up and, besides being messy and dangerous, can irreparably injure your freezer.
11 Try not to spill things in the freezer – and if you do, mop up any spills immediately!
12 Do not put items wrapped in ordinary paper into the freezer as the paper will stick to the walls. It will not protect the food sufficiently, either.
13 Never be tempted to scrape ice off the inside with a metal object. It can so easily slip and a punctured lining means a new freezer. Help defrosting, if necessary, by placing a bowl of warm water in the empty freezer.
14 Defrost the freezer regularly and wipe it out with a solution of bicarbonate of soda and warm water – not hot soapy water – and dry it thoroughly.
15 After cleaning, or when new, make sure the freezer is down to the right temperature before you put the food in.

16 In the case of a breakdown, call in help immediately. (This should hardly, if ever, happen as there is so little to go wrong in a freezer.)

17 Try and take out some sort of insurance policy against food spoilage through a faulty freezer or accidentally switching the current off. Far too much money is at stake these days to risk being uninsured. It is also worth noting that the smell of rotten food is virtually unshiftable and often necessitates a replacement freezer as well as food.

Food Care

1 Choose prime quality food (see 'Seasonal Savings').

2 Make sure that everything connected with freezing is very clean as most 'bugs' are not killed off by freezing, they merely hibernate. This is another reason for reconstituting food carefully.

3 Since the accent in this book is on speed and the small freezer, do keep a good balance of prepared basics and commercially frozen foods as relevant to your eating habits (see 'Food for Freezing').

4 Prepare it properly (see 'Food for Freezing').

5 Portion food, if appropriate, before it is frozen.

6 Avoid commodities that won't freeze (see 'Food for Freezing').

7 Package it properly (see 'Wrap It Up').

8 When carrying commercially frozen foods home from the supermarket, do wrap them in plenty of newspaper to help keep them cold, or carry the food in one of these special thermal bags, or ask for it to be packed with a piece of dry ice as is the practice of some of the more expensive stores. N.B. On no account handle the dry ice without gloves; it would burn you badly!

9 Do not refreeze thawed food unless it still has some ice crystals in it or unless it is cooked before being refrozen.

10 When defrosting the freezer, remove any food, wrap it in several thicknesses of chilled newspaper and put it in a cold place. It will last for up to 10 hours easily like this.

11 If the freezer does break down or there is an electricity cut,

keep the lid closed. The food will last a good 18 hours like this.

12 Do not keep frozen food beyond the recommended time (see 'Food for Freezing').

13 Allow pâtés, game, fruit cakes and Christmas puddings to mature before freezing, as they will not do so either during freezing or on thawing.

14 Make sure you reconstitute, thaw or reheat the frozen food properly (see 'Food for Freezing' and 'Food for Eating').

15 Do experiment – but in small quantities until you are sure it works!

16 Remember that freezing does not alter the nutritional value of food, but your cooking or handling might – so do things correctly!

Pay attention to all these bits and pieces of advice and I reckon that even those who profess to 'hate frozen food' won't know it is anything other than prime quality fresh produce. Then you can smile sweetly and say, 'Of course, my dear!'!

CHAPTER 7

Seasonal Savings

The limited freezer space, to say nothing of the limited time available, presupposes that most of the stocks of food in your freezer will be commercially prepared. However, there will be occasions when you are either given or feel like buying the fresh article and then want to pop it in the freezer for future use. Or you may not be able to find some of the more unusual foodstuffs in commercial food packs and will want to buy the fresh item.

As already mentioned, it is important to put only prime quality fresh produce into the freezer for best results. So here are some hints on choosing for quality, followed by a chart showing when certain foods are at their fresh best for freezing. This is in no way meant to be a comprehensive list of all fresh foods – only some of those that may be less readily available in commercially frozen packs.

Quality Pointers for Fresh Food

All commodities should look and smell fresh.

Beef lean should be darkish red with 'marbling' of fat through it; and the fat should be firm and creamy yellow.

Lamb should have creamy-yellow hard fat and the lean may be any shade from medium pink to cherry red.

Pork should have firm, pinkish lean meat with any fat firm and creamy.

Veal should be pale pink and such fat as there is should be firm and white.

Poultry should be plump and firm. The flesh ought to be creamy-white and free of bruises. The skin must be undamaged. In a young bird, the breast bone should feel pliable.

White fish ought to feel firm and be an unblemished white.

Oily fish should again smell fresh, feel firm but pliable and the skin must be bright and silvery.

Shellfish may smell distinctly of the sea, but it should still seem fresh. The shells ought to be undamaged and clear coloured. The flesh inside should be firm and again clear coloured – either pink, white or whatever depending on the species.

Green vegetables should be crisp and firm without any discoloured parts.

Root vegetables should look neither dry and wizened nor damp and mouldy. They ought to feel firm, and be free of blemishes, hacks and extra soil adhering to them.

Salad vegetables must be firm and crisp without blemish or discoloration.

Hard fruits are again firm, unbruised and the appropriate bright colour.

Semi-soft fruits such as pears, melons and avocados ought to be free of blemishes and bruises but, for ripeness, should yield a little to gentle pressure at the stalk end.

Soft fruits should be firm and dry as well as unblemished. The colour should be even.

Citrus fruits ought to be on the soft side for maximum juiciness, and have thin skins. If you wish to use the rind, obviously it ought to be a good clear, unblemished colour; but blemished skin does not mean that the inside is necessarily less than first class.

At Their Fresh Best for Freezing in UK

Fruit	*January*	*February*	*March*	*April*	*May*	*June*	*July*	*August*	*September*	*October*	*November*	*December*
Apricots	●	●			●	●	●	●				
Blackberries								●	●			
Blackcurrants							●	●				
Cherries						●	●	●				
Cranberries	●										●	●
Damsons									●	●		
Figs							●	●	●			
Gooseberries							●	●				
Grapes							●	●				
Limes							●	●				

	January	*February*	*March*	*April*	*May*	*June*	*July*	*August*	*September*	*October*	*November*	*December*
Loganberries								●				
Mangoes						●	●					
Melons									●	●		
Nectarines and Peaches						●	●	●				
Oranges – Seville	●	●										
Pears									●	●		
Pineapples	●	●	●		●	●						
Plums								●	●	●		
Pumpkin										●		
Raspberries						●	●					
Redcurrants							●	●				
Rhubarb				●	●	●						
Strawberries						●	●					
Vegetables												
Artichokes							●	●	●			
Asparagus					●	●						
Aubergines	●	●	●	●	●	●	●	●	●	●		
Avocados		●										●
Beetroot						●	●	●	●	●		
Broccoli	●	●			●	●			●		●	●
Celery	●	●									●	●
Chestnuts										●	●	
Herbs							●					
Horseradish	●	●	●					●		●	●	●
Leeks	●	●										
Marrow								●	●	●		
Tomatoes					●	●	●	●	●			
Fish & Game												
Crab						●	●	●				
Grouse								●	●	●	●	
Guinea Fowl	●			●		●	●	●	●			
Halibut	●	●	●	●	●	●						

	January	*February*	*March*	*April*	*May*	*June*	*July*	*August*	*September*	*October*	*November*	*December*
Lobster						●	●	●				
Partridge	●									●	●	●
Pheasant	●									●	●	●
Pigeon	●		●	●		●	●	●	●			
Salmon		●	●	●	●	●	●	●				
Scallops	●	●	●							●	●	●
Turkey			●	●						●	●	
Venison						●	●	●	●	●	●	●
Wild Duck	●								●	●	●	●

Part 2

CHAPTER 8

Food for Freezing

The idea behind this book is to get sophisticated meals easily and quickly from the small freezer – so everything should be to hand. Thus, I have drawn up a list of freezer contents from which, in conjunction with a good store cupboard and comprehensive spice rack, you could prepare any recipe from the next two chapters at the drop of a hat.

The amount of each commodity that you decide to keep will depend on how often you are likely to use it.

A final word of warning – ***do not try to freeze:***

items with a high gelatine content such as jelly or aspic shapes

green salad vegetables with a high water content like lettuce, cucumber or watercress

avocados or bananas unless puréed and mixed with lemon juice or something else such as cream, flour, etc.

single cream

water melon

eggs still in their shells – they'll burst!

Freezer Stock:

	Preparation	*Packing*	*Thawing*
Vegetables:			
artichoke bottoms	blanched 8 minutes	polythene bag	use frozen
asparagus	commercial pack		
aubergine	sliced & blanched 3 minutes	plastic box	use frozen
avocado purée	lemon juice added	plastic tub	3–4 hours

	Preparation	*Packing*	*Thawing*
baby beetroots	commercial pack		
baby roast potatoes	commercial pack		
broad beans	commercial pack		
brussels sprouts	commercial pack		
carrots	commercial pack		
cauliflower	commercial pack		
chips	commercial pack		
chopped celery	commercial pack		
courgettes	commercial pack		
green beans	commercial pack		
horseradish	grated	plastic tub	3–4 hours
leeks	chopped & blanched 2 minutes	polythene bag	use frozen
mushrooms	commercial pack		
onion – chopped	commercial pack		
peas	commercial pack		
potato whirls	see basic recipe		
pumpkin purée	as for fruit purée	plastic tub	1 hour
sauté potatoes	commercial pack		
shredded cabbage	commercial pack		
spinach – leaf	commercial pack		
stew pack mixed	commercial pack		
sweetcorn	commercial pack		
sweet peppers	commercial pack		
tomatoes	commercial pack		
tomato purée	see basic recipe		

Fruit:

apple slices	blanched 2 minutes	polythene bag	2 hours
apricot halves	in basic syrup	plastic box	4 hours
cherries	stoned, in basic syrup	plastic box	3 hours
chestnut purée	see basic recipe		
citrus fruit shells	empty and washed	polythene bag	2 hours
fruit – selection	commercial packs		
fruit purées	see basic recipe		
grapefruit – juice	commercial pack (concentrated)		

	Preparation	*Packing*	*Thawing*
grapefruit – rind	in thin strips	plastic tub	none
icecreams	commercial packs or see 'Food for Eating'		
lemon – juice	pips removed	plastic tub	2 hours
lemon – rind	in thin strips	plastic tub	none
lemon – slices	packed tightly	plastic tub	use frozen
melon balls	commercial pack		
mousses – various	commercial packs or see 'Food for Eating'		
orange – juice	commercial pack (concentrated)		
orange – rind	in thin strips	plastic tub	none
orange – slices	packed tightly	plastic tub	use frozen
peach halves	in basic syrup	plastic box	5 hours
rhubarb	commercial pack		
sorbets – various	commercial or see 'Food for Eating'		
Stocks & Sauces:			
béchamel sauce	see basic recipe		
beef stock	see basic recipe		
chicken stock	see basic recipe		
espagnol sauce	see basic recipe		
fish stock	see basic recipe		
St Honoré cream	see Gâteau St Honoré p. 188		
velouté sauce	see basic recipe		
Meat:			
bacon	unopened vacuum pack	in pack	4 hours
chicken – joints	cooked and uncooked	foil	overnight
chicken – roll	cooked	foil	overnight
chicken – whole	uncooked	foil	overnight
gammon – roll	cooked or uncooked	foil	overnight
guinea fowl	uncooked	foil	overnight
leftover meat or game – selection	cooked	polythene bag	6–8 hours
sausages	uncooked	polythene bag	6–8 hours

	Preparation	*Packing*	*Thawing*
small cuts of beef, lamb, veal, pork including offal	commercial packs		
turkey – roll	cooked or uncooked	foil	overnight
Fish:			
herrings	clean and wash	polythene bag	4–6 hours
kipper fillets	commercial pack		
prawns	commercial pack		
salmon – meat	cooked leftover	foil	3–4 hours
salmon – steaks	commercial pack		
salmon – smoked	commercial pack		
salmon trout	clean and wash	foil	overnight
smoked cod's roe	cooked	plastic box	3–4 hours
smoked haddock	commercial pack		
smoked mackerel	none	foil	3–4 hours
trout	commercial pack		
whitebait	commercial pack		
white fish – various	commercial packs		
Bakery Items:			
basic sponge	see basic recipe		
bread	whole or sliced	polythene bag	3 hours or use slices frozen
breadcrumbs	brown and white	polythene bag	none
bread – dough	commercial pack		
choux pastry puffs	see White Swans p. 201		
croûtons	dice and fry bread	plastic box	use frozen
flaky pastry	see basic recipe		
fritter batter	see Surprise Apricot Fritters p. 164		
pancakes	see basic recipe		
puff pastry	commercial pack		
shortcrust pastry	commercial pack		
yeast	fresh	polythene bag	none

	Preparation	*Packing*	*Thawing*
Dairy Produce:			
cheese – grated	none	polythene bag	none
cheese – hard	cut in blocks	foil	time dependent on size
cream – double	whip lightly	plastic tub	2 hours
cream – soured	none	in tub	2 hours
cream – whirls	whip, sweeten and pipe on to tray	plastic box	use frozen
flavoured butters	see basic recipes		
meringue shells	see basic recipe		
milk	use homogenized	in carton	3–4 hours
yogurt – various	none	in tub	1–2 hours beat to blend
Miscellaneous:			
chocolate curls	see 'Looking Good'	plastic box	none
herbs – various	see 'Looking Good'	polythene bag	use frozen
ice cubes – plain and fancy	spray with soda water	polythene bag	use frozen
nuts – various	see 'Looking Good'	plastic tub	none
rice – cooked	see basic recipe		

Keeping Times

In order to preserve the first-class colour, texture and flavour of frozen foods, it is important to know how long they will keep. On commercially frozen packs it is usually marked for how long they will store in tip-top condition in your freezer. Here is a guide to keeping times for commodities you freeze yourself.

Meat	beef, lamb and poultry	12 months
	pork	10 months
	game	6 months
	bacon, sausages, offal	4 months
Fish	white fish	12 months
	shellfish	10 months
	oily fish	8 months

Vegetables	all	12 months
Fruit	most	12 months
	citrus	6 months
Dairy produce	eggs (lightly beaten)	12 months
	cheese	6 months
	soft cheese, cream	4 months
	icecream, butter	3 months
	homogenized milk	1 month
Bakery items	yeast, sponges, batter	8 months
	pastry	3 months
Made-up dishes	cooked meat or poultry	1 month
	others	4 months

CHAPTER 9

Cook for Freezing

So much for the stock list and keeping times. Now here are the *Basic Recipes* you may need:

Basic Sponge

Take *an egg* (see p. 16) and its weight in *self-raising flour, soft margarine* and *caster sugar*

To make Put everything into a basin and whisk it all together until it is light and fluffy and the consistency of whipped cream.

Divide the mixture into lined sandwich tins or bun tins and bake in the oven preheated to 360°F, Gas 4–5 (185°C), for 10–12 minutes for buns and 30–35 minutes for cakes.

To freeze Cool thoroughly and pack in polythene bags, separating the sandwiches with foil. Seal, label, date and freeze.

To use Take the required amount from the freezer and allow to thaw at room temperature and still wrapped for 2 hours.

Note One egg makes 9–12 buns and 3 eggs make 2 7-inch (17-cm.) sponge sandwiches. Endless variations are possible from this basic; just remember to keep the proportions of dry ingredients to the other ingredients constant. However, you may safely add 1 tablespoon of liquid such as coffee or orange juice without destroying the proportions.

Basic Syrup

1 lb (400 gm) granulated sugar
1 pt (500 ml.) water

To make Boil the sugar and the water together for 10 minutes.

To freeze Do not freeze this basic syrup unless it is being used to freeze fruits such as peaches; it is not worth it.

To use Use this as the basis of water ices, etc., or add flavouring such as rum to make a useful sauce.

Béchamel Sauce

1 pt (500 ml.) milk
1 bayleaf
1 small onion
6 cloves
½ teaspoon salt
2 oz (50 gm) butter
2 oz (50 gm) flour
salt & pepper

To make Put all the ingredients except the last three into a small saucepan and bring gently to the boil. Remove from the heat and set aside to cool. Meantime, melt the butter gently in another saucepan and beat in the flour. Cook, stirring constantly, until the mixture thickens. This is called a roux. Take the pan off the heat and gradually beat in the strained milk. Make sure no lumps form at this stage. Return the pan to a low heat and stir constantly until the sauce coats the back of the spoon and is very smooth and shiny. Season with salt and pepper.

To freeze Pack the sauce into appropriately sized plastic pots with lids. Leave ½ inch (1 cm.) space at the top. Seal, label, date and freeze.

To use Take the required amount of sauce from the freezer, turn it into a saucepan and heat very gently until thawed. If it separates out, beat it very well until it is smooth again. This is a coating sauce so you may want to thin it down; in which case, beat in a little warm milk or vegetable liquor until it is the consistency required.

Note Béchamel sauce made with cornflour instead of flour is less apt to separate but I prefer the flavour and consistency of this method.

Butters

Take:	4 oz (100 gm) butter
for *Maître d'Hôtel* add:	2 teaspoons crumbled parsley 2 teaspoons lemon juice salt & pepper ¼ teaspoon cayenne pepper
Tarragon	2 teaspoons crumbled tarragon salt & pepper
Lemon (*Meunière*)	3 teaspoons lemon juice 2 teaspoons grated lemon rind salt & pepper
Tomato	2 tablespoons tomato purée
Sweet Pepper	3 tablespoons puréed sweet peppers

Mustard	1 tablespoon made mustard
Paprika	1 dessertspoon paprika pepper
Horseradish	1 tablespoon finely grated horseradish
Chive	1 tablespoon finely chopped chives
Anchovy	1 tablespoon anchovy essence

To make In all cases, soften the butter in a small basin using a spatula, then blend in thoroughly the appropriate flavouring. Shape the butter into a roll ¾ inch (2 cm.) in diameter. Wrap in foil.

To freeze Overwrap in a polythene bag, seal, label, date and freeze.

To use Take the appropriate butter from the freezer, unwrap it and cut off the necessary number of slices. Use these pats to top hot or cold food.

Note Sweet butters such as rum, cinnamon, hazelnut, almond, pistachio, chocolate, are made in the same way but adding sugar if necessary and chopping ingredients very finely if appropriate.

Cooked Rice

rice
double its volume of water
salt
1 teaspoon oil

To make Measure out the rice then set it aside. Using the same container, measure out double that quantity of water and put it into a saucepan. Salt it lightly and then add the oil. Bring the water to the boil. Throw in the rice, stir it and then cover the pan with a close-fitting lid. Lower the heat a little and leave the rice to cook for 10–15 minutes, depending on the quantity, when all the water should have been absorbed and the rice should be dry and fluffy and separate. To 'fluff' it a little more, shake it vigorously in the pan with the lid held on firmly. Resist the temptation to lift the lid during cooking time.

To freeze If the rice is to be frozen, then as soon as it is cooked, turn it into a basin of cold water to cool it rapidly. Drain it thoroughly and then pack it in convenient quantities in polythene bags. Seal, label, date and freeze.

To use Take the required quantity from the freezer. Put ⅛ of the original quantity of water plus a small knob of butter into a frying pan. Turn the rice into it and heat very gently, stirring now and again.

Espagnol Sauce

2 oz (50 gm) butter
3 oz (75 gm) streaky bacon – chopped
1 tablespoon chopped carrot
1 tablespoon chopped onion
1 dessertspoon chopped mushrooms
2 oz (50 gm) flour
1 pt (500 ml.) beef stock
2 tablespoons tomato purée
salt & pepper
1 teaspoon mixed herbs

To make Melt the butter in a saucepan and add the bacon and vegetables. Fry gently for 5 minutes. Stir in the flour and cook very slowly until the mixture is a light brown. Gradually stir in the stock, tomato purée, seasoning and herbs. Simmer for half an hour skimming off froth as it rises to the surface. Liquidize the sauce or rub it through a sieve.

To freeze Pack the sauce into plastic pots with lids leaving ½ inch (1 cm.) space at the top. Seal, label, date and freeze.

To use Take the required amount of espagnol sauce from the freezer and turn it into a small saucepan. Heat it gently to thaw. Beat in a tablespoon of sherry to every ½ pint (250 ml.) of sauce, heat thoroughly and use the sauce as necessary.

Flaky Pastry

8 oz (200 gm) flour
pinch salt
3 oz (75 gm) butter
3 oz (75 gm) lard
½ teaspoon lemon juice
4 tablespoons water

To make Sift the flour into a basin with the salt and rub in 1½ oz (37 gm) of the butter and lard mixed. Add lemon juice to the water and mix it into the flour and fat using a round-bladed knife. Mix to an elastic dough. Turn the pastry out on to a well-floured board, knead it and roll it to an oblong about three times as long as it is wide. Using a knife, spread little pats of ⅓ of the remaining fats on to the lower ⅔ of the pastry. Fold the top ⅓ down on to the middle ⅓ and the bottom ⅓ up over both. Seal the edges, distribute the air enclosed by pressing in several places with the rolling pin. Half-turn the pastry and roll it out as before. Repeat the process another twice until all the fat is used.

To freeze Wrap the pastry in convenient quantities in a floured polythene bag or in foil. Seal, label, date and freeze.

To use Take the required amount of pastry from the freezer and allow it to thaw in the fridge for 24 hours. Roll out and fold once more and then use as required. As with all pastry, it requires a hot oven to bake but whatever recipe you use will tell you exactly at what temperature and for how long.

Note This recipe is included because it is not available in commercially frozen packs and some things really are better with this than with puff or shortcrust pastry, e.g. eccles cakes and sausage rolls.

Fruit Purées

1 lb (400 gm) fruit
basic syrup as necessary

To make Wash the fruit, cut it up and put it into a saucepan. Add a little basic syrup if it is a rather dry, sour fruit. Add sugar only to such fruit as apples – and there is no need to skin or core the fruit at this stage. For rhubarb, add a knob of butter to take the acidity off it. Cook the fruit over a low heat and when it is soft remove any stones and liquidize it or rub it through a fine sieve. (Use a sieve for apples so that skins and cores are left behind.)

To freeze Pack the purée into plastic pots with lids leaving ½ inch (1 cm.) space at the top. Seal, label, date and freeze.

To use Take the required amount of purée from the freezer. If it is to be used hot, turn it into a saucepan and heat it very gently to thaw and heat; if cold, allow 4–5 hours at room temperature to thaw out.

Note 1 lb (400 gm) fruit gives ½ pint (250 ml.) purée.

Meringue Shells

To every *egg white* allow *2 oz (50 gm) caster sugar*

To make Whisk the egg white until it is standing in soft peaks. Add a third of the sugar and whisk again until stiff. Fold in another third of the sugar. Using two dessertspoons dipped in cold water, put spoons of the mixture on to a lightly oiled and sugared sheet of greaseproof on a baking tray. Otherwise, use a ½ inch (1 cm.) star pipe and pipe out rounds of the mixture. Sprinkle the remaining sugar over and bake the meringue shells in the oven at 200°F, Gas ¼ (100°C), for at least three hours until crisp and dry.

To freeze Pack the meringues into plastic boxes with plenty of paper padding for protection. Seal, label, date and freeze. However, meringues will keep perfectly in a sealed tin for several weeks if your freezer is rather full.

To use Take the required number of meringues from the freezer and use as you wish. They need no time to thaw.

Note For variety, a few drops of food colouring or flavouring may be added to the mixture at the whisking stage. And if making a meringue base, merely spread the mixture out into a circle on the greaseproof before baking. In this case, it is a good idea to add 1 teaspoon of lemon juice and 1 dessertspoon of cornflour for each egg white – it makes the resulting meringue softer and more easily cut.

Pancakes

4 oz (100 gm) flour
¼ teaspoon salt
1 egg
½ pt (250 ml.) milk

To make Sift the flour and salt into a basin and make a 'well' (dip) in the centre. Drop the egg into the well with a little of the milk. Gradually incorporate the flour by stirring the egg and milk rapidly in the well. Add the rest of the milk gradually and beat the batter until very smooth. Set it aside for 15 minutes. Meantime, lightly grease and heat a pancake pan. Have handy two large plates and nine pieces of greaseproof paper. Transfer the batter to a measuring jug. Pour enough batter into the hot pan to just cover the base. Cook until the top is dry and the underneath lightly browned. Turn it out on to one piece of the paper on one of the plates. Cover with another piece of paper and the other plate. This keeps the pancakes from becoming leathery. Repeat the process layering pancakes and paper between the two plates until all the batter is used. This quantity should make 8 pancakes.

To freeze When the pancakes are cold, replace the greaseproof paper with polythene film, butcher's paper or oiled greaseproof and pack in convenient quantities in polythene bags. Seal, label, date and freeze.

To use Take the required number of pancakes from the freezer. They need almost no thawing time when separated out. Use the pancakes with the uncooked side outermost so that on reheating they become a good colour and not over brown.

Potato Whirls (Duchess potatoes)

1 $2\frac{1}{4}$-oz (64-gm) pkt instant potato
1 egg yolk
1 tablespoon milk
$\frac{1}{2}$ oz (13 gm) butter
pepper

To make Make up the potato according to the instructions. Beat in the remaining ingredients and put the mixture into a piping bag fitted with a $\frac{1}{2}$ inch (1 cm.) star nozzle. On to a greased tray pipe out 6 or 8 rather high whirls. Leave them to get cold.

To freeze Lift the whole tray into the freezer and leave there until the whirls are frozen solid. Remove them from the tray and pack in a plastic box. Seal, label, date and return to the freezer.

To use Take the required number of whirls (Duchess potatoes) from the freezer, set them on a baking tray and heat and brown in the oven preheated to 400°F, Gas 6 (200°C), for 10–15 minutes.

Stocks

ham, meat, poultry or fish bones – raw or cooked
cold water to cover
1 small carrot – roughly chopped
1 small onion – roughly chopped
6 peppercorns
2 bayleaves
salt

To make Put everything into a large saucepan with a close-fitting lid. Bring slowly to the boil, then simmer for 3–4 hours. Set aside to cool thoroughly, then repeat the process. Strain the stock into a basin, cover and set aside to cool. This stock is then fairly concentrated so may need to be diluted for use later. For further concentration and consequent reduction in volume, boil the stock rapidly to reduce it appropriately.

To freeze When cold, pack into waxed cartons or polythene-lined foil bags. Seal, label, date and freeze.

To use Take the required quantity from the freezer, turn it into a saucepan and heat gently until thawed. Add water if necessary to dilute and then use according to requirement.

Sweetened Chestnut Purée

1 lb (400 gm) chestnuts
½ pt (250 ml.) milk
1 teaspoon vanilla essence
2 oz (50 gm) butter
3 oz (75 gm) sugar

To make Put a cut through the skin of each chestnut then put on a tray in the oven at 425°F, Gas 7 (210°C), for about 15 minutes until all the skins crack open. Remove the skins quickly and cook the chestnuts in already-boiling milk and vanilla essence until soft. Drain the chestnuts and rub through a wire sieve or liquidize to a fine purée. Put this into a saucepan with the butter and sugar and cook over a low heat for 6 or 7 minutes until it dries and so thickens a little. Cool.

To freeze Pack into suitably sized plastic pots with lids leaving ½ inch (1 cm.) space at the top. Seal, label, date and freeze.

To use Take the required quantity of purée from the freezer and if it is to be used cold, allow it 3–4 hours at room temperature to thaw. Beat it smooth before use. If it is to be used hot, turn the frozen purée into a saucepan and heat it gently over a low heat. Beat it well.

Note This has many uses as the basis of a sauce with icecream, as a cake decoration or as a hot or cold pudding almost in its own right, e.g. Chestnut Mont Blanc, p. 98.

Tomato Purée

1 lb (400 gm) tomatoes
½ oz (13 gm) butter
1 tablespoon finely chopped onion
salt & pepper
pinch mixed herbs

To make Skin and chop the tomatoes. Melt the butter in a small saucepan and fry the onion until soft but not browned. Put all the ingredients into the liquidizer and blend to a purée. Alternatively, add the tomato, seasoning and herbs to the butter and onion in the pan and cook gently until soft before rubbing through a sieve to a purée.

To freeze Pack the purée into plastic pots with lids leaving ½ inch (1 cm.) space at the top. Seal, label, date and freeze.

To use Take the required amount of purée from the freezer and turn it into a saucepan. Heat gently over a low heat to thaw and then use according to requirement.

Velouté Sauce

2 oz (50 gm) butter
2 oz (50 gm) flour
1 pt (500 ml.) well flavoured chicken stock
1 teaspoon lemon juice

To make Melt the butter in a saucepan and beat in the flour, off the heat. Gradually beat in the stock making sure that no lumps form. Return the pan to the heat and stir constantly over a low heat until the sauce is smooth and thick enough to coat the back of the spoon. Beat in the lemon juice.

To freeze Pack the sauce into appropriately sized plastic pots with lids, leaving ½ inch (1 cm.) space at the top. Seal, label, date and freeze.

To use Take the required quantity from the freezer and turn it into a saucepan. Heat gently to thaw it out and beat constantly. The sauce may separate out but a brisk beating will reconstitute it. This is a coating sauce which you may want to thin down a little, in which case beat in the appropriate amount of warm chicken stock.

Note For fish dishes, a fish velouté is preferable. In this case, make it in the same way using fish stock instead of chicken stock.

Now that you have your freezer fully stocked, it's full steam ahead into all those delicious recipes – with ease!

CHAPTER 10

Food for Eating

Most of the recipes that follow are fairly sophisticated, but all are very simple to make. The ingredients should already be in your freezer or store cupboard – if you have read, noted and carried out the advice in the previous chapter!

Unless 'fresh' is specifically stated and unless the item cannot be frozen at all, I am presuming use of the frozen variety.

All the recipes are marked with either an 'A' or an 'F'. 'A' is for 'assembly' and indicates that the recipe is designed to be put together quickly from basics already in the freezer. 'F' is for 'freeze' and indicates that this recipe is designed to be wholly or partly made up before putting into the freezer; but it is still usually made from frozen basics.

You will see that the number of servings varies. The purpose behind that is not only to give variety but also to enable you to save yet more time by leaving a little extra for tomorrow's supper.

There are very few joints of meat. They take up both space and time – neither of which you have.

The whole menus at the end of each section have been put together for nutritional balance – but they are only meant as suggestions.

I hope, having read the book thus far, that you will now enjoy preparing and eating many of my own favourite recipes and that you will find them delicious!

COLD AND HUNGRY

F or A *Cabbage and Sausage Soup*

8 portions

4 oz (100 gm) streaky bacon
8 oz (200 gm) pork sausages
6 baby roast potatoes
2 pts (1 litre) diluted chicken stock
2 bouquet garnis
2 bayleaves
salt & pepper
6 oz (150 gm) shredded cabbage

To make Take the required ingredients from the freezer. Chop the bacon, put it in a large saucepan and fry it gently. Cut the sausages and potatoes into chunks. Add to the bacon and fry gently until almost thawed out. Add all the other ingredients, bring to the boil and simmer gently for 30 minutes. Remove the herbs.

To freeze Divide the soup between a relevant number of polythene-lined foil bags or waxed cartons. Seal, label, date and freeze.

To finish and serve Take the required amount from the freezer and reheat it gently. Can be served hot as a substantial meal in itself.

A *Bread Soup*

6 portions

2 pts (1 litre) diluted chicken stock
8 oz (200 gm) stale bread
salt & pepper
2 eggs
1 pt (500 ml.) milk
2 oz (50 gm) butter

To make Take the required ingredients from the freezer. Put the stock into a saucepan and very quickly melt it over a low heat. As soon as it is melted, add the bread, salt and pepper. Over a very low heat bring the mixture to the boil. The bread will absorb most of the stock. Whisk the mixture until it is smooth. Whisk together the eggs and half the milk and add to the bread and stock along with the butter.

To finish and serve Bring the soup slowly to boiling point, whisking continuously. Stir in the remaining milk and serve with a sprig of parsley on top.

A *Cullen Skink*

6–8 portions

1 10-oz (250-gm) pkt smoked haddock
½ pt (250 ml.) water
3 oz (75 gm) chopped onion
½ pt (250 ml.) fish stock
2 bayleaves
1 blade mace
6 peppercorns
salt
1 2¼-oz (64-gm) pkt instant potato
½ pt (250 ml.) milk
1 oz (25 gm) butter
1 tablespoon crumbled parsley

To make Take the required ingredients from the freezer. Take the fish out of the packet and poach it for 10 minutes until soft. Lift the fish from the water, scrape off any skin and bones and return these to the water. Add the onion, stock and seasonings and simmer the stock for 20 minutes. Meantime, flake the fish and make up the instant potato according to the pack. Stir in the milk and butter so that the potato is puréed. Strain the stock on to the puréed potato, stir in the flaked fish and the parsley. Return the pan to the cooker and heat the soup thoroughly.

To finish and serve Serve in soup bowls with lots of crusty bread at hand.

A *Savoury Whitebait*

4 portions

8 oz (200 gm) whitebait
salt & pepper
1 oz (25 gm) white breadcrumbs
1 oz (25 gm) grated cheese
½ teaspoon mixed herbs
2 oz (50 gm) butter
1 tablespoon orange juice
2½ fl. oz (63 ml.) tomato purée

To make Take the required ingredients from the freezer. Sprinkle the fish with salt and pepper and toss it in a mixture of the crumbs, cheese and herbs. Fry in hot butter until crisp and browned. Drain. Mix together the orange juice and tomato purée. Add salt and pepper to taste.

To finish and serve Pile the whitebait into the centre of a warm dish and pour the sauce over the fish. Serve immediately as a starter.

A *Angus Creams*

6–8 portions

1 12-oz (300-gm) pkt smoked haddock fillet
4 tomatoes
½ pt (250 ml.) fish velouté sauce
2½ fl. oz (63 ml.) cream
1½ oz (37 gm) butter
6–8 lemon slices
parsley sprigs

To make Take the required ingredients from the freezer. Cook the smoked haddock fillets according to the instructions on the packet or, if fresh, cover fish with boiling water and allow to stand for 5 minutes, then drain. Discard any skin from the fish, turn it into a basin and flake it with a fork. Chop the tomatoes and add to the fish along with the sauce and cream. Divide mixture between the relevant number of cocotte dishes.

To finish and serve Dot the tops of the creams with butter and put under a medium grill to heat thoroughly, and brown the tops lightly. Garnish with a lemon twist and a tiny parsley sprig. Serve hot or cold.

A *Timbale of Game*

2 portions

6 oz (150 gm) cooked game meat
1 2½-oz (63-gm) jar stuffed olives
2 oz (50 gm) soft breadcrumbs
2 teaspoons crumbled parsley
salt & pepper
egg yolk
⅓ pt (175 ml.) appropriate gravy

To make Cut up the cooked game into fairly small pieces. Grease 2 ¼-pint (125-ml.) or 1 ½-pint (250-ml.) foil pudding basin. Drain the olives and cut in half. Line the pudding basin with halved olives stuck to the base and sides so that the cut side is next to the foil. In a small basin make a stuffing from the crumbs, parsley, seasoning and sufficient egg yolk to bind. With a wet hand press a layer of stuffing over the olives lining the basin. Leave aside sufficient to make a lid. Mix the game meat with just sufficient gravy to moisten and pack it into the basin. Use the remaining stuffing to spread over the top. Seal the edges.

To freeze Cover the basin with greased foil. Turn the rest of the gravy into a small tub. Seal, label, date and freeze.

To finish and serve Take the timbales and gravy from the freezer. Steam the timbales still covered over boiling water for 40–45 minutes to thaw, cook the stuffing and thoroughly heat through. Meantime turn the gravy into a small saucepan and heat gently. Remove the cover from the basin, turn the timbales on to a warm platter and serve with the gravy poured over.

A *Best End Lamb Casserole*

2 portions

1 lb (400 gm) best end of neck chops
salt & pepper
flour
1 oz (25 gm) butter
2 oz (50 gm) sliced onions
¼ pt (125 ml.) espagnol sauce
½ green pepper – chopped
4 tablespoons water
2 oz (50 gm) courgettes

To make Take the required ingredients from the freezer. Dip the chops in the flour mixed with salt and pepper. Fry in the butter for 7 minutes on each side and turn the chops into a casserole dish. Fry the onions and add to the chops. Turn the sauce and the peppers into the frying pan over a low heat and blend in 4 tablespoons of water. Bring to the boil stirring constantly. Pour over the chops, cover the dish and cook in the oven preheated to 325°F, Gas 3 (160°C), for 25 minutes. Add the courgettes and cook for a further 15 minutes.

To finish and serve Serve the casserole hot, accompanied by croquette potatoes heated in the oven with the casserole.

A *Aubergine Beef Pot*

2 portions

4 oz (100 gm) aubergine slices
2 rashers streaky bacon
½ green pepper
2 oz (50 gm) chopped onion
1 clove garlic
8 oz (200 gm) minced beef
¼ pt (125 ml.) tomato purée
1 tablespoon tomato ketchup
½ teaspoon oregano
salt & pepper
½ tablespoon flour
4 oz (100 gm) grated cheese

To make Take the required ingredients from the freezer. Put half the aubergine slices into a well greased casserole dish. Chop the bacon and fry until it is crisp. Drain and set aside. Deseed and chop the green pepper and fry in the bacon fat along with the onion and crushed garlic. Add the mince and brown it over a low heat using a wooden spoon to break it up as it thaws. Add all the other ingredients except the flour, cheese and bacon. Blend the flour with a little water and stir it in. Spoon half this mixture into the casserole dish, on top of the aubergine. Sprinkle with half the grated cheese. Then repeat with the rest of the aubergine, meat and cheese. Bake uncovered in the oven preheated to 350°F, Gas 4 (180°C), for 30 minutes.

To finish and serve Serve the Pot with the crispy bacon sprinkled on top.

F *Stuffed Cabbage Leaves*

8 portions

16 cabbage leaves
3 oz (75 gm) butter
8 oz (200 gm) chopped onion
3 oz (75 gm) raw rice
¾ pt (375 ml.) chicken stock
1½ lb (600 gm) minced beef
2 teaspoons mixed herbs
salt & pepper
4 tablespoons soft brown sugar
4 tablespoons lemon juice
½ pt (250 ml.) tomato purée
strips lemon rind

To make Cut the coarse stalk out of each leaf and blanch them in boiling, salted water to set the colour. Run under cold water to cool quickly. Melt the butter in a frying pan and add the onion which may have to be chopped more finely. Add the rice, stir and cook for 2 minutes. Stir in the stock and cook gently until the stock is absorbed. Turn the rice into a basin, mix in the mince and herbs. Season with salt and pepper. Divide the mixture into 16 balls and wrap one in each cabbage leaf. Press to seal. Place them in a foil-lined casserole. Mix together the other ingredients except the rind and pour over the cabbage parcels. Cover tightly and bake in an oven preheated to 300°F, Gas 2 (150°C), for 2 hours. Set aside to cool.

To freeze Put the casserole into the freezer and when the food is solid, lift it out of the dish and overwrap it in foil. Seal, label, date and return to the freezer.

To finish and serve Take the Stuffed Cabbage Leaves from the freezer, unwrap the food and place in a casserole. Put the dish, tightly covered, into the oven preheated to 400°F, Gas 6 (200°C), for 35 minutes. Uncover the dish and cook for a further 15 minutes to thicken the sauce and brown the tops of the leaves. Sprinkle with strips of rind. Serve hot as a complete dish.

F Beef and Potato Loaf

6 portions

1½ lb (600 gm) minced beef
4 oz (100 gm) breadcrumbs
1 dessertspoon mixed herbs
2 oz (50 gm) finely chopped onion
2 oz (50 gm) finely chopped green pepper
2 teaspoons lemon juice
2 tablespoons tomato ketchup
1 teaspoon mild curry powder
2 egg yolks
1 2¼-oz (64-gm) pkt instant potato
1 oz (25 gm) butter
salt & pepper

To make Take the required ingredients from the freezer and allow to thaw sufficiently to enable handling. In a basin mix together the first 8 ingredients and bind with the egg yolks. Make up the potato according to the instructions on the packet. Beat in the butter and a little more salt and pepper. Line 2 1-lb (400-gm) loaf tins or 1 2-lb (1-kilo) loaf tin with well buttered foil. Layer the potato and the meat mixture into the tin(s) so that potato is on the base, then meat, potato, meat, potato and ending with meat. Press firmly, cover and bake in the oven preheated to 400°F, Gas 6 (200°C), for 1 hour. It may be carefully turned out and eaten hot at this stage.

To freeze Allow the loaf to cool in the tin. Lift it out, overwrap it in foil, seal, label, date and freeze. Or slice up the loaf and pack it with foil between each slice in convenient quantities in polythene bags.

To finish and serve Take the required quantity of Beef and Potato Loaf from the freezer. To serve cold, allow slices 30 minutes to thaw when spread out on a platter, allow the whole loaf 2–3 hours to thaw at room temperature. Serve with salad. To serve the loaf hot, put it still wrapped in foil into the original loaf tin and bake it in the oven preheated to 400°F, Gas 6 (200°C), for 35 minutes. Turn out on to a warm platter and slice to serve. Accompany by creamed spinach or green beans.

A *Chilli con Carne*

6 portions

2 oz (50 gm) butter
6 oz (150 gm) chopped onion
1½ lb (600 gm) minced beef
2 teaspoons chilli powder
1 teaspoon cumin seeds
1 tablespoon sugar
salt
¼ pt (125 ml.) tomato purée
4 tomatoes – chopped
¼ pt (125 ml.) espagnol sauce
lemon slices

To make Take the required ingredients from the freezer. Melt the butter in a strong saucepan and fry the onion until soft and lightly browned. Put the mince in the saucepan over a low heat and gradually thaw it. Turn up the heat and brown the mince. Stir in all the other ingredients, cover and cook over a medium heat for 15–20 minutes.

To finish and serve Turn the Chilli con Carne out on to a large warm platter and surround with rice or noodles. Garnish with lemon slices and serve hot. Accompany with a salad of Chinese Leaves.

A *Mild Curried Mince and Rice*

2 portions

½ oz (13 gm) butter
1 teaspoon salt
1 teaspoon Masala
½ teaspoon ground ginger
½ teaspoon coriander powder
2 oz (50 gm) chopped onion
8 oz (200 gm) mince
½ pt (250 ml.) water
12 oz (300 gm) cooked rice
crumbled parsley

To make Put the butter and spices in a saucepan and fry for 3 minutes. Add the onion and continue frying until the onion is soft. Turn the mince into the pan and work at it with a wooden spoon to break it down over a low heat. When it is broken down, turn up the heat to brown the mince, add the water, cover the pan and simmer for about 15 minutes. Meantime, reheat the frozen rice (p. 49).

To finish and serve Put the rice on to a platter, pour the mince into the middle, garnish with parsley or a frozen lemon slice and serve very hot.

A or F *Veal and Corn Pie*

4 portions

1 lb (400 gm) minced veal
8 oz (200 gm) minced bacon
1 oz (25 gm) butter
4 oz (100 gm) chopped onion
1 teaspoon thyme
salt & pepper
¼ teaspoon mixed spice
1 egg – hard-boiled & sliced
1 oz (25 gm) raisins
8 oz (200 gm) sweetcorn
¼ pt (125 ml.) cream
crumbled parsley

To make Take the required ingredients from the freezer. Put the meats into a frying pan over a gentle heat and break down with a wooden spoon as they thaw. Turn up the heat and cook. Put half the meat into the bottom of a well greased pie dish. Melt the butter in the pan and fry the onion. Mix in the salt, pepper, thyme and spice. Pour over the meat. Spread over a layer of the egg and the raisins. Cover with a layer of the rest of the meat. Top with the corn, pour over the cream and cover with a well buttered piece of foil. Bake in the oven preheated to 375°F, Gas 5 (190°C), for 30 minutes.

To freeze The pie may be frozen at this stage, in which case make it in a foil pie dish and cool it thoroughly. Overwrap it in a polythene bag. Seal, label, date and freeze.

To finish and serve If it has been frozen, take it from the freezer, remove the polythene bag and put the pie, still covered, into the oven, preheated to 400°F, Gas 6 (200°C), for 30 minutes. In both cases, give the pie a further 10 minutes uncovered at 425°F, Gas 7

(220°C), to brown the top. Put the pie dish on a serving platter and sprinkle with crumbled parsley to serve.

A *Risi-Pisi*

2 portions

10 oz (250 gm) cooked rice
2½ fl. oz (63 ml.) tomato purée
2½ fl. oz (63 ml.) good beef stock
½ oz (13 gm) butter
1 oz (25 gm) finely chopped onion
1 clove garlic – crushed
2 sausages
10 oz (250 gm) peas
salt & pepper
1 lemon

To make Take the required ingredients from the freezer. Put the rice into a deep frying pan and add the tomato purée and stock. Cook gently until the liquid is absorbed and the rice hot. Melt the butter in another small frying pan and fry the onion and garlic. Add the sausages and fry until cooked. Lift the sausages out, cut them up into small pieces and add along with the onion, garlic and peas to the rice. Mix well and check the seasoning.

To finish and serve Pile the Risi-Pisi on to a warm platter, garnish with the lemon cut in wedges and serve immediately.

A *Salmon Maître d'Hôtel Pie*

4 portions

1 7½-oz (187-gm) pkt puff pastry
meat from 2 cooked salmon heads
¼ pt (125 ml.) fish velouté sauce or béchamel sauce
2 teaspoons lemon juice
1 dessertspoon crumbled parsley
egg yolk to glaze

To make Take the required ingredients from the freezer and allow them to thaw out sufficiently to enable handling. Roll out half the pastry and use it to line a 6-inch (15-cm.) sandwich tin with a removable base. Pick the salmon meat off the heads and use the bones to make fish stock for the freezer. Mix together the fish, sauce, lemon juice and parsley. Check the seasoning and pour the mixture into the lined sandwich tin. Roll the remaining pastry and use it to cover the pie. Seal the edges and decorate. Brush over with egg yolk.

To finish and serve Bake the pie in the oven preheated to 400°F, Gas 6 (200°C), for 35 minutes. Serve hot or cold with courgettes in tomato sauce or a cucumber and endive salad.

F *Russian Fish Pie*

6 portions

1 7½-oz (187-gm) pkt puff pastry
8 oz (200 gm) cooked haddock fillets
2 oz (50 gm) peeled prawns
4 fl. oz (100 ml.) fish velouté sauce
1 tablespoon tomato purée
2 tablespoons capers
2 teaspoons horseradish sauce
salt & pepper
egg to glaze

To make Take the required ingredients from the freezer and allow to thaw sufficiently to enable handling. Roll the pastry out to 12 inches (30 cm.) square. Flake the haddock finely and mix with all the other ingredients except the egg. Check the seasoning. Pile the fish mixture into the centre of the pastry square. Damp the edges of the pastry and bring each corner to the centre over the fish so that the corners join. Pinch the four edges together to form a square parcel with four 'seams' running from the centre to each corner. Decorate with pastry leaves. Brush with beaten egg to glaze, lift the pie carefully on to a baking tray and bake it in the oven preheated to 400°F, Gas 6 (200°C), for 25 minutes, almost to cook the pie. Set it aside to cool.

To freeze Put the pie carefully into a rigid plastic container. If you put it on the lid and then put the base on top, it will be easier to get out without damage. Seal, label, date and freeze.

To finish and serve Take the pie from the freezer and allow it to thaw overnight in the fridge. Put the pie on a baking tray and complete the baking in the oven preheated to 375°F, Gas 5 (190°C), for 20 minutes. Serve hot with buttered carrots and peas.

A *St George's Eggs*

4 portions

2 oz (50 gm) bacon-fat or butter
1½ lb (600 gm) chopped onions
4 tomatoes – chopped
1 medium green pepper – chopped
salt & pepper
2 dessertspoons mild curry powder
¼ pt (125 ml.) water
2 bananas – sliced
2 oz (50 gm) apple slices
1 teaspoon sugar
3 eggs
1¼ lb (500 gm) cooked rice
crumbled parsley

To make Take the required ingredients from the freezer. Melt the fat in a deep frying pan. Fry the onion, tomato and pepper until soft and well browned. Add salt, pepper and curry powder. Stir in well. Stir in the water and simmer gently until almost all of the water is absorbed or driven off. Meantime, reheat the rice (p. 49). Stir the bananas, apple and sugar into the onion mixture and boil rapidly. Break the eggs into a basin and whisk with a fork to break them up a little. Using the fork, very quickly stir the eggs into the rapidly boiling mixture until the eggs are invisible.

To finish and serve Put a ring of rice on to a warm platter and pour the St George's Eggs into the centre. Sprinkle liberally with crumbled parsley and serve immediately.

A *Smetana Pie*

4 portions

4 oz (100 gm) flour
1 oz (25 gm) butter
1 oz (25 gm) lard
3 oz (75 gm) grated cheese
½ teaspoon cayenne pepper
½ teaspoon salt
2 tablespoons water
¼ pt (125 ml.) béchamel sauce
2 teaspoons flour
2½ fl. oz (63 ml.) soured cream
2 tablespoons dry white wine
ground pepper
4 oz (100 gm) chopped onion
4 oz (100 gm) peas and carrots
2 oz (50 gm) chopped celery
2 oz (50 gm) broad beans
2 oz (50 gm) green beans
2 oz (50 gm) beetroot – chopped

To make Take the required ingredients from the freezer. Rub the butter and lard into the flour, mix in the cheese and seasonings. Mix to a stiff dough with the water. Knead and roll two-thirds of it to fit a 1½-pint (750-ml.) pie dish. Heat the sauce gently and then beat in the flour blended with a little water and cook until the sauce thickens rather more than normally. Stir in the soured cream and wine. Season highly with pepper. Mix in all the vegetables and pour into the pie dish. Wet the edges of the dish and cover the dish with the remaining cheese pastry. Decorate the edges and the top. Brush with milk and bake in the oven preheated to 400°F, Gas 6 (200°C), for 15–20 minutes until the top is golden brown.

To finish and serve Serve the Smetana Pie very hot on its own.

A *Redcurrant Upsidedown Pudding*

4–6 portions

2 eggs
4 oz (100 gm) self-raising flour
4 oz (100 gm) soft margarine
6 oz (150 gm) caster sugar
8 oz (200 gm) redcurrants

To make Take the redcurrants from the freezer and sprinkle with 2 oz (50 gm) of the sugar. With well greased foil, line a 6–inch (15-cm.) cake tin with a removable base. Spread half the redcurrants over the base. Whisk together the remaining ingredients until light and fluffy. Spoon half the mixture on top of the redcurrants. Put in a layer of the remaining fruit and then the rest of the sponge mixture. Bake in the oven preheated to 360°F, Gas 4–5 (185°C), for 35 minutes.

To finish and serve Turn the pudding out on to a warm dish and serve hot or cold with cream.

A *Pumpkin Pie*

4–6 portions

1 7½-oz (187-gm) pkt shortcrust pastry
¾ pt (375 ml.) pumpkin purée
¾ pt (375 ml.) milk
8 oz (200 gm) sugar
1 oz (25 gm) butter – melted
pinch of salt
1 teaspoon lemon juice
½ teaspoon grated nutmeg
2 eggs – separated

To make Take the ingredients from the freezer and allow to thaw sufficiently to enable handling. Roll the pastry and use to line a deep 7-inch (17-cm.) pie plate. Roll the scraps and cut in strips for the top. Mix together all the other ingredients except the egg whites. Whisk the whites until standing in soft peaks, then fold into the pumpkin mixture. Pour into the pastry case and use the strips twisted to decorate the top. Bake in the oven preheated to 400°F, Gas 6 (200°C), for 20 minutes.

To finish and serve Serve immediately whilst it is risen and fluffy.

A *French Cherry Pudding*

6–8 portions

1 lb (400 gm) cherries
2½ fl. oz (63 ml.) red wine
4 oz (100 gm) breadcrumbs
3½ oz (90 gm) butter
5 oz (125 gm) caster sugar
½ teaspoon vanilla essence
5 eggs
1 tablespoon apricot purée
1 tablespoon gin

To make Take the required ingredients from the freezer. Put the cherries, 2 tablespoons of the syrup they were frozen in, the wine and 1½ oz (37 gm) of the sugar in a small saucepan and simmer gently to cook the cherries a little and to thicken the wine syrup. Drain them and keep this wine syrup as well as the cherries. Cool. Put 3½ oz (90 gm) of the crumbs into a basin and mix with the melted butter. Mix in the remaining sugar and the vanilla. Separate the eggs and gradually work 3 of the yolks into the breadcrumbs. Mix in the cherries. Beat the 5 whites until stiff and fold into the cherry mixture. Pour into a well buttered mould that has been coated inside with the remaining bread-crumbs. Place the mould in a roasting tin of hot water and bake in the oven preheated to 375°F, Gas 5 (190°C), for 40–45 minutes.

To finish and serve Allow the pudding to shrink for a minute or two then turn out carefully on to a warm serving platter. Mix together and gently heat the cherry and wine syrup, the apricot purée and the gin. Serve the French Cherry Pudding with this sauce poured over.

F *Iced Strawberry Soufflé*

10 portions

10 oz (250 gm) sugar
3 tablespoons water
3 egg whites
12 oz (300 gm) strawberry purée
1 pt (500 ml.) lightly whipped cream
strawberry slices

To make Dissolve the sugar in the water and boil for 10 minutes. Meantime whisk the egg whites until very stiff, pour over the sugar and water syrup and whisk at the same time. Fold in the strawberry purée and cream.

To freeze Wrap a collar of foil or lightly oiled paper round two 1-pint (500-ml.) or one 2-pint (1-litre) soufflé dish so that the collar extends above the rim. Pour the soufflé into the dish or dishes. Put it in the freezer. It needs at least 2 hours but ought only to be kept a few days. When it is frozen, take it out, overwrap it in a polythene bag, seal, label, date and return to the freezer.

To finish and serve Take the soufflé from the freezer, unwrap it and take the collar off. Set the dish on a folded napkin on a platter and serve decorated with one or two strawberry slices on top.

F *Honey and Almond Cream*

10 portions

10 oz (250 gm) clear honey
6 egg yolks
1 pt (500 ml.) lightly whipped cream
4 oz (100 gm) toasted chopped almonds
lemon juice or very dry white wine

To make Melt the honey in a basin over hot water, add the egg yolks and whisk until the mixture is thick and creamy. Take it off the heat and allow it to cool by continuing to whisk and adding 1 tablespoon cold water. Fold in the whipped cream and the nuts.

To freeze Pack the cream into suitably sized plastic containers. Cover, seal, label, date and freeze.

To finish and serve Take the required quantity from the freezer when needed. Spoon it into tall glasses and pour over a little lemon juice or very dry white wine to serve.

F *Chocolate Mousse*

4 portions

6 oz (150 gm) dark chocolate
2 tablespoons water
1 tablespoon Crême de Menthe
4 eggs
6 peppermint meringue shells

To make Carefully melt the chocolate and gradually add the water and liqueur, beating constantly. Separate the eggs and beat the yolks into the chocolate. Turn the mixture into a basin and set aside to cool. Meantime whisk the egg whites until stiff. Fold the chocolate mixture and 2 roughly crumbled meringue shells into the whites.

To freeze Divide the mixture between 4 plastic mousse pots or foil-lined sundae glasses which are strong enough to withstand the low temperature. When the mousse is frozen, you may remove the sundae glasses and overwrap the mousse. Seal, label, date and freeze.

To finish and serve Take the required number of mousses from the freezer, take each out of its wrappings whilst still frozen and put into glasses. Top each with a meringue shell or a cream whirl and allow to thaw for 30–60 minutes.

F *Granita*

6 portions

3 tablespoons instant coffee
4 tablespoons soft brown sugar
½ pt (250 ml.) water
¼ pt (125 ml.) cream
1 miniature Tia Maria

To make In a small pan, mix the coffee, sugar and half the water. Dissolve over a low heat and then boil for 5 minutes. Stir in the rest of the water. Pour the strong, sweet coffee into a foil-lined 7-inch (17-cm.) sandwich tin and freeze. When it is mushy, take it from the freezer and turn it into a basin. Whisk it very well. It will become the colour of coffee cream and will double in bulk.

To freeze Return the mixture to a freshly lined, 7-inch (17-cm.) tin, and freeze. When solid, remove the tin and overwrap the Granita. Seal, label, date and return to the freezer.

To finish and serve Take the cream from the freezer and whisk it. Turn the Granita on to a round, shallow dish and remove the foil. Pipe the top with cream as if it were a cake. Pour the liqueur over it. Cut in wedges to serve.

SUGGESTED MENUS

Chilli con Carne
Pumpkin Pie

Salmon Maître d'Hôtel Pie
Redcurrant Upsidedown Pudding

Savoury Whitebait
Veal and Corn Pie
Chocolate Mousse

Angus Creams
Stuffed Cabbage Leaves
French Cherry Pudding

Cullen Skink
Beef and Potato Loaf
Iced Strawberry Soufflé

Cabbage and Sausage Soup
St George's Eggs
Granita

Bread Soup
Russian Fish Pie
Honey and Almond Cream

FANCY SOMETHING TASTY

A *Tomato and Orange Soup*

2 portions

½ pt (250 ml.) diluted chicken stock
4 tomatoes
1 oz (25 gm) sliced onions
¼ oz (6 gm) butter
¼ pt (125 ml.) reconstituted orange juice
salt & pepper to taste
a few strips of orange rind

To make Take the required ingredients from the freezer. Melt the butter in a saucepan and gently fry the onions until tender but not brown. Add all the other ingredients except the orange rind. Bring the mixture slowly to the boil. Simmer for 10 minutes to soften the tomato. Put the soup through a liquidizer or sieve. Return it to the saucepan.

To finish and serve Bring the soup to the boil and add a few fine strips of orange rind, pour the soup into warm bowls and serve with a crusty roll.

A *Angel Soup*

2 portions

½ pt (250 ml.) chicken stock
salt & pepper
1 pancake
parsley or thyme

To make Take the ingredients from the freezer. Turn the chicken stock into a saucepan and heat it very gently to thaw. Season it to taste and make sure that it is very clear. If not, then strain it through a very clean tea towel or coffee filter paper and reheat it. Roll the pancake up and using a very sharp knife, cut it into thin strips. Add these to the boiling stock.

To finish and serve Check the flavouring. Put crumbled parsley or thyme into the bottom of two warm soup bowls and pour in the very hot soup. Serve with warm crusty bread.

F *Quenelles of Whiting*

6–8 portions

10 oz (250 gm) fillets of whiting
4 oz (100 gm) breadcrumbs
2 egg yolks
1 egg white
1 tablespoon anchovy essence
salt & pepper
6 oz (150 gm) garden peas
¼ pt (125 ml.) fish velouté sauce
2½ fl. oz (63 ml.) soured cream
crumbled parsley

To make Take the required ingredients from the freezer except the peas, sauce, cream and parsley. Poach the fish gently in enough water just to cover it. Drain the fish and flake it very finely or liquidize it. Turn the fish into a basin, add 2 tablespoons of the fish stock, the crumbs, beaten egg, essence, salt and pepper. Using two spoons dipped in hot water, shape the mixture into quenelles (small egg shapes) and set on a greased tray.

To freeze Put the tray in the freezer and when the quenelles are solid, pack them in polythene bags. Seal, label, date and return to the freezer.

To finish and serve Take the required quenelles and proportionate quantity of the other ingredients from the freezer. Unwrap the quenelles and put them into a thickly buttered deep frying pan. Pour over just enough boiling water to cover and cook the quenelles at simmering point for about 15 minutes to cook thoroughly. Cook the peas in the usual way. Meantime heat the sauce very gently to thaw thoroughly. Stir in the soured cream and parsley and heat but do not boil. Drain the quenelles on kitchen paper, put them in a circle on a warm platter, pour the sauce over and pile the peas in the centre to serve.

A *Curried Cauliflower*

6 portions

2 oz (50 gm) butter
2 oz (50 gm) chopped onion
1 dessertspoon mild curry powder
1 oz (25 gm) sultanas
2 teaspoons grated lemon rind
2½ fl. oz (63 ml.) water
12 oz (300 gm) cauliflower florets
10 oz (250 gm) cooked rice
pinch of saffron
crumbled parsley

To make Take the required ingredients from the freezer. Melt the butter in a pan and fry the onion. Stir in the curry powder and cook for 5 minutes. Add the sultanas, lemon rind and water. Break the cauliflower up into very small florets and toss into the pan. Stir well and then cover the pan and cook gently for 5 minutes. Meantime reheat the rice (p. 49), stirring in the saffron blended in a little of the water.

To finish and serve Make a border of the rice on a warm platter, pile the cauliflower in the centre and sprinkle liberally with crumbled parsley and serve as a starter.

A *Pork Spare Ribs in Barbecue Sauce*

2 portions

2 English-cut spare rib chops
salt & pepper
2 tablespoons oil
2 oz (50 gm) chopped onion
2 tablespoons tomato ketchup
3 teaspoons French mustard
1 tablespoon soft brown sugar
1 tablespoon Worcestershire sauce
1 tablespoon malt vinegar
¼ teaspoon chilli powder
2½ fl. oz (63 ml.) tomato purée

To make Take the required ingredients from the freezer. Rub the chops with salt and pepper on both sides and grill under a medium grill for about 10 minutes on each side until thoroughly cooked. Turn up the grill to crisp and brown the fat on the chops. Meantime, heat the oil in a small saucepan and fry the onion finely chopped until it is soft and lightly brown. Take the saucepan off the heat and stir in the remaining ingredients. Heat very gently, stirring constantly.

To finish and serve Arrange the chops on a warm platter and pour the sauce over. Serve hot, accompanied by a green salad and rice or creamed potatoes.

A *Kidneys Chasseur*

2 portions

3 lamb kidneys
salt & pepper
1 oz (25 gm) flour
1 oz (25 gm) butter
¼ pt (125 ml.) espagnol sauce
1 dessertspoon redcurrant jelly
¼ teaspoon cayenne pepper
1 teaspoon lemon juice
1 tablespoon sweet vermouth
1 2¼-oz (64-gm) pkt instant potato
parsley sprigs

To make Take the required ingredients from the freezer and allow to thaw. Core and split the kidneys in half. Mix the salt and pepper with the flour and dip the kidneys in it. Melt the butter in a frying pan and brown the kidneys. Add the sauce, jelly, cayenne, lemon and vermouth to the pan and simmer gently for 10 minutes to cook but not toughen the kidneys. Meantime, make up the potato according to the pack instructions and put into a piping bag with a ½-inch (1-cm.) star nozzle.

To finish and serve Pipe a border of potato round a serving platter, pour the Kidneys Chasseur into the centre, garnish with parsley sprigs and serve very hot.

A Chicken Giblets with Rice

2 portions

2 sets chicken giblets
½ oz (13 gm) butter
2 oz (50 gm) chopped onion
flour
salt & pepper
1 clove garlic – crushed
1 dessertspoon tomato purée
½ teaspoon mixed herbs
¼ pt (125 ml.) chicken stock
12 oz (300 gm) cooked rice
parsley

To make Take the ingredients from the freezer. Clean all the giblets carefully and cut up roughly. Melt the butter in a pan, add the giblets and onion and cook gently. Sprinkle with a little flour and with salt and pepper. Toss to brown. Mix in all the other ingredients except the rice and parsley. Cook gently for 20 minutes. Meantime, reheat the rice (p. 49).

To finish and serve Mix together the rice and giblets and cook for a further 5 minutes. Turn on to warm plates and serve sprinkled with crumbled frozen parsley and with fresh lettuce.

A Chicken Fritters

2 portions

6 oz (150 gm) left-over cooked chicken meat
3 tablespoons oil
3 tablespoons lemon juice
3 tablespoons crumbled parsley
¼ pt (125 ml.) fritter batter
lemon slices

To make Take the required ingredients from the freezer. Cut the chicken up into 2-inch (5-cm.) strips and marinade in a mixture of the oil, juice and parsley. When the batter is thawed out, drain the chicken pieces, dip each in batter and fry in oil. Drain on kitchen paper.

To finish and serve Serve the Chicken Fritters piled high and garnished with lemon twists on a platter. Accompany with a salad.

F or A *Chicken and Courgette Casserole*

6–8 portions

1 3-lb (1½-kilo) chicken
butter
8 oz (200 gm) courgette slices
2 oz (50 gm) sliced onion
2 oz (50 gm) sliced mushrooms
1 teaspoon thyme
¼ pt (125 ml.) béchamel sauce
½ pt (250 ml.) water
salt & pepper
crumbled parsley

To make Take the required ingredients from the freezer. Cut the chicken into 10 pieces, i.e. 2 drumsticks, 2 thighs, 2 wings and 2 breasts, each cut in half. Brush each piece with melted butter and cook under a medium grill for 10 minutes on each side until a golden colour. Put aside the wings to eat immediately. Put the remaining 8 pieces of chicken into a casserole dish. Scatter with the vegetables, herbs and salt and pepper. Very gently heat the sauce to melt it and then blend in the water. Pour this over the chicken and vegetables. Cover the dish.

To freeze The casserole may be frozen at this stage. Divide it into appropriately sized foil dishes. Seal, label, date and freeze.

To finish and serve If the casserole has been frozen, take it from the freezer and put it into an oven preheated to 400°F, Gas 6 (200°C), for 40 minutes. If not, cook it in the oven at 350°F, Gas 4 (180°C), for 30 minutes. Remove the cover, stir the contents and serve with crumbled parsley sprinkled on top.

A *Prawns Américaine*

4 portions

1¼ lb (500 gm) cooked rice
¼ teaspoon saffron
12 oz (300 gm) peeled prawns
2 tablespoons olive oil
1 oz (25 gm) finely chopped onions
1 clove garlic – crushed
1 tablespoon brandy
¼ pt (125 ml.) dry white wine
2½ fl. oz (63 ml.) tomato purée
salt & pepper
1 teaspoon crumbled tarragon
2 teaspoons crumbled parsley
½ teaspoon arrowroot

To make Take the required ingredients from the freezer. Put the rice on to reheat (p. 49) having stirred into it the saffron blended with a little water. Set aside four well shaped prawns for garnish. Heat the oil in a frying pan. Toss the prawns in the oil. Add the onion and garlic to the pan and cook gently. Pour in the brandy, increase the heat and burn off the alcohol by setting the contents of the pan alight. When the flame has gone out, lower the heat a little and carefully pour in the wine and tomato purée. Add salt and pepper and cook for 5–10 minutes. Remove the prawns and keep warm. Add the herbs and the arrowroot blended in a little water. Simmer 2–3 minutes to thicken the sauce very slightly.

To finish and serve Make a border of saffron rice round an oval platter, put the prawns in the centre and pour the sauce over the prawns. Serve hot with a salad.

A *Prawn and Raisin Pancakes*

2 portions

4 pancakes
8 oz (200 gm) peeled prawns
1 oz (25 gm) raisins
2½ fl. oz (63 ml.) béchamel sauce
1 tablespoon lemon juice
salt & pepper
crumbled parsley

To make Take the required ingredients from the freezer, and thaw sufficiently to allow handling. Meantime soak the raisins in boiling water to soften and swell. Drain them and mix with the prawns, sauce and lemon juice. Check the seasoning. Divide the mixture between the 4 pancakes and roll up so that the pale side is outside. Place in a greased pie dish.

To finish and serve Heat the pancakes and brown uncovered in the oven preheated to 375°F, Gas 5 (190°C), for 20 minutes. Serve hot, sprinkled with crumbled parsley and accompanied by a tomato and cucumber salad or buttered broad beans.

A *Grilled Trout with Savoury Cabbage*

2 portions

2 trout
salt & pepper
3 tablespoons olive oil
1 oz (25 gm) chopped onion
1 clove garlic – crushed
6 oz (150 gm) chopped cabbage
2 tomatoes, chopped
1 oz (25 gm) chopped toasted almonds

To make Take the ingredients from the freezer. Rub the trout with salt and pepper and make several diagonal cuts through the skin and flesh along both sides. Brush with oil and put to grill under a low grill for 5 minutes on each side and then turn the grill up to hot and grill the fish for a further 5 minutes on each side. Meantime heat the oil in the frying pan and fry the onion and garlic until soft and slightly brown. Add the cabbage and tomato to the pan with salt and pepper to taste. Toss the mixture over a medium heat until it is thoroughly heated through but still fairly crisp.

To finish and serve When the cabbage is ready, put it on to a warm oval platter and place the grilled fish on top. Sprinkle the whole dish with toasted almonds.

A *Ratatouille Slice*

4–6 portions

1 7½-oz (187-gm) pkt puff pastry
2½ fl. oz (63 ml.) olive oil
2 cloves garlic
1 oz (25 gm) finely chopped onion
6 oz (150 gm) aubergine slices
6 oz (150 gm) courgette slices
1 small green pepper – chopped
4 tomatoes – quartered
1 teaspoon sweet mixed herbs
¼ pt (125 ml.) béchamel sauce
2 tablespoons dry white wine

To make Take the required ingredients from the freezer and allow to thaw sufficiently to enable handling. Roll the pastry to double its width, trim off the edges using a hot knife and turn it upside-down on to a wetted baking tray. Bake in the oven pre-heated to 425°F, Gas 7 (220°C), for 15 minutes until well risen and cooked through. Meantime, heat the oil in a deep frying pan and gently fry the garlic and onion. Add the aubergine, courgette and pepper and cook gently, being careful not to break up the vegetables too much. Mix in the tomatoes and herbs. Keep warm. Turn the sauce into a small pan and beat in the wine. Heat it thoroughly but do not boil.

To finish and serve Take the pastry from the oven and split it in half. Place on a warm platter. Carefully spoon the ratatouille into the lower half, cover with the pastry top and pour the sauce over the whole Ratatouille Slice. Serve hot on its own as a tasty meal.

A *Chilli Rice au Gratin*

2 portions

12 oz (300 gm) cooked rice
1 oz (25 gm) butter
4 oz (100 gm) chopped onion
2 oz (50 gm) chopped celery
1 small green pepper
2 tomatoes
1 oz (25 gm) peas
2 tablespoons tomato purée
2½ fl. oz (63 ml.) water
½ teaspoon chilli powder
salt & pepper
1 teaspoon soft brown sugar
2 oz (50 gm) grated cheese

To make Take the ingredients from the freezer. Melt the butter in a frying pan and add the onion and celery. Cook gently. De-seed and chop the pepper. Chop the tomatoes. Add the pepper, tomatoes and all the other ingredients except the cheese to the pan. Cook gently, stirring constantly.

To finish and serve Turn the rice on to a warm dish, sprinkle the top liberally with the cheese and brown under a hot grill. Serve hot with fried chicken drumsticks, also from the freezer.

A *Rhubarb Cheese Swans*

6 portions

12 oz (300 gm) rhubarb
4 oz (100 gm) caster sugar
2 eggs
8 oz (200 gm) cottage cheese
¼ pt (120 ml.) cream
12 choux pastry swans (p. 201: White Swans)

To make Take the required ingredients from the freezer. Stew the rhubarb gently and liquidize it to a purée. Blend in the sugar and eggs, then cook over a gentle heat, stirring continuously until the mixture thickens. Cool. Sieve the cottage cheese and lightly whip the cream. Fold both into the cold rhubarb. Spoon the mixture into the choux pastries and assemble the swans.

To finish and serve Arrange the swans decoratively on a platter and dust with icing sugar before serving.

A *Peach and Almond Blush*

2 portions

2 portions White Lady (p. 129)
2 peach halves
2½ fl. oz (63 ml.) raspberry purée
2 teaspoons toasted chopped almonds

To make Take the peaches and the raspberry purée from the freezer and allow them to thaw. Drain the peaches. Into each of 2 well chilled glasses put a portion of White Lady, top with a peach-half, rounded side up, pour over the raspberry purée and top with a few toasted almonds. Serve immediately.

A *Yogurt and Strawberry Flan*

4–6 portions

1 small pkt digestive biscuits
2 oz (50 gm) butter
8 oz (200 gm) cottage cheese
¼ pt (125 ml.) sweetened natural yogurt
1 dessertspoon Cointreau
8 oz (200 gm) strawberries
1 tablespoon jelly marmalade

To make Take the required ingredients from the freezer. Crush the biscuits with a rolling pin and mix in the melted butter. Press the mixture into a flan ring and chill. Meantime sieve the cottage cheese into a basin. Add the yogurt and Cointreau and beat till smooth. Pour this into the flan base and chill in the freezer for 10–15 minutes.

To finish and serve Remove the flan ring and place the flan on a serving dish. Pile the strawberries on top of the yogurt mixture and brush with a little melted jelly marmalade to glaze.

F *Vanilla Mousse*

6–8 portions

4 oz (100 gm) sugar
4 egg yolks
½ pt (250 ml.) milk
vanilla
¾ pt (375 ml.) whipped cream

To make Whisk the sugar and yolks together. Gently heat the milk to boiling point and then pour it over the eggs, whisking constantly. Strain the custard into a saucepan and continue stirring over a low heat until it thickens. Make sure it is thoroughly cooked and thick but not boiled. If insufficiently cooked, it is dry when frozen. Add vanilla essence to taste, cover and set aside to cool. When cold fold in the cream.

To freeze Pack the mousse into suitably sized plastic containers. Cover, seal, label, date and freeze.

To finish and serve Take the Vanilla Mousse from the freezer and serve spooned into glasses, with almost any fruit purée or a chocolate sauce poured over; or use as a basis for more complicated iced sweets.

SUGGESTED MENUS

Curried Cauliflower
Chicken and Courgette Casserole

Prawns Américaine
Rhubarb Cheese Swans

Quenelles of Whiting
Pork Spare Ribs in Barbecue Sauce
Vanilla Mousse

Tomato and Orange Soup
Prawn and Raisin Pancakes
Peach and Almond Blush

Angel Soup
Grilled Trout with Savoury Cabbage
Yogurt and Strawberry Flan

IN A RUSH

A *Lemon and Watercress Soup*

6 portions

2 pts (1 litre) chicken stock
1 bunch watercress
6 oz (150 gm) cooked rice
2½ fl. oz (63 ml.) lemon juice
2 eggs
salt & pepper
a few strips lemon rind

To make Wash the watercress and chop it roughly. Put the stock and watercress in a pan and heat it very gently to boiling point. Cool it slightly and liquidize it or rub the soup through a sieve. Add the rice to the soup and return it to a gentle heat to soften the rice. Meantime, beat together the lemon juice and eggs. Whisk in 3 tablespoons of hot soup. Then, over a low heat, whisk the egg mixture into the soup. Bring to the boil and immediately take off the heat.

To finish and serve Check the seasoning and make sure the soup is very hot but not boiling. Pour the soup into warm bowls and serve topped with a few fine strips of lemon rind.

A *Easy Taramosalata*

4–6 portions

6 oz (150 gm) smoked cod roe
1 tablespoon olive oil
¼ pt (125 ml.) soured cream
1 dessertspoon crumbled parsley
1 clove garlic – crushed
black pepper to taste
lemon slices

To make Take the required ingredients from the freezer. Put the roe (in its wrapping) in a basin and cover with cold water to thaw and soften the roe. Leave it for 1–1½ hours. Drain the roe, skin it and mash it in a basin. Using an electric whisk, beat the roe and oil together until smooth. Very lightly whisk in the remaining ingredients except the lemon slices.

To finish and serve Pile the Taramosalata on to a platter or into small individual cocotte dishes. Garnish with a slice of lemon and serve cold with crusty brown bread rolls or potato scones (p. 195).

A *Prawn Bisque with Rice*

6 portions

1½ pts (750 ml.) fish stock
2 oz (50 gm) tomato purée
2 oz (50 gm) cooked rice
3 oz (75 gm) peeled prawns
1 oz (25 gm) butter
½ oz (13 gm) flour
crumbled parsley

To make Take the necessary ingredients from the freezer. Turn the stock into a saucepan and heat very gently to thaw. Put six nicely shaped prawns aside for garnish. Chop the rest fairly finely. Add the tomato purée, rice and chopped prawns to the stock and simmer gently. Meantime melt the butter in a small pan, beat in the flour and cook for 3 minutes. Gradually beat in a little hot soup to give a thin, smooth sauce. Stir the sauce into the soup.

To finish and serve Bring the soup to the boil, pour into warm soup bowls and garnish each with a whole prawn and a light sprinkling of crumbled parsley.

A Guinea Fowl in Lemon Sauce

6–8 portions

2 guinea fowl	**¼ pt (125 ml.) milk**
salt	**½ oz (13 gm) butter**
bouquet garni	**1 oz (25 gm) cornflour**
1 blade mace	**2½ fl. oz (63 ml.) lemon juice**
1 bayleaf	**sugar**
6 peppercorns	**2½ fl. oz (63 ml.) cream**
1 small green pepper	**strips of lemon rind**

To make Rub the guinea fowl with salt and put into a large saucepan with enough water just to cover the birds. Add the bouquet garni, mace, bayleaf and peppercorns. Take the green pepper from the freezer and trim off a few very thin strips for garnish. Put these into a polythene bag and return to the freezer. Chop the rest of the pepper, discarding the seeds, and add to the saucepan. Bring the saucepan to the boil, cover and simmer very gently for about 45 minutes until the birds are tender. Lift them out and cut up into joints. Put into a foil container. Blend the cornflour with a little of the milk. Put the rest into a small saucepan along with the butter and ¼ pint (125 ml.) strained stock. Heat it gently and mix in the blended cornflour. Stir constantly until the sauce thickens. Add the lemon juice. Check the seasoning, adding a little sugar if necessary. Pour the sauce over the guinea fowl.

To freeze Set the guinea fowl container aside to cool. Seal, label, date and freeze.

To finish and serve Take the guinea fowl, green pepper and lemon strips and cream from the freezer. Put the guinea fowl into the oven preheated to 400°F, Gas 6 (200°C), for 35 minutes to thaw and heat through thoroughly. Lift the pieces of guinea fowl on to a serving platter, leaving as much of the sauce as possible in the container. Into this, stir the cream and check the seasoning. Put the container on top of a hotplate on the cooker to make sure it is thoroughly hot. Stir constantly but do not boil.

Pour the sauce over the guinea fowl and serve decorated with the strips of green pepper and lemon rind.

A *Cyrano Cutlets*

2 portions

4 lamb cutlets	**2 oz (50 gm) sliced mushrooms**
salt & pepper	**¼ pt (125 ml.) béchamel sauce**
2 lamb kidneys	**2½ fl. oz (63 ml.) cream**
12 asparagus spears	**4 whole mushrooms**

To make Take the ingredients from the freezer. Rub the cutlets with salt and pepper and, if still frozen, fry slowly in butter for 7–10 minutes on each side. If thawed, grill for 5 minutes on each side. Split the kidneys in half and remove the core. Fry or grill them as for the cutlets but for only 5 minutes and 2 minutes respectively. Meantime, tie the asparagus in a bundle and cook in simmering salted water for 5 minutes. Drain well and keep warm. In another small pan, heat together the sliced mushrooms and the béchamel sauce. Liquidize it or rub through a sieve to give a smooth mushroom cream. Stir in the cream and return the sauce to the pan to heat thoroughly, but do not boil. Check the seasoning. Put the whole mushrooms into the frying pan or under the grill just long enough to heat them.

To finish and serve On to a warm platter, arrange four groups of three asparagus spears and place a cutlet on each group. Place ½ a kidney on each cutlet so that the smooth side is uppermost. Mask the kidney, cutlets and asparagus with the sauce so that only the tips of the asparagus show. Garnish each group with an upturned whole mushroom. Serve hot with peas and croquette potatoes.

A *Veal and Ham Flan*

4 portions

1 7-inch (15-cm.) cooked short-crust pastry flan case
4 oz (100 gm) cooked roast veal
4 oz (100 gm) cooked boiled ham
¼ pt (125 ml.) béchamel sauce
2½ fl. oz (63 ml.) soured cream
1 oz (25 gm) peas
1 oz (25 gm) sliced mushrooms
½ small red sweet pepper – chopped
2 teaspoons chopped chives
salt & pepper
crumbled parsley

To make Take the required ingredients from the freezer and allow to thaw. Chop the meats and mix with the sauce, cream, vegetables and chives. Check the seasoning and spoon the mixture into the flan case. This flan may also be served hot, in which case, heat the flan case under a medium grill but covered with a piece of foil to prevent over-browning. Meantime heat all the other ingredients (except the parsley) gently together in a saucepan. Pour the hot meat mixture into a warm flan case.

To finish and serve Whether served hot or cold, put the flan on to a serving platter and garnish with crumbled parsley.

A *Blanquette of Veal*

4 portions

1 lb (400 gm) pie veal
3 oz (75 gm) chopped onion
6 cloves
5 peppercorns
1 teaspoon dill
1 bayleaf
2 tablespoons lemon juice
1 pt (500 ml.) water
1 pt (500 ml.) béchamel sauce
2 egg yolks
¼ pt (125 ml.) cream
crumbled parsley
1 lemon

To make Take the required ingredients from the freezer. Trim and cut up the veal. Put it and the next seven ingredients all into a saucepan, bring to the boil, skim, then simmer for 1 hour. Meantime gently thaw the sauce over a gentle heat. Lightly whisk together the eggs and cream and beat into the sauce. Heat but do not boil.

To finish and serve Lift the veal out of the stock (strain the stock and freeze it for other uses at a later date), put it into a warm serving dish, pour the sauce over and sprinkle liberally with crumbled parsley. Serve hot with the lemon cut in wedges and served separately. Accompany by leaf spinach or courgettes and creamed potatoes.

F *Chickenburgers*

8 portions

2 lb (1 kilo) chicken pieces
4 oz (100 gm) white breadcrumbs
1 teaspoon dried tarragon
salt & pepper
1 egg

To make Using a sharp knife take the chicken meat off the bones and mince it coarsely. (Use the bones for stock.) Mix together the chicken, crumbs, herbs and seasoning. Whisk the egg lightly and use sufficient to bind the chicken mixture. Divide it into eight, roll each into a ball and flatten to about ½ inch (1 cm.) thick, making sure the edges are the same thickness as the middle.

To freeze Interleaf the Chickenburgers with greased greaseproof paper, butcher's paper or polythene film, overwrap in polythene bags in convenient quantities. Seal, label, date and freeze.

To finish and serve Take the required number from the freezer. Fry from frozen in little melted butter for 5 minutes on each side. Serve with a salad and chutney or with fried onions inside a soft roll.

A *Chicken Choux*

2 portions

4 large choux pastry puffs
6 oz (150 gm) cooked chicken – chopped
½ pt (250 ml.) béchamel sauce
1 oz (25 gm) chopped celery
4 oz (100 gm) grated cheese
salt & pepper

To make Take the required ingredients from the freezer. Put the choux puffs on a baking tray and into the oven preheated to 325°F, Gas 3 (160°C), to warm through. Meantime turn the chicken, sauce and celery into a saucepan and stir over a very gentle heat to thaw and heat through. Stir in 3 oz (75 gm) of the cheese and check the seasoning. Take the choux puffs from the oven and turn the oven up to 425°F, Gas 7 (220°C). Split the choux puffs and fill each with the chicken mixture.

To finish and serve Place the filled choux puffs on a greased serving dish, sprinkle the tops with the remaining cheese and put into the hot oven to melt and brown the tops. Serve hot with green vegetables or salad.

F *Chicken Goulash*

4 portions

½ pt (250 ml.) chicken stock
4 small chicken quarters
salt & pepper
1 oz (25 gm) butter
2 oz (50 gm) chopped onion
2 teaspoons paprika pepper
¼ pt (125 ml.) tomato purée
3 tomatoes
1 tablespoon cornflour
¼ pt (125 ml.) natural yogurt
lemon slices for garnish

To make Take from the freezer all the ingredients required except the yogurt and lemon. Put the stock into a saucepan and heat it very gently to thaw it out. Put the frozen chicken joints into the warm stock, cover and leave for 30 minutes. Lift the joints out of the stock and dry them. Season each with salt and pepper and grill under a medium grill for 10 minutes on each side until golden. Meantime melt the butter in a medium saucepan and gently fry the onion until soft. Stir in the paprika, tomato purée and roughly chopped tomatoes. Blend the cornflour with a little of the chicken stock, make up to ¼ pint (125 ml.) with remaining stock and pour this into the saucepan. Add the chicken, cover and simmer gently for 30 minutes. Set aside to cool.

To freeze Turn the mixture into appropriately sized foil containers. Seal, label, date and freeze.

To finish and serve Take the required quantity of chicken mixture from the freezer and a proportionate quantity of yogurt. Turn the chicken and sauce into a saucepan and heat very gently until thawed and heated through. Thaw the yogurt (p. 45). Lift the chicken pieces on to a warm serving dish. Stir the yogurt into the tomato and paprika sauce and pour this goulash sauce over the chicken. Garnish with lemon slices.

A *Apple Stuffed Herrings*

portions

small filleted herrings
pt (125 ml.) cider or dry white wine
oz (50 gm) brown breadcrumbs
½ oz (13 gm) chopped toasted almonds
2 oz (50 gm) apple slices – chopped finely
salt & pepper

To make Take the required ingredients from the freezer. Put the herrings in a dish, pour over the cider or wine and allow the fish to thaw in this marinade. Drain the fish and lay on a greased oven-proof dish. Mix together the other ingredients using a little of the marinade to hold the stuffing mixture together very lightly. Set aside a very little of the stuffing to use as a topping later. Divide the rest of the stuffing between the fish, fold the fish lengthwise over the stuffing, cover the dish with greased foil.

To finish and serve Bake the fish in the oven, preheated to 350°F, Gas 4 (180°C), for 20 minutes. Remove the foil, sprinkle the rest of the stuffing over the fish, turn the oven up to 400°F, Gas 6 (200°C), and bake for a further 10 minutes to crisp and brown the top. Garnish with a couple of apple slices and serve hot with celery.

A *Chinese Fried Rice with Prawns*

2 portions

2 oz (50 gm) bacon rashers
2 tablespoons olive oil
1 oz (25 gm) chopped onion
12 oz (300 gm) cooked rice
salt & pepper
4 oz (100 gm) peeled prawns
2 eggs
1 tablespoon Soy sauce
1 tablespoon crumbled parsley

To make Take the ingredients from the freezer, chop the bacon into small pieces and fry gently in a frying pan. Add the oil and onions (which may need to be chopped more finely) to the bacon and fry until the onion and bacon are cooked and slightly crispy. Add the rice to the pan and season with salt and pepper to taste. Add the prawns and cook gently until thoroughly hot. Make a space in the centre of the rice and break the eggs into it. Using a fork or spatula, cook the egg until it begins to look like soft scrambled egg and then mix it through the rice. Mix in the sauce and parsley.

To finish and serve Turn the Chinese Fried Rice with Prawns on to a platter and serve hot or cold with shredded fried lettuce or raw beanshoots.

A *Spiced Eve's Pudding*

4 portions

1 lb (400 gm) apple slices
2 oz (50 gm) soft brown sugar
2 teaspoons ground cinnamon
½ teaspoon ground cloves
1 tablespoon lemon juice
2 teaspoons grated lemon rind
1 egg
2 oz (50 gm) soft margarine
2 oz (50 gm) caster sugar
2 oz (50 gm) self-raising flour

To make Take the apples from the freezer and put half in the bottom of a greased 1½-pint (750-ml.) pie dish. Mix together the sugar, half the cinnamon, the cloves, lemon juice and rind and sprinkle on top of the apples. Put the rest of the apples on top. Put the four remaining ingredients and the rest of the cinnamon all into a basin and whisk until light and fluffy. Spoon this mixture over the apples so as to seal the edges, and bake in the oven preheated to 360°F, Gas 4–5 (185°C), for 30 minutes until the sponge top is risen and springy to the touch.

To finish and serve Serve the Spiced Eve's Pudding hot or cold with lightly beaten cream.

F *Cinnamon and Lemon Rice Balls*

4–6 portions

4 oz (100 gm) raw rice
1 pt (500 ml.) milk
5 oz (125 gm) sugar
2 eggs
4 teaspoons ground cinnamon
2 teaspoons finely grated lemon rind
1 oz (25 gm) white breadcrumbs
¼ pt (125 ml.) lemon juice
¼ pt (125 ml.) water
2 teaspoons arrowroot

To make Take the required ingredients except the lemon juice from the freezer. Put the rice into a pan of plenty of cold water, bring quickly to the boil and boil rapidly for 10 minutes. Drain it well, pour in the milk and simmer until all the milk is absorbed.

Mix in 1 oz (25 gm) of the sugar, 1 egg, 2 teaspoons of the cinnamon and the lemon rind. Spread the mixture out on a platter and put into the freezer for 10 minutes or so to cool thoroughly and solidify a bit. Shape the mixture into small balls and coat in the remaining egg beaten and the white crumbs.

To freeze Place the rice balls on a tray and freeze. When solid, pack in convenient quantities in plastic boxes. Seal, label, date and return to the freezer.

To finish and serve Take the lemon juice and the required number of rice balls from the freezer and immediately fry in hot oil until heated through and golden brown. Toss in a mixture of the remaining sugar and cinnamon. Pile on to a warm dish and keep warm. Meantime gently heat together the lemon juice, water and sugar to taste, and stir in the arrowroot blended with a little of the water. Boil until it thickens and clears. Stir well. Serve the Cinnamon and Lemon Rice Balls with the hot lemon sauce poured over.

A *Chestnut Mont Blanc*

4 portions

¾ pt (375 ml.) sweetened chestnut purée
3 tablespoons basic syrup (p. 47)
½ pt (250 ml.) cream
1 egg white
1 oz (25 gm) sugar
½ teaspoon vanilla essence

To make Take the required ingredients from the freezer and heat the purée gently. Beat well. Beat in the basic syrup. Put this purée into a piping bag with a small plain nozzle. Butter and sugar a ring mould or a savarin mould and then run the warm chestnut purée out of the bag all higgledy-piggledy into the mould so that it looks like spaghetti. Leave it aside for a minute or two. Whisk the cream and the egg white separately then fold them together along with the sugar and vanilla. This is Chantilly Cream.

To finish and serve Turn the chestnut out on to a very cold serving platter. Fill the centre with a mound of the Chantilly Cream at the very last moment before serving.

A *Meringue Cream Pancakes*

2 portions

4 pancakes	**1 egg white**
½ pt (250 ml.) St Honoré Cream (p. 188: Gâteau St Honoré)	**2 oz (50 gm) caster sugar**
	lemon juice

To make Take the required ingredients from the freezer. Spread some cream on the cooked side of each pancake. Fold up the sides all round to enclose the cream and form a rectangle. Place the pancakes on a greased and sugared tray. Whisk the egg white and fold in ⅔ of the sugar. Pile this meringue on top of each pancake, sprinkle with the remaining sugar and bake in the oven preheated to 300°F, Gas 2 (150°C), for ¾–1 hour until crisp and dry. Alternatively and for speed, the pancakes may be baked in the oven preheated to 400°F, Gas 6 (200°C), for 5–6 minutes to brown and crisp the top.

To finish and serve Carefully lift the pancakes on to a platter and, if the meringue has been cooked by the quick method, then serve them immediately; if by the slower method, the Meringue Cream Pancakes may be served hot or cold. Hand pure lemon juice separately.

F Rum Baba

6–8 portions

8 oz (200 gm) flour
½ oz (13 gm) yeast
1 oz (25 gm) caster sugar
¼ pt (125 ml.) lukewarm milk and water, mixed
2 eggs
2 oz (50 gm) butter
3 oz (75 gm) shredded almonds
¾ pt (375 ml.) rum syrup
½ pt (250 ml.) whipped cream in whirls

To make Sift the flour into a warm basin. In a cup, cream the yeast with 1 teaspoon of the sugar and mix with 3 tablespoons of the liquid. Pour this into a well in the centre of the flour and cover with flour. Set aside in a warm place for 10 minutes when the yeast will crack through the flour. Lightly whisk the eggs with the remaining liquid and pour this into the flour. Knead to an elastic dough. With the hand, work in the rest of the sugar, the melted butter and 2 oz (50 gm) of the almonds and beat until the mixture is like a very thick batter. Butter thickly a ring mould or 6–8 small moulds and coat with the rest of the almonds. Turn the dough into the mould(s) and set aside in a warm place until risen to double the size. Bake in the oven preheated to 400°F, Gas 6 (200°C), for 45 minutes. Turn out, prick all over and pour over half the syrup (p. 47).

To freeze When thoroughly cold, place the Rum Babas on a tray and freeze. When solid, wrap separately in a square of foil and in a polythene bag. Seal, label, date and return to the freezer.

To finish and serve Take the Baba from the freezer, unwrap and place on a serving dish. Prick with a fork and pour over the proportionate amount of the rest of the rum syrup and decorate with frozen cream whirls. Allow 2 hours for the whole dish to thaw before serving.

SUGGESTED MENUS

Chicken Goulash
Cinnamon and Lemon Rice Balls

Apple Stuffed Herrings
Meringue Cream Pancakes

Easy Taramosalata
Veal and Ham Flan
Rum Baba

Lemon and Watercress Soup
Blanquette of Veal
Spiced Eve's Pudding

Prawn Bisque with Rice
Guinea Fowl in Lemon Sauce
Chestnut Mont Blanc

LEAVE HIM TO IT

F *Goatherd's Soup*

6–8 portions

4 oz (100 gm) dried red kidney beans
1 pt (500 ml.) water
2 oz (50 gm) sliced onion
2 oz (50 gm) sliced carrots
½ pt (250 ml.) chicken stock
½ pt (250 ml.) milk
2 oz (50 gm) butter
salt & pepper
fried croûtons (p. 22)

To make Take the necessary ingredients from the freezer and put the first four items into a saucepan. Bring to the boil and simmer for 30 minutes until the beans and vegetables are very tender. Liquidize the soup or rub it through a fine sieve. Add the stock, milk and butter to make a creamy soup. Stir well, season and set aside to cool.

To freeze Turn the soup into conveniently sized lined waxed cartons or polythene-lined foil bags. Seal, label, date and freeze.

To finish and serve Take the required quantity of soup and the proportionate amount of fried croûtons from the freezer. Turn the soup into a saucepan and heat slowly but thoroughly, stirring constantly. Meantime heat the croûtons then pour the soup into warm bowls and sprinkle with hot croûtons.

F *Pork Pâté*

8–10 portions

8 oz (200 gm) streaky bacon rashers
1½ lb (600 gm) pork fillet
8 oz (200 gm) pigs' liver
8 oz (200 gm) belly pork
2 oz (50 gm) chopped onion
salt
1 teaspoon ground black pepper
¼ teaspoon ground mace
1 teaspoon rosemary
4 oz (100 gm) white breadcrumbs
1 egg – beaten
melted butter to cover
2 cloves garlic – crushed
lemon slices

To make Line one 2-pint (1-litre) casserole dish or two or more smaller ones with foil and then line with the bacon rashers, de-rinded. Mince the fillet, liver, belly and onion all together and fairly finely. Mix in all the other ingredients except the butter, garlic and lemon adding a little water if necessary to give a soft dropping consistency. Pack the pâté into the lined casserole(s) and cover with a piece of greased foil. Put the lid on and set the dish(es) in a roasting tin of hot water. Bake in the oven pre-heated to 325°F, Gas 3 (160°C), for 3–4 hours depending on the size of the casserole(s) used. Remove the lid and foil. Replace with another piece of buttered foil and put a plate with a weight on top of the pâté. Cover and set aside to cool. Leave for 2 days before freezing to allow flavours to mature.

To freeze Lift the pâté plus foil lining carefully out of the casserole(s), overwrap in foil, seal, label, date and freeze.

To finish and serve Take the required quantity of Pork Pâté from the freezer, unwrap it and put into the original casserole. Melt the butter and mix in the garlic. Pour over the pâté to fill the gaps and give a seal. Set aside overnight to allow the butter to harden and the pâté itself to thaw. Garnish with lemon slices and serve with toast or crusty bread as a starter, with a salad as a main course, or spread on biscuits as a cocktail savoury.

A *Pumpkin au Gratin*

2–4 portions

1 2¼-oz (64-gm) pkt instant potato
8 oz (200 gm) broad beans
salt & pepper
½ pt (250 ml.) pumpkin purée
2 tomatoes – sliced
¼ pt (125 ml.) béchamel sauce
2 oz (50 gm) grated cheese
1 oz (25 gm) breadcrumbs

To make Take the required ingredients from the freezer. Grease a 1½-pint (750-ml.) pie dish. Make up the potato according to the pack instructions and spread in the bottom of the pie dish. Spread out the beans on top of this and sprinkle with salt and pepper. Spoon in the pumpkin purée and top with the tomato slices. Pour over the sauce and top with a mixture of the cheese and breadcrumbs. Bake in the oven preheated to 375°F, Gas 5 (190°C), for 20 minutes until the top is crispy and brown and the whole dish is thoroughly heated through.

To finish and serve Put the pie dish on an oval platter and serve accompanied with a green salad.

F *Rabbit with Green Sauce*

6 portions

1 rabbit
salt & pepper
2 chicken livers
½ pt (250 ml.) dry cider
water
1 oz (25 gm) butter
½ teaspoon marjoram
½ teaspoon thyme
1 oz (25 gm) cornflour
1 large bunch parsley
2½ fl. oz (63 ml.) soured cream
lemon wedges
parsley sprigs

To make Wipe the rabbit, rub with salt and pepper, put the chicken livers into the carcase and place in a saucepan. Pour over the cider and sufficient water to cover the rabbit. Cover, bring to the boil and simmer for about 1 hour until the rabbit is cooked.

Lift the rabbit out of the liquid and cut it into 6 portions. Discard the livers. Put the joints into appropriately sized foil dishes. Meantime, melt the butter in a small saucepan, add the thyme and marjoram. Strain ½ pint (250 ml.) of the liquor from the rabbit into the melted butter. Heat gently. Use a little water to blend the cornflour, pour it into the liquid, bring to the boil stirring constantly until the sauce thickens. Crumble in the parsley and mix it well so that the sauce is green. Pour this over the rabbit. Cover and set aside to cool.

To freeze Seal, label, date and freeze.

To finish and serve Take the rabbit from the freezer and, still covered, put it into the oven preheated to 400°F, Gas 6 (200°C), for 30–40 minutes until thoroughly hot. Lift the rabbit joints out of the sauce on to a warm serving dish and keep warm. Then put the sauce in the foil dish over a gentle heat and stir in the soured cream. Heat but do not boil. Pour over the rabbit and garnish with lemon wedges and parsley sprigs to serve.

A or F *Lamb Creole*

4 portions

2 tablespoons oil
6 oz (150 gm) chopped onion
2½ lb (1 kilo) neck of lamb
2 teaspoons mild curry powder
1 teaspoon flour
¼ pt (125 ml.) stock or water
1 oz (25 gm) sultanas
1 bouquet garni
2 teaspoons coconut
1 banana – sliced
1¼ lb (500 gm) cooked rice

To make Heat the oil in a stewpan and fry the onion until soft. Meantime cut the neck from the bones and into chunks. Brown in the oil with the onion. Lift the lamb out and set aside. To the pan add the curry and flour. Cook gently in the oil for 2–3 minutes stirring constantly. Stir in the water or stock, add the sultanas and herbs. Return the meat to the pan, cover it and simmer gently for 45 minutes.

To freeze The Lamb Creole may be frozen at this stage. Cool it, turn it into a foil or plastic container, cover, seal, label, date and freeze.

To finish and serve If frozen, the lamb will require gentle cooking in a stewpan for 35 minutes before the addition of the coconut and banana. Take the rice from the freezer and reheat it (p. 49). Pile it into a dish and keep it warm. Add the coconut and banana to the lamb and cook for a further 5 minutes without the lid. Remove the herbs and turn the Lamb Creole into a serving dish. Serve hot with the rice, and a green salad on the side.

A *Lamb Chops and Redcurrants*

2 portions

2 lamb loin chops
salt & pepper
4 oz (100 gm) redcurrants
4 tablespoons water
1 tablespoon sugar
4 tablespoons stock
4 tablespoons vinegar
1 teaspoon arrowroot

To make Take the required ingredients from the freezer. Rub the chops with salt and pepper and cook under a medium grill for 7–10 minutes on each side. Meantime put all the other ingredients except the arrowroot into a small saucepan. Bring it to the boil slowly. Blend the arrowroot with a little water and pour it into the redcurrants. Stir until it thickens.

To finish and serve Arrange the chops on a platter and pour the sauce over. Serve hot with a salad of endive and mushroom slices.

F *Greek Bitockes*

6–8 portions

4 oz (100 gm) breadcrumbs
2½ fl. oz (63 ml.) milk
12 oz (300 gm) minced middle neck of lamb
salt & pepper
3 oz (75 gm) Boursin cheese or any rich cream cheese with herbs
1 egg – lightly beaten
2 oz (50 gm) flour
¾ pt (375 ml.) tomato purée

To make Take the crumbs from the freezer and soak in the milk. Add the minced lamb and salt and pepper. Press the cheese through a sieve and mix into the meat mixture. Mix with sufficient of the egg to hold the mixture together. Shape the mixture into 18–24 balls and flatten to about ½-inch (1-cm.) thickness. Dip in flour and set on polythene film or waxed paper on a tray.

To freeze Put the tray into the freezer. When the bitockes are solid, take them from the freezer and repack them in convenient quantities in polythene bags. Seal, label, date and return to the freezer.

To finish and serve Take the required amount of bitockes and tomato purée from the freezer. Turn the tomato purée into a saucepan and heat it gently. Check the seasoning. Keep it warm. Then fry the bitockes in hot oil for 2–3 minutes on each side until cooked and lightly browned. Serve the Greek Bitockes on a warm platter and with the hot tomato purée poured over. Accompany with rice, macaroni or simply lots of chopped fresh cucumber and endive.

A *Grilled Chicken Portuguaise*

2 portions

2 chicken quarters
2 oz (50 gm) butter
½ oz (13 gm) chopped onion
½ clove garlic
salt & pepper
¼ pt (125 ml.) espagnol sauce
1 tomato
1 teaspoon crumbled parsley

To make Take the chicken from the freezer 24 hours before needed and thaw slowly in the refrigerator. Take the other ingredients from the freezer. Melt the butter in a small saucepan, chop the onion more finely and gently fry it with the crushed garlic clove in the butter. Use some of the butter to brush the chicken joints liberally, sprinkle with salt and pepper and put them to cook for 10 minutes on each side under a medium grill. Turn the sauce into the pan with the onion and turn down the heat very low so that the sauce thaws. Add the tomato and when it is soft, take it out, skin it, chop it and return it to the sauce. Add the parsley and heat the sauce thoroughly.

To finish and serve When the chicken is cooked and golden brown and the sauce is hot, put the chicken on to a dish and pour the sauce over. Accompany with Duchess potatoes and a green salad.

F *Granny's Chicken Pie*

2 portions

1 large fresh breast of chicken
2 rashers back bacon
1 oz (25 gm) flour
salt & pepper
2 eggs
¼ pt (125 ml.) chicken stock
1 oz (25 gm) white breadcrumbs
1 teaspoon sage
1 7½-oz (187-gm) pkt shortcrust pastry

To make Take the required ingredients from the freezer. Cut the chicken meat off the bones and into small cubes. Chop the bacon and fry it gently. Mix the flour with salt and pepper and toss the chicken pieces in it. Add chicken to the bacon and fry gently to cook through. Meantime hardboil and chop one of the eggs. Lightly whisk the other egg and use a little of it to blend together the breadcrumbs and sage to make a stuffing. Shape the stuffing into four small balls and fry them also. Lift the chicken, bacon and stuffing into a 1-pint (½-litre) pie dish and stir the remaining flour into the juices in the pan. Add the stock and stir until the sauce thickens. Add the chopped egg to the sauce then pour it over the chicken in the pie dish. Roll the pastry to fit the top of the dish and decorate.

To freeze Put the pie into the freezer and when it is solid, slide it into a polythene bag, seal, label, date and return to freezer.

To finish and serve Preheat the oven to 425°F, Gas 7 (220°C). Take the pie from the freezer, remove the bag and brush the pastry with beaten egg or milk to glaze. Bake in the oven for 30–35 minutes. Serve hot or cold with salad.

A *Chicken and Lemon Pancakes*

2 portions

6 oz (150 gm) cooked chicken meat
¼ pt (125 ml.) béchamel sauce
1 tablespoon lemon juice
½ teaspoon dried tarragon
1 oz (25 gm) green beans
salt & pepper
4 pancakes
melted butter
4 lemon slices

To make Take the required ingredients from the freezer. Put the chicken and sauce into a saucepan over a very gentle heat to thaw out. When thawed, add the lemon juice, tarragon and beans (these may need to be chopped more finely). Check the seasoning. Divide the mixture between the pancakes. Roll them up and place in a greased pie dish, brush the top of the pancakes with melted butter and heat thoroughly in the oven preheated to 400°F, Gas 6 (200°C), for 15 minutes.

To finish and serve Put a slice of lemon on each pancake and serve very hot with a salad.

F Neapolitan Macaroni

4 portions

8 oz (200 gm) macaroni
8–10 oz (200–250 gm) cooked roast meat – minced
¼ pt (125 ml.) espagnol sauce
¼ pt (125 ml.) tomato purée
powdered garlic
salt & pepper
4 oz (100 gm) grated cheese
2 tomatoes
parsley sprigs

To make Take the required ingredients from the freezer. Cook the macaroni in the usual fashion in boiling salted water with a knob of butter added to prevent its sticking together. Drain well. In a basin mix together the next five ingredients but using only half the tomato purée. Check the seasoning. Put half the cheese into the bottom of a well greased foil pie dish and spread the meat mixture over this. Add the macaroni and then a layer of the remaining cheese. Chop the tomatoes roughly and add to the remaining tomato purée. Season well and pour over the cheese-topped macaroni.

To freeze Cover the pie dish. Seal, label, date and freeze. If more appropriate, divide the macaroni, etc. between two smaller pie dishes suitable for 2 portions.

To finish and serve Take the Neapolitan Macaroni from the freezer, uncover and bake in the oven preheated to 425°F, Gas 7 (220°C), for 25 minutes until thoroughly heated through. Serve immediately, garnished with a parsley sprig.

F Stuffed Peppers

2 portions

6 oz (150 gm) minced beef
2 oz (50 gm) ox kidney – chopped
1 oz (25 gm) finely chopped onion
1 teaspoon sage
salt & pepper
2½ fl. oz (63 ml.) tomato purée
6 oz (150 gm) cooked rice
2 large green peppers
¼ pt (125 ml.) béchamel sauce
2 oz (50 gm) grated cheese

To make Take the mince and kidney from the freezer and turn into a small saucepan over a gentle heat. Break the meat down with a wooden spoon as it thaws. Then turn up the heat a little to brown the meat. Add the onion, sage, salt and pepper and tomato purée. Cook for 5 minutes. Allow it to cool, pouring off any excess fat. Take the rice and the peppers from the freezer. Mix the still frozen rice into the meat. Cut the tops off the still frozen peppers and cut away the insides. Pack the mince and rice mixture into the peppers. Put the tops on as lids.

To freeze Wrap the peppers individually in foil, overwrap in a polythene bag, seal, label, date and freeze.

To finish and serve Take the required number of peppers from the freezer and remove the polythene bag but not the foil. Take the proportionate amount of sauce and cheese from the freezer. Put the peppers into the oven preheated to 400°F, Gas 6 (200°C), for 30 minutes to heat through thoroughly. Meantime turn the sauce into a small saucepan and thaw and heat through over a gentle heat. Beat in the cheese. Unwrap the peppers, take the lids off and put peppers on a warm plate. Pour the cheese sauce over and then set the lids of the peppers on top at an angle for garnish.

F *Apricot Cream Fluff*

4 portions

8 fresh sweet apricots
¼ pt (125 ml.) sweet white wine
¼ pt (125 ml.) cream
1 egg white
mint leaves

To make Take the cream from the freezer to thaw. Remove the stones from the apricots and soak them in the wine. Liquidize them or rub through a sieve to a purée. Lightly whip the cream and, separately, the egg white to the same consistency as the purée. Fold the three mixtures together.

To freeze Pack the fluff into conveniently sized plastic yogurt pots or foil-lined moulds. Cover, seal, label, date and freeze.

To finish and serve Take the required amount from the freezer and serve frozen, spooned into glasses and garnished with a mint leaf.

F *Orange Rice Brûlée*

4 portions

2 oz (50 gm) pudding rice
1 oz (25 gm) sugar
½ oz (13 gm) butter
1 pt (500 ml.) milk
4 tablespoons marmalade
2½ fl. oz (63 ml.) cream
4 oz (100 gm) demerara sugar
strips of orange rind

To make Grease a 1-pint (500-ml.) pie dish and put the first 4 ingredients into it. Cover and bake in the oven preheated to 300°F, Gas 2 (150°C), for 2½ hours. When cooked, stir in the marmalade and cream. Divide the pudding into suitable foil-lined cocotte dishes, sprinkle each with 1 oz (25 gm) of the sugar and put under a hot grill to melt and caramelize the toppings. Set aside to cool.

To freeze Put the dishes in the freezer and when the rice is solid, remove the dishes and overwrap the Orange Rice Brûlées. Seal, label, date and return to the freezer.

To finish and serve Take the required number of brûlées from the freezer, unwrap and set each in a glass. Allow to thaw. Top each with a twist of orange rind to serve.

F *Chocolate Lemon Bombe*

6 portions

6 oz (150 gm) dark chocolate
1 large lemon
4 oz (100 gm) loaf sugar
½ pt (250 ml.) water
½ beaten egg white
6 twists of lemon rind

To make Grease or carefully foil-line 6 individual pudding moulds. Melt the chocolate over hot water. Pour some melted chocolate into each mould, one at a time, and very quickly run the chocolate round the inside of the mould so that it coats the inside surface before it sets. Do this over the pan of melted chocolate so as not to waste any. Set the moulds aside to harden. Meantime, using a potato peeler, take the zest off the lemon and put it in a pan with the sugar and water. Dissolve and boil for 10 minutes. Add the strained juice from the lemon. Pour this into a plastic container, cover and put in the freezer. When it is mushy, take it out and turn it into a basin, whisk it well and fold in the lightly beaten egg white. Divide this lemon sorbet between the chocolate-lined moulds.

To freeze Cover each bombe, seal, label, date and freeze.

To finish and serve Take the required number of bombes from the freezer, unwrap and turn out on to attractive dishes. Decorate with a twist of lemon rind.

F *Sauterne Spoom*

6–8 portions

5 oz (125 gm) sugar
½ pt (250 ml.) water
⅓ pt (200 ml.) Sauterne wine
2 tablespoons lemon juice
2 egg whites
strips lemon rind

To make Dissolve the sugar in the water and boil for 10 minutes to make a syrup. Add the wine and lemon juice. Turn this into a shallow container and put in the freezer. When it is mushy, take it from the freezer, turn it into a basin and whisk it lightly. In another basin whisk the egg whites until soft peak consistency. Fold the two mixtures together.

To freeze Pack the spoom in a plastic container, cover, seal, label, date and freeze.

To finish and serve Take the Sauterne Spoom from the freezer and spoon the required amount into the appropriate number of tall, chilled, wine glasses. Decorate each with twisted strips of lemon rind and serve immediately as a palate-clearer after a strongly flavoured first course and before a delicately flavoured second course; or as a sweet accompanied with sponge fingers.

SUGGESTED MENUS

Rabbit with Green Sauce
Chocolate Lemon Bombe

Pumpkin au Gratin
Lamb Chops and Redcurrants
Sauterne Spoom

Pork Pâté
Grilled Chicken Portuguaise
Orange Rice Brûlée

Goatherd's Soup
Greek Bitockes
Apricot Cream Fluff

TOO TIRED TO BE BOTHERED

F *Suzette Soup*

6–8 portions

2 pts (1 litre) ham stock
2 oz (50 gm) butter
8 oz (200 gm) chopped leeks
2 blades mace
6 peppercorns
2 inches (5 cm.) cinnamon stick
$2\frac{1}{4}$-oz (64-gm) pkt instant potato
2 egg yolks
salt & pepper
6–8 cream whirls

To make Take the required ingredients from the freezer. Melt the butter and gently fry the leeks until tender. Add the stock and seasonings and cook gently for 10 minutes. Liquidize the soup or rub through a sieve discarding the spices as you go. Turn the potato powder into a basin and beat in half the soup to make a potato purée. Whisk the yolks and whisk in a little of the hot soup to make a smooth cream. Put everything except the cream into the one saucepan, heat it, stirring continuously. Season to taste and add a few drops of green food colouring if necessary.

To freeze Set the soup aside to cool. Pour it into appropriately sized waxed cartons or polythene-lined foil bags. Seal, label, date and freeze.

To finish and serve Take the required amount of soup and the cream whirls from the freezer and turn the soup into a saucepan. Heat gently and thoroughly but do not boil. Stir constantly. Pour into warmed bowls and top each with a cream whirl.

F *Lettuce and Lemon Soup*

4–6 portions

2 pts (1 litre) chicken stock
1 round lettuce
1 oz (25 gm) butter
2 oz (50 gm) chopped onion
½ oz (13 gm) flour
1 blade mace
2 tablespoons lemon juice
2 egg yolks
¼ pt (125 ml.) double cream
salt & pepper
green colouring
parsley
lemon rind strips

To make Take the required ingredients from the freezer. Put the stock into a saucepan and heat it gently to thaw out. Wash the lettuce and shred it finely. Melt the butter in a large pan and gently fry the onion and lettuce until soft. Blend the flour with a little stock and beat it into the onion and lettuce mixture. Gradually beat in all the stock, add the mace and simmer the soup for about 20 minutes. Liquidize the soup or rub it through a sieve, discarding the mace as you go. Return the soup to the saucepan and season. Beat together the lemon juice, yolks and cream and blend in a little hot soup to give a creamy mixture. Beat this carefully into the soup. Add a few drops of colouring if necessary. Check seasoning and set aside to cool.

To freeze Divide the soup between appropriately sized waxed cartons or polythene-lined foil bags. Seal, label, date and freeze.

To finish and serve Take the required amount of soup from the freezer and turn it into a saucepan. Heat it very gently, stirring constantly. Pour the hot soup into warm bowls and garnish each with a sprinkling of crumbled frozen parsley and a few very small strips of lemon rind.

Note This soup can equally well be made using Chinese Leaves instead of lettuce.

F or A *Hot Chick Pea Broth*

6–8 portions

4 oz (100 gm) chick peas
1 pt (500 ml.) water
2 teaspoons salt
pinch bicarbonate of soda
½ teaspoon ground coriander
½ teaspoon chilli powder
½ teaspoon ground ginger
½ teaspoon cumin powder
1 pt (500 ml.) diluted beef stock
2 oz (50 gm) chopped onion
1 teaspoon dried chopped chilli peppers
2 teaspoons crumbled parsley

To make Put the first four ingredients into a saucepan to soak overnight. Next day add the four spices, bring the pan to the boil and simmer for 30 minutes until the peas are tender. Meantime take the stock and onion from the freezer and gently melt them together in a large saucepan. Simmer gently to cook the onion. Liquidize the chick peas with any liquid remaining in the pan or rub them through a sieve and add to the onion and stock. Add the peppers and parsley and simmer gently for 10 minutes. Check the seasoning.

To freeze This is quick to assemble from basics in the freezer if you remember to soak the peas. Turn the soup into conveniently sized waxed cartons or polythene-lined foil bags. Seal, label, date and freeze.

To finish and serve Take the required quantity from the freezer and heat gently. Serve with crusty bread.

F Lambs' Liver Pâté

6 portions

1 lb (400 gm) lambs' liver
8 oz (200 gm) streaky bacon rashers
2 oz (50 gm) chopped onion
salt & pepper
1 tablespoon lemon juice
1 tablespoon brandy
½ teaspoon marjoram
½ teaspoon thyme
2 oz (50 gm) butter – melted
1 egg – beaten
2½ fl. oz (63 ml.) made aspic jelly
2 bayleaves
2 lemon slices
6 peppercorns

To make Chop finely the liver, bacon and onion. In a basin mix together all the ingredients except the last four. Line and grease a straight-sided 1-pint (500-ml.) casserole dish and pack the liver mixture into it. Cover with greased foil and place in a roasting tin with hot water. Bake in the oven preheated to 350°F, Gas 4 (180°C), for 1 hour. Put a plate and a weight on top of the pâté and set it aside to cool. Leave for 2 days before freezing to allow flavours to mature.

To freeze When cold, lift the pâté and foil out of the casserole dish, overwrap the pâté in foil and seal, label, date and freeze.

To finish and serve Take the pâté from the freezer, unwrap it and put it into the original casserole. Pour over the melted aspic and when just beginning to set, garnish with bayleaves, lemon slices, and peppercorns, all glazed with aspic. Set aside, overnight, for the aspic to set and the pâté to thaw and regain its flavour. Serve cold in the casserole as a main course with salad or as a starter with hot toast.

F *Dubarry Cream*

5–8 portions

3 pts (1½ litres) ham stock
1 lb (½ kilo) cauliflower florets
bouquet garni
2 bayleaves
1 blade mace
6 peppercorns
salt
½ pt (250 ml.) béchamel sauce
1 pt (500 ml.) milk

To make Take the required ingredients from the freezer. Turn the stock into a saucepan and heat very gently to thaw. Add all the other ingredients except the sauce and milk. Bring the soup to boiling point and simmer for 20–30 minutes. Liquidize or sieve the soup, picking out and discarding the herbs and spices as you go. Meantime, blend a little hot soup with the sauce and beat it well so that it is quite thin. Bring the soup back to boiling point and whisk in the sauce.

To freeze Cool the soup then divide it between appropriately sized waxed containers. Seal, label, date and freeze.

To finish and serve Take the required amount of soup from the freezer and turn into a saucepan. Heat very gently to thaw. Add to every pint of soup a few tiny cauliflower florets and ¼ pint (125 ml.) milk. Bring it to boiling point and serve very hot.

A or F *Pigeon Pie*

–4 portions

rashers bacon
oz (50 gm) butter
pigeons
salt & pepper
oz (50 gm) sautéed potatoes
4 oz (100 gm) sliced mushrooms
1 egg – hard boiled
4 tablespoons chicken stock
1 7½-oz (187-gm) pkt puff pastry

To make Take the required ingredients from the freezer and if the pigeons have been frozen, allow them to thaw out as for chicken. Chop the bacon and fry gently until crisp. Lift out the bacon. Add the butter to the pan to melt. Using a sharp knife, cut back and wings off the pigeons and discard. Cut the legs and thighs away from the breasts and divide the breasts into 2 pieces. Sprinkle the pieces with salt and pepper and sauté gently in the butter to cook partially. Lift out and put with the bacon. Chop the potatoes more finely and toss in the hot fat to crisp. Mix together the bacon and pigeon and the mushrooms and potato. Chop the egg and mix into the pigeon mixture with the chicken stock. Roll out half the pastry to line a 7-inch (17-cm.) foil dish. Turn in the pigeon filling. Roll out the remaining pastry and use to cover the pie. Seal the edges and decorate with scraps of pastry. Make a small hole in the centre.

To freeze The pie may be frozen at this stage, in which case put it into a polythene bag, seal, label, date and freeze.

To finish and serve If frozen, take the pie from the freezer, unwrap it, brush over with milk, and bake it in the oven preheated to 425°F, Gas 7 (220°C) for 40–45 minutes. If the pie is not frozen, brush the top with milk and bake in the oven preheated to 400°F, Gas 6 (200°C), for 25 minutes. Serve hot or cold with a salad.

F *Marga*

4 portions

1 poussin
1 lb (½ kilo) neck of lamb
2 oz (50 gm) black-eye beans
½ teaspoon dried chilli peppers
½ teaspoon allspice
½ teaspoon ground ginger
2 teaspoons salt
1 pt (500 ml.) water
2 tomatoes – chopped
2 Jerusalem artichokes or potatoes – chopped
8 oz (200 gm) courgette slices
1 small green pepper
6 oz (150 gm) mixed stew pack vegetables
1 oz (25 gm) broad beans
1 oz (25 gm) peas

To make Put the poussin, lamb, spices, salt, black-eye beans and water into a stew pan and bring it slowly to the boil. Simmer for 1 hour until the meat and the beans are very tender. Lift out the meats and strip the meat from the bones (they can be used again to make stock). Chop the meat into conveniently sized pieces and put it back into the pan with the beans. Thicken the stock with a little blended cornflour if you wish.

To freeze It is sensible to freeze the basic stew at this stage so that it is more versatile should you want to swop the additional ingredients around. So pour the stew into one or two foil-lined casserole dishes and freeze. When solid, lift the foil and stew out of the dish, overwrap, seal, label, date and freeze.

To finish and serve Take the required quantity from the freezer and put it in a stew pan over a gentle heat. Add all the other ingredients in proportion to the amount of basic stew used. Mix well and heat thoroughly. Check seasoning and serve with rice or bread.

A *Bolognaise Pancakes*

2 portions

8 oz (200 gm) minced beef
2 oz (50 gm) finely chopped onions
salt & pepper
2 teaspoons oregano
¼ pt (125 ml.) tomato purée
1 teaspoon flour
1 teaspoon Worcestershire sauce
4 pancakes
2 oz (50 gm) grated cheese
1 tomato – sliced

To make Take the required ingredients from the freezer. Put the mince into a saucepan over a low heat and break it down with a wooden spoon as it thaws. Turn up the heat to brown the mince. Add the onion, salt, pepper and herbs and cook for 5 minutes. Add the tomato purée. Blend the flour with a little water and stir in this and the Worcestershire sauce. Simmer for 20 minutes.

To finish and serve Put the pancakes, cooked side uppermost, on to a platter, spoon ¼ of the Bolognaise sauce on to each pancake and wrap over the meat. Sprinkle the top with grated cheese and put under a medium grill for 5 minutes to heat the pancakes and melt and brown the cheese. Garnish with tomato slices. Serve hot with a green vegetable or a salad.

A *Gammon Fritters with Dutch Sauce*

2 portions

¼ pt (125 ml.) fluffy fritter batter (p. 164: Surprise Apricot Fritters)
2 cooked gammon steaks or 8 oz (200 gm) boiled gammon
¼ pt (125 ml.) velouté sauce
1 egg yolk
1 dessertspoon natural yogurt
lemon wedges

To make Make up the batter and cut the gammon into 1-inch (2½-cm.) pieces. Dip in batter and fry in hot oil until crisp and golden. Drain and keep warm. Thaw the sauce by stirring in a saucepan over a gentle heat. Beat in the egg yolk and yogurt and cook a minute or two longer but do not boil.

To finish and serve Pile the Gammon Fritters on to a warm platter and garnish with lemon wedges. Put the sauce in a sauceboat and hand separately. Accompany by a salad of endive, green pepper and chopped almonds.

A *Chicken Véronique*

2 portions

8 oz (200 gm) cooked chicken meat
¼ pt (125 ml.) béchamel sauce
2 oz (50 gm) green grapes
2 tablespoons sweet white wine (optional)
2½ fl. oz (63 ml.) cream
1 6-inch (14-cm.) cooked shortcrust pastry case or 2 slices fresh toast

To make Take the required ingredients from the freezer. Cut the chicken into bite-sized pieces. Turn the sauce into a saucepan and thaw very gently over a low heat. Cut the grapes in half. Stir the chicken and grapes into the sauce and continue to heat gently until the mixture is thoroughly hot. Stir in the wine (if used) and the cream. Continue heating but do not boil.

To finish and serve Heat the pastry case in the oven or make the toast. Serve the Chicken Véronique piled into the pastry case or on top of trimmed toast and with a subtle vegetable such as green beans or broccoli.

A *Chicken Pilau*

2 portions

12 oz (300 gm) cooked rice
2 oz (50 gm) butter
water
1 oz (25 gm) chopped onion
1 oz (25 gm) peas
½ teaspoon dried chopped chilli peppers
6 oz (150 gm) shredded cooked chicken meat
1 egg – hard boiled
1 teaspoon dry mustard
salt & pepper

To make Take the required ingredients from the freezer. Melt half the butter in a frying pan and half in a small saucepan. Add 3 tablespoons water and rice to the butter in the frying pan and turn it gently with a fork to thaw and heat through thoroughly. Gently cook the onion in the butter in the saucepan. Mix together the mustard, chilli peppers and 2 teaspoons water and mix into the butter and onion. Add the chicken and turn it gently to thaw, heat through and flavour it. Add the chicken mixture, chopped hard boiled egg and peas to the rice, mix carefully, check seasoning.

To finish and serve Make sure the pilau is very hot and serve it with a shredded lettuce or raw cabbage vinaigrette.

A *Redcurrant Chicken*

2 portions

2 small chicken breasts
salt & pepper
1 oz (25 gm) butter
2 dessertspoons demerara sugar
1 teaspoon cinnamon
4 oz (100 gm) redcurrants
2 tablespoons water

To make Take the chicken from the freezer and allow it to thaw out completely. Rub the chicken breasts with salt and pepper and half of the butter. Grill slowly under a medium grill for 10 minutes on either side. Meantime mix together the sugar and cinnamon and rub half of the mixture into the upper side of the chicken. Turn the grill up to hot and continue to grill the chicken for 5 minutes so that the sugar topping melts and crisps slightly. At the same time take the redcurrants from the freezer and put them into a small saucepan with the remaining butter and sugar mixture. Heat the fruit mixture gently to thaw, soften slightly and thoroughly heat.

To finish and serve Lift the chicken on to a platter and spoon the spiced redcurrants over.

F *Smoked Mackerel Portuguaise*

6 portions

2 small smoked mackerel
2 tablespoons lemon juice
2 dessertspoons crumbled parsley
salt & pepper
1 7½-oz (187-gm) pkt puff pastry
¼ pt (125 ml.) espagnol sauce
2½ fl. oz (63 ml.) tomato purée
1 oz (25 gm) chopped onion
1 tablespoon oil
1 teaspoon oregano

To make Take the first three ingredients from the freezer and allow to thaw. Skin and bone the mackerel. Mash in a basin with the juice, parsley, salt and pepper to taste. Cut the pastry in half and roll each piece to a thin 7½-inch (18-cm.) square. Cut each into five 1½-inch (3½-cm.) squares, put a small spoonful of fish mixture on half the squares, damp the edges, cover with the other pastry squares. Seal the edges.

To freeze Put into the freezer on a tray and when frozen transfer to polythene bags. Seal, label, date and freeze.

To finish and serve Take the appropriate amount of sauce, purée and onion from the freezer and gently heat the sauce and purée together to thaw. Fry the onion, which may need to be chopped more finely, in a tablespoon of oil, add the herbs and then stir this mixture into the sauce and heat thoroughly. Meantime take the required number of fish parcels from the freezer and deep fry from frozen in hot oil for 10 minutes to cook the pastry, heat the filling and brown the outside lightly. Drain, serve piled on a warm platter with a little of the sauce poured over and the rest handed separately in a sauceboat.

F *Goujons of Plaice with Horseradish*

6–8 portions

6 whole fresh plaice
2 tablespoons lemon juice
salt & pepper
2 oz (50 gm) flour
2 eggs – beaten
dried breadcrumbs
2 teaspoons lemon rind
½ pt (250 ml.) horseradish sauce
parsley sprigs
lemon slices

To make Using a thin, very sharp knife, make a cut through the skin and flesh of the fish down the backbone on each side. Holding the tail, insert the point of the knife into this cut at the head end and keeping the blade resting against the bones, radiating from the backbone, slide the knife down to the tail so as to free the flesh on one side of the backbone from the side bones. Cut this fillet free of the fine side bones. Repeat this process for the other fillet on the upper side of the fish, then turn the fish over and cut away the two fillets from the other side. (There are four fillets to each fish.) Then, holding each fillet in turn by the tail, cut diagonally through the flesh to the skin very near the tail. Using the knife in a series of stroking motions and held so that the blade is almost flat against the skin, free the flesh from the skin. It should come free in a roll and the skin should be left clean of flesh. When all the plaice have been filleted and skinned in this way, cut them into thin strips. Cut each strip in half. Sprinkle them with salt and pepper and lemon juice. Dip each goujon in flour, then in egg, then in crumbs mixed with the lemon rind. Deep fry the strips, a few at a time, in hot oil for 3 minutes. Drain and cool.

To freeze Pack the goujons in waxed cartons or in plastic containers in appropriate amounts. Seal, label, date and freeze.

To finish and serve Take the required amount of horseradish sauce from the freezer and allow it to thaw out. Just before they are required, take the required amount of goujons from the freezer and fry from frozen in hot oil for 3 minutes. Drain. Pile on to a warm platter, garnish with parsley sprigs and lemon slices and serve with the horseradish sauce and french beans.

F or A *Pizza*

1–2 portions

3 oz (75 gm) self-raising flour
1 oz (25 gm) butter
salt & pepper
1 teaspoon oregano
4 tablespoons milk
2 oz (50 gm) sliced mushrooms
2 tomatoes – sliced
1 oz (25 gm) grated cheese
2 oz (50 gm) streaky bacon rashers or 8 anchovies
4 stuffed olives

To make Take the required ingredients from the freezer. Rub the butter into the flour, seasonings and herbs and mix to a fairly soft dough with the milk. Knead the dough lightly and then shape it into a 7- or 8-inch (17–20 cm.) round. Turn up the edges and decorate to form a 'wall'. Put in a layer of mushrooms and then of tomato slices. Pack the grated cheese on top and then decorate with the bacon cut in thin strips (or the anchovies) to form a spiral or lattice effect. Cut the olives in half and place them decoratively, cut-side up, on top of the Pizza. Bake in the oven preheated to 400°F, Gas 6 (200°C), for 15–20 minutes until cooked.

To freeze The Pizza may be frozen at this stage though there seems little point as it is so quick to make and it would only clutter the freezer unnecessarily. However, to freeze, merely cool the Pizza thoroughly and put it into a polythene bag. Seal, label, date and freeze.

To finish and serve If it has been frozen, take it from the freezer, unwrap it and place it on a baking tray. Reheat in the oven preheated to 350°F, Gas 4 (180°C), for 20 minutes. Serve the Pizza hot with a salad.

A *Martiniques*

4 portions

2 small bananas
2½ fl. oz (63 ml.) rum
¼ pt (125 ml.) cream
1 oz (25 gm) sugar
2 drops vanilla essence
4 portions orange water ice (p. 150: Maltese Bombe)

To make Peel and slice the bananas and marinade in the rum for 10 minutes if possible. Whisk together the cream, sugar and vanilla until it stands in soft peaks.

To finish and serve Take the orange water ice from the freezer and, using an icecream scoop (or a large tablespoon will do), put one portion on each of four teaplates (blue or green look nice) so that the ice is piled high. Very quickly, using a large star nozzle, pipe slightly off-line whirls of cream round the base of the ice so as to resemble waves. Put slices of banana on top of the ice. Serve immediately with rum marinade poured over.

F or A *Iced Rice*

4 portions

6 oz (150 gm) sweetened blackberries
¼ pt (125 ml.) cream
½ egg white
14 oz (350 gm) can creamed rice
1 tablespoon lemon juice
strips lemon rind

To make Set aside 8 whole blackberries to use for decoration. Purée the fruit by rubbing through a sieve or liquidizing. Whisk the cream to soft peak consistency. Whisk the egg white similarly. Fold the three mixtures together.

To freeze Turn the blackberry cream into a plastic container. Cover, seal, label, date and freeze.

To finish and serve Turn the creamed rice into a basin and mix in the lemon juice and the rind cut into about ½-inch (1-cm.) strips. Take the blackberry icecream from the freezer and in chilled tulip glasses, layer spoons of lemon rice and the fruit icecream ending with the blackberry icecream. Decorate with the whole blackberries set aside at the beginning.

A *Florida Meringue*

2 portions

2 empty half-grapefruit shells
1 portion lemon sorbet (p. 113: Chocolate and Lemon Bombe)
1 portion orange water ice (p. 150: Maltese Bombe)
1 egg white
2 oz (50 gm) caster sugar

To make Scrape out the grapefruit shells very well and wash thoroughly. Chill in the freezer. Fill each with half a portion each of the lemon and the orange ice. Return to the freezer.

To finish and serve Just before serving, whisk the egg white until stiff. Quickly fold in the sugar and pile ½ this meringue on top of each grapefruit shell. Make sure the edges are well sealed. Pop into the oven preheated to 400°F, Gas 6 (200°C), for 3–5 minutes to brown the meringue. Put into grapefruit glasses and serve immediately.

F *White Lady*

6–8 portions

4 oz (100 gm) almonds
2 tablespoons water
5 oz (125 gm) caster sugar
1 pt (500 ml.) milk
4 drops vanilla essence
¼ pt (125 ml.) fresh double cream
6–8 toasted almonds

To make Skin the almonds by letting them sit in boiling water for 2 minutes and then sliding the skins off. Chop the nuts as finely as possible and put into a small basin with the water. Pound the nuts to a paste as best you can with the handle of a heavy knife. (A pestle and mortar is best for this if you have one.) Dissolve the sugar in the milk and bring it to the boil. Flavour it with vanilla and then pour it over the pounded almonds. Steep until the milk is cold. Strain the milk into a basin and mix in the (unwhipped) double cream. Pour into a shallow container and freeze until mushy. Whisk thoroughly until it is smooth.

To freeze Turn the White Lady into conveniently sized plastic containers. Cover, seal, label, date and freeze.

To finish and serve When required take the necessary amount from the freezer. Spoon into champagne glasses. Decorate each with a toasted almond and serve immediately. This makes a delicious sweet or is an excellent basis for many other sweets, e.g. Peach and Almond Blush (p. 85).

F *Tea Mousse*

10 portions

⅓ pt (200 ml.) very strong Earl Grey, Elsenham Evening or your favourite special tea
6 egg yolks
6 oz (150 gm) caster sugar
1 pt (500 ml.) lightly whipped cream
mint leaves

To make Cool the tea and put it in a basin with the yolks and sugar. Whisk these together over warm water until thick and creamy. Cool the mixture, whisking into it 1 tablespoon cold water. Fold in the cream.

To freeze Turn the Tea Mousse into an appropriate mould or a plastic container. Cover, seal, label, date and freeze.

To finish and serve Take the mousse from the freezer when required and either turn out on to a large platter or spoon into individual glasses. Decorate with mint leaves.

F *Beer Soup*

6–8 portions

1¾ pts (875 ml.) beer
1 oz (25 gm) caster sugar
2 inches (5 cm.) cinnamon stick
¼ teaspoon ground ginger
8 slices of lemon
1 oz (25 gm) flour
½ oz (13 gm) butter
1 pt (500 ml.) milk
1 egg
1 tablespoon rum

To make Put the first five ingredients into a saucepan and bring slowly to the boil. Simmer for 5 minutes. Meantime melt the butter in a pan, beat in the flour and then half the milk and the egg and rum. Take the beer mixture off the heat and strain it. Whisk the strained liquid into the milk mixture. Return to the heat and cook for 10 minutes stirring constantly.

To freeze Divide the mixture between appropriately sized plastic pots or waxed cartons. Cool. Seal, label, date and freeze.

To finish and serve Turn the soup into a saucepan and heat very gently to thaw and warm through. In another pan bring a proportionate amount of the remaining ½ pint (250 ml.) milk to the boil. Stir it into the Beer Soup and serve very hot in warm bowls or toddy glasses.

SUGGESTED MENUS

Lambs' Liver Pâté
Redcurrant Chicken
Iced Rice

Hot Chick Pea Broth
Marga
Tea Mousse

Dubarry Cream
Smoked Mackerel Portuguaise
Florida Meringues

Suzette Soup
Goujons of Plaice with Horseradish
Martinique

Lettuce and Lemon Soup
Pigeon Pie
White Lady

Pizza
Beer Soup

ON A DIET – AGAIN

F *Lightning Soup*

8 portions

3 pts (1½ litres) water	**pepper**
3 teaspoons salt	**3 eggs**
4 oz (100 gm) broken vermicelli	**½ pt (250 ml.) warm milk**

To make Put the water, salt and vermicelli into a saucepan and bring to the boil. Simmer until the vermicelli is soft and the soup thick. Add pepper. In a large basin, whisk the eggs lightly and pour over the warm milk whisking continuously. Whisk in the soup gradually.

To freeze The soup may be frozen in waxed cartons at this stage but, as it is so quick, there seems little point.

To finish and serve Pour the soup back into the saucepan and reheat thoroughly but do not boil. Serve in warm soup bowls with a small sprig of parsley for garnish.

A *Consommé Colbert*

2 portions

½ pt (250 ml.) beef stock	**2 celery leaves**
2 oz (50 gm) mixed vegetables, i.e. carrot, turnip, green beans & peas	**salt & pepper**
	2 eggs

To make Take the required ingredients from the freezer. Turn the stock into a saucepan and heat it very gently to thaw it out.

Check that it is really clear. If not, strain it through a very clean tea towel or a coffee filter paper. Cut the carrot and turnip into small dice and the beans into small diamonds. Cook all the vegetables in lightly salted water for 3 minutes. Drain them and add to the stock. Chop the celery leaves and add to the soup. Season the soup to taste. Meantime, poach the eggs very lightly in a little water in a separate pan.

To finish and serve Drain the eggs and carefully put one in each of two warmed soup bowls. Very quickly pour the hot soup over the eggs and serve immediately.

F *Mince Soup*

6–8 portions

2 pts (1 litre) beef stock
6 oz (150 gm) raw minced beef
2 oz (50 gm) chopped onion
salt & pepper
1 oz (25 gm) macaroni

To make Take the required ingredients from the freezer. Turn the stock into a saucepan to heat gently and thaw out. Meantime in another pan gently heat the mince to thaw it out and brown it. Work it constantly with a wooden spoon. Add the mince, onion and seasoning to the stock and simmer gently for 1 hour. Meantime cook the macaroni separately in boiling, salted water. Drain it. Strain the stock, add the macaroni and set the soup aside to cool.

To freeze Divide the soup between appropriately sized waxed cartons or polythene-lined foil bags. Seal, label, date and freeze.

To finish and serve Take the required quantity of soup from the freezer and turn it into a saucepan to heat gently and thaw. Bring to the boil and pour into warm bowls. Sprinkle each with crumbled parsley.

A *St Clement's Lamb*

2 portions

2 chump chops
2 tablespoons lemon juice
2 tablespoons orange juice
4 drops liquid sweetener
1 teaspoon powdered garlic
2 twists lemon rind

To make Take the chops from the freezer and put unwrapped in a dish. Mix together the other ingredients and pour over the chops. Let the meat marinade in a warm place for 30 minutes if possible. Turn the chops frequently. Put the chops on the grill rack, set the rind aside and spoon the marinade over the meat. Grill under a medium grill for 7–10 minutes on each side, basting frequently with the juices.

To finish and serve Put the chops on to a warm platter, pour the juices over and garnish with the lemon rind. Serve hot with broccoli or an orange and cucumber salad.

A *Shoulder Skillet*

2 portions

12 oz (300 gm) shoulder steak
salt & pepper
2 oz (50 gm) butter
1 clove garlic – crushed
1 oz (25 gm) mushrooms finely chopped
2 tablespoons lemon juice
2 teaspoons grated lemon rind
2 tablespoons crumbled parsley

To make Take the required ingredients from the freezer and thaw sufficiently to enable handling. Beat the meat very well with a meat hammer or large wooden spoon. Trim the meat and cut it up into chunks. Sprinkle it well with salt and pepper. Melt the butter in a frying pan and toss in the meat. Brown it, then add all the other ingredients and fry gently for 10 minutes, keeping it constantly moving by shaking the pan gently.

To finish and serve Turn the steak on to a warm serving platter and serve alone with broccoli or with green salad containing orange slices.

A *Chicken and Sprout Crunch*

2 portions

4 cooked chicken drumsticks
4 oz (100 gm) brussels sprouts
2 tomatoes
2 tablespoons olive oil
2 tablespoons lemon juice
1 teaspoon sugar
salt & pepper
½ teaspoon marjoram
4 oz (100 gm) chopped toasted almonds

To make Take the required ingredients from the freezer. Strip the meat off the chicken drumsticks and shred it. Roughly chop the sprouts and tomatoes and mix with the chicken. In a small basin blend together all the other ingredients except the almonds.

To finish and serve Toss together the chicken mixture and the dressing. Turn into a dish and sprinkle liberally with the nuts.

A *Orange and Tomato Chicken*

4 portions

4 chicken pieces
salt & pepper
2 oz (50 gm) soft margarine
2 oz (50 gm) chopped onion
2½ fl. oz (63 ml.) concentrated orange juice
¼ pt (125 ml.) tomato purée
2 teaspoons Worcestershire sauce
crumbled parsley

To make Thaw the chicken completely and rub the pieces with salt and pepper. Melt the margarine in a frying pan and fry the onion until transparent. Add the other ingredients except the chicken and parsley and stir well. Place the chicken in the pan and baste thoroughly. Cover the pan with a lid or foil and cook very gently for about 30 minutes until the chicken is cooked. Turn the meat once or twice during this time.

To finish and serve Remove the cover of the frying pan, stir the sauce well, turn the chicken so that the skin side is downwards, turn up the heat and continue frying the chicken to brown the skin side. Lift the pieces out on to a warm platter and arrange attractively, browned side uppermost. If necessary, stir a little more orange juice into the juices remaining in the pan, check the seasoning and pour over the chicken. Serve hot, sprinkled with crumbled parsley and accompanied by a salad or green beans.

A *Liver with Rosemary and Lemon Cream*

2 portions

8 oz (200 gm) calves' liver
salt & pepper
2 oz (50 gm) butter
2 teaspoons grated lemon rind
1 teaspoon rosemary
1 tablespoon lemon juice
$2\frac{1}{2}$ fl. oz (63 ml.) cream

To make Take the required ingredients from the freezer and allow to thaw. Slice the liver and rub with salt and pepper. Melt the butter in a frying pan and gently fry the liver with the other ingredients, except the cream, for 2–3 minutes on each side. Do not over-cook the liver.

To finish and serve Lift the liver out on to a warm platter and keep warm. Take the frying pan off the heat and rapidly stir in the cream to give a smooth sauce. Pour this sauce over the liver and serve accompanied by cooked rice (p. 49) with a pinch of saffron added.

A *Sole and Apple in Cider*

2 portions

5 small fillets of sole – skinned	**¼ pt (125 ml.) dry cider**
salt & pepper	**6 cloves**
1 tablespoon lemon juice	**1 teaspoon arrowroot**
4 oz (100 gm) apple slices	

To make Take the required ingredients from the freezer and allow the sole to thaw just sufficiently to be able to roll it. With the side on which the skin was uppermost, sprinkle the fish with salt, pepper and lemon juice. Put a couple of apple slices on each fillet and roll the fillets up to enclose the apple, making sure the tail is on the outside. Tuck the tail under the roll so that the fillets will stand steady on one end. Put the fish into a greased pie dish, spoon over the extra apple and pour over the cider and cloves. Cover with greased foil and bake in the oven, preheated to 350°F, Gas 4 (180°C), for 20–30 minutes.

To finish and serve When cooked, carefully lift the fish on to a platter and keep warm. Strain the juices into a small saucepan and rub any pieces of apple through a sieve into the liquid. Use a little water to blend the arrowroot and use it to thicken the sauce slightly; this should be boiled for 1 minute to thicken and clear it. Pour this sauce over the fish and serve hot with Duchess potatoes and courgettes.

A *Paris Omelet*

portions

oz (25 gm) butter	**2½ fl. oz (63 ml.) cream**
small green pepper	**salt & pepper**
oz (50 gm) sliced mushrooms	**3 eggs**
oz (150 gm) leaf spinach	**1 oz (25 gm) grated cheese**
tablespoons dry white wine	**crumbled parsley**

To make Take the required ingredients from the freezer. Me the butter in a saucepan. Deseed and chop the pepper finel Add to the butter and cook gently until soft. Add the mushroom spinach and wine. Check the seasoning. Cook gently until all very soft. Mix in the cream and turn the spinach mixture out o to a warm serving platter. Shape it into a round and keep warm Meantime separate the eggs, add salt and pepper and whisk th yolks and whites in separate basins – the whites until standing i soft peaks. Fold the yolks and whites together and pour into hot, greased omelet pan. Cook for 2–3 minutes then sprinkle th cheese on top of the omelet and put the pan under a hot grill t cook the fluffy cheesy top of the omelet.

To finish and serve Slide the fluffy omelet on to the top of th spinach on the serving dish. Sprinkle liberally with crumble parsley and serve immediately. Cut like a cake to serve.

A *Hot Sprout Sala*

2 portions

4 rashers streaky bacon
1 clove garlic
1 tablespoon olive oil
1 tablespoon lemon juice
1 teaspoon sugar
salt & pepper
1 teaspoon powdered rosemary
2½ fl. oz (63 ml.) tomato purée
8 oz (200 gm) brussels sprouts
2 oz (50 gm) apple slices
4 oz (100 gm) chopped toasted almonds

To make Take the required ingredients from the freezer. Gri the bacon until crispy, chop and set aside. Crush the garlic an put in a deep frying pan along with the next five ingredient Blend them together well and cook for 2 minutes. Stir in th tomato purée, the sprouts (halved if necessary) and the appl Cook, turning gently, for 5 minutes until thoroughly warme Mix in the bacon and almonds.

To finish and serve Turn the Sprout Salad on to a warm platte and serve hot with crusty bread.

F *Melon Water Ice*

8 portions

1 lb (400 gm) orange melon balls	**4 drops vanilla essence**
½ pt (250 ml.) water	**1 tablespoon lemon juice**
5 oz (125 gm) sugar	**mint leaves or pistachio nuts**

To make Take the melon and lemon juice from the freezer and allow to thaw out. Dissolve the sugar in the water and add ¼ pint (125 ml.) of the juice drained from the melon. Bring to the boil and boil for 5 minutes. Set this syrup aside to cool, then add vanilla essence and lemon juice. Rub the melon through a sieve or liquidize it to give a smooth purée. Mix the syrup into the melon purée.

To freeze Pour the melon mixture into a shallow container and freeze. When it is set to the mushy stage, take it from the freezer and whisk it to break up the ice and make it smooth. Divide the mixture into suitably sized plastic containers, cover, seal, label, date and return to freezer.

To finish and serve When required, take the necessary amount of Melon Water Ice from the freezer and spoon it into well-chilled glasses the rims of which have been dipped in egg white and then delicately coloured with green caster sugar. Top each portion with a mint leaf or a few skinned, chopped, pistachio nuts. The pale orange colour is complemented by the delicate green. Serve the Melon Water Ice as a sweet or as a 'palate-clearer' between a strongly flavoured first course and a more delicate second course.

A *Raspberry Iced Mousse*

6–8 portions

¾ pt (375 ml.) raspberry purée
8 oz (200 gm) icing sugar
2 tablespoons lemon juice
¾ pt (375 ml.) whipped cream
a few whole raspberries

To make Take the required ingredients from the freezer and allow them to thaw until usable. Fold together all the ingredients except the whole fruit.

To freeze Pack into a 1½-pint (750-ml.) mould, cover and freeze for at least 2 hours. For best results it should not be kept in the freezer for any more than a week or so.

To finish and serve When required, turn the Raspberry Iced Mousse out on to a platter and decorate with a few whole raspberries. Serve cut like a cake and with sponge fingers or shortbread.

F *Devon Spoom*

10–15 portions

5 oz (125 gm) caster sugar
½ pt (250 ml.) water
½ pt (250 ml.) sweet cider
1 tablespoon lemon juice
2 egg whites
fresh apple slices

To make Dissolve the sugar in the water and then boil for 5 minutes. Cool it and then add the cider and lemon juice. Pour it into a shallow container and put in the freezer until mushy and half set. Whisk up the egg whites and fold into the iced cider mixture.

To freeze Pack into conveniently sized plastic containers, cover, seal, label, date and freeze.

To finish and serve Take the required quantity of Devon Spoom from the freezer and spoon it into tall wine glasses. Decorate with a slice of fresh apple.

SUGGESTED MENUS

Lightning Soup
Hot Sprout Salad
Melon Water Ice

Consommé Colbert
Liver with Rosemary and Lemon Cream
Raspberry Iced Mousse

Mince Soup
Paris Omelet
Devon Spoom

SPOIL YOURSELF

A *Egg and Cabbage in Lemo*

2–4 portions

4 eggs
6 oz (150 gm) chopped cabbage
1 small red pepper
1 tablespoon lemon juice
1 teaspoon grated lemon rind
½ teaspoon crumbled tarragon
3 tablespoons good mayonnaise

To make Hard-boil the eggs. Take the ingredients from th freezer and allow them to thaw out. Chop the cabbage mo finely if necessary. Deseed and finely chop the pepper. Mi together. In a small basin blend together the lemon juice, rin tarragon and mayonnaise. Pour the dressing over the cabbag and pepper and mix lightly.

To finish and serve Pile the dressed cabbage into a woode bowl, shell and halve the eggs and place them cut side uppe most around the edge of the cabbage. Serve with crusty brea as a starter.

A *Stuffed Lamb Kidne*

4 portions

6 lamb kidneys
salt & pepper
oil to brush
2 oz (50 gm) breadcrumbs
1 teaspoon lemon rind
1 teaspoon Worcestershire sauce
pinch chilli powder
1 tablespoon tomato ketchup
½ teaspoon oregano
4 slices fresh toast
4 lemon slices

To make Take the required ingredients from the freezer. Split the kidneys carefully in half and remove any cores, sprinkle with salt and pepper, brush with oil and grill the kidneys for 2–3 minutes on each side. Make the toast at the same time. Meantime, mix together all the other ingredients except the lemon slices. Check the seasoning. Heat this stuffing in a small saucepan.

To finish and serve Place 3 half-kidneys, rough sides uppermost diagonally across each slice of toast. Spoon stuffing mixture on top of each kidney half. Cut each lemon slice in half and put one piece each side of the kidneys on the toast. Arrange on individual plates and serve hot as a starter. Or serve as a savoury at the end of a meal, using only 2 halves of kidney and half a slice of toast per person.

A *Smoked Salmon Rolls*

4 portions

4 slices brown bread
8 thin slices smoked salmon
8 asparagus tips
¼ pt (125 ml.) soured cream
1 tablespoon lemon juice
1 teaspoon finely chopped chives
1 dessertspoon fine strips lemon rind

To make Take the required ingredients from the freezer. Trim the crusts from the bread and cut the bread into 8 fingers. Roll a piece of salmon round each asparagus tip. Mix together the remaining ingredients keeping a few pieces of chives and rind for garnish.

To finish and serve Place each salmon roll on a finger of bread and set them attractively on a platter or individual plates. Pour some of the sauce over the salmon and garnish with chives and rind. Hand the remaining sauce in a small dish also garnished with chives and rind.

A Guinea Fowl Calvados

2–4 portions

1 small guinea fowl
1 oz (25 gm) chopped onion
4 oz (100 gm) bacon rashers
1 oz (25 gm) butter
2 oz (50 gm) unsweetened apple slices
3–4 oz (75–100 gm) cooked rice
¼ pt (125 ml.) chicken stock
salt & pepper
¼ pt (125 ml.) béchamel sauce
1 egg yolk
2½ fl. oz (63 ml.) double cream
2½ fl. oz (63 ml.) calvados (or apple juice)

To make Thaw the guinea fowl as for chicken. Take the other ingredients from the freezer. Chop the onion more finely and brown it in the butter. Add 1 oz (25 gm) of the bacon and the apples, both finely chopped. Add the rice and stock. Bring to the boil and cook gently until the stock is absorbed and the rice rather sticky. When cool enough to handle, use this mixture to stuff the guinea fowl at the neck end. Secure the skin. Season the fowl. Lay the remaining bacon over the breast of the bird and roast it in the oven preheated to 375°F, Gas 5 (190°C), for approximately 50 minutes until tender. Meantime gently thaw and heat the béchamel sauce in a small saucepan. Beat in the egg yolk and the cream. Do not boil.

To finish and serve Lift the guinea fowl on to a platter, discard the bacon, pour the calvados over and set it alight as it is served. Serve the cream sauce separately in a sauceboat.

A Turkish Lamb Kebabs

2 portions

1 small neck fillet of lamb
2 tablespoons oil
¼ pt (125 ml.) milk
6–8 button onions or chunks of onion
6–8 bayleaves
2 fresh whole tomatoes
10 oz (250 gm) cooked rice
crumbled thyme or powdered thyme
5 fl. oz (125 ml.) soured cream

To make Take the required ingredients except the rice from the freezer and allow to thaw out overnight. Cut the fillet into chunks, put in a dish and pour over a mixture of the oil and milk. Soak for up to 2 hours if possible. Drain the meat and thread decoratively on to long skewers, alternating with the onion and bayleaves and with the tomato in the middle. Cook under a hot grill for 10 minutes, turning constantly. Meantime take the rice from the freezer and heat it up as usual (p. 49).

To finish and serve Spread the rice out on a warm platter and lay the two skewers on top. Using a fork to keep the meat, etc., in place, carefully draw out the skewers. Sprinkle the whole dish generously with crumbled, frozen thyme or with powdered thyme. Serve the dish hot and hand the soured cream separately in a small bowl. Accompany with a raw cabbage and red pepper salad.

A *Sweetbreads in Wine Sauce*

4 portions

1 lb (400 gm) lamb sweetbreads
¾ pt (375 ml.) chicken or veal stock
1 oz (25 gm) chopped onion
2 oz (50 gm) celery
strips of lemon rind from ½ a lemon
6 peppercorns
2 bayleaves
1 oz (25 gm) carrot
1 blade mace
¾ pt (375 ml.) béchamel sauce
¼ pt (125 ml.) soured cream
6 tablespoons dry white wine
1¼ lb (500 gm) cooked rice
crumbled parsley
8 lemon slices

To make Take the required ingredients from the freezer. The sweetbreads will usually have been blanched and cleaned before freezing. If not, do so. Put the sweetbreads into a pan with the stock and the next 7 ingredients. Bring to the boil and simmer for 30 minutes until cooked. On the rare occasion that the sweetbreads are still whole, the cooking time will be 1–2 hours depending on size. Meantime reheat the rice (p. 49) and make a border of rice on a warm serving dish. When cooked, lift the sweetbreads out of the stock and put in the centre of the rice border. Pour over half the wine. Keep warm. Gently heat the béchamel sauce and beat in the soured cream and the rest of the wine. Heat but do not boil.

To finish and serve Pour the sauce over the sweetbreads and sprinkle liberally with crumbled parsley. Garnish with lemon slices.

A *Sirloin Piquant*

2 portions

2 sirloin steaks
salt & pepper
¼ pt (125 ml.) espagnol sauce
8 peppercorns
1 gherkin – chopped
8 capers
1 dessertspoon lemon juice
1 teaspoon crumbled parsley

To make Take the required ingredients from the freezer. Rub the steaks with salt and pepper and grill according to preference. Meantime, simmer the peppercorns in the sauce until it is well flavoured (about 5 minutes is enough). Strain the sauce into another saucepan and stir in the other ingredients.

To finish and serve Lift the steaks on to a warm platter and pour the sauce over. Serve hot, accompanied by a fresh salad.

A *Veal Chops with Cucumber Sauce*

2 portions

2 veal chops
salt & pepper
½ cucumber
1 oz (25 gm) butter
¼ pt (125 ml.) béchamel sauce
2½ fl. oz (63 ml.) soured cream
1 teaspoon chopped chives
green colouring

To make Take the required ingredients from the freezer. Rub the chops well on both sides with salt and pepper. Grill for 10 minutes on each side under a medium grill. Meantime, skin and chop the cucumber and cook gently in the butter until soft. Rub through a sieve or liquidize to give a cucumber purée. Gently heat the béchamel sauce and stir in the cucumber purée, soured cream, chives and a few drops of green colouring. Heat thoroughly but do not boil. Check the seasoning.

To finish and serve Arrange the chops on a warm platter and pour the sauce over or hand the sauce separately. Accompany by sauté potatoes and grilled tomatoes.

A *Salmon Steaks in Champagne Cream*

2 portions

2 salmon steaks
salt & pepper
1 oz (25 gm) butter
$\frac{1}{4}$ pt (125 ml.) sweet champagne or sparkling wine
$2\frac{1}{2}$ fl. oz (63 ml.) cream
8–10 grapes or 4–5 apple slices

To make Take the ingredients from the freezer. Place each salmon steak on a square of buttered foil. Sprinkle with salt and pepper and half the champagne or wine. Wrap the steaks in the foil, sealing the edges very well. Put the parcels into a pan of gently boiling water, bring the water back to the boil and simmer for 20–25 minutes. Meantime, whip the remaining champagne or wine and the cream together until it stands in soft peaks. Fold in the halved, deseeded grapes or roughly chopped apple slices.

To finish and serve Unwrap the salmon steaks and serve on to a warm platter. Pour the juices over. Hand the champagne cream separately and accompany with french beans or a spinach salad.

A *Lemon and Tarragon Plaice*

4 portions

8 plaice fillets – skinned
salt & pepper
3 tablespoons lemon juice
3 oz (75 gm) white breadcrumbs
3 teaspoons crumbled tarragon
1 tablespoon oil
½ pt (250 ml.) béchamel sauce
thin strips lemon rind

To make Take the required ingredients from the freezer and allow to thaw just sufficiently to handle. Lay the plaice fillets flat on a board with the side that had the skin on uppermost. Sprinkle with salt and pepper. Mix together 2 tablespoons of the juice, 2 oz (50 gm) crumbs and 2 teaspoons of tarragon. Press this stuffing so it holds loosely together. Divide it between the fillets and fold each in half to cover the stuffing. Place on a grill-rack, brush each fillet with oil and grill for 15 minutes under a medium grill. Transfer to a shallow ovenproof dish so that the uncooked side of the fish is uppermost. Mix the remaining juice and herbs into the sauce and coat the fish. Sprinkle with the remaining crumbs.

To finish and serve Put the dish under a hot grill for 5–10 minutes to heat the sauce and crisp the top. Serve very hot and garnished with strips of lemon rind. Accompany by lightly cooked cabbage.

F *Javanese Bombe*

4–6 portions

3 bananas
2 teaspoons lemon juice
4 oz (100 gm) icing sugar
¼ pt (125 ml.) lightly whipped cream
4 drops rum essence
½ oz (13 gm) dark coffee sugar beans
2–3 portions Granita (p. 74)

To make First of all, put a simple metal mould in the freezer.

Peel and mash the bananas. Mix in the lemon juice and sugar and fold in the cream, essence and sugar beans. Take the mould from the freezer and also the required quantity of Granita. Put the Granita into the mould and, using a spoon and working very quickly, spread it on the bottom of the mould and up the sides in an even layer to the top. Fill the centre with the banana mousse, pack it down well and, finally, cover it with a little more granita.

To freeze Cover the mould very tightly using greased foil and freeze the bombe for at least 2 hours. For best results, it should not be kept much longer than a week or so in the freezer and if this is to be the case, make sure it is well sealed, labelled, and dated.

To finish and serve Just before it is needed, take the Javanese Bombe from the freezer, uncover, dip the mould into warm water for 1 second to loosen it. Turn it upsidedown on to a very cold platter, decorate it with a few slices of banana dipped in lemon juice and cut like a cake to serve.

A *Chocolate Flake*

4–6 portions

3 portions Granita (p. 74)
2 oz (50 gm) chopped toasted almonds
¼ pt (125 ml.) cream
1 tablespoon Benedictine or Drambuie
1 oz (25 gm) caster sugar
½ egg white
1½ oz (37 gm) dark chocolate

To make Line 4 or 6 chilled individual moulds with Granita as for a bombe (p. 148). Press the nuts against the Granita. Put the moulds in the freezer. Meantime, whisk the cream until it is just stiff and beginning to lose its gloss. Fold in the liqueur and sugar. Beat the egg white until it stands in soft peaks. Fold this into the cream as well. Grate the chocolate. Take the moulds from the freezer and fill each with the cream. Make a hollow in the middle of the cream and pack with some grated chocolate, being careful not to mix the cream and chocolate together. Cover the chocolate with a little cream and, in turn, the cream with a little more Granita. Cover the moulds and return them to the freezer for at least 1 hour.

To finish and serve Take the Chocolate Flake from the freezer just before serving. Turn out on to individual glass dishes and decorate with a few coarse gratings of chocolate.

F *Maltese Bombe*

6–8 portions

4 oz (100 gm) caster sugar
½ pt (250 ml.) water
¼ pt (125 ml.) undiluted orange juice
1 egg white
3–4 portions Vanilla Mousse (p. 86)
orange slices

To make Dissolve the sugar in the water and boil for 10 minutes to make a syrup. Pour this over the orange juice in a basin. Mix it well and turn it into an ice-cube tray or a shallow plastic container. Put it in the freezer. When it is frozen but still soft, take it from the freezer and whisk it. Then fold in the egg white beaten to soft peak stage. Return the water ice to the freezer and freeze till solid. This is now an orange water ice. Use it to line 6–8 chilled individual bombe moulds or one larger mould (p. 148 Javanese Bombe). Fill the centre with Vanilla Mousse, cover the top with orange water ice.

To freeze Cover, seal and freeze for at least 2 hours. If it is to be kept longer, label and date it, but for best results it should not be kept for much more than a week or so.

To finish and serve Just before it is required, take the bombe from the freezer and turn out on to individual plates or on to a larger round platter. Decorate with halved orange slices.

SUGGESTED MENUS

Egg and Cabbage in Lemon
Salmon Steaks in Champagne Cream
Maltese Bombe

Stuffed Lamb Kidneys
Lemon and Tarragon Plaice
Javanese Bombe

Smoked Salmon Rolls
Sweetbreads in Wine Sauce
Chocolate Flake

PEOPLE TO DINNER

F *Chicken Liver Bites*

6–8 portions

12 oz (300 gm) chicken livers
4 oz (100 gm) sliced mushrooms
4 tablespoons oil
½ teaspoon oregano
1 clove garlic – crushed
¼ pt (125 ml.) milk
6 peppercorns
1 oz (25 gm) sliced onion
2 cloves
salt & pepper
1 oz (25 gm) butter
1 oz (25 gm) flour
3 oz (75 gm) coarse oatmeal

To make Take the required ingredients from the freezer. Dice the livers and mushrooms very small and toss in hot oil mixed with the oregano and garlic. Meantime put the milk, peppercorns, onion, cloves, salt and pepper into a small saucepan and bring very slowly to the boil. Melt the butter in a saucepan and stir in the flour. Beat in the strained, flavoured milk. Cook, stirring constantly until the sauce is very thick. Drain the chicken livers and mushrooms and blend into the sauce. Set aside to cool. When cool enough to handle, shape into 24 small balls and roll in oatmeal to cover very well.

To freeze Pack the Bites in a rigid container. Seal, label, date and freeze.

To finish and serve Take the required number of Bites from the freezer and deep fry from frozen in hot oil for 5 minutes. Drain and serve piled high on a platter garnished with lemon wedges and lettuce as a starter or on cocktail sticks as a cocktail savoury.

A *Kipper Creams*

8–10 portions

1 12-oz (300-gm) pkt kipper fillets
1 small green pepper
¼ pt (125 ml.) horseradish sauce
2½ fl. oz (63 ml.) cream – lightly whipped
2 teaspoons lemon juice
salt & pepper
16–20 small pastry cases
strips lemon rind
crumbled parsley

To make Take the ingredients from the freezer. Cook the kipper fillets in the packet according to the instructions. Turn them out on to a board and scrape off the skin and remove any bones. Flake the fish very finely and put in a basin. Deseed and finely chop the green pepper. Add it to the fish and mix in the sauce, cream and lemon juice. Season with salt and pepper.

To finish and serve Pile a small amount into each pastry case, garnish with a thin strip of rind and crumbled parsley. Arrange on a large lettuce-lined platter and serve as a starter or cocktail savoury.

F *Kipper Mousse*

4–6 portions

1 6-oz (150-gm) pkt kipper fillets
½ oz (13 gm) aspic powder
½ teaspoon powdered gelatine
¼ pt (125 ml.) warm water
¼ pt (125 ml.) mayonnaise
¼ pt (125 ml.) cream
2 teaspoons crumbled parsley
salt & pepper
lemon slices

To make Cook the kipper fillets according to the instructions on the packet. Discard any skin. Meantime dissolve the aspic and gelatine in the warm water and set it aside. When the fish and the aspic mixture are roughly the same temperature, blend them together in the liquidizer, or with a rotary whisk, until smooth. Fold in the mayonnaise, lightly whipped cream an parsley. Check the seasoning.

To freeze Turn the mixture into a foil-lined 1-pint (500-ml. mould, cover and freeze. When frozen solid, remove the mouss in the foil from the dish, overwrap it, seal, label, date and retur to the freezer.

To finish and serve Take the mousse from the freezer, unwra and turn carefully on to a platter, allow to thaw overnight in th refrigerator, serve garnished with lemon slices and with brow bread and butter.

A *Glazed Shoulder of Lam*

4–6 portions

4½ lb (2 kilo) shoulder of lamb
salt & pepper
12 whole cloves
¼ pt (125 ml.) dry red wine
2 oz (50 gm) demerara sugar
1 teaspoon ground cloves
1 teaspoon mixed spice
1 teaspoon ground ginger
2½ fl. oz (63 ml.) tomato purée
2 teaspoons flour

To make Take the meat from the freezer and allow it to tha overnight. Rub the skin with salt and pepper and stud it wit cloves. Pour over the wine, cover with foil and roast in the ove preheated to 350°F, Gas 4 (180°C), for 2 hours. Meantime mi together the sugar and spices. After the 2 hours, remove the fo from the meat, press the sugar mixture on to the skin of th lamb, put the oven up to 425°F, Gas 7 (220°C), and roast th meat for a further 15–20 minutes to caramelize the topping.

To finish and serve Transfer the meat to a warm platter. T the juices in the roasting tin add the tomato purée and abou ¼ pint (125 ml.) water. Blend the flour with a little cold wate and pour it into the roasting tin. Put the roasting tin over a lo heat on top of the cooker and bring to the boil stirring con stantly and scraping up any sediment stuck to the roasting tin. Cook until it thickens a little. Check the seasoning. Strain the gravy into a sauceboat and serve with the glazed shoulder of lamb. This dish is nice accompanied by sauté potatoes, courgettes and an orange and grapefruit salad.

A or F *Lamb Gueveche*

8 portions

2 lb (1 kilo) scrag end of lamb
8 oz (200 gm) chopped onions
1 dessertspoon mixed sweet herbs
4 tablespoons oil
salt & pepper
8 oz (200 gm) green beans – chopped
8 oz (200 gm) courgettes – thickly sliced
8 oz (200 gm) aubergine – thickly sliced
8 oz (200 gm) Jerusalem artichokes or fresh potatoes – thickly sliced
2 oz (50 gm) green peppers – cut in strips
4 large tomatoes
2 oz (50 gm) chopped toasted nuts

To make Take the ingredients, except the tomatoes and nuts, from the freezer. Cut the meat up and put it into a frying pan over a low heat until the meat thaws and the fat begins to run. Turn up the heat a little, add the onions and herbs and brown the meat and onions. Drain and put in a deep foil-lined casserole dish. In another pan, heat the oil and fry separately (adding salt and pepper at each stage) the beans, courgettes, aubergine, artichokes (or fresh potatoes) and green pepper, until each is lightly browned. As each vegetable is cooked, drain it and spread it out in a layer on top of the meat in the casserole, ending with the green pepper. Cover the casserole tightly and cook in the oven preheated to 300°F, Gas 2 (150°C), for 2 hours. No liquid is added as sufficient comes from the vegetables. The stew need not be frozen, in which case add the tomato slices at this stage and cook at 350°F, Gas 4 (180°C) for a further 30 minutes.

To freeze Cool the dish thoroughly and put it in the freezer as it is, or divide it into suitably sized portions and put in foil containers. In the latter case, seal, label, date and freeze. In the former, when the stew is quite frozen, lift it, plus the foil lining, out of the dish and overwrap the stew in a polythene bag. Seal, label, date and return to the freezer.

To finish and serve Take the required quantity of stew from the freezer, unwrap, put in a dish and lay the proportionate amount of tomato slices over the top. Cover and cook in the oven pre-heated to 350°F, Gas 4 (180°C), for 1 hour. To serve, remove the lid and sprinkle the top with the proportionate amount of nuts. Serve as a complete dish with crusty rolls.

A *Orange and Lemon Fillet*

4 portions

2 small neck fillets of lamb
salt & pepper
1 oz (25 gm) butter
¼ pt (125 ml.) orange juice
1 tablespoon lemon juice
2 tablespoons dry white wine
fine strips orange rind
fine strips lemon rind
1 teaspoon arrowroot
1 lb (400 gm) cooked rice
crumbled parsley

To make Take the required ingredients from the freezer. Cut the lamb fillets into small chunks, sprinkle with salt and pepper. Fry gently in the butter until browned. To the pan add all the other ingredients except the arrowroot, rice and parsley. Cover the pan and let the lamb simmer gently in the liquid for 10 minutes. Blend the arrowroot with a little water and stir it into the sauce to thicken it slightly. Meantime, heat the rice (p. 49).

To finish and serve Put a border of rice on a platter and pour the Orange and Lemon Fillet into the centre. Garnish with crumbled parsley.

A *Steak Chasseur*

6 portions

6 rump steaks
salt & pepper
1 clove garlic – cut
oil
$\frac{1}{2}$ pt (250 ml.) espagnol sauce
2 oz (50 gm) redcurrant jelly
$\frac{1}{2}$ teaspoon powdered gelatine
1 teaspoon lemon juice
$2\frac{1}{2}$ fl. oz (63 ml.) port, cream sherry or sweet red vermouth
$\frac{1}{4}$ teaspoon cayenne pepper
parsley sprigs

To make Take the required ingredients from the freezer and allow to thaw out. Rub the steaks with salt, pepper, garlic and oil, and set aside whilst the sauce is made. Turn the espagnol sauce into a saucepan over a low heat. Add the redcurrant jelly. Dissolve the gelatine in the lemon juice and alcohol. Stir into the sauce, add the cayenne pepper and boil until it is reduced to about $\frac{1}{2}$ pint (250 ml.). Grill the steaks according to preference.

To finish and serve Arrange the steaks on a warm platter and strain the hot sauce over them. Garnish with parsley sprigs and accompany by new boiled potatoes and spinach or a salad.

A *Topper*

2 portions

10 oz (250 gm) chuck steak
2 oz (50 gm) peas
4 oz (100 gm) baby carrots
2 oz (50 gm) chopped onion
$\frac{1}{4}$ pt (125 ml.) espagnol sauce
3 oz (75 ml.) self-raising flour
1 oz (25 gm) margarine
salt & pepper
1 teaspoon mixed herbs
4 tablespoons milk

To make Take the required ingredients from the freezer and allow the meat to thaw sufficiently to enable cutting. Cut the meat up into fairly small thin pieces and fry gently in oil to brown and cook almost completely. Sprinkle with salt and pepper. Transfer to a 1-pint (500-ml.) pie dish and mix in the vegetables and sauce which may need to be thawed by gently heating in a small saucepan. Put the pie dish into the oven preheated to 425°F, Gas 7 (220°C), whilst the topping is made very quickly. Put the flour into a basin and rub in the margarine. Mix in the salt, pepper and herbs. Using a knife, mix in the milk to form a rather soft dough. Turn this out on to a floured board and shape it to fit the top of the pie dish. Take the pie dish from the oven, wet the edges of the dough and lift it quickly on to the top of the meat so that the wet edges stick to the lip of the pie dish. Make a small cut in the top of the pie and return it to the oven. Bake for a further 15 minutes until the top is crusty, risen and lightly browned.

To finish and serve As this is a quick dish, complete in itself, no other garnishing or accompaniment is necessary. Serve the Topper very hot.

A *Brandied Sweetbreads en Croûte*

4 portions

1 lb (400 gm) sweetbreads
1 oz (25 gm) flour
salt & pepper
2 oz (50 gm) butter
¼ pt (125 ml.) soured cream
1 liqueur glass of brandy
8 oz (200 gm) sliced mushrooms
4 2-inch (5-cm.) wide slices of white bread from a small loaf
4 lemon slices
parsley sprigs

To make Take the required ingredients from the freezer and toss the sweetbread pieces in the flour mixed with plenty of salt and pepper. Melt the butter in a frying pan and fry the sweetbreads gently for about 15 minutes. Meantime, trim the crusts from the bread slices and hollow out the centre of each piece of bread so that you have 4 rather squat 'boxes'. Deep fry these in oil, drain and keep hot. Lift the sweetbreads out of the pan and divide between the four 'boxes'. Keep warm. To the juices in the pan, stir in the soured cream and brandy. Cook, stirring constantly, until the quantity is reduced to about half. Toss in the sliced mushrooms and cook for a minute or two so as to heat the mushrooms but not destroy their shape or discolour the sauce.

To finish and serve Lift the croûtes on to a serving platter and pour the sauce over the sweetbreads in each. Top each with a twisted lemon slice and a tiny sprig of parsley. Serve hot accompanied by a crisp celery and apple salad. This is nice done 'in miniature' as a starter or cocktail savoury.

A *Tarragon Roast Chicken*

4–6 portions

1 3-lb 14-oz (1¾-kilo) chicken
3 oz (75 gm) small mushrooms
3 sprigs tarragon
or 3 teaspoons dried tarragon
salt & pepper
2 oz (50 gm) brown breadcrumbs
1 oz (25 gm) butter
egg yolk
2 teaspoons flour

To make Take the chicken from the freezer and allow it to thaw out thoroughly, preferably slowly in the fridge. Take the mushrooms, tarragon and breadcrumbs from the freezer. Finely chop 1 oz (25 gm) of the mushrooms and 1 sprig of tarragon and mix with the breadcrumbs, some salt and pepper and enough egg to bind. Divide the stuffing into small balls. When the chicken is thawed out, gently loosen the skin from the breast and from the top of the legs by carefully sliding your index finger between the skin and the flesh from the neck end. Slide 8 mushrooms, smooth side uppermost, between the flesh and the skin so that there are 3 along either side of the breast bone and 1 on top of each leg. Tuck the skin at the neck end back under the bird to secure it. Put 2 sprigs of tarragon inside the carcase. Rub the bird with salt, pepper and butter. Wrap the bird loosely in kitchen foil, place it in a roasting tin and roast it in the oven preheated to 350°F, Gas 4 (180°C), for ¾ hour. Open the foil, put the stuffing balls around the chicken, turn the oven up to 400°F, Gas 6 (200°C), and roast for a further 30 minutes.

To finish and serve Lift the chicken and stuffing balls on to a hot platter and keep warm. Turn the juices into a saucepan, taking care to scrape the foil well. Blend 2 teaspoons flour with a little water, pour into the juices, make up to about ½ pint (250 ml.) with water and bring to the boil stirring constantly. Pour the gravy into a sauceboat. Serve the chicken, stuffing and gravy with baby roast potatoes, courgettes and baby onions in white sauce.

A *Turkey and Ham Casserole*

6–8 portions

12 oz (300 gm) turkey roll
12 oz (300 gm) gammon roll
3 oz (75 gm) flour
2 teaspoons mixed herbs
salt & pepper
2 oz (50 gm) butter
½ pt (250 ml.) chicken stock
8 oz (200 gm) sliced mushrooms
2 oz (50 gm) green beans
4 oz (100 gm) grated cheese

To make Take the meats and stock from the freezer and thaw. Cut the meats up into irregular-shaped pieces. Mix the flour with the herbs and salt and pepper. Toss the meats in this and fry until brown in the butter melted in a stewpan. Sprinkle with the rest of the flour. Add the stock, cover the stewpan and simmer gently for 40 minutes. Add the vegetables, stir and simmer a further 10 minutes.

To finish and serve Turn the casserole into an oblong serving dish about 2 inches (5 cm.) deep, sprinkle the top liberally with the cheese and put under a grill preheated to hot in order to melt and slightly brown the topping. Serve hot with Duchess potatoes (p. 54).

A *Turkey Kebabs with Orange Rice*

2 portions

12 oz (300 gm) cooked turkey roll
4 rashers streaky bacon
2 fresh tomatoes
4 large mushrooms
1 green pepper
4 tablespoons olive oil
2 tablespoons lemon juice
1 teaspoon dry mustard
1 teaspoon ground cinnamon
1 teaspoon soft brown sugar
½ oz (13 gm) butter
12 oz (300 gm) cooked rice
4 tablespoons orange juice
pinch saffron
orange & lemon rind

To make Take required ingredients from the freezer. Cut the turkey into 1-inch (2-cm.) cubes. Cut the bacon rashers in half and roll them. Halve the tomatoes. Cut the pepper into 8. Thread the first 5 ingredients alternately on to long skewers. Set them in the base of the grill pan. In a small basin and using a wooden spoon, blend together the oil, lemon juice, mustard, cinnamon and brown sugar. Pour this over the kebabs and allow them to marinade for at least 10 minutes but up to an hour if possible. Turn frequently. Melt the butter in a frying pan and blend in the saffron and orange juice. Add the rice and turn it gently until it is thawed and thoroughly hot. Meantime, put the kebabs on to the rack in the grill pan or on to the spit and grill them under a medium grill for 15–20 minutes, turning them frequently and basting with marinade.

To finish and serve Turn the rice out on to a large platter then place the kebabs on top. Pour the kebab juices over and scatter with small strips of lemon and orange rind. Serve hot with a lettuce and cucumber salad.

F Roast Duck in Grapefruit Sauce

4 portions

1 4½-lb (2-kilo) duck
salt & pepper
1 grapefruit
4 oz (100 gm) butter
4 tablespoons crumbled mint
4 oz (100 gm) demerara sugar
½ pt (250 ml.) water
strips grapefruit rind

To make Thaw the duck as for chicken. Rub it with salt and pepper and prick the skin all over. Grate the rind from the grapefruit and squeeze the juice. Mix both with the mint and sugar. Blend half the mixture with the butter and spread over the breast of the duck. Place the duck on a grill rack in a roasting tin, pour in ¼ pint (125 ml.) water and roast in the oven preheated to 375°F, Gas 5 (190°C), for about 1½ hours. Baste the duck frequently. When cooked, lift the duck out and cut it up into portions using scissors. Put into an appropriately sized foil dish. Let the juices in the roasting tin settle and then pour off the excess fat. Add to the juices the remaining grapefruit and mint mixture and the ¼ pint (125 ml.) water. Heat the gravy on top of the cooker and stir constantly. Boil it rapidly so as to reduce the volume and thicken the sauce a little. Pour the sauce over the duck.

To freeze Cover the dish and set it aside to cool. Seal, label, date and freeze.

To finish and serve Take the required quantity from the freezer and reheat in oven, preheated to 400°F, Gas 6 (200°C), for 35–40 minutes. Turn on to a warm platter and serve garnished with strips of rind.

A Haddock Crisp

3–4 portions

1 12-oz (300-gm) pkt haddock fillets
salt & pepper
1 tablespoon lemon juice
2 oz (50 gm) sliced mushrooms
¼ pt (125 ml.) béchamel sauce
3 oz (75 gm) white breadcrumbs
3 oz (75 gm) grated cheese
parsley sprigs

To make Take the required ingredients from the freezer and cook the pack of haddock fillets in boiling water according to the instructions. Meantime, gently thaw and heat the sauce in a small saucepan. Mix in the mushrooms. Turn the hot fish into a greased pie dish and flake it very roughly. Season with salt, pepper and lemon juice, spread the sauce over the fish and top with a fairly thick layer of breadcrumbs and cheese mixed.

To finish and serve Put the dish under a hot grill to crisp and brown the topping. Serve hot. Garnish with parsley sprigs. Accompany with spinach.

A Grilled Haddock Suprême

6 portions

6 fillets haddock
oil to brush
salt & pepper
½ teaspoon crumbled thyme
½ pt (250 ml.) fish velouté sauce
4 oz (100 gm) sliced mushrooms
¼ pt (125 ml.) cream

To make Take the required ingredients from the freezer. Brush the fillets with oil and sprinkle with salt, pepper and thyme. Set aside. Meantime, turn the sauce into a saucepan and thaw it out gently over a very low heat. When thawed, add all but 12 small slices of mushroom. Simmer the sauce for 30 minutes. Rub the sauce through a fine sieve, stir in the cream and reheat it very gently but do not boil. At the same time, put the fish under a medium grill and cook until thawed and cooked through, about 20 minutes depending on size.

To finish and serve Arrange the fish attractively on a platter and coat with the suprême sauce. Garnish with the mushroom slices that were set aside earlier. Serve hot with a delicately flavoured green vegetable and new potatoes.

A *Strawberry and Orange Fool*

4 portions

4 trifle sponges or small slices orange cake
4 tablespoons orange juice or 1 miniature bottle Cointreau
½ pt (250 ml.) cream
4 oz (100 gm) strawberry purée
sugar to taste
strips orange rind

To make Take the required ingredients from the freezer and allow to thaw. Put the sponge into the bottom of 4 saucer champagne glasses or sundae glasses. Pour over the orange juice or Cointreau. Whip the cream until it stands in soft peaks. Fold in the strawberry purée and sweeten if necessary. Divide the mixture between the 4 glasses, piling it up attractively on top of the sponge.

To finish and serve Decorate each with fine strips of orange rind and serve lightly chilled.

A *Surprise Apricot Fritters*

3–4 portions

36–40 apricot halves
¼ pt (125 ml.) St Honoré Cream (p. 188: Gâteau St Honoré)
2½ fl. oz (63 ml.) apricot brandy
2 oz (50 gm) flour
pinch salt
2½ fl. oz (63 ml.) water
1 dessertspoon corn oil
1 egg white
caster sugar

To make Take the required ingredients from the freezer. Drain the apricots and wipe dry. Sandwich the halves together with the St Honoré Cream and sprinkle with the apricot brandy. Set aside to soak for a few minutes. Meantime, to make the fluffy fritter batter, sift the flour and salt into a basin and beat in the water and oil. Whisk the egg white stiffly and fold into the flour mixture. Heat the oil for frying. Dip each apricot in the batter and fry until crisp, fluffy and evenly golden. Drain on soft paper.

To finish and serve Pile the Surprise Apricot Fritters on to a napkin on a serving platter and sprinkle the fritters liberally with caster sugar. Serve immediately.

F *Crispy Apple Cream*

4–6 portions

1 7½-oz (187-gm) pkt shortcrust pastry
12 oz (300 gm) apple slices
½ oz (13 gm) butter
1 teaspoon ground ginger
1 oz (25 gm) caster sugar
2 oz (50 gm) ginger marmalade
¼ pt (125 ml.) cream
2 oz (50 gm) demerara sugar

To make Take the required ingredients from the freezer and thaw sufficiently to enable handling. Roll the pastry and use to line a 7-inch (17-cm.) flan ring. Bake blind in the oven preheated to 400°F, Gas 6 (200°C), for 10–15 minutes. Meantime, set aside 4 oz (100 gm) of well shaped apple slices and stew the rest in a small saucepan along with the butter, ginger and sugar. Beat the apple mixture smooth. When the flan is cooked, spread the cooked apple in the base and arrange the other apple slices on top. Spread with the marmalade. Whisk the cream and spread it thickly over the top of the apples leaving a 2-inch (5-cm.) circle of apple showing in the centre.

To freeze Remove the flan ring and pack the flan into a box, seal, label, date and freeze.

To finish and serve Take the flan from the freezer and immediately sprinkle the top liberally with demerara sugar. Put the flan under a hot grill to heat it a little but mainly to caramelize the sugar topping. Serve immediately.

F *Iced Pineapple Surprise*

8–10 portions

1 fresh pineapple with a good green top
2½ fl. oz (63 ml.) gin
4 oz (100 gm) sugar
½ pt (250 ml.) water
1 egg white
2 tablespoons lemon juice

To make Slice the top off a good, ripe pineapple and, using a sharp knife, cut the flesh out of the skin. Choose a few pieces, cut them up very small and steep in the gin. Put the rest of the pineapple into the liquidizer and make into a purée. Dissolve the sugar in the water, bring to the boil and boil for 5 minutes. Cool. Beat the egg white until it stands in soft peaks. Fold everything together.

To freeze Pour the ice into a plastic container, cover and freeze for at least 2 hours. If it is to be kept longer, seal, label, date and freeze and also wrap the pineapple shell in foil and put in the freezer.

To finish and serve Take the pineapple and the ice from the freezer. Spoon the ice into the pineapple shell and pack well. Set the lid with its green leaves on top and set the whole pineapple upright on a folded napkin on a dish to serve.

A *Queen of Hearts*

4 portions

4 tablespoons redcurrants
3 dessertspoons caster sugar
¼ pt (125 ml.) cream
2 drops vanilla essence
4 portions Granita (p. 74)

To make Take the fruit and cream from the freezer and allow to thaw sufficiently to handle. Mix 2 dessertspoons of the sugar into the fruit and allow to stand. Whisk the cream and fold in the remaining sugar and the vanilla. Put the cream in a piping bag with a large star nozzle.

To finish and serve Spoon a portion of Granita into each of 4 well chilled glasses. Make a hollow in the ice and put in a tablespoon of sweetened redcurrants. Pipe a heart-shape of cream round the fruit so as to hide the Granita. Serve immediately, with heart-shaped shortbread biscuits for added glamour.

A *Chestnut Soufflé Pudding*

3–4 portions

¾ pt (375 ml.) sweetened chestnut purée (p. 55)
4 eggs
pinch salt
¼ pt (125 ml.) basic syrup (p. 47)
1 tablespoon apricot purée
½ teaspoon rum essence

To make Take the required ingredients from the freezer. Gently heat the chestnut purée. Separate the eggs and beat 3 of the yolks into the chestnut. Take the chestnut purée off the heat and fold in the four egg whites stiffly beaten. Turn the mixture into a buttered and sugared 2-pint (1-litre) metal mould. Place the mould in a roasting tin of hot water and cook like this in the oven preheated to 375°F, Gas 5 (190°C), for 50 minutes. Meantime, mix the syrup, apricot and rum essence together and heat gently.

To finish and serve When the pudding is firm to the touch, take it from the oven and set the dish on a board for a minute or two to allow the pudding to shrink a little. Turn the Chestnut Soufflé Pudding out on to a warm platter and pour the hot rum apricot sauce over it. Serve immediately.

A *Falstaff*

4–6 portions

2 portions Vanilla Mousse (p. 86)
3 oz (75 gm) chopped toasted almonds
3 portions Raspberry Mousse (p. 140)

To make Line a well chilled mould with vanilla mousse as for a bombe (p. 113). Press 2 oz (50 gm) of the nuts on to the vanilla mousse to cover it fairly well. Pack the raspberry mousse into the centre, cover with a little more vanilla mousse. Cover the mould and put it into the freezer for at least 30 minutes. The more quickly you work, the less time it will need to be back in the freezer.

To finish and serve Take the Falstaff from the freezer and turn it out on to an attractive round glass dish. Sprinkle the top with the rest of the almonds and serve immediately. Cut like a cake to serve.

F or A *Mint and Chocolate Igloo*

8–10 portions

3 whole eggs & 2 whites
6 oz (150 gm) caster sugar
1 miniature crême de menthe
2 teaspoons powdered gelatine
3 tablespoons water
¼ pt (125 ml.) cream
2 oz (50 gm) dark chocolate
1 6-inch (15-cm.) thin, basic sponge cake (p. 46)

To make Set aside the 2 egg whites as these are not required until the end. Separate the 3 whole eggs. Put the 3 yolks, 2 oz (50 gm) sugar and the liqueur into a basin and whisk the mixture over hot water until it becomes thick and the consistency of lightly whipped cream. It will become paler as it thickens. Meanwhile dissolve the gelatine in 2 tablespoons of the water. When the egg and liqueur mixture is thick, take it off the heat, add a tablespoon of the water and continue whisking until it is cool. Whisk in the dissolved gelatine and set aside for a minute or two. Meantime whisk the cream and the 3 egg whites in 2 separate basins until standing in soft peaks. Fold both into the crême de menthe mixture. Pour half of this mousse into a wetted 1-pint (500-ml.) dome-shaped mould. Grate the chocolate coarsely and put it in a thick layer on top of the mousse. Pour the rest on top of the chocolate.

To freeze Cover the mould, seal, label, date and freeze. If you need the mould, it may be turned out carefully when solid, wrapped carefully and quickly in foil, overwrapped in a polythene bag, sealed, labelled, dated, and returned to the freezer.

To finish and serve Take the cake from the freezer and allow it to thaw for an hour. Just before the pudding is required, whisk the other 2 egg whites and fold in the remaining 4 oz (100 gm) sugar to make a meringue. Take the iced mousse from the freezer, unwrap or unmould it and put it on top of the cake on a large oven-proof dish and, using a large star nozzle, very quickly pipe the meringue over the mousse to cover it so that there are *no* gaps. Put the Igloo immediately into the oven preheated to 425°F, Gas 7 (220°C), for 3–5 minutes to crisp and brown the meringue slightly. Serve immediately and cut like a cake.

A *Crêpes Suzette*

4 portions

8 pancakes
¼ pt (125 ml.) curaçao
2 oz (50 gm) butter
2 oz (50 gm) sugar
1 tablespoon grated orange rind
brandy – optional

To make Take the pancakes from the freezer. Put ¾ of the curaçao into a pancake pan to heat very gently. Beat together the butter, sugar, orange rind and remaining curaçao until light and creamy. Spread each pancake on the uncooked side with some of this cream. Dealing with each pancake in turn, put it into the curaçao in the pan so that the pancake is flat with the creamed side uppermost and heat it over a fairly high flame for a minute. Then fold it quickly in four and push it to the side of the pan to keep warm whilst you deal with the others. If the pan is not big enough to do this, then serve the pancakes as they are ready.

To finish and serve When all the Crêpes Suzette are ready, serve them immediately with the juices from the pan poured over. For added drama if you are cooking in front of your guests, throw a little brandy into the hot pan at the last moment before you lift the crêpes out, turn up the heat and 'flame' it. Serve from the still-flaming pan.

SUGGESTED MENUS

Brandied Sweetbreads en Croûte
Strawberry and Orange Fool

Tarragon Roast Chicken
Surprise Apricot Fritters

Roast Duck in Grapefruit Sauce
Chestnut Soufflé Pudding

Chicken Liver Bites
Haddock Crisp
Queen of Hearts

Turkey and Ham Casserole
Crispy Apple Cream

Grilled Haddock Suprême
Iced Pineapple Surprise

Lamb Gueveche
Mint and Chocolate Igloo

Kipper Creams
Steak Chasseur
Falstaff

Kipper Mousse
Glazed Shoulder of Lamb
Crêpes Suzette

INSTANT PARTIES

A *French Onion Soup*

6–8 portions

2 oz (50 gm) butter
6 oz (300 gm) sliced onions
½ oz (13 gm) flour
2½ pts (1¼ litres) water
salt & pepper
6 thin slices french bread
6 thin slices Gruyère cheese
2 oz (50 gm) butter

To make Take the required ingredients from the freezer. Melt the butter in a strong saucepan. Gently fry the onions until they are soft and well browned. Sprinkle with the flour, stir well and brown a little more. Add the water and seasoning. Cook for 10 minutes.

To finish and serve Put a slice of cheese on each piece of bread and dot the tops with butter. Put a cheese and bread slice in each of six warm soup bowls and pour over a portion of soup. Leave it to stand in a warm oven for 5 minutes before serving.

A *Asparagus Malta*

6 portions

12 pancakes
36 asparagus spears
3 tablespoons vinegar
2 tablespoons water
2 egg yolks
2 oz (50 gm) butter
salt & pepper
1 tablespoon orange juice
a few strips of finely cut orange rind

To make Take the required ingredients from the freezer. Unwrap the pancakes but leave interleaved with foil. Put them between two plates and reheat in the oven preheated to 350°F,

Gas 4 (180°C), for 20 minutes. Meantime, tie the asparagus in bundles and cook in boiling, salted water for 3 minutes. Drain. Wrap three asparagus spears in each pancake and set in a serving dish. Cover and keep warm. Put the vinegar into a small saucepan and boil to reduce it to 1 tablespoon. Add the water and pour over the egg yolks in a small basin. Whisk. Melt the butter and whisk half of it into the eggs and vinegar. Put the basin in a pan of hot water and whisk over a gentle heat until the eggs thicken. Season to taste. Take the sauce off the heat and stir in the rest of the butter, the orange juice and strips of rind.

To finish and serve Take the asparagus pancakes from the oven, uncover, pour over the Malta sauce and serve immediately as a starter or as a main course with cold meat.

A or F *Breast of Lamb with Apple and Oatmeal*

4–6 portions

2 breasts of lamb
salt & pepper
4 oz (100 gm) white breadcrumbs
2 oz (50 gm) apple slices – chopped finely
1 teaspoon ground cloves
1 oz (25 gm) raisins
1 egg yolk
2 oz (50 gm) coarse oatmeal
apple sauce (purée)

To make Take the required ingredients from the freezer and allow to thaw sufficiently to enable handling. Rub the meat with salt and pepper. Mix together the crumbs, apple, cloves and raisins and mix with sufficient egg yolk to hold the stuffing together. Wrap the breasts of lamb round the stuffing, tie it well and put it in a dry roasting tin. Roast in the oven preheated to 375°F, Gas 5 (190°C), for 30 minutes to the lb (400 gm). Take the lamb from the oven, roll it in oatmeal to coat the outside, turn the oven up to 425°F, Gas 7 (220°C), and put the meat back in for 10 minutes to crisp and brown the oatmeal.

To freeze If the lamb is to be served cold, it may be frozen at this stage. Cool it thoroughly, slice it down, wrap in foil in convenient quantities and overwrap in a polythene bag. Seal, label, date and freeze. When required, spread out the slices to thaw for at least 1 hour before serving.

To finish and serve Serve the lamb hot, or cold, sliced down and with the apple sauce handed separately.

A *Minty Roast Leg of Lamb with Green Sauce*

6–8 portions

4½ lb (2 kilos) leg of lamb
salt & pepper
2 tablespoons vinegar
1 tablespoon crumbled mint leaves
1 teaspoon sugar
1 pt (500 ml.) béchamel sauce
1 tablespoon crumbled parsley
2 teaspoons lemon juice
a few fine strips lemon rind
a small bunch of mint

To make Take the lamb from the freezer and allow it to thaw, unwrapped, in the fridge for 24 hours. Rub the skin with salt and pepper. Place the lamb on a large square of foil and spoon over the mixture of vinegar, mint and sugar. Wrap the foil round the meat and roast the lamb in the oven preheated to 350°F, Gas 4 (180°C), for 2½ hours, opening up the foil for the last ½ hour. Meantime, take the other ingredients from the freezer, thaw, mix everything together except the mint. Heat the sauce gently, adding a little milk to thin if necessary.

To finish and serve Drain the lamb and place it on a warm platter. Garnish with the bunch of mint and hand the sauce separately, with the juices from the meat in another sauceboat.

F *Topside Poivrade*

6 portions

2 lb (1 kilo) piece topside
salt & pepper
2 tablespoons oil
¼ pt (125 ml.) lemon juice
12 peppercorns
1 oz (25 gm) chopped onion
¼ pt (125 ml.) espagnol sauce
lemon twists

To make Take the required ingredients from the freezer and thaw sufficiently to enable handling. Slice the topside in ½-inch (1-cm.) slices and lay in a dish. Pour over a mixture of all the other ingredients except the espagnol sauce and leave to marinade for 24 hours, if possible. Cover the dish and bake in the oven preheated to 325°F, Gas 3 (160°C), for 1 hour. Lift the meat out into suitably sized foil dishes, pour the marinade into a small saucepan and boil until the quantity is reduced to about 2½ fl. oz (63 ml.). Mix in the espagnol sauce and strain the mixture over the meat. Cool.

To freeze Cover the foil dishes. Seal, label, date and freeze.

To finish and serve Take the required quantity from the freezer and reheat in the oven preheated to 400°F, Gas 6 (200°C), for 30 minutes. Carefully transfer the meat to a warm serving platter, pour the sauce over and garnish with lemon twists.

F *Shepherds' Delight*

6 portions

1½ lb (600 gm) cold roast beef
2 oz (50 gm) salami
1 teaspoon chopped dried chilli peppers
2 oz (50 gm) peas
½ pt (250 ml.) espagnol sauce
8 oz (200 gm) sliced carrots
2 2¼-oz (64-gm) pkts instant potato
2 oz (50 gm) butter
crumbled parsley

To make Mince the cold roast beef coarsely and finely chop the salami. In a basin, mix together the first four ingredients. Melt the sauce over a low heat and mix into the meat mixture. Cook the carrots in boiling, salted water until soft. Drain and mash very well. Make up the potato according to the pack instructions and then beat in half the butter and the carrot. Divide the meat mixture between 3 foil pie dishes and top each with ⅓ of the carrot and potato mixture. Fork the topping attractively. Dot the remaining butter on top of each pie. Cool.

To freeze Cover each foil dish carefully with foil. Seal, label, date and freeze.

To finish and serve Take the required amount of Shepherds' Delight from the freezer and bake in the oven preheated to 400°F, Gas 6 (200°C), for 30 minutes. Uncover the pie dish for the last 10 minutes to allow the topping to crisp and brown slightly. Sprinkle liberally with crumbled frozen parsley.

F *Pork Pie*

12 portions

4 lb (2 kilos) English spare ribs
salt & pepper
2 teaspoons powdered bayleaves
1 teaspoon anchovy essence
12 oz (300 gm) lard
½ pt (250 ml.) milk and water mixed
2 lb (1 kilo) flour
1 teaspoon salt
beaten egg to glaze

To make Trim, bone and cut up the pork. Put the trimmings and bones into a saucepan, cover with water and simmer gently for 1 hour. Strain this stock and season it with salt and pepper Put it aside to set to a stiff jelly. Put the lard, milk and water into a saucepan and bring to the boil. Sift the flour and salt into a basin, make a well in the centre and pour in the liquid. Using a wooden spoon, mix it well to a soft dough. Set aside a ¼ of the dough and keep warm. Allow the rest to cool sufficiently to enable handling. Knead well and roll out slightly. Use it to line a greased 7-inch (17-cm.) cake tin with a loose base. Line by pressing the dough up the sides of the tin to within ½ inch (1 cm.) of the top. Cut the meat up finely and mix with salt, pepper, bay-leaves and anchovy essence. Pack firmly into the pastry case. Use the rest of the pastry to make a lid. Seal the edges decoratively and carefully. Make a small hole in the centre of the lid. Make some leaves and a rose out of the pastry scraps and place on top of the pie. Brush the top over with the beaten egg and bake in the oven preheated to 300°F, Gas 2 (150°C), for 3 hours. When cooked, carefully pour some heated jellied stock into the pie through the hole in the top until it is full. Set aside to cool and set. This Pork Pie may be made into smaller versions using a jar or a glass around which to shape the pastry before filling and wrapping a strip of the foil round each before baking to hold the shape. The baking time would be reduced proportionately to a minimum of 1 hour for individual-sized pies.

To freeze Remove the pie from the tin and wrap in foil or a polythene bag. Seal, label, date and freeze.

To finish and serve Take the pie from the freezer and, still wrapped, allow 24 hours at room temperature for it to thaw and regain its full flavour. Unwrap it and serve with salad.

A *Lemon and Garlic Chicken*

4–5 portions

1 3-lb 14-oz (1¾-kilo) chicken
salt & pepper
2 cloves garlic
2½ fl. oz (63 ml.) lemon juice
strips of rind from 2 lemons
½ pt (250 ml.) water and chicken juices
1 teaspoon arrowroot
1 teaspoon sugar
parsley sprigs

To make Take the required ingredients from the freezer. Thaw the chicken out thoroughly. Rub the skin with salt and pepper. Peel the garlic. Halve one clove and put it inside the carcase. Cut the other clove into long spikes. Using a skewer, make holes over the breast and legs of the bird and push a spike of garlic into each hole. Sprinkle half the lemon juice and half the rind over the chicken and wrap the bird in foil. Roast it in the oven preheated to 375°F, Gas 5 (190°C), for 1¼ hours. Open the foil, baste the breast with the juices and continue baking for 15–20 minutes to crisp and brown the skin.

To finish and serve Lift the chicken on to a platter and keep warm. Strain the juices from the chicken into a small saucepan and make up to ½ pint (250 ml.). Blend the remaining lemon juice with the arrowroot and a little of the water. Heat the juices gently, add the blended arrowroot and bring to the boil stirring continuously until the sauce is thickened and clear. Stir in remaining rind and sugar to taste. Garnish the chicken with parsley sprigs and serve with the sauce handed separately in a sauceboat.

F *Chicken Bilbao*

6 portions

6 fresh chicken joints
salt & pepper
4 tablespoons olive oil
4 oz (100 gm) chopped onion
2 cloves garlic – crushed
6 oz (150 gm) streaky bacon rashers
10 oz (250 gm) raw rice
1¼ pts (625 ml.) chicken stock
½ pt (250 ml.) tomato purée
1 dessertspoon brown sugar
10 oz (250 gm) peas
lemon slices

To make Skin the chicken joints and rub with salt and pepper. Heat the oil in a frying pan and fry the chicken joints slowly until partly cooked and golden brown. Remove the chicken to a casserole dish. Add the onion and garlic to the juices in the pan and cook till soft. Chop the bacon and add to the frying pan with the rice. Stir and fry until the bacon crisps and the rice is lightly browned. Add the stock, tomato purée and sugar, and salt and pepper to taste. Turn the rice mixture into a foil-lined casserole, cover and set aside to cool.

To freeze Put the chicken in the casserole into the freezer. When frozen, lift out the chicken in the foil and overwrap it in foil. Seal, label, date and return to the freezer.

To finish and serve Take the chicken from the freezer, take off the foil and put the frozen block into the original casserole dish. Cover it tightly and put it in the oven preheated to 375°F, Gas 5 (190°C), for 1 hour until the rice is cooked through and the whole dish is hot. Stir the peas into the rice, return to the oven for 5 minutes then serve Chicken Bilbao very hot and garnished with lemon slices.

F *Chicken Kiev*

8 portions

8 chicken breasts
salt & pepper
8 oz (200 gm) butter
2 cloves garlic
1 bunch watercress
1 oz (25 gm) mushrooms
2 oz (50 gm) flour
2 eggs
breadcrumbs
lemon wedges

To make If using frozen chicken, allow it to thaw. Take the skin off the chicken breasts and remove carcase bone if necessary. Rub with salt and pepper. Lay them out on a board with inside uppermost. Put the butter into a small basin, add the garlic cloves crushed, the watercress leaves and mushrooms, both very finely chopped. Blend together with the butter. Divide the butter into 8 pieces and shape into a small sausage. Put one on each chicken breast and wrap up in the chicken so that the wing bone, still attached to the chicken meat, sticks out at one corner. Smooth the edges of the chicken meat with your fingers to seal the butter inside. Dip each piece of chicken in flour seasoned with salt and pepper, then coat in beaten egg and breadcrumbs. Dip again in egg and then crumbs. Deep fry for 10–15 minutes. Drain and set aside to cool.

To freeze Pack each piece individually in a small polythene bag or foil to protect the coating. Then put into larger polythene bags in convenient quantities. Seal, label, date and freeze.

To finish and serve Take the required number from the freezer, unwrap and put on a baking tray. Thaw and heat through in the oven preheated to 425°F, Gas 7 (220°C), for 20 minutes. Serve garnished with a lemon wedge.

F or A *Ox Tongue Soubise*

8–10 portions

1 ox tongue
salt
6 peppercorns
1 pt (500 ml.) béchamel sauce
1 lb (400 gm) chopped onions
2½ fl. oz (63 ml.) cream
crumbled parsley

To make Put the ox tongue into a large saucepan and cover with cold water. Add the salt and peppercorns. Bring it slowly to the boil and simmer for 35 minutes to the pound (400 gm) and 35 minutes over. Lift the tongue out on to a board and cut away the bones and gristle at the root of the tongue. Carefully lift off the rough skin and then bend the tongue round so that the tip is over the root and fit into a deep cake tin. Fill up with tongue stock to just cover the meat. Put a plate with a weight on it on top of the tongue to press it into shape and set it aside to cool and set overnight.

To freeze The tongue may be frozen at this stage, in which case when it is set, turn it out and wrap it carefully in foil and then overwrap in a polythene bag. Or slice it down, interleave the slices with foil and pack in convenient quantities in polythene bags. Seal, label, date and freeze.

To finish and serve Take the required number of tongue slices and a proportionate amount of the other ingredients from the freezer and allow to thaw sufficiently to enable handling. If not already sliced, slice the tongue down and lay in a deep serving platter. Gently heat the sauce. Boil the onions in water until soft and then drain and rub through a sieve or liquidize to give an onion purée. Stir this into the sauce, check the seasoning and pour over the tongue slices. Cover and heat in the oven preheated to 350°F, Gas 4 (180°C), for 20 minutes. Stir in the cream, sprinkle with crumbled parsley and serve hot with Duchess potatoes and broad beans.

F *Salmon Trout in Classic Dress*

8–10 portions

1 fresh salmon trout	**¼ pt (125 ml.) water**
bouquet garni	**lemon slices**
6 peppercorns	**1 egg – hard boiled**
1 small jar Danish lumpfish	**crumbled parsley**
1 teaspoon powdered gelatine	**parsley sprigs**

To make Clean the fish and wipe well but do not remove the head, tail or scales. Three-quarters fill a fish-kettle with water, add the bouquet garni and peppercorns and bring the water to the boil. If you have no fish-kettle, use a strong, fairly deep roasting tin and foil to cover. Set the fish on the fish-kettle rack or on the rack from the roasting tin so that the fish stands on its belly. Using a larding needle and a piece of fine string, shape the fish into an S-shape by threading the string through the head, middle and tail. When the water is boiling, lower the fish into it, cover the pan, bring the water back to the boil, simmer for 5 minutes, then immediately remove the pan from the heat and set it aside to cool, preferably overnight. Lift the fish out and very carefully remove the string, body skin, fins, eyes and the ridge of fat along the edges of the belly and the top of the backbone.

To freeze Wrap the fish very carefully and very closely in well-oiled foil or polythene film. Overwrap it, seal, label, date and freeze.

To finish and serve Take the salmon trout and the other ingredients from the freezer. Unwrap the fish and set it on a serving platter. Put a line of lumpfish along the groove on the top of the fish from which the fat was removed. Dissolve the gelatine in the water and use it to brush over the salmon trout and lumpfish to glaze it. Dip the lemon slices in the gelatine, halve the slices and use to edge the platter. Separate the hard-boiled yolk and white. Press the yolk through a sieve and, using the blade of a small knife and the little finger, press on to the salmon trout just below the lumpfish in a long line on either side of the backbone. Finely chop the egg white and press a line on to the fish along the middle of each side. Use crumbled parsley for similar lines below and above the egg white. Tuck more glazed halved lemon slices along the belly of the fish if it is rather untidy. Put parsley sprigs in the eye sockets. Serve the fish cold with creamy horseradish sauce and a selection of salads and new potatoes.

F *Champagne Marquise*

8–10 portions

½ pt (250 ml.) water
½ pt (250 ml.) champagne or sparkling wine
4–6 oz (100–150 gm) sugar
¼ pt (125 ml.) cream
16–20 fresh strawberries

To make Take the cream from the freezer and thaw sufficiently to whip it lightly. Meantime, dissolve the sugar in the water with almost all the champagne added. The amount of sugar depends on whether you are using a sweet or a dry wine. Boil the syrup for 10 minutes. Turn the syrup into a foil-lined tin or a plastic container and freeze. When it is mushy, take it from the freezer, turn it into a basin and whisk it thoroughly. Fold in the whipped cream.

To freeze Pack in plastic containers, seal, label, date and return to the freezer.

To finish and serve Slice the strawberries and soak in the remaining champagne. Take the Marquise from the freezer and spoon portions into chilled champagne glasses. Decorate with the strawberries and serve immediately.

A *Raspberry Vacherin*

8–10 portions

3 egg whites
1 tablespoon cornflour
1 teaspoon lemon juice
6 oz (150 gm) caster sugar
½ pt (250 ml.) cream
1 miniature Tia Maria
1 lb (400 gm) raspberries

To make Whisk the egg whites until stiff then fold in the sifted cornflour, the lemon juice and half the sugar. Whisk again, then fold in ½ the remaining sugar. Use ⅓ of the meringue mixture to spread out to an 8-inch (20-cm.) circle on a lightly oiled sheet of paper on a baking tray. Pipe the rest in whirls so that eight are largest, seven smaller, five smaller still and one tiny one. Sprinkle the remaining sugar over the meringue. Bake in the oven at its lowest setting for 3 hours.

To finish and serve Take the cream and raspberries from the freezer. Whisk the cream and Tia Maria until thick. Set aside a few well-shaped raspberries, fold in the rest. Remove the meringue from the paper and put the base soft side uppermost on a serving platter. Pile the raspberry mixture high on top and stick the meringue shells round the cream so that the larger shells are near the base and decrease in size to the smallest one on top. Push the whole raspberries, previously set aside, into spaces between the meringue shells to give an attractive finish.

A or F *Iced Vanilla Trifle*

6–8 portions

3 oz (75 gm) redcurrants
2 oz (75 gm) apple slices
6 trifle sponges
2 miniature Kirsch
6 portions Vanilla Mousse (p. 86)
redcurrants and apple slices to decorate

To make Take the fruit from the freezer. Cut the apple into small dice and mix with the currants. Soak the fruit until thawed in the Kirsch from 1 of the bottles. Split the sponges. In another shallow dish soak the trifle sponges in the rest of the Kirsch until it has all been soaked up. Pack 2 portions of the Vanilla Mousse into the base of a 1-pound (500-gm) loaf tin and spread it flat. Spoon in 2 oz (50 gm) of the fruit and spread flat, and top with 4 halves of sponge. Repeat this process twice to end with a layer of sponge.

To freeze Cover and return to the freezer for at least 30 minutes. Because this is simple and quick to make, it can be made when required, but you can keep it in the freezer for a week or so at this stage; in which case, seal, label and date it.

To finish and serve Take the trifle from the freezer when it is required. Uncover it and turn it out of the loaf tin on to an oblong platter. Decorate with a line of redcurrants along the top and a few apple slices at the base. Slice like a loaf to serve.

F or A *Very Easy Icecream*

8–10 portions

1 large tin evaporated milk
2 oz (50 gm) caster sugar
1 egg white

To make Put the tin of evaporated milk in the freezer for 3 or 4 hours. Open the tin and pour the contents into a basin. Whisk it until it has trebled in volume. Gradually add the sugar, whisking constantly. Whisk the egg white until very stiff, then fold it into the milk and sugar. Pour into plastic containers.

To freeze Cover, seal, label, date and freeze the icecream.

To finish and serve Take the required quantity from the freezer as you need it. Spoon into glasses and serve with chocolate sauce or fruit or use to accompany fruit pies. This basic ice-cream may have almost any flavouring added, either before freezing or as required, but allowing 1 hour for it to be returned to refreeze before serving. Suggested flavours are 1 dessert-spoon blended instant coffee, chocolate chips, 2 bananas crushed, or nuts or fresh fruit.

F *Jamaican Cream*

6–8 portions

1 pt (500 ml.) milk
1 oz (25 gm) raisins
1½ oz (37 gm) cornflour
1½ oz (37 gm) soft brown sugar
2 tablespoons instant coffee
3 eggs – separated
1 oz (25 gm) butter
cream whirls
chopped roasted almonds

To make Pour almost all the milk and the raisins into a sauce-pan and heat it gently. Use the remainder to blend the cornflour. Add the sugar and coffee to the cornflour. Then pour the mixture into the warm milk, stirring constantly until it thickens. Take it off the heat and beat in the egg yolks and butter. Turn the coffee mixture into a basin to cool. Meantime, whisk the egg whites then fold them into the coffee mixture.

To freeze Divide the Jamaican Cream into six or eight small foil pots or clean empty plastic mousse tubs. Cover, seal, label, date and freeze.

To finish and serve Take the required number of Jamaican Creams from the freezer one hour before required. Turn out into glasses or appropriate dishes, top with a frozen cream whirl and chopped, roasted almonds and set aside to thaw out.

A *Chocolate Profiteroles*

10–15 portions

30–40 2-inch (50-cm.) choux pastry puffs (p. 201: White Swans)	**8 oz (200 gm) caster sugar**
2 pts (1 litre) St Honoré Cream (p. 188: Gâteau St Honoré)	**1 large can evaporated milk**
8 oz (200 gm) dark chocolate	**1 oz (25 gm) butter**
	1 egg yolk
	2½ fl. oz (63 ml.) brandy

To make Take required ingredients from the freezer and allow to thaw sufficiently to enable handling. Fill the choux puffs with St Honoré Cream using a piping bag and a plain ½-inch (1-cm.) nozzle. Pile them high on a serving platter. In a basin over hot water, melt the chocolate. Whisk in the sugar, evaporated milk, butter, egg yolk and brandy.

To finish and serve Pour the hot sauce over the filled choux puffs and serve immediately. Or, if the dish has to sit for a bit, then pour only a very little sauce over the puffs to decorate and hand the rest of the sauce separately. This prevents sogginess!

A or F *Iced Chocolate Hedgehog*

4–6 portions

1 7-inch (17-cm.) plain basic sponge (p. 46)
2 10-fl. oz (250-ml.) chocolate icecream
1 lb (½ kilo) icing sugar
1 tablespoon cocoa powder
1 tablespoon drinking chocolate
2 tablespoons water
1 small can sweetened condensed milk
1 oz (25 gm) toasted spikes of almonds

To make Split the cake in half and cut in thin triangles. Use these to line a well-chilled, simple, dome-shaped 1-pint (500-ml.) mould. Spoon the icecream into the mould and pack it down well. Cover and seal the mould and put it in the freezer for at least 30 minutes whilst you make the chocolate fondant icing. Sift the icing sugar, cocoa and drinking chocolate into a basin and blend in the water and condensed milk. Beat well until a smooth, shiny icing results.

To finish and serve Take the mould from the freezer and turn out the cake-covered icecream on to a board and very quickly cover it with the chocolate fondant icing. Stick the almond spikes into the icing so it looks like a hedgehog. Cut the hedgehog free of the board round the base so as to neaten the edge, and transfer it to a platter. Use the scraps of icing to make a small head for the hedgehog by rolling the bits into a ball, shaping a snout, putting 2 currants for eyes and 1 for a nose and pressing this head against the base of the sweet.

To freeze This may be frozen at this stage but is better iced as you need it as the icing will 'weep' a little when you take it from the freezer and though this would dry out in time, with an icecream centre it would thaw too much. If you do decide to freeze it in its completed state, then put the finished Iced Chocolate Hedgehog on a cake board instead of a platter and put it back in the freezer. When solid, wrap it carefully in a large polythene bag or put it in a rigid plastic container. Seal, label, date and freeze. When required, unwrap it and serve it straight from the freezer.

F or A *Gâteau St Honoré*

6–8 portions

2 oz (50 gm) sugar
4 oz (100 gm) butter
6 oz (150 gm) flour
8 eggs
12 oz (300 gm) sugar
2½ oz (63 gm) flour
1 pt (500 ml.) milk
1 teaspoon vanilla essence
21 medium-sized choux pastry puffs (p. 201: White Swans)
2½ fl. oz (63 ml.) water

To make Cream the butter and sugar together and work in the flour. Press the paste into an 8-inch (20-cm.) flan ring, prick with a fork and pinch the edges. Bake in the oven preheated to 350°F, Gas 4 (180°C), for 1 hour. Cool on a wire tray. Meantime, make the St Honoré Cream. Separate the eggs and whisk 4 of the yolks and 7 oz (175 gm) of the sugar in a basin over hot water until pale and creamy. Fold in the sifted flour. Bring the milk and vanilla to the boil and pour over the eggs and sugar whisking constantly. Cook gently over hot water, stirring with the whisk, until cooked and thickened. Whisk the eight egg whites until stiff and fold into the cream. Set the St Honoré Cream aside to cool. (This cream packed, in plastic tubs, freezes well at this stage.) Use this cream to fill the choux puffs and pile the rest in a tall peak on top of the shortbread base. Stick the filled puffs round the base and up the sides of the pile of cream. Then make a light toffee by boiling together for 10–15 minutes the remaining 5 oz (125 gm) of sugar dissolved in the water. Drizzle this toffee over the whole gâteau so that it makes the choux pastry puffs stick together and looks attractive. Set aside to cool and harden.

To freeze Carefully wrap the whole gâteau in a cone of foil. Seal, label, date and freeze. To save space, the base, choux puffs and the St Honoré Cream may all be frozen separately and assembled and decorated with the toffee when required.

To finish and serve Take from the freezer, unwrap and allow 4 hours to thaw, whether the Gâteau St Honoré is already complete or has yet to be assembled.

SUGGESTED MENUS

Lemon and Garlic Chicken
Very Easy Icecream

Chicken Bilbao
Jamaican Cream

Chicken Kiev
Raspberry Vacherin

Breast of Lamb with Apple and Oatmeal
Iced Vanilla Trifle

Minty Roast Leg of Lamb with Green Sauce
Chocolate Profiteroles

Ox Tongue Soubise
Iced Chocolate Hedgehog

Asparagus Malta
Salmon Trout in Classic Dress
Champagne Marquise

French Onion Soup
Topside Poivrade
Gâteau St Honoré

CHILDREN'S HOUR

F *Home-made French Bread*

1 or 2 loaves

8 oz (200 gm) flour
1 teaspoon salt
¼ oz (6 gm) yeast
1 teaspoon sugar
¼ pt (125 ml.) milk
½ oz (13 gm) butter
1 egg

To make Sift together the flour and salt into a warm mixing bowl. In a small basin cream together the yeast and sugar. In a small saucepan, gently heat the milk and butter to lukewarm. Whisk the egg and set half of it aside for glaze. Add the remaining half to the warm milk and then pour it over the creamed yeast. Make a well in the centre of the flour and pour in the mixture of liquids. Mix well to an elastic dough using a little more milk if necessary. Turn the dough out on to a floured board and knead it until it is smooth. Put it into a floured polythene bag, close the bag loosely and set the dough aside for 30 minutes to rise. Knead it again to get rid of any air bubbles, shape into one or two loaves, make cuts across, put on a greased tray, cover with a polythene bag and again set aside in a warm place for 10 minutes then brush with the rest of the egg and bake in the oven preheated to 475°F, Gas 9 (240°C), for 10–15 minutes. Allow the bread to cool thoroughly.

To freeze When cold, wrap each loaf closely in foil, label, date and freeze. It may be convenient to freeze the bread in even smaller pieces suitable for one or two servings, or indeed to preslice it ready to be spread with garlic butter as soon as it comes from the freezer when it would otherwise be rather difficult to slice.

To finish and serve Take the required quantity of Home-made French Bread from the freezer. If it is a whole loaf, unwrap it and allow it to thaw for about 1 hour then crisp in the oven preheated to 400°F, Gas 6 (200°C), for 5–10 minutes. If it has been cut in pieces, refresh it still wrapped in the oven preheated to 450°F, Gas 8 (230°C), for 15 minutes. For garlic bread, unwrap it, butter the slices, rewrap it in the foil and proceed as for bread cut in pieces.

F *Banana Bread*

1 loaf

3 oz (75 gm) butter
6 oz (150 gm) sugar
1 egg
3 bananas
2½ fl. oz (63 ml.) natural yogurt
10 oz (250 gm) self-raising flour
1 teaspoon baking powder
1 teaspoon salt

To make Cream the butter and sugar together until soft and creamy. Gradually beat in the egg. Mash the bananas and mix with the yogurt. Stir this into the creamed mixture. Sift the flour, baking powder and salt and fold into the banana mixture. Turn the bread mixture into a lined loaf tin or a 7-inch (17-cm.) cake tin. Bake in the oven preheated to 350°F, Gas 4 (180°C), for 1 hour until risen, lightly browned and springy to the touch. Allow the Banana Bread to shrink slightly in the tin then turn it out on to a cooling tray.

To freeze Cool the bread thoroughly then put into a polythene bag, seal, label, date and freeze.

To finish and serve Take the Banana Bread from the freezer at least 2 hours before it is required and leave it to thaw still wrapped. To serve, cut it down like a loaf. It may be sliced and spread with butter or peanut butter but it is nice alone.

F *Coconut Bread*

2 loaves

1 lb (400 gm) flour
½ teaspoon salt
3 teaspoons baking powder
7 oz (175 gm) sugar
4 oz (100 gm) butter
¼ pt (125 ml.) milk
4 oz (100 gm) desiccated coconut
1 egg

To make Sift the flour, salt and baking powder into a basin. Mix in the sugar and rub in the butter. Soak the coconut in the milk for a few minutes then mix it with the egg lightly beaten. Using a knife, work this liquid mixture into the flour and butter mixture. This will make a fairly wet dough. Turn it out on to a floured board, knead it and divide it into two. Shape each piece into a loaf and put each into a lined loaf tin. Bake in the oven preheated to 350°F, Gas 4 (180°C), for 1 hour until risen, lightly browned and springy to the touch. Allow the Coconut Bread to shrink slightly in the tin, then turn out on to a cooling tray.

To freeze Cool thoroughly then put into a polythene bag, seal, label, date and freeze.

To finish and serve Take the bread from the freezer at least 2 hours before it is required. Slice like a loaf to serve. Besides being delicious at coffee break or tea time, the Coconut Bread makes a good base for orange water ice for a sweet.

F *Ginger Iced Peanut Bread*

2 loaves

1 lb (400 gm) flour
4 teaspoons baking powder
5 oz (125 gm) soft brown sugar
3 oz (75 gm) salted peanuts
¾ pt (375 ml.) milk
10 oz (250 gm) icing sugar
2 teaspoons ground ginger
a few nuts and crystallized ginger pieces

To make Sift the flour and baking powder into a basin. Add the sugar. Chop the nuts very finely or grind coarsely in the coffee grinder. Mix the nuts into the dry ingredients in the basin. Mix in the milk and divide the mixture between 2 lined loaf tins. Set them aside, cover with a clean tea towel and allow them to rise for 20 minutes. Bake in the oven preheated to 350°F, Gas 4 (180°C), for about 35 minutes until lightly browned and springy to the touch. Allow to shrink slightly in the tin, then turn out and cool. Sift the icing sugar and ginger together and blend with a little water to make a firm icing. When the loaves are cool, use this icing to coat the top of each. Decorate simply with a few peanuts and pieces of crystallized ginger. Allow to set.

To freeze Put each loaf into a polythene bag, seal, label, date and freeze.

To finish and serve Take the peanut bread from the freezer at least 2 hours before you need it and unwrap it to thaw. The icing will probably weep a little but will dry out as the bread comes to room temperature. Serve the Ginger Iced Peanut Bread thickly sliced.

F *Treacle Scones*

8–12 scones

1 lb (400 gm) self-raising flour
½ teaspoon salt
3 teaspoons mixed spice
2 teaspoons ground cinnamon
2 teaspoons bicarbonate of soda
3 oz (75 gm) butter
½ pt (250 ml.) milk
2 tablespoons treacle
milk to glaze

To make Sift the first five ingredients into a baking bowl. Rub in the butter. Mix the treacle and milk together and pour into a well in the centre of the rubbed-in mixture. Mix to a dough using a knife. This will make a very sticky, wet dough so scrape it out on to a well floured board and lightly knead with the finger tips dipped in flour. Push the dough out to about ½ inch (1½ cm.) thick and cut into rounds using a plain 1½–2 inch (3½–5 cm.) cutter. Put on a baking tray, brush with milk and bake in the oven preheated to 425°F, Gas 7 (220°C), for 12–15 minutes. Cool on a wire tray.

To freeze Pack in convenient quantities in polythene bags. Seal, label, date and freeze.

To finish and serve Take the required scones from the freezer and allow them to thaw for about 2 hours at room temperature. Split and butter the Treacle Scones to serve. In my childhood, Treacle Scones were the basis of a traditional Hallowe'en game; the scones were dipped in yet more treacle and were then suspended on long strings from the pulley in the kitchen. The children, with hands behind backs, tried to take a bite from the scones whilst a malevolent grown-up jerked the pulley! A glorious sticky mess and a great deal of fun resulted. Perhaps you might like to try it!

F *Walnut Scones*

6–8 scones

4 oz (100 gm) self-raising flour
4 oz (100 gm) fine oatmeal
2 teaspoons baking powder
½ teaspoon salt
1 oz (25 gm) sugar
1½ oz (37 gm) butter
1½–2 oz (37–50 gm) chopped walnuts
scant ¼ pt (125 ml.) milk

To make In a baking bowl, mix together the first five ingredients. Rub in the butter and mix in the nuts. Using a knife, mix the milk into the ingredients so that a light elastic dough is formed. Turn this out on to a board dusted with oatmeal and using the finger tips gently and quickly push the dough out to about ½ inch (1½ cm.) thick. Cut with a plain round 1½–2 inch (3½–5 cm.) cutter. Put the scones on to a baking tray and bake in the oven preheated to 425°F, Gas 7 (220°C), for 10 minutes. Cool on a wire tray.

To freeze When the scones are thoroughly cold, pack them in convenient quantities in polythene bags. Seal, label, date and freeze.

To finish and serve Take the required quantity from the freezer and allow to thaw unopened for at least 1 hour at room temperature. Serve the scones split and buttered.

F *Potato Scones*

4–8 scones

1 2¼-oz (64-gm) pkt instant potato
½ oz (13 gm) butter
½ pt (250 ml.) milk and water mixed
2 oz (50 gm) fine oatmeal
pinch baking powder

To make Put the potato powder and butter into a basin. With a fork mix in the milk and water at boiling point. Let it cool a little, then, with the fork, work in the oatmeal – or as much of it as the potato will take. Turn the dough out on to a board and roll it out to a circle about ¼ inch (½ cm.) thick. Cut into 4 triangles. (If you want smaller scones, divide the mixture in two and roll out and cut as described twice.) Prick well with a fork. Lightly grease a large frying pan, or the solid plate on the cooker or a girdle, and heat it until hot. Cook the scones on this for 3 minutes on each side. Cool on a wire tray and between the folds of a clean tea towel.

To freeze When thoroughly cold, pack interleaved with polythene or foil in convenient quantities in polythene bags. Seal, label, date and freeze.

To finish and serve Take the required quantity from the freezer, unwrap and thaw at room temperature for at least 30 minutes. Spread with butter, roll up and halve to serve. They are also lovely dipped in blackcurrant jam. Fried flat in bacon fat, they make a change from fried bread for Sunday breakfast. This Potato Scone mixture rolled slightly thicker, cut in large rounds and cooked for about 5–6 minutes on either side, makes an excellent alternative to traditional Pitta bread to serve with a savoury mousse or Taramosalata (p. 88).

F *Pumpkin Muffins*

18–20 muffins

4 oz (100 gm) cooked mashed pumpkin
¼ pt (125 ml.) milk
1 egg
6 oz (150 gm) self-raising flour
1 teaspoon salt
3 teaspoons baking powder
1 teaspoon ground cinnamon

To make Put the thawed pumpkin into a baking bowl. Warm the milk and mix it into the pumpkin. Beat in the egg. Sift in the remaining ingredients and mix well using a metal spoon. Put a well rounded teaspoon of the mixture into paper cases or greased bun tins and bake in the oven at 400°F, Gas 6 (200°C), for 30 minutes until risen and lightly browned. Cool on a wire tray.

To freeze Pack in polythene bags in convenient quantities. Seal, label, date and freeze.

To finish and serve Take the required quantity from the freezer, unwrap them and put them still frozen on to a baking tray. Revive in the oven preheated to 400°F, Gas 6 (200°C), for 5–10 minutes. Cut off the tops, spread with butter and serve hot still in the paper cases if used.

This may be made with 3 small bananas mashed instead of the pumpkin.

F *Cyril the Centipede*

4×12 biscuits

8 oz (200 gm) flour
1 teaspoon baking powder
½ teaspoon salt
3 oz (75 gm) lard
3 oz (75 gm) butter
2 oz (50 gm) dark soft brown sugar
2 oz (50 gm) granulated sugar
1 egg
4 drops vanilla essence
2 oz (50 gm) mixed peel – finely chopped
coloured water icing for decoration
Liquorice Allsorts for decoration
orange rind for decoration

To make Sift the first 3 ingredients into a baking bowl. In another basin, cream together the sugars and fats. Whisk the egg and vanilla together and gradually beat into the creamed mixture. Beat well. Fold in the dry ingredients and the peel. Divide the mixture in 4. Place each amount on a square of lightly-oiled foil or waxed paper and shape into rolls about 1½ inches (3½ cm.) in diameter. Wrap up in the foil.

To freeze Overwrap the rolls, seal, label, date and freeze until required.

To finish and serve Take the required amount from the freezer, unwrap and when sufficiently thawed to enable handling, cut the pastry into rounds about ¼ inch (½ cm.) thick. Place on a greased tray and bake in the oven preheated to 425°F, Gas 7 (220°C), for 5–7 minutes. Cool. Ice with an ordinary pale pink or chocolate water icing and decorate with icing to make different faces on each. Or make a centipede by standing the biscuits up on end and linking them together with a small piece of round Liquorice Allsort each end dipped in icing and stuck between each biscuit. The last biscuit should have a tail of a twist of orange rind and the front biscuit a face drawn in icing and two antennae of strips of rind. Assemble the centipede in a curve on a cake board. It may be refrozen at this stage, wrapped in polythene so as not to damage it. For more ordinary occasions, dust the biscuits with soft brown sugar as soon as they come out of the oven, or sandwich together in twos with jam.

A *Matches*

8 matches

1 13½-oz (337-gm) pkt puff pastry
½ pt (250 ml.) milk
¾ oz (18 gm) cornflour
2 egg yolks
1 oz (25 gm) caster sugar
4 drops vanilla essence
4 oz (100 gm) icing sugar
1 dessertspoon water
1 teaspoon lemon juice
1 teaspoon cocoa powder

To make Take the pastry from the freezer and let it thaw just sufficiently to enable handling. Roll it to about ¼ inch (½ cm.) thick, then, with a warm knife, cut it into oblongs, 4 inches (10 cm.) by 1½ inches (3½ cm.). Place these upside down on to a wetted tray and bake in the oven preheated to 425°F, Gas 7 (220°C), for 10–15 minutes until well risen and golden. Cool on a wire tray. Meantime, make the Confectioners' Custard filling: put nearly all the milk into a saucepan to heat. Use the rest to blend the cornflour; mix the yolks, vanilla and the sugar in with the blended cornflour; add it to the warm milk, beating constantly; beat the custard over a low heat until it cooks and thickens. Put a piece of foil on top of the custard to exclude any air and set it aside to cool.

To finish and serve When both the pastry and the custard are quite cold, split the pastry Matches and fill each with a very generous portion of custard. Make up a thick water icing using the icing sugar, water and lemon juice. Set aside 3 teaspoons of the icing and colour it chocolate by blending in the cocoa powder. Use the white icing to coat the top of each match. Put the chocolate icing into a tiny piping bag made from greaseproof paper with a very small hole in the point. Draw lines of chocolate icing 1 inch (2½ cm.) apart across the width of the top of each Match whilst the white icing is still wet. Then, to 'feather' the icing, draw the point of a meat skewer back and forth along the length of each Match through the chocolate lines so as to 'smudge' the icing and get a 'feather iced' topping. Matches can be served for tea or as a sweet.

F *Hazelnut Soldiers*

10–12 soldiers

4 oz (100 gm) shelled hazelnuts
8 oz (200 gm) sugar
½ teaspoon vanilla essence
2 egg whites
2 oz (50 gm) dark chocolate

To make Finely chop the nuts or coarsely grind them in the coffee grinder and mix with the sugar. Whisk together the vanilla and egg whites until very stiff. Mix in the nuts and sugar. Turn the mixture on to a very well floured board and roll to ½ inch (1 cm.) thick. Cut in strips about 3 inches (7½ cm.) long and 1 inch (2½ cm.) wide. Lift carefully on to a greased baking tray and bake in the oven preheated to 350°F, Gas 4 (180°C), for about 20 minutes until lightly golden. Allow to set on the tray for 2 or 3 minutes before lifting the soldiers on to a wire tray to cool.

To freeze Pack in a plastic box to protect the soldiers. Seal, label, date and freeze.

To finish and serve Take required number of soldiers out of the box in the freezer and reseal the box. Allow the Hazelnut Soldiers to thaw out at room temperature for 2 hours or pop into the oven preheated to 425°F, Gas 7 (220°C), for 5 minutes to thaw and crisp up again. Cool them, dip the ends in melted chocolate. Set by resting on a wire tray before serving.

F *Apple Diamonds*

12–14 pastries

4 oz (100 gm) butter
2 oz (50 gm) sugar
8 oz (200 gm) finely chopped apple slices
4 oz (100 gm) lemon rind – minced
½ teaspoon mixed spice
1 13½-oz (337-gm) pkt puff pastry
egg white and caster sugar for topping

To make Cream the butter and sugar until light and fluffy. Mix in the fruit, rind and spice. Roll the pastry out thinly and cut in strips 2 inches (5 cm.) wide and then into diamond shapes. Put a little of the fruit mixture on each of half the number of diamond shapes, wet the edges and use the other diamonds to cover each. Pinch the edges together to give a fluted effect. Place the Apple Diamonds on a wetted baking tray and bake in the oven preheated to 425°F, Gas 7 (220°C), for 15 minutes. Cool on a wire tray.

To freeze Pack in a plastic box. Seal, label, date and freeze.

To finish and serve Take the required number of Apple Diamonds from the box in the freezer and put them on a baking tray. Brush each with egg white and dust with caster sugar then put into the oven preheated to 350°F, Gas 4 (180°C), for 15 minutes to thaw them out and also crisp the topping. Serve cold for tea or hot with cream or icecream as a sweet.

F *Bakewell Tarts*

12 cakes

1 7½-oz (187-gm) pkt shortcrust pastry
2 tablespoons raspberry jam
1 egg
1½ oz (37 gm) self-raising flour
2 oz (50 gm) soft margarine
½ oz (13 gm) ground almonds
2 oz (50 gm) caster sugar

To make Roll the pastry and cut with a fluted cutter. Use these to line 12 patty tins. Put a very small dot of jam in each pastry case. Using a whisk, blend all the remaining ingredients together until light and fluffy. Put a rounded teaspoon of this mixture into each pastry case on top of the jam. Bake in the oven preheated to 360°F, Gas 4–5 (185°C), for 15 minutes until lightly browned and springy to the touch. Cool on a wire tray.

To freeze Pack in convenient quantities in polythene bags.

Seal, label, date and freeze.

To finish and serve Take the required number from the freezer and allow them to thaw out for about 2 hours still in the polythene bag. Dust each with icing sugar before serving for tea.

F *White Swans*

Makes 20–24

½ pt (250 ml.) water
4 oz (100 gm) butter
7 oz (175 gm) flour
1 teaspoon salt
4 eggs
1 pt (500 ml.) cream
sugar to taste
vanilla essence
icing sugar

To make Put the water and butter in a saucepan and bring it slowly to the boil. Sift the flour and salt on to a piece of paper. Take the saucepan off the heat and shoot the flour quickly into the liquid. Beat it very well. When smooth, beat the eggs in gradually. Beat the mixture very well until it is smooth and elastic. The result is dependent on good and sufficient beating at this stage. Put ¾ of the choux paste into a piping bag with a plain ½-inch (1-cm.) nozzle. Pipe about 20 rounds on to a well-greased baking tray. Put the remaining paste into another bag with a ¼-inch (½-cm.) plain nozzle and pipe a similar number of elongated S-shapes on to the baking tray. Bake in the oven preheated to 400°F, Gas 6 (200°C), for 25 minutes. Take the S-shapes out and cool on a wire tray. Puncture the side of each of the rounds to allow the air to escape and put them back into the bottom of the oven for 6–7 minutes to allow them to dry out. Cool on a wire tray.

To freeze This is a good stage to freeze the choux paste as it freezes well. It is extremely versatile, of use as a basis of savoury or sweet dishes in the 'swan' shape or simply as 'buns', either of this standard size, larger to serve several people, or as a meal centrepiece or in miniature as petits fours or cocktail savouries. Pack the pastries in polythene bags, seal, label, date and freeze.

To finish and serve Take the required number of choux 'rounds' and the corresponding number of S-shapes from the freezer. They require virtually no time to thaw out; handling to finish is sufficient to thaw. Whisk the appropriate quantity of cream until standing in soft peaks. Add sugar and vanilla to taste. Slice the top off each round and fill with cream. Set the S-shape in one side of the cream to resemble the swan's neck. Cut the top slice in half and stick in the top of the cream to resemble wings. Dust with icing sugar and serve for tea.

A *Cream Palmiers*

10–12 pastries

1 7½-oz (187-gm) pkt puff pastry
1 egg white
3 oz (75 gm) caster sugar
2 tablespoons jam
½ pt (250 ml.) cream

To make Take the pastry from the freezer and allow it to thaw just sufficiently to enable handling. Roll it so that the oblong becomes a square of about 8 or 9 inches (20–22 cm.). Sprinkle with 1 oz (25 gm) of the sugar. Roll two opposite sides up and in towards the middle so that a double roll is formed. Using a hot knife, slice this double roll into ⅓-inch (1-cm.) pieces. Put them flat on a wetted tray and bake in the oven preheated to 450°F, Gas 8 (230°C), for 10–12 minutes. Brush each with egg white and dust with caster sugar. Return them to the oven reduced to 300°F, Gas 2 (150°C), for 10 minutes to crisp and glaze the tops. Cool on a wire tray.

To finish and serve Spread half the number of pastries with jam on the unglazed side. Whip the cream and spoon or pipe a portion on top of the jam. Cover with the remaining pastries, glazed side uppermost. Serve the Cream Palmiers in paper cases for tea.

These may be frozen at almost any stage but are so quick to make that there seems little point.

F *Eccles Cakes*

6–8 cakes

8 oz (200 gm) flaky pastry (p. 51)	**4 oz (100 gm) currants**
1 oz (25 gm) butter	**½ teaspoon ground cinnamon**
2 oz (50 gm) sugar	**1 egg white and sugar for topping**

To make Roll the pastry out to about 3 inches (7 cm.), and cut into 3-inch (7-cm.) rounds. Mix together the next 4 ingredients and put a little in the middle of each pastry round. Gather up the edges of the pastry and pinch them well together. Turn each round over so that the gathered up edges are underneath. Press flat and roll slightly until the currants just begin to show. Put two diagonal cuts across each Eccles Cake, brush with egg white and dust with sugar. Place on a wetted baking tray and bake in the oven preheated to 425°F, Gas 7 (220°C), for 15–20 minutes until risen and lightly browned. Cool on a wire tray.

To freeze Pack the Eccles Cakes into plastic boxes in convenient quantities. Seal, label, date and freeze.

To finish and serve Take the required number of Eccles Cakes from the box in the freezer. Place them on a baking tray and crisp up in the oven preheated to 425°F, Gas 7 (220°C), for 5 minutes. Serve slightly warm if possible.

F Cinnamon and Lemon Cake

3 eggs
6 oz (150 gm) self-raising flour
6 oz (150 gm) soft margarine
6 oz (150 gm) caster sugar
1 lemon
2 egg whites
12 oz (300 gm) dark soft brown sugar
pinch cream of tartar
3 teaspoons ground cinnamon
4 tablespoons water

To make Line 2 7-inch (18-cm.) sandwich tins. Put the eggs, flour, margarine, sugar, grated rind and the juice of the lemon all into a baking bowl. Whisk for a minute or two until smooth and fluffy. Divide the mixture between the two tins and bake in the oven preheated to 360°F, Gas 4–5 (185°C), for 35 minutes until lightly brown and springy to the touch. Turn out, remove the paper and cool on a wire tray. Split each cake in two. Put all the remaining ingredients into a basin and whisk over hot water until thick and creamy. Remove from the heat and continue whisking until cold and a little stiffer. Use ⅓ of this frosting to sandwich the four pieces of cake together. And use the remaining ⅔ to swirl generously over the sides and top of the cake.

To freeze Set the cake on a board and freeze. When quite solid, wrap it in a polythene bag or put it in a box for protection. Seal, label, date and freeze. If relevant, the cake may be cut up in portions and frozen with each slice separately wrapped in waxed paper before putting it all into one polythene bag.

To finish and serve Take the cake from the freezer, unwrap it and allow it to thaw out at room temperature for at least 3 hours.

F *Sticky Chocolate Cake*

3 eggs
4 oz (100 gm) self-raising flour
2 oz (50 gm) drinking chocolate powder
6 oz (150 gm) soft brown sugar
6 oz (150 gm) soft margarine
1 teaspoon Angostura Bitters
1 tablespoon chocolate sauce (commercial)
2 tablespoons medium sherry
1½ tablespoons cocoa powder
1½ tablespoons drinking chocolate powder
1½ tablespoons soft brown sugar
2 oz (50 gm) soft margarine

To make Line 2 7-inch (18-cm.) sandwich tins. Put the first 7 ingredients and 1 tablespoon of the sherry into a basin and whisk until thoroughly blended and fluffy. Divide the mixture between the 2 tins and bake in the oven preheated to 360°F, Gas 4–5 (185°C), for 35–40 minutes until risen and springy to the touch. Turn them out and cool on a wire tray. In a small basin, whisk together the other tablespoon of sherry and all the remaining ingredients until smooth and creamy. Sandwich the two cakes together with ⅔ of the chocolate cream. Put the rest into a piping bag with a large star nozzle and use to pipe large whirls of the cream round the edge of the top of the cake.

To freeze Put the cake on a plate into the freezer. When it is solid, put it in a polythene bag or a box. Seal, label, date and return to the freezer.

To finish and serve Take the Sticky Chocolate Cake from the freezer, unwrap it and allow at least 3 hours at room temperature for it to thaw out. Serve for tea.

F or A *Easter Sponge*

3 eggs
3 oz (75 gm) caster sugar
3 oz (75 gm) self-raising flour
8 oz (200 gm) coffee butter icing
pale green water icing
chocolate eggs and fluffy chickens

To make In a basin over warm water, whisk together the eggs and sugar until thick and creamy. Fold in the sifted flour and turn the mixture into a non-stick fluted ring mould. Bake in the oven preheated to 400°F, Gas 6 (200°C), for 15–20 minutes until well risen and spongy to the touch. Turn the sponge out on to a wire tray to cool. This is a fatless sponge and may be baked in 2 sandwich tins for a straightforward jam or cream sponge, or in a swiss roll tin.

To freeze Wrap the sponge in a polythene bag, seal, label, date and freeze.

To finish and serve Take the ring sponge from the freezer, split it and use ⅔ of the coffee butter icing to sandwich the pieces together. Make up the pale green water icing and pour this roughly over the sponge so that it drips irregularly down the sides. When dry, put the rest of the coffee butter icing into a piping bag with a very small plain nozzle and pipe squiggles over the sponge to resemble twigs of a bird's nest. Put the sponge on a plate and fill the centre with lots of little chocolate Easter eggs with one or two fluffy chickens perched on the side. Serve for a special Easter tea party.

A similar sponge may be made for almost any occasion, only varying the icing colour and the general decoration.

The Easter Sponge may be packed in a box and frozen at the finished stage. In which case, allow 2 hours unwrapped for it to thaw out and the icing to dry out completely.

F *Orange and Praline Gâteau*

1 pkt trifle sponges
2 dessertspoons instant coffee powder
¼ pt (125 ml.) water
3 tablespoons Cointreau
3 oz (75 gm) butter
4 oz (100 gm) icing sugar
1½ oz (37 gm) drinking chocolate
6 oz (150 gm) chopped toasted almonds
1 egg – separated
milk to mix
¼ pt (125 ml.) cream
1 orange
chocolate shavings and orange rind twists

To make Line a 9-inch (22-cm.) cake tin with a removable base. Put the trifle sponges in a shallow dish and pour over a mixture of the coffee, water and Cointreau. Use ⅓ of the sponges to line the base of the cake tin. Cream the butter and 3 oz (75 gm) of the icing sugar. Mix in the drinking chocolate and half of the nuts. Beat to a soft consistency using the yolk of the egg and a little milk. Spread half of this mixture over the sponge base. Set in another layer of sponge and spread over the rest of the chocolate mixture. Cover with a final layer of sponges.

To freeze Cover the tin and put it in the freezer for 3 or 4 hours to set thoroughly. If you want to store it in the freezer at this stage, turn it out when set, and overwrap it in a polythene bag. Seal, label, date and freeze. The cake may also be stored in the freezer when completely finished as follows. (In which case, freeze the whole unwrapped and, when solid, wrap it in a larger polythene bag, seal, label, date and freeze.)

To finish and serve When set, turn the cake out on to a cake board and remove the paper. Whip the cream and the white of the egg in separate basins until both are fairly stiff. Fold them together. Fold in the remaining 1 oz (25 gm) of icing sugar and the juice from ½ the orange. Spread half this icing round the sides of the cake and then dip the sides of the cake in the rest of the chopped toasted almonds so that they stick lightly. Use the rest of the icing to top the cake and decorate the centre of the top with a small heap of chocolate shavings and some twists of orange rind round the edge.

F or A *Lutetia Gâteau*

4 eggs
3 oz (75 gm) caster sugar
3 oz (75 gm) butter
3 oz (75 gm) flour
8 oz (200 gm) shelled walnuts
2 tablespoons brandy
1 egg white
2 oz (50 gm) icing sugar
5 oz (125 gm) butter
2 tablespoons apricot jam
chocolate fondant icing (p. 187: Iced Chocolate Hedgehog)
¼ pt (125 ml.) sweetened chestnut purée (p. 55)

To make Line an 8-inch (20-cm.) cake tin. In a basin over hot water, beat together the eggs and sugar until thick and creamy. Meantime, melt the butter gently and skim the froth off the top. Warm the flour a little so that the egg mixture, butter and flour are all at about the same temperature. Fold half the butter and half the flour into the thickened egg mixture. Fold in the rest and then turn the mixture into the tin. Bake in the oven preheated to 360°F, Gas 4–5 (185°C), for about 40 minutes until lightly brown and springy to the touch.

To freeze This is Genoese pastry which at this stage may be cooled and frozen in a polythene bag. It is an excellent basis for many cakes or puddings.

To finish and serve If the gâteau is to be completed at this stage, pound to a purée or chop *very* finely 4 oz (100 gm) of the walnuts mixed with the brandy. Whisk together the egg white and the icing sugar in a basin over hot water until it is thick and creamy. Mix in the nuts. Melt the 5 oz (125 gm) butter until just very soft but not quite liquid and mix that in also. Split the cake in three and use this cream to sandwich the layers together. Spread the whole cake with the jam. Heat the chocolate fondant icing slightly to make it just spreadable and use it to cover the entire cake. Stick the remaining nuts over the sides of the cake. Allow the chestnut purée from the freezer to thaw. Beat it well and put it into a piping bag with a small, plain nozzle. Pipe a great and generous heap of 'squiggles' like spaghetti over the top of the cake. Serve the Lutetia Gâteau as a very special tea time treat or as an elegant dinner party sweet. It may be frozen at the finished stage, in which case freeze it in a box for protection and allow 3 hours unwrapped for it to thaw.

SUGGESTED MENUS

Banana Bread
Bakewell Tarts
Lutetia Gâteau
Hazelnut Soldiers

Coconut Bread
Orange and Praline Gâteau
White Swans

Walnut Scones
Cream Palmiers
Cinnamon and Lemon Cake

Potato Scones
Ginger Iced Peanut Bread
Apple Diamonds
Cyril the Centipede

Home-made French Bread
Pumpkin Muffins
Eccles Cakes
Sticky Chocolate Cake

Treacle Scones
Matches
Easter Sponge

CHAPTER 11

Looking Good

Good cooking is as much a question of presentation as of following the recipe accurately and not burning the food. If a dish looks good, people are prepared to like it, whereas if it looks messy, it can be off-putting no matter how delicious it may eventually taste.

The very first thing in good presentation of food, of course, is to make sure the serving platter is sparkling clean and free of drips and greasy fingermarks. If the food does happen to drip on its way to the plate, use a clean cloth and wipe off the offending smudges immediately. Dried-on food spills are easily removed if you rub them with a little wet salt on the edge of a cloth.

Placement of the food is also important. On a serving dish, make sure it is not only attractively set out but also that the person who is going to dish it can easily see what's what – and do supply the appropriate serving cutlery! If you are serving food direct on to the plate, don't heap it on any old how. Basically, the plate should look like this:

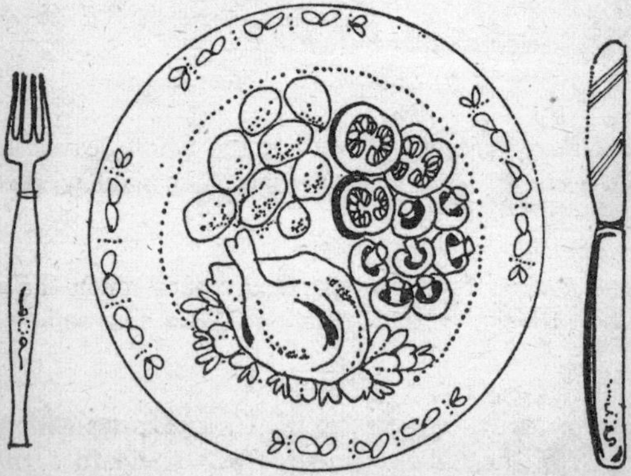

That's all very elementary, so let's see how to add that bit of extra style to the presentation of food – the garnish or decoration. As a rule, garnish applies to savoury dishes and decoration to sweet. It should always be relevant or complementary to the ingredients of the dish in question.

Simple Savoury Garnishes

Pastry leaves diamond shapes of pastry, marked with leaf-like veins. Used to stick on top of pies before baking, or baked separately and set around the edge of a sauced meat or fish dish.

Bayleaves nicely shaped bayleaves are used, plain or dipped in aspic, for the top of pâté or meat loaves – very often in conjunction with a few peppercorns and a lemon slice.

Parsley possibly the most usual garnish; and what a difference it can make to dishes that look rather plain, such as shepherd's pie, fish in white sauce, a meat stew, a plate of sandwiches or a pastry pie. Use parsley in sprigs or chopped; but be bold. If you use a sprig, make it a decent sized sprig or a clump of fresh looking leaves (with the long main stalks cut off) and put in one strategic place – the middle or the side, for example. If you use chopped parsley, then chop just the leaves in a cup with scissors. Chop it very finely and then sprinkle it liberally over the dish. Do not dot a dish with lots of tiny hand-picked parsley leaves – it looks dreadful! Parsley, like all fresh herbs, keeps well in the freezer, and all you need do is crumble a piece of the frozen article between your fingers for a chopped effect.

Mint and Other Herbs as above but the whole leaves are also sometimes used. If using a herb other than parsley, do choose one appropriate to the dish.

Chives and Onion Tails use these chopped finely as a tasty alternative to parsley. Can also be sprinkled over salads and in sauces.

Watercress normally only used in fairly large sprigs with just the very coarsest of the stalks trimmed off. A standard garnish for grilled steaks and cheese. Winter watercress is a bit scraggy and not much use. This does not keep in a freezer but will keep fresh for several days if upside down in a jug of water.

Lettuce young leaves are used either whole or finely shredded but usually as a base on which to put food such as seafood, cheese or cold meats. When using whole leaves, it is sometimes a good idea to snap the stalk to make it sit properly on the platter. To crisp limp lettuce, put it in cold water for a few minutes or in an enclosed pan with a teaspoonful of sugar overnight.

Cucumber usually used thinly sliced either with the skin removed or not. I think it gives more colour if the skin is left on. Drawing a cannelling knife down the cucumber at regular intervals round it before slicing gives a most attractive edging to each slice. A fork used in the same way gives almost the same effect. Remember that the grater often has a cucumber slicer on it. Use the slices halved or whole and overlapping around the edge of a dish or down the centre. It is traditional with cold salmon. Cucumber twists on top of individual dishes or meat loaves look attractive. To make a twist, take one thin slice, cut it through from the skin to the centre then stand it upright on the food by pulling the edges of the cut in opposite directions.

Tomato slices and wedges are most decorative and useful for any pale dish. Set overlapping slices or groups of slices round the edge of a dish, down the middle or in the centre. Similarly with wedges. The skins really ought to be removed first but most people don't bother. To skin, impale the tomato on a fork and hold it over a gas flame or in a pan of boiling water until the skin splits. Then it just lifts off. To cut tomato wedges, cut down through where the stalk was; to slice a whole tomato, lay it on its side on the board and slice it down that way. In both cases, such cutting helps prevent the inside from falling out of the wedges or slices. Tomato twists can be made in the same way as cucumber twists. Another popular way of using tomatoes either for garnish or for salads is van-dyked. To van-dyke a tomato, insert the point of a small sharp knife into the tomato in zig-zags round the middle of it, holding the tomato upright between the thumb and first finger of the other hand. Do make sure the knife is pushed right into the centre. When cut thus, all the way round, pull the two halves gently apart. Sometimes the seeds are scooped out and the tomato shells filled with peas, corn or a meat or fish mixture for a rather opulent garnish.

Eggs are hardboiled and may be sliced, quartered or van-dyked. Sometimes the cooked yolk and white are separated and the white finely chopped, whilst the yolk is pressed through a wire sieve. This makes a very attractive garnish for cold fish or a dark green vegetable. Egg slices are often used on top of pies or flans if appropriate to the contents.

Cream double cream poured attractively over the surface of sauced dishes or thick puréed soups can look super. Also, whisked with a little salt and pepper, it can be piped on top of cold meat or vegetable flans.

Lemons are used a great deal in garnishing almost any dish but most particularly fish dishes. In slices, either overlapping, in groups or singly, lemon looks fabulous. Use wedges, with the ends cut off to facilitate squeezing, with fried or grilled fish. These are cut by first slicing off the ends of the fruit, standing it on its end and then cutting it downwards into 4, 6 or 8 depending on the size. Lemon twists, made in the same way as those of cucumber, are used a great deal and to excellent effect on top of fried or sauced fish or veal or avocado. Lemon butterflies are more delicate and as such are only used for the more delicate foods such as sole or veal in wine sauce. To make them, take a thin slice and *halve* it. Then cut it from the skin side *to* the centre, but not through, and then pull it open into a butterfly shape.

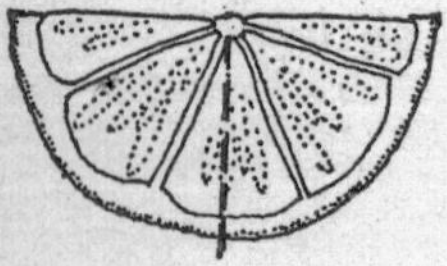

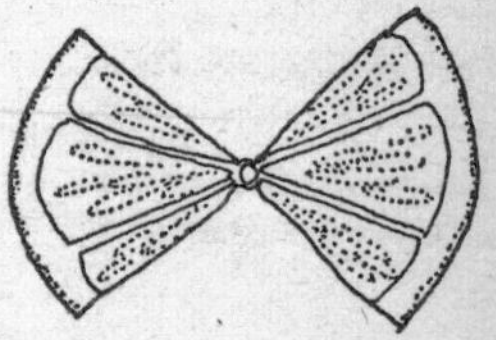

Lemons can also be van-dyked like tomatoes and similarly used. There are many other professional ways of cutting lemons, such as in baskets. Make a cut down through the lemon from each pointed end so that the cuts come within ½ inch (1 cm.) of meeting. Then make two cuts through the side of the lemon to meet the ends of the previous cuts at right-angles. Lift out the small triangular shapes of lemon and use as wedges. To complete the basket, cut the flesh away from the inside to form a handle and as much of a basket as you require. It may be filled with vegetables, fruit or even just parsley to make an interesting garnish.

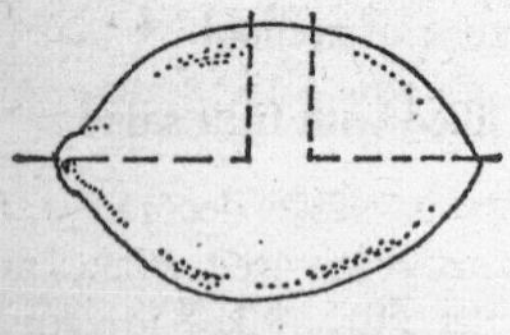

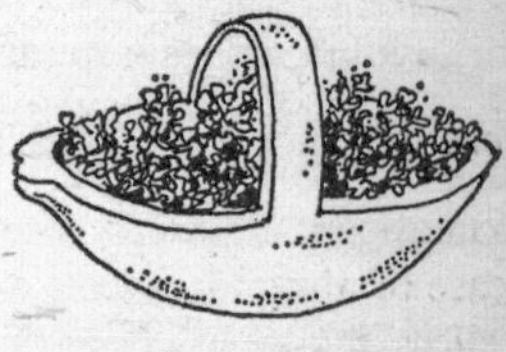

Lemons are often used along with parsley. But do always remember to flick out the pips. Very thin strips of rind, strewn over the top of a dish, look super.

Oranges and Limes can effectively be used in the same way as lemons if appropriate.

Grapefruit van-dyked looks good as a starter but it does take some practice to make sure the incisions are going to meet!

Simple Sweet Decorations

Sugar is the most useful and is simply sprinkled over the surface. Sprinkle caster sugar on biscuits and sponge cakes while they are still warm so that the sugar sticks. Icing sugar is used on cold sponges or biscuits. Sieve it over plain or through a very open cut paper or plastic doily for a fancy effect. Do not use sugar on a damp surface – it will simply disappear.

Cream is whipped and may be spread flat over a surface and further decorated; or piled on roughly and lifted into attractive peaks with the end of a knife blade. Piping cream requires a degree of practice particularly for intricate work using small nozzles. The most useful and easy to use is a ½ inch (1 cm.) star pipe for whirls on cakes, buns and puddings of all sorts. Make the piping bold and either make just a few whirls or else cover the whole surface. A half-way measure looks messy and small decorations have to be perfectly formed to be effective. Time enough after some practice to try more intricate designs with small pipes. If you can't use pipes at all, a blob of whipped cream assisted off the end of a dessertspoon can look just as good on an individual sweet. Use whipped cream only for cold sweets.

Lemons, Oranges and Limes may be used in exactly the same way as for savoury dishes – minus the parsley, of course!

Melons look good cut in baskets and filled with fruit salad.

Nuts chopped, halved or whole are tasty as well as decorative. In the case of almonds, flakes and spikes are often used. Flakes are flat slices taken from the length of the nut; spikes are long, chunky slices obtained by cutting down the nut from end to end, from front to back as it were. Nuts are always skinned (see 'blanche' in 'In a Word') and sometimes toasted until lightly browned. Use nuts liberally – sprinkle chopped nuts, dig in ends of flakes or spikes or edge with whole or halved nuts. Nuts look and taste good with chocolate or lemon sweets.

Pastry Leaves make and use as for savoury dishes.

Mint leaves or small sprigs look fabulous with chocolate, coffee, peppermint or any pale coloured cold sweet. Lovely also in cold drinks or on ices.

Crystallized Fruits and Flowers make most colourful and attractive decorations when the colour combinations are chosen carefully. Do not overdo either the amount or the colour variety. In the case of angelica, or indeed any strips of decoration, cut it delicately. Glacé cherries and angelica are traditional on trifle and cold meringue-topped puddings – though violets and mimosa look better, I think.

Chocolate is normally used grated. Whether you grate it finely or coarsely depends on the dish and your own preference. Chocolate leaves are available in most good grocery or confectionery shops. They look good either whole or cut in triangles, and stuck upright on the top of individual cream sweets. Chocolate buttons may be more easily obtainable and are almost as effective. Curls of chocolate look very professional and are not too hard to make if you can be bothered. They freeze well but need to be packed carefully as they are very fragile. To make curls, melt the chocolate and then pour it out on to a really cold smooth surface and spread thinly. When almost completely set, scrape strips of it off the surface using the blade of a thin knife held firmly and at an angle of 45° to the table, the sharp edge of the blade towards you and resting on the table. The chocolate will roll into curls. A warm butter curler, drawn along a block of slightly soft chocolate, can also work well.

What a difference even a bit of parsley can make – it's not for nothing that it's known as the cook's best friend! Garnishes and decorations also do a marvellous cover-up job on otherwise disasters. But the amateurs' watchwords for all garnishing and decoration are fresh foodstuffs and bold simplicity.

Index of Recipes

Books about Food and Drink in Fontana

Beer and Skittles Richard Boston

A book about beer in all its aspects. Full of facts and humour to delight those who are fond of beer and to convert those who are not.

Scotch Whisky David Daiches

A complete history of Scotch whisky from its early days as a cottage industry to the triumph of the great blending firms and the decline in popularity of the single malts in this century.

The Sunday Gardener Alan Gemmell (Ed.)

Contains chapters on how to grow fruit and vegetables (as well as flowers, grass and shrubs) if you only have time to garden at busy weekends.

Food for Free Richard Mabey

An illustrated guide to the astonishing range of wild British foods, with information on how to find, gather and cook each one.

Eat Fat and Grow Slim Richard Mackarness

A revolutionary and fully tested approach to slimming that encourages you to eat as much food as you want while ignoring the calorie problem completely.

Country Bazaar Andy Pittaway & Bernard Scofield

This handbook of country pleasures – ranging from brass-rubbing, weaving and smocking to animal-tracking, hedgerow-dating and goat-keeping – includes sections on how to make wine, cheese (cottage, pot, cream, Quark and Indian), cream, butter, yoghurt and honey-medicine.

The Complete Urban Farmer David Wickers

Tells town-dwellers how to grow their own fruit and vegetables for year-round pleasure and economic benefit.

Use Your Loaf Ursel & Derek Norman

Twenty-six step-by-step recipes for baking bread from the Old English Farmhouse Loaf and Grandma's Milk Bread to Croissants and Viennese Gugelhupf.

Salad Days Ursel & Derek Norman

Delicious step-by-step recipes for crisp, refreshing salads.

Not Just a Load of Old Lentils Rose Elliot

Four hundred varied vegetarian recipes which stimulate the converted to be more adventuresome and provide bored meat-eaters with appetizing ideas.

Simply Delicious Rose Elliot

'One of the best vegetarian cookery books available' – *The Vegetarian*; '. . . does for vegetarian cooking what Henry Ford's Model T did for vehicular transportation' – *Jewish Gazette*

Simple Freezer Cookery Caroline Rennie

Specially written for the growing number of people who regard a freezer as a necessity rather than a luxury. Practical information about freezers is followed by delicious but simple recipes for all occasions.

THE INC

"She never lov … know of love?" The small Frenc … red in the face with emotion and rag … William heard the blood drumming in his own ears. "She has never in her life known happiness except with me, you comprehend? Perhaps you cannot do so, you who preach always of misery and sin and the fire to come. Pah! You are your own god, in your pulpit, in your bed; a woman made of marble would be all the same to you. I will leave tonight; I will go away with Marie and we will make love together always, you hear me? She loves me in such a way——"

It was then that the red mist descended before William's eyes. He could remember, afterwards, only the recollection of his boyhood's sight of the fully-fired anvil, the flames cherry-red beneath, and the one occasion his mother had permitted him to use the great air-forced bellows of leather and brass. The air hissed out of the bellows' mouth and made the fire glow brighter. It took a strong man's hands to squeeze and work the bellows, to elicit that long final hiss of expired air.

Also by the same author, and available in Coronet Books:

THE MALVIE INHERITANCE

The Incumbent

Pamela Hill

CORONET BOOKS
Hodder and Stoughton

First published in Great Britain 1974
by Hodder and Stoughton Limited

Coronet Edition 1976

Printed and bound in Great Britain
for Coronet Books,
Hodder and Stoughton, London,
by Richard Clay (The Chaucer Press) Ltd
Bungay, Suffolk

ISBN 0 340 20489 3

FOREWORD

As no one of the characters in this book is fictitious except Paul, it is perhaps redundant to state that I am aware that it was Robert Napier who made possible the first steam crossing of the Atlantic. He was my great-great-great-uncle, and, apart from having been, certainly, one of the last people to walk through his empty onetime palace of Shandon before it was pulled down, I have had access both to family anecdotes and letters, which relate much of the extraordinary history of marriages and elopements, interwoven with the story of Robert and his wife and their involvement with his younger brother's families. I can remember seeing the crayon portraits of the two old parents which I have described, together with a wealth of remembered detail from my eldest great-aunt and, later, from both branches of a curiously estranged race of descendants; the only thread binding the whole together being the common memory, or legend, of a deranged woman with an iron will. I have used every possible detail which has been given me, including the descriptions of wedding-dresses; the whole tale, with one exception, is as it may have happened; no more can perhaps be expected after a hundred and fifty years.

I

I

The death of the second wife of the Reverend William Heatherton, D.D., incumbent in the living of Savill's Old Kirk in the heart of the city, had not been unexpected. Margaret Heatherton had been known to be in her late seventies, and for some years now had endured a lingering and painful illness with great fortitude. On the day after the sad event itself, parishioners, acquaintances—Mrs. Heatherton had not encouraged friends beyond the family—and almost the entire genteel curious of the city called, in their carriages, to view the body laid out in the coffin, leave mourning-cards and drink the manse madeira.

The widower himself meantime mounted alone to his study, which contrary to convention was on the topmost floor of the house. In all other ways William Heatherton was a conventional man, and it could not, accordingly, be due to eccentricity that he had, some years previously, purchased from his Session the manse itself, which was outmoded, as well as already owning the separate house adjoining. Dr. Heatherton had bought the latter many years before on the death of its owner, and speculation, which had reason to regard the financial acumen of the Heatherton family with great respect, was then rife as to the impending rise in value of land in that quarter, as otherwise William Heatherton would not have invested in it. When he firmly refused, some years later, to consider moving himself and his family to a new manse the Session intended purchasing in a superior district of town, his employers gladly sold him his present one, and let the other profitably meantime. However, murmurs were heard, not for the first time, to the effect that it would be better if Dr. Heatherton retired, and let a new man with fresh ideas come into the new house as Savill's minister; the fact that the old gentleman declined to listen to such proposals may have been due to the unwillingness of any present member to put them to him. For the meantime, at least, William continued to hold the living, and no doubt it suited him to have the two adjoining tall grey houses, if only for room. He, at the time a widower with three daughters, had many years since married a widow with a large family of her own. A third child of the double second marriage had been added to what must already have been an extremely crowded household; and with servants also to find quarters for, accommodation might have been a problem had not Dr. Heatherton, in his far-seeing way, purchased the second house when it was available. The city genteel leant back, gratified, on this assumption, and speculated no more. It was true that, by now, Dr. Heatherton's three girls by his first wife were married and gone; gossip still raised its head, a trifle, about the manner of those marriages, except for young Mrs. Urquhart's to which no breath of scandal could attach itself, despite the extraordinary behaviour of her stepmother at the ceremony. To appear in black crape! It was odd; but one must remember that Mrs. Heatherton was, by now, confronting her Maker. As to her own daughters, by her earlier marriage to Howie the wealthy shipowner, they had remained spinsters, every one.

What the enquiring public did not know was that the adjoining house was kept shut up; no one used it. Occasionally the big spare figure of the minister would be observed to ascend its front steps, faultlessly attired as he always was in tall hat, gloves and cane; and turn the key of the house, go in and close the door after him, emerging again after perhaps three-quarters of an hour. No doubt he used it nowadays for offices. Other paths of enquiry were closed, as Mrs. Heatherton, her family and her husband had been—though, again, one did not speak ill of the dead—a trifle stand-offish, always formal; no one knew them or could achieve much more than a stiff acknowledgement to a bow in the street, or the steady declining of a polite invitation to drink tea. It was, folk knew, a long time since Dr. Heatherton himself had first come to Savill's; in their way they were proud of him, as one may take pride in a monument of some unyielding material; he had seen many changes, and had weathered them all; but it was undoubtedly time a younger man came soon to Savill's. Dr. Heatherton's sermons, it was true, retained all their fire and thunder; but, as was increasingly realised nowadays, sermons were not everything. "It'll be hard on him, though, his wife's death," was the general comment. And so they had come, the curious, to see.

William Heatherton had evaded them by his ascent of the upper staircase, leaving Margaret's daughters silent at their post below, in the death-chamber. As he opened the locked study door sunlight met and blinded him, streaming on to the familiar, scholarly things among which of late years he had passed almost all his waking hours. Moving cautiously, as old men will, Dr. Heatherton went across and jerked shut the heavy green felt curtains which framed the window, giving a limited view of the street far below, with its whitewashed carriage-blocks and tall polished lamp-standards. He frowned; it had been an omission of propriety to leave the curtains undrawn, with every other room in the house respectfully darkened and shuttered, as was the rest of the street. In this room, of all rooms! But it was true he discouraged the servants from coming up here.

Groping his way back in the artificially induced dark to his desk, one of William Heatherton's hands encountered the bulk of the large indexed Bible which lay there. It contained entries of every event connected with his family, the births and deaths, the marriages, yes, those also ... And Margaret's death, once it was certain, he had entered carefully yesterday in his own hand; the ink would still be black, with the date inscribed by her name.

William's other hand touched a shelf. This he knew—was there anything in the room he did not know, or could have failed to find blindfold?—to be a part of a plain, solid oak bookcase devoid of glass, purchased by William himself in his student days, so that he had always been fond of it. It had been an item in a displenishing sale held publicly at a farmhouse some miles to the south of what was now the city; William Heatherton in those days had bought the bookcase for a shilling. On having it delivered to his lodgings at that time, he had found, pasted to the under-surface, a yellowing label with the name of a mansion long untenanted. The signature written in flowing copperplate on the label was that of the last laird, killed at Waterloo. The discovery had increased William's initial satisfaction with the bookcase, making a kind of bond between it, himself and history. It also gave him a third-hand association, as he recognised soberly, with folk in high places. This awed William less than it might have done; for generations, long before the dead laird's disused furniture had found its way to a farm-steading, William Heatherton's forebears had wrought at the anvil on the estates of a duke.

"The Duke would oft-times come by on a fine day, and aye removed his bonnet." The smug, repeated phrase had been his mother's, whose own folk had little time for dukes; but she hoarded anecdotes of her old husband's boyhood farther north. Hearing her carping, familiar voice now in the induced dark, as though she had not been dead these thirty years, William stretched out his hands in a gesture which seemed to include both books and wood. The printed word had, when all was said, been his consolation, more than children, more than wives. It was his mother he had to thank for that, for her determination had made him a minister. William's eyes, rendered dim by their lifetime's study, stared down now through the thick lenses of the spectacles he wore, trying to assess the change in his flesh, the flesh his mother had long ago borne. Soon now, in the nature of such things, it would undergo the further change already to be found in Margaret's body, lying dead downstairs. Curious that he should feel the vitality in himself the more abundant for her death, as though for many years he had been imprisoned, suppressed, like a river forced to run underground. Folly! But his hands, at least, were unchanged. They were by now, had been for years, pallid, soft; run to fat with easy living, like the muscles of a retired athlete. The palms were cushioned, the nails well-kept and square; good hands for the sweeping, eloquent gestures for which he, William Heatherton, the blacksmith's son, had become famous as year followed year, and his sermons were printed and the demand for them grew, the time of the Disruption—how long ago that distressing business seemed, and how little, despite all prayer, he himself had been able to do, in the event, to stay that rending apart of the garment of the reformed Church, which should have remained whole!

He had already accepted the call, by then, to Savill's Old Presbyterian Kirk. He still ministered there in the pulpit Sunday after Sunday. There were those, he knew, who said, had done almost from the beginning, that his manners were outmoded, that a younger man with liberal ideas would cater for a wider cross-section of the populace, and that William, concerned with preaching still to the élite of the city, should make way for a successor. But he knew, had always known what to say to those who, like himself, mistrusted change. For them he was the symbol of convention, formality, stability; like a granite pillar, unyielding to whatever winds might blow.

And he could still, even at his age, preach a fine sermon. He could still crowd the fashionable pews. The well-to-do parishioner had seen to it, during his long ministry, that Savill's became and remained the first church of the city, despite the fact that more and still more dwellings were building to the west ... they'd drive down, nevertheless, from those to Savill's still, of a Sunday, crowding the stately grey street where the houses, including the pair he'd purchased for himself, were Regency in style, with graceful pillars and fanlight doors, and coachman's quarters to the rear, in the narrow lane. Margaret had always kept a coachman, though William himself liked to walk down to the services twice on a Sunday, to clear his thoughts and make ready for the sermon he was about to preach, the extempore prayers he would sometimes say, though generally he prepared these also.

A volume of extracts from the best of his printed sermons lay nearby his hand now, on the shelf. Devoid of the personality of direct address, for reading, they contained stern admonition. There was no softness in them, no easy way of escape for the evil-doer. James, William's elder brother, the famous shipbuilder now dead, had first recommended that the sermons be privately printed, and later had shown them to friends in England, among them a bishop; William, though his denomination did not allow him to recognise such authority, was proud of this, and that the bishop had admired the sermons and had written to him. James Heatherton had done all he could to foster his brother William's prosperity, both in material and other things.

It seemed incredible that James was dead. He had barely outlived his wife and cousin Alicia by the space of a summer; like the trunk and the root, those two had been to one another. If William himself had ever known such joy in marriage, would he have ended differently from the man he now was? Would he have been softer, kindlier?

James himself had been the kindest man alive. William missed him more than he could ever express, despite the fact that, of latter years, because of the feud with Margaret, they saw less of one another than formerly, except by chance.

Margaret! The harm she had wrought, or was part of the fault his own?

His fault; again, his hands. He continued to stare down at them in the half-dark, as though by doing so he must in the end come to terms with himself, perhaps even with Margaret's memory. For, more than ever now that she was dead, he must resolutely think no evil of her; must not remember her hardness, her estrangement in body and spirit from him these many years, as though that earlier marriage of hers to George Howie had been the only one she ever made, the children of it her only children. The year Wilhelmine was born Margaret had ended by disowning her daughter. Strange now to recall that he himself had made a child with Margaret: that they must once have loved together.

"It is so long a time," William Heatherton thought. He left grasping the shelf for support and, standing squarely, brought the palms of his hands to face one another within view of his myopic sight. It was as though, in nearly eighty years, he had never before taken leisure to regard them, his hands, or think of the things they had done.

His hands. They'd once been strong; were still so, for an old man and a scholar. Their strength, long ago, could have forged iron at an anvil, as his father and James had done. He could still, he knew, lift weights that were marvellously heavy.

His father, Nathan, had wanted him also, like the older son, to be an ironmaster. There had only been the two of them, however, James and himself; and their mother Jean had been adamant. "How she ruled us all, even my father!" William thought. And he, like the infant Samuel, was to be set aside for the service of the Church, his mother said, instead of channelling his genius in the ways of James and all his kin. It would be a social step upwards to have a son in the pulpit. William's long lip puckered; he had never had illusions about his mother. He heard, again, her voice, with the note of steel behind the soft riverside accent of her kinsfolk; and that was as it should be, in a family of foundry-workers for many generations. Jean Dyce had been born and reared in the west-coast town to which in the end the smith Heatherton, searching for a wife to suit him, came, having left his northern heritage and anvil, and the Duke's doffed bonnet. He had bigged himself a cottage of clay to which to bring his bride from among her near kin, the lean hard men who wrought with iron; and of iron James and William themselves were got. "Keep at your books, Willie lad! Keep at them, and be a minister when ye're grown," and so, given her determination and his own, it had in the end fallen out. He'd done well at his books, and better at the ministry.

He was glad that his mother, before she died, had seen him don the bright robes of a Doctor of Divinity. As it was an honour conferred on him from high places, because of his scholarship, Jean had died content. She had been proud of William rather than loving him. Had anyone ever loved him?

Margaret? Marie, his first wife, back in the shadows?

He could see himself clearly in his own mind now. It was as though he held a mirror up to catch the light, perhaps the mirror at which he still shaved himself daily. That was downstairs, but he could still see himself as though he held it. His thick curling hair—neither he nor James had ever balded—had bleached from grey to white these last years. Otherwise there was as little outward change in his face as in his hands. It was as though all experience lay within, as though William had determined from the beginning to show a mask to all the world, no more. A large bland face with a scholar's pallor, it was now, though he had been high-coloured as a young man. Little in the way of lines or wrinkles showed; the long upper lip, inherited from his father's folk, was less marked in him than it had been in James. The pebble-thick glasses combined to shut out, from an avid world today, whatever William Heatherton might be feeling. He had shed no tears at his wife's death.

Had he shed them that time for Marie? He could not remember, it was so long ago . . .

Folk outside spoke of him, he was aware, by repute, for they did not know him, as a stern and formal man. To picture him as having fathered children was perhaps impossible. He was the figurehead, again the granite pillar; since the death of his brother he had virtually ceased to feel. Finally withdrawn by himself into an impenetrable shell, the circumstances of his family life, of his calling, had aided him; his step-children looked on him as a stranger in his own house; his own daughters by the first marriage had been driven out long ago. Before that, he had not known them well, had not succeeded, through Margaret's own bitter silences, in breaking down, by mere table-talk, the wall arisen between them; and it was only at meals the family met. Those, formally served with the panoply of crystal and silver, silver salvers, engraved with his name, silver gravy-spoon warmers shaped like great conch shells; gleaming mahogany of table and sideboard, and the maids in their white aprons serving in silence and taking away the plates, had been no occasion for getting to know his children.

Kate, the eldest of all, lately had been kind to him. On hearing of her stepmother's death she had sent at once to bid him come and make his home with her and Richard, and the children. William had refused with courtesy; he was too old, he said, for a change of residence now. He let it be thought that the vociferous little girls—Kate had no son as yet—might disturb him; he could not otherwise explain why it was that he could not leave, must never leave this house.

Safeguarded, this tall house and the other! Safe till his own death! After that it would not matter...

He made his thoughts return to his children. There had been the three by the first wife, all daughters. Alicia, the second girl, was in China now, on her husband's mission-station. Jenny, the third ... he had not seen Jenny since her wedding-day.

She had not crossed his threshold again, because of Margaret. But now that John Howie, the bridegroom and reason for the quarrel, Margaret's only son, was dead, like his mother, then maybe...

William's mind jerked itself away from contemplation of those three plain, downtrodden daughters of his first marriage, to himself. He was by now, he knew, a kind of talisman to his congregation, even to those members of it who did not approve his reactionary views. They would watch, Sunday after Sunday, with a kind of awed pride as the big, old figure, scarcely stooping beneath its added weight of laundered bands, hood and gown, mounted the pulpit-steps. An engraving had been made of Dr. Heatherton thus, some years back; it showed William somewhat leaner and greyer than he now was, and the stern eyes and long-lipped face were those of a prophet, looking out from the walls of many a devout household. Did its presence serve to deter wrongdoers from persisting in the evil tenor of their ways? or to reassure the righteous that they would enter heaven?

A copy hung downstairs; though not in Margaret's room. He hadn't set foot, apart from yesterday as she was dying, in Margaret's room since she had told him, all those years ago, that their marriage, save for outward show, was at an end.

Had it affected him, by now, at all to watch Margaret die?

One hand fingered William's high mourning-cravat. However that might be, one must still at all costs preserve appearances: let no least whisper, by this date so long afterwards, make known the truth that he and she had lived as strangers under one roof for many years, almost since the birth of Wilhelmine. Before that...

How old was Wilhelmine? Time passed so subtly! William calculated, and reminded himself that his youngest child, the sole fruit of his second marriage, was by now thirty-eight. Thirty-eight years he and the mother had lived as strangers. And, like the rest of Margaret's daughters, but unlike his own, Wilhelmine had never been permitted, perhaps never tempted, to marry.

Marie's daughters by him had broken away, had made their own lives despite their stepmother. William was glad of that.

The stepmother. Margaret, his dead wife. Where at this moment was her strange soul journeying? Had she come face to face with that God of hers who forbade and recorded so much, the God without mercy or forgiveness, the God of petty things? Perhaps the same God, for it was possible. Whom he himself painstakingly concerned himself with interpreting in the pulpit each Sunday, as if his own wrestlings with the things in his mind had defeated any notion he might once have had of a loving Father, when he himself as a parent had so greatly failed.

But it was, William knew, every orthodox person's belief. If one encountered inner doubt, it must be concealed. His own mission was to point out the error to the sinner, to make such a person repent ... and himself? Himself? He, that time long ago ... and then the other ...

"It was only a moment's anger, a moment's lust," William thought. The years between, the virtuously lived and upright years, had erased, had atoned for both sins; would surely count on his behalf at the very Judgment. Yet who was he to know how God would judge? How would God regard what lay *here*, beyond the inner wall?

He had crept almost furtively down to the death-chamber yesterday when they had sent for him, as though his long-buried weakness must be openly manifest to everyone now that Margaret would shortly stand before God, and would by then know, perhaps, all things that should be known.

She would still, he was certain, forgive nothing.

He remembered the past years without rancour, merely with a kind of weariness, recollecting how in a thousand small ways, as well as the greater ones, she had erased him, William, from her life. It had been on a similar pattern to her later denial of John Howie, her only son. In a way he himself had been a model for John, an overture to the main tragedy; for was not youth peerless? But Margaret had denied her only son his inheritance on his marriage, so that John died a beggar. There was more than that; since that forbidden marriage of Margaret's son and his, William's, daughter, the young pair had attended church Sunday after Sunday, sat beside Margaret in the manse pew, and she had never turned her head, or acknowledged them. She had never spoken of her son again, or addressed him. When he was dying at last she refused to go to his death-bed, though Jenny had sent word in time.

How the years passed, William thought: it must be eleven, now, since the grandchild's birth. As though a knell rang in his own ears, reminding him of the nearness of the grave, William thought of that unknown grandson of his, of Margaret's. That child would be running about actively, playing games with boys of his own age, no doubt, that son of theirs, an only child with the formidable double heritage of Howie and Heatherton in his veins. A unique blend, unless . . .

Ah, perish the doubt that rose! He had already told himself that *that* supposition, that he himself was not Jenny's father, was forbidden. He remembered well enough, for his dates were precise, the last time he had fathered a child on Marie.

Marie . . . his early bride, dead so long ago that her memory was like thin paper, faded yellow with the years . . .

Marie had done her duty, he reflected, in bearing his children. It was neither her fault nor his that there had been no living sons. That had been the will of God; there had been Kate, born to them within the first year of marriage, while he himself was still in his early charge of Gowanmount. Then Alicia, known always as Lissy, called after his brother James's wife, a year later; less than a year. Then the boy who had died, then Jenny . . . all of them with dark hair, like their mother's. William reflected on the fecundity of his race.

Why should he not see Jenny's boy for himself, now Margaret was dead? "It is my own house, after all," he thought, "and I may bid whom I choose to it." The thought, he knew, would not have occurred to him in Margaret's lifetime; nor was it proper quite yet, before her coffin left the house for burial. They would say, the Howie women and the congregation, he knew, that he hadn't waited till her body was cold before inviting her rival to visit here.

To visit! Why should Jenny and her son not stay always with him, now Margaret's daughters, all of them, were departing, his own included, together after the funeral? He had tried to consider their standards, treat them as his own family and not George Howie's; they hadn't responded. Madam Georgina, the eldest, with her waxy beauty a trifle blurred by time and grief, had ordered the other sisters to this conclusion, he didn't doubt. Georgy had her mother's strong will; the more miraculous that she should have remained, through all these years, as subservient to her mother, foreseeing every least of Margaret's wishes and carrying them out, even to the point of never marrying, remaining here as adoptive parent to young Wilhelmine. It was as though Margaret had chosen, by every feasible means, to repudiate *him*, her husband, and the flesh they had made together.

Jenny's son. It was better to think of him, the heir, than of Wilhelmine.

He would do it, would invite them both by letter tomorrow, mother and son, after the funeral. If Jenny refused the offer, nothing in any case could hurt him, William, any more. If she should accept, there would be light and life again about the place, with the boy in the house, perhaps coming to him, his grandfather, for help with his lessons. None of his own children had ever so come; there'd been a governess. But boys needed a man's help in the things they must learn. He'd like it, he admitted, if Jenny and the boy came here.

It should be done, William was increasingly resolved; and felt the great surge of renewed freedom overwhelm him. As soon as the hearse, sent by the foremost undertakers in the city, had conveyed Margaret behind nodding sable-plumed horses and hired mourners to its chosen place in the mausoleum, beside George Howie, tomorrow, he himself would write to Jenny, begging her to bring the boy, and make their home with him.

His grandson! The joy of his old age! "It is the will of God, no doubt, all of it," William said again aloud. Before they came, he must see to the ... the other matter; there couldn't be much left now, but a prying boy might glimpse, as children of an earlier generation had done, some matter he perhaps should not. The trouble there'd been over that! Best ensure, once he himself was alone after the Howie women and Wilhelmine had gone, that *that* didn't repeat itself ... Could he do it? It must be done, without a doubt, and now if ever. God would give him strength. William's hands strayed absently once more about the bookshelves, at last fingering a familiar rough place in the wood, where a knot might long ago have been mended. He would look ... he would break open the inner door and look, later on, from the other house, the house kept always empty.

A knock sounded at the door. William answered, a slight hardening of the pallid face and guarded eyes indicating his displeasure. It had been made fully clear to the maids that they must not come up here, not even to dust the furniture unless under his supervision; the books he did for himself. In any case, all housework was suspended till after the funeral. It must be a matter of urgency or importance; some prominent caller, no doubt, to sympathise, waiting now below-stairs. William was already weary of these and their mouthings of condolence, folk who had known neither him nor Margaret well. But one had to maintain appearances, if only for Margaret's sake. She had never, whatever flaws their private life together might contain, failed William in public show; the congregation, and all others in the city, would remember Mrs. Heatherton as a constant, edifying presence in the manse pew, faultlessly dressed, her large capable hands gloved in kid, her millinery notable, her gowns made to fit her still fine figure by a leading modiste; and the legend of her first wealthy marriage still about her, like a drift of expensive scent. Folk had bidden Margaret Heatherton good-morning, and later good-day; had nodded from their carriages, and perhaps had the nod returned, if they were socially suitable; later, there might come an invitation to a church soirée where everyone sipped tea. William himself had played his part at such things, with difficulty as he never found ease in conversation. Apart from that, all they knew——

How dared they come? The highest in the land had not known him, or Margaret.

He went now and opened the study door. It revealed a very old servant in laundered cap and apron, indrawn mouth hostile as ever, eyes unafraid. William downed the unworthy fear which always rose in him at sight of Sarah Court, his late wife's confidential servant, seldom met with nowadays. Sarah had come with Margaret from George Howie's opulent house to the Savill's manse when her mistress, then a widow, married William Heatherton: there was little about the family and its ways Sarah did not know, or would not have discussed with her mistress. The old witch, to climb alone up here! She seldom, William knew, need stir nowadays from her own quarters, for the younger servants did the work; she had attended Margaret constantly during the latter's illness and death, and in company with Georgina Howie had at last laid out the dead body. Margaret's eldest daughter would not, even now, leave the coffin before it was closed. Why had Sarah done so?

Anger that he should feel fear of any servant made William's voice curt. "Did I not give orders that I was on no account to be disturbed up here?" he said. He had taken out a book as if for protection, and was fingering the gilt-edged leaves as though he could see what he read. He would have to light the lamp, he knew, when Sarah had gone. The depth of his own fear was evident to him in the fact that he dared not, now she was standing here, bid her go and light it.

"I'd not have come for any but an urgent matter." Court was an Englishwoman, as her dead mistress had been. She had never lost the unfamiliar vowel-sounds, the difference both in intonation and outlook, for all her years in the north. No doubt part of her open contempt for himself stemmed from that she felt for all Scots. William stared down at the black ribbons threaded through her mourning-cap, forgetting his book.

"What is it, then?" he said, as though indulging a child. Nothing, as he had told himself already, could be of such import as to rouse feeling in him any more. He had lived beyond desire, betrayal, grief, envy, lust, resurgence of love, acceptance of its loss. Over the years, through every imaginable personal disaster, he had become marble to himself, granite to others. He almost smiled. No doubt it was a message from the undertakers to say that one of the horses was lame of a foot, and they would have to take a less well-matched member tomorrow; or perhaps one of the mourners had fallen sick, so that there would be fewer weepers about the hearse. What did it matter? What did anything matter now, except the plan he had promised himself to fulfil? William waited. The old woman seemed to find difficulty in framing her reply for some moments; the toothless mouth mumbled.

At last she said, tonelessly, "Miss Jenny is here, and asking if she may see you."

A great rush of blood to the heart brought feeling back to William Heatherton. Through it all he was aware of the presence of impropriety. "You mean Mrs. Howie, Sarah, do you not?" he said stiffly. He should also reproach the woman, he knew, for failing to observe the customary terms of respect to himself: "doctor" or "sir". But he did neither of those things. He knew, none better, that Sarah had for her mistress's sake hated that marriage between his own youngest daughter by his first wife, and Margaret's only son. Since John Howie died his young widow had not come back again to Savill's, to sit alone with them all in the bitterly divided pew. He himself hadn't spoken with her since, since—when was it he had last had speech with Jenny?

"Mrs. Howie is below, you say?"

He might have been inculcating a lesson in a stubborn child. It was purposeless; Sarah obstinately said nothing. William turned wordlessly, with care replacing, in its customary place on the shelf, the book he had lately chosen. After all these years, to see Jenny again! Had his thoughts brought her today?

"She came on foot," said Sarah, implying that other folk had come in their carriages. Anger burned suddenly in William.

"Tell Mrs. Howie that I will join her directly. Show her into the parlour, if you please, and give her a glass of wine."

"That's been done." Sarah was triumphant at having forestalled his instructions, William knew; and, suddenly wishing the enmity between them gone, he tried to carry the woman's mood along with him; if she would, even now, to befriend her.

"Last time Mrs. Howie—Miss Jenny—came to this house it was for her wedding to Master John, Sarah, if you remember?" He had by now emerged on to the upper landing where she stood, and closed and locked the study door behind him. "Much has happened since then," he added sententiously.

Much indeed, he was thinking; John, the erstwhile bridegroom and the only one who, earlier, could banish his mother's grim moods; laughing John, dead of an inflammation of the lungs caught with working daily long hot hours down at James's yards, then coming out tired into the open air. If Margaret blamed the Heathertons for her son's death she had never spoken of it. John Howie, reared like a young prince until the time came when at last he glimpsed Jenny again, after all those years apart . . . John, able hitherto to do nothing except divert himself and spend the ungrudging pocket-money his mother gave him, then thrown suddenly, at her whim, as a beggar on the world, to earn a living for himself and a young, ignorant wife! He, William, should perhaps have done more; but what? James at least had provided employment for the boy, made him self-respecting. A self-respecting corpse in a cheap pine coffin. Where were his own thoughts taking him, William Heatherton, today?

But he should have done more for Jenny and John, granted that they were proud, would not perhaps have accepted charity. He—the girl's father—hadn't offered even that. He had done nothing.

He leaned forward, and grasped the mahogany newel at the head of the stairs, preparing to go down. As he did so Sarah's voice spoke behind him out of the shadows.

"*Her* head lies now over the very spot they stood on that day, that brought her her greatest grief. Broke her heart, it did, that marriage of Master John's to—to——"

Sarah Court flung back her head, and he could once again glimpse the woman she had been. "Began ailing a year later to the day, *he* did, they say, off and on; a sorry coupling they've had, and small joy he got out of it, or her either, that shameful wedding."

"Be silent," William said sternly; but knew she would not obey. She never had heeded anyone in all her life except Margaret. He preceded her downstairs and heard her voice, like a raven's croak, continue behind him.

"You'll see a difference in Miss Jenny. Lost her looks, she has, not that she ever had much. A stout little body, she is now, for all her blacks; a servant to a rich gentleman, they say she is, and keeps the boy with her."

William did not reply, or chide her further. He was making his customary way downstairs, with caution; down to the rich, the opulent world of everyday, enhanced rather than dimmed for the present by mourning, never for any cause banished far; the world of mahogany, plush and new paraffin oil-lamps, with three heavy comfortable meals served daily. It occurred to William, for the first time in all of his ministry, that never in his eighty years had he known hunger, privation, cold, the things that charity assiduously provided for in the circles lately patronised by Margaret Heatherton; her work-party at Savill's catered mostly for the heathen, the naked abroad in Africa and China, who must be induced to better their ways.

William saw Sarah Court compress her lips as finally, on the hall landing, her black skirts brushed past him to return to her own quarters. He had preferred to see her down to her own place himself; otherwise, for all he knew, she'd have tried the handle of the locked study door, perhaps even looked through the keyhole to that place where, behind the books, the wood was rough. William moved on, with his dignified gait, the key safe in his pocket; never once turning his white head to admit that he left, had on each occasion, consciously or not, done so, an unnamed horror behind him upstairs, among the deserted bookshelves.

He felt some hesitant shyness before entering the parlour; but as he did so Jenny left her chair, came forward, and held up her face for him to kiss her. She'd always been a warm-hearted thing, he remembered; coldly, for he could act now in no other fashion, William bent and kissed her cheek.

As he did so, time fell away and he saw himself, an old cadaver. So long was it since his dry lips had touched flesh that it was like a contact between the dead and the living; as though he, not the corpse lying orderly next door, had known death, and had returned from it to a moment's renewal of life, love, flavourful things. He recalled now that it had been Jenny's wedding-day when he last exchanged a word with her. He'd come out to meet her when the carriage had arrived with her, the bride, and James who had brought her over, and had taken her into the drawing-room on his arm, long ago.

Memories crowded in on William. He'd insisted, triumphing for once over Margaret's demented obstinacy, that the marriage take place here, in what should have been Jenny's home. A child she'd been, no more, when she ran away years before to James and Alicia at Imrie; they, not he and Margaret, had been father and mother to the girl ever since.

"Dearest Papa," said Jenny, "are you well, despite the sadness? I came as soon as I heard; perhaps I should not have done so?"

James, his dead brother, had become a parent to his own lost daughter: James, tall and spare, his presence real as if it were with them in the room today, the long-lipped face, grey hair—and side-chops already whitening, as on that day he had given Jenny away as a bride while he, William, read the service over the pair. Margaret had refused to be present; she remained in her room. The bride had worn, William remembered, a bonnet with bunched straw trimming, and a plaid dress. Now Jenny was in black, a widow. It was true that, as Sarah Court had said, she had grown stouter. The awareness gave William a feeling of warmth towards her, this little, stoutening, plain, no longer young woman. She anchored him to the things of earth.

"How old are you?" he said, hearing his own voice sound as a cold precise whisper in the overloaded room; there was no place here for echoes. It had, in any case, now he thought of it, been a strange, almost a discourteous question. His own blurting thoughts had trespassed on courtesy. He should have asked her, in his turn, how she did; if she also were well.

"This is a sad business," he made himself say. It shouldn't happen again, that intrusion of his constant, buried self; he must mind his words, like a schoolboy learning manners. But to see her again had for the time unmanned him.

"I am forty-one, Papa; and my son Johnny is eleven years old." She spoke equably, answering without rancour a question many women would have coquetted over, or resented. The notes of her voice were still sweet, he heard, like the strings of a harp beneath fine fingers. It might have been one thing that had charmed Margaret's son John Howie, rich, handsome, sought-after young John. Many prettier women had angled for him, despite his mother's fiat concerning marriage. But for such as Jenny to entrap so spoilt a lad! She'd always been plain, and was so still, he recognised; her dark hair showed no more grey than either of her sisters', though it had more curl than theirs; it was parted doucely under her unfashionable bonnet. She looked what she was, a housekeeper.

"Is that man good to you?" he heard himself ask. He led her to a chair, with his customary old-world courtesy placing her in it, and turning to where the decanter sat, ready to pour her out more wine. He felt his hands tremble against the chill of the crystal. He heard her reply.

"Why, yes, Papa, Mr. Macdonald is extremely kind. He has no family of his own, you see, and he allows me to have

Johnny with me in the house, provided the child doesn't trouble him; we bide belowstairs mostly, the pair of us, when Johnny isn't at school, and there's the garden. Oh, Papa, they already gave me some wine; and a piece of cake, while I was waiting. I do not think that I had better have any more." She made pretence, politely, to sip the wine he had nevertheless poured; William watched her hungrily. He hadn't felt like this about Kate, while she was here yesterday; but that eldest of his girls had had her husband by her, anxious and hovering lest she injure herself or the unborn third, or was it fourth, child. Jenny had no one at all to protect her. She'd been brave; yes, it was true enough.

He forced himself to more talk; had she brought the boy today? His soul yearned; then he remembered, too late, that Sarah Court had sneered at Jenny for having come here on foot. There would be no child's face peering anxiously from behind the glass of a carriage-window, waiting till the great panelled door should open again, to reveal his bonneted, gloved mama emerging and waiting, expensive skirts held sideways out of the mud, upon the clean-washed mounting-block for the coachman to assist her inside her equipage.

He found himself unable to ask further concerning Jenny's rich employer, or the conditions of her humdrum life. He watched her turn the wine-glass in her hand, still making pretence to drink. The hand was small, William noticed; smaller than her sisters', who were both big women; and roughened, no doubt with housework. A wave of remorse enveloped William again as he thought of how, during the years since John Howie's death, he himself had been too greatly immersed in his books, shutting out personal life, to enquire concerning Jenny. But the conditions here had perhaps been sufficient excuse, "They're good to you where you are, then?" he heard himself repeating. "I'm glad of that."

Jenny gave her small calm smile, and answered the question he had not asked openly. "I didn't bring Johnny today, Papa. Death can be a difficult matter for a child; frightening, perhaps. When John was dying, I sent our boy meantime to a neighbour. And my son never knew his grandmother."

Did any of us? thought William, in detached admiration of her calm. His myopic eyes had focussed themselves at last on

Jenny's gloves, left nervously folded in her lap while she drank her wine. They were carefully darned in places, and were made of cheap black cotton. He remembered Margaret telling her daughters that no lady would contemplate being seen in public in gloves, or shoes either, made of any but the finest possible kid. "If she cannot acquire such things, she should not be seen abroad." Jenny's small foot, protruding below her braided skirts, revealed a laced shoe with a patch on it.

"The wine is to your taste?" he asked her formally. It was, he knew, the finest obtainable in Madeira; brought in personally by Richard Urquhart, Kate's husband, who was an importer of choice foreign goods. The crystal glasses and decanter sat on a silver tray, well polished. The tray itself had been engraved and presented to William on withdrawal from his earlier charge of Gowanmount in order to sustain the call to Savill's Old, forty-odd years ago. The inlaid clock which ticked on the marble mantelpiece had been a later, more expensive gift from the well-endowed congregation of Savill's, on the occasion of their minister's prosperous second wedding to the widow of the shipowner.

Nobody here now would remember Marie, the first wife. She had died at Jenny's birth.

William returned, with determination, to the present. Most of the furniture in this room, he reflected wryly, was Margaret's own, and would be removed, perhaps, by the Howie women when they left forthwith with Wilhelmine. Well, he could afford to dispense with furniture; he had enough for his own needs, and the house next door had needed no more than he bought with it on the death of old Miss Hyslop, the former owner. How she had used to hirple with difficulty up and down the street, always in the same bonnet and shawl!

"Ye've aye been good to old folk, minister; good, too, ye've been over the matter of the French mooseer. Who'd have thocht he'd gaun sae quick, leaving his gear, and a month's rent still owed to me? Ah, minister, ye've enough to dae wi' money..."

But she had taken it, that sum he'd handed her long ago for Paul Chantel's arrears. Better that than enquiry, following perhaps to France...

He'd bought that house soon afterwards; no one, since the

old woman's death, had entered it since except himself. They thought he was eccentric, no doubt, to buy that, and own the manse as well, when he need not have owned either; they'd have set him up, the Savill's congregation, in the new place they'd long since purchased south of here, but he would not go...

"Papa, may I see her?"

William raised his eyes; he had forgotten Jenny's presence. His gaze was blurred when he tried to regard her more closely; had she tears in her eyes? How much wrong had he, Margaret, all of them, done to Jenny from the beginning? Was it because of the memory of Chantal? No, it had all of it been pride, pride. And she, like her elder sisters, had fled his house and the woman who came to rule it. Margaret had, he now saw, ruled in all ways like a tyrant queen. Had he himself lived out half his life in fear?

"You may see her if you wish," he answered Jenny. They rose; she set down her glass. The thought recurred to him of her lifelong enemies, the full Howie sisterhood, Margaret's daughters, John's sisters, spinsters all, in a black-clad unforgiving covey in that room across the hallway. The portrait of handsome John would still be hanging on the wall. His mother had never taken it down: she clung to possessions.

Georgy would be, he knew, seated by the coffin. Wilhelmine, who had been Jenny's bridal attendant, at William's order, loved Georgy and would never now leave her side. Should he ever have remarried? Should he ever have fathered Wilhelmine?

It had been the urges of the flesh, he knew. It was as if Jenny's presence helped him see many things clear, as Margaret had done.

Wilhelmine. Why must they, all of them, treat her as a child still, at thirty-eight? Why had he acquiesced in that? That day of John and Jenny's wedding the child had, despite her mothers' prohibition, come to the ceremony at his bidding, worn a pink gown...

"I have forgiven her long ago, Papa. I should like to see her once more and make my peace. That is why I came."

Margaret, always Margaret, the old man thought bitterly. Her supremacy in his house had not ceased now she was dead.

It had not been to see *him*, her father, that Jenny had returned today, or to comfort and sustain him in any sorrow he might feel. It had been to view her dead stepmother, no more. "Come, then," he said, "let us go and see her."

There was no daylight in the death-chamber. According to custom the coffin had been placed across its trestles in the drawing-room, on whose walls hung portraits of the Howie family. Georgina Howie, the dead woman's eldest daughter, had given orders that paraffin-lamps be placed at the head and sides, rather than wax candles, which would have savoured too greatly of Popery. Georgy herself, seated at the coffin's head, kept her eyes fixed on her dead mother's face. Georgy by now was herself like an effigy in wax, its erstwhile prettiness preserved behind glass from erosion and dust. She, the Howie first-born, was in fact fifty-two. She had in youth, during the brief season allowed her, been a noted beauty; the cream-satin quality of her plump arms and bosom, and her large dark eyes, had attracted, it was whispered to this day, a proposal of marriage from a baronet from England. The eyes, scarcely marred by time, were dry and had shed no tears; likewise Georgy's hair, smooth and dark as ever, gave back the gleam of a blackbird's wing in the lamplight. It had used, during her season, her hair, to be brushed and polished daily afterwards with silk; now she spent less time on it. She remained as still as an effigy as the father and daughter entered, Jenny in her shabby black dress on William's arm. Behind them, in the lamplit shadows, handsome John's portrait smiled on. He wore a frilled shirt of a fashion the generation past had favoured; one languid hand fingered a gold-topped cane. Jenny did not raise her eyes to the portrait.

As they came in there was a disturbance in the quietness; from among the other black-clad figures in the room, Wilhelmine Heatherton, the baby of the family, flung herself sobbing towards William's other side.

"Papa! Oh, oh, Papa, how sad it all seems," and the tears coursed down her cheeks. Absently, he let himself caress her and smooth her hair; he also made her kiss Jenny. Wilhelmine's hair was light-brown and curly, like his own had been, he thought. When she had been a tiny thing she had used sometimes to perch, if Georgy were elsewhere, on William's knee while he wrote out his sermons; now and again while he pondered some point of doctrine he would pull gently at the ringlets, ordered and fine as silk floss. The fact, as though he had only now realised it, that Wilhelmine had changed not at all with the years shocked William today. Her voice was still high and petulant, like a child's; her manners were not, had never been or would be, those of a grown woman. She was regarding Jenny now with a thumb in her mouth, her close-set grey eyes vacant. The other sisters encouraged and petted her, he knew. Somewhere upstairs, Wilhelmine still kept her doll's house, and she and Georgy played with it daily by custom, except for today and yesterday, with the death and coming funeral. No doubt Wilhelmine was perturbed by the lack of her day's treat more than by her mother's death. What had he fathered? Was there a devil in him, or in Margaret?

He walked towards the body. It was the first time he had seen it since it had been coffined; as the widower, it would be understood by the visiting public that his grief had made him withdraw. But now he faced the truth; with Jenny by him, he could see many things truly.

He no longer felt any fear of viewing the dead woman. Margaret Heatherton had died in her sleep, and he could still remember the deep, snoring breaths followed at last by the death-rattle. Perhaps he had expected Margaret to look, still, as though she slept. But his view was interrupted; Wilhelmine barred his progress, jumping up and down a little, irreverently; a spoilt child, out of place here.

"Papa, make Georgy eat some dinner and come away. Please make her come. She's sat by Mama since ... since ... like a stone, and won't move, or speak to me."

William forbore to rebuke his youngest daughter. It must, he knew, be strange and terrifying for this creature, pampered as a fish in a heated tank, to come face to face, suddenly, with reality. And Georgy, since the thing had happened that had changed all their lives here, had acted as a mother, no less, to Wilhelmine. He spoke soothingly to the pathetic, young–old creature, noting how like her mother's the narrowly set eyes seemed, even now when they were reddened with crying; and spared a moment to lead her back to the other half-sisters, who withdrew, taking her with them. Only Georgy remained, as if she had heard nothing of what was said, and had not seen the pair enter. William made his way back to Jenny, who stood by the coffin, looking down at her stepmother's face.

Margaret Heatherton's expression still told no one anything; she remained in death as in life, inscrutable to all enquirers. The smoothed face, with its small eyes finally closed beneath paper-thin lids, and the long whimsical upper lip were much as they had been; yellowed somewhat with the change death brings, and with the steady glow of the oil-lamps in the thickly curtained room. It had been a witty face, handsome and to be reckoned with. Now it met, without reservation or fear, the greatest challenge of all to continued identity, and overcame it; she was still Margaret. Her hair, for long now palest silver that had once been gold, was parted smoothly under a lace cap whose lappets lay carefully disposed on either side of the head. She wore her two wedding-rings; a concession to propriety, William found himself thinking. *That* had never been lacking in her; nor had efficiency; nothing those ringed, large hands had undertaken had ever yet been bungled, half done, or set aside. Everything Margaret set out to do had been concluded, even the ruin of her children's lives, each separate one.

William thought of all this, and of how by rights the sight of her face, seen now for the last time till they met before God, should move him more deeply: as if by rights all that had passed of late years to separate him from Margaret should be, by his will and perhaps by hers, already wiped clean. Yet he could feel no act of will, nor any message from her. They might have been strangers. He himself felt nothing that he would not have felt for anyone else's dead.

"You should not be here."

It might have been the voice in his own mind, but it was Georgy Howie who spoke aloud; and not to him, but directly to Jenny, who stood by his side and whom he had forgotten. William made a slight, protesting movement and some demur; to behave thus, over the corpse! But Georgy ignored him as though he were not present. Her dark eyes gazed at Jenny without expression; she rose to her feet. Jenny faced her, withdrawn at last from her long staring down at the coffin. To both of the women, William knew, he himself was no longer present. Even John Howie was elsewhere, back in the shadows; weak handsome John. There was only the coffined dead and the two living women, confronting one another after years in which nothing that had happened had been forgotten, nothing forgiven or mitigated. "Can you not leave us with our grief?" said Georgy's ageless face. "Do you suppose that I too have lost nothing and no one?" replied the other's silence.

The silence almost conquered. One did not bicker openly in the presence of death. But shortly Georgy said, speaking in a low voice as though the corpse might hear her and waken, "Had *she* been alive you would not have entered this house again, you—you harlot," and then tears began to trickle unbidden down her face. As if an unbearable tension had been relieved with their coming, she made no effort to remove or stop them; they splashed down at last on to the rich lace lappets of the dead woman's cap. William took Jenny again by the arm and led her from the room, in silence.

When they were alone he said, "You must excuse her; she is distraught. She should not have said what she did."

"It was true, though, was it not?" said Jenny defiantly. He saw that her cheeks were suddenly bright as carnations; it made her seem almost handsome. William shook his head, deeply grieved and disturbed; how did one answer such a thing? They'd been young, the two of them, when it had happened; and he recalled that he must write to Jenny, when all this was done with. "Leave your direction with me, when you go," he told her gently. "I—I would wish to write and——"

He could not even say it, so great was his perturbation; could not tell her, even now, that his heart's desire, when the rest had gone, was to have her always near him, and her son. He watched her go, with Georgy's lapse unmentioned again between them; and having seen the small, shabby figure depart on its way down the street went back into his house, and gave orders that the coffin was to be closed at once instead of waiting till tomorrow, as was expected. "Miss Howie is overwrought, and must have her rest," he said coldly. He then went upstairs to his study, alone; he would finish the day as other days, reading. Reading brought a man solace and forgetfulness ... who should know that if not himself?

But there was to be no rest for William Heatherton that night, not even the light sleep which is all that old men need. The events of the day had revealed a chain of memories that dragged, link upon backward link, into the intolerable places his mind would not ordinarily admit or recognise. Through every hour that chimed from the city's many clocks he lay awake, remembering.

II

THE IMAGES IN WILLIAM'S MIND ROSE, MINGLED, COALESCED and then resolved, like pondweed in muddy water that has been briefly stirred. Unsubstantial shapes wavered vaguely in his mind's eye, centring at last about a single figure, that of a young girl of about eighteen, slender and solitary, walking uphill. The chill wind of long ago whipped her narrow, dove-coloured skirts and caught at her silk shawl's fringes. It had been, after first noting her, one of the things William's mind registered early, that shawl. So rich a piece of apparel could only be an heirloom of good family; anyone who possessed it would not readily part with it, for instance to give it away to a servant. And she herself, the young girl, walked like a lady; not with resolute peasant strides, but tentatively, as if uncertain of her surroundings; perhaps a stranger to the place. Why was she out alone? Had she no maid, to follow a pace or two behind? The anomaly struck William; it was not then customary for young ladies of such a sort to go out unaccompanied.

Later he would consider, in his already considering mind, all of it; but for the present he was instantly, fully aware of the girl. The hue of her shawl was ivory, the colour of very old silk which has been carefully kept. It struck him that she was all ivory, like a carved figurine he had seen portrayed in a book brought back by a China missionary. Her complexion altogether lacked the rosy, garish hue so boasted of by Scotswomen, its sallow quality relieved only by the heart-shaped mouth, which was subtly and naturally red. Dark eyes, straight dark hair knotted plainly beneath a shabby bonnet which did not accord with the status of the shawl; but it was, William had already convinced himself, impossible that she should be a servant. The impertinent wind revealed small narrow ankles, with the criss-crossed ribbons which tied on her flat slippers showing black against the white cotton hose. William's mind went further; upwards to the calf, to the unseen garter; his thoughts grew unseemly, and he directed them back. Her gloves were black also, of some cheap material; she carried a small bunch of asters in her hands. William knew he would never forget the colours of the flowers; lavender, rose, blue, white, crimson. An ivory girl, with a rainbow between her hands, and a neatly turned ankle and fringed silk shawl.

A small sound recalled him to awareness of himself, and to propriety; the faint, metallic click of the latched side-gate leading to Gowanmount vestry, from which he had lately emerged; the elders, who were discussing a measure by vote in his requested absence, would soon follow. Without thinking what he did William held open the gate to leave it ready for the others; these men were his employers, he their chosen servant, who did their bidding in the pulpit each Sunday and made them duly tremble, and drank tea with their wives, on weekdays, about his parish in the city.

If they had not been about to come after him, would he have followed the girl uphill? William acknowledged to himself that he would; and the thought itself caused an unwonted flush to stain his handsome, stolid, clean-shaven face, already a little too staid for his years, between the clerical bands, which he wore about his throat beneath the stock, and the tall hat which sat soberly on his light-brown curls. He was thirty, and was not ill-looking.

And the girl was real, not a dream of inchoate form, an urge of the flesh such as still came to William sometimes, though he downed it. But today beyond control, habit, conscience, duty and prudence came the desire to follow her.

What did he want of her? He already knew.

The awareness was with him as he heard the murmur of the elders' voices behind the door, and then saw it open. He had forgotten them; so alien a thing, this sudden desire, foreign to everything he stood for, already, to numberless folk!

He must marry, he knew, when the time came, some suitable young woman. But who was to say that *she* was unsuitable? That shawl——

But he might not have followed the matter to its conclusion, after all, if at that moment the Session Clerk, Joseph Craik, and the Treasurer, one George Howie, had not come out to tell him the decision to which they had all come to at the close of the meeting. They formed a tall-hatted knot about their young minister, and chaffed him; a process William could not appreciate, for he took himself solemnly, as most others took him. But not George Howie; Howie, the upcome shipowner and financier, cock-a-hoop. "They wouldna have passed the motion contrary to your wishes, minister, had ye had a wife to make them known to the congregation as should be done. When are we to name the day? Man, it isna for lack of making known a wheen bonny lasses; any of them wad be proud to name hersel' mistress o' Gowanmount manse, and the cost o' improvements wad be met then, I don't doubt, for the ladies arena blate, and wad gi'e us no peace till the thing was richt done." The small, twinkling eyes surveyed William knowledgeably, and the big young minister shrank into himself with inherent shy dislike; a forward, insensitive creature, George Howie, and William himself would have disliked him even more without the constant exercise of Christian charity.

That the minister of Gowanmount was thirty, and still unwed, was perhaps less of a tribute to the good-natured tolerance of the elders than to the undying hopefulness of their wives. The prospect of having a niece or daughter installed as mistress of the large, half-used manse near by was elevating; nevertheless, such hopes by now had wary overtones. Various means had been used at the outset to entrap the well-spoken, well-fleshed young minister, who, partly because his brother was already a famed ship's engineer, had been chosen over the heads of several older, drier man who had, four years previously, answered the call to fill the advertised vacancy at Gowanmount. But William Heatherton had, without a doubt, preached the finest sermon; and he sustained the call, in local parlance. But he still—and this was the cause of some whispering among the matrons at missionary-meetings, and following morning and afternoon church—William still had his manse kept clean and well-ordered by a middle-aged housekeeper, chosen by his mother, Mrs. Nathan Heatherton. That was all very well for a year or two, and the congregation had no fault to find with Mrs. Prescott, who otherwise kept herself respectfully to herself; but it was time the manse had its own proper mistress. Since the Reformation, with the resulting ban on celibacy and priests, it was obligatory on a preacher to be a family man. Soon, if the next few years passed as rapidly and uneventfully as the last, the minister of Gowanmount would have become something of a joke, let alone a perennial target for hopeful spinsters at prayer-meetings. It was time he settled down; and this both Craik and Howie made clear, not for the first time, today with winks and nudges.

"It doesna do to let the ladies think ye are afeared o' them, minister! What say ye to——" but on the near utterance of a certain young lady's name, Craik put a finger to the side of his nose, and looked sly; it was not the approved practice to name an unmarried girl in men's company. "Ah, well, ye'll ken who I mean," said the clerk, and received the formal smile, and dropped lids over almost colourless eyes, of the tall young minister whom he was beginning, and had done for some time now, to think a cold fish, maybe; one who was out for himself, at any rate, and on his way up the social scale without a doubt. They said the brother had married well; a cousin, was it not? The whole family had genius of an unexpected kind; there was David Heatherton, the eccentric, who also designed ships; maybe that accounted partly for the young minister's innate lack of approachability, which kept most folk, even the optimistic ladies, at a distance. Joe Craik would take the whole question later to his wife, for sympathy over the wordless set-down he had just received; that good lady duly bridled at it. "Willie Heatherton needna think himsel' better than plain folk; his ain were smiths. Why, his father and mither bide yet in the auld clay bigging down-bye, honest folk they are enough; the auld wife sets her nose high. He's a fine figure in the pulpit, to be sure, is Willie; but in his nightshirt he'll look no better than you do, Joe, I believe."

"His brother James is civil enough, for all his rich marriage," concluded her spouse thoughtfully. For some reason it was disrespectful to have to think of the minister in his nightshirt; but there, the ladies would never be diverted!

George Howie's dart had stabbed deeper than the clerk's had done, and William afterwards wondered if the brisk, bumptious little session treasurer had set him on the path he was to follow, without further decision of his own. Afraid of women! There might be reason, William did not doubt, to fear George Howie's own lady; he kept her like a queen on a showy, palatial house in the best residential quarter of the city. William had, on two somewhat formal occasions now, admired the hearth with its shining fire-irons, whose value as a smith's son he could well assess; and the red Turkey carpet, over which the full satin skirts of Mrs. Howie herself dragged richly. Such a hushing noise of richness, a faint awareness besides of verbena and lavender, were about Mrs. George Howie whether at home, in church in their central pew, or at mission-meetings; the latter Margaret Howie patronised with generosity, and William knew—and the session, having made George their treasurer, knew also—that Howie and his grand English wife were among the foremost givers to good causes, and to Gowanmount in general. William himself would be foolish to offend George Howie by showing how greatly he resented his banter.

"Afeared, minister..." It was like the effrontery of the man to persist; William did not speak again, and let the other prate on. "It micht well ha'e been that *I* was afeared, the time I took Margaret from her grand kin in the south parts. A castle they lived in, or near enough; anyone micht ha'e thought her too high-set for the likes o' me. But now we're crouse and cantie, as the Bard said: and never a doubt in anyone's mind who's master." George Howie inflated his chest, set off by a brocade waistcoat somewhat less conspicuous than he would have chosen for himself a year or two ago, before his vaunted marriage; Margaret had done her best to tone down her spouse's sartorial aspirations. "Say it I will, for all that; no man ever had a better helpmeet! She's a good head under her feathered bonnet, Margaret has; many's the time I've gone to her for her opinion on some thing I couldna myself fathom, and have not regretted it: no man could jalouse better than she. There's no jewel like a good woman, minister; tak' the advice of one who didna marry the first, nor the second either; but if I'd met Margaret sooner it'd maybe have been the better for us baith." He clapped his thick-fingered hand on William's black sleeve, lifted his tall hat and made an elaborate farewell; walking thereafter a few yards to where his polished carriage waited, with the liveried coachman impervious above a groomed and shining chestnut pair.

"It's no' muckle far till his house," mouthed a lesser emerging light, behind William and near enough for him, within his customary frigid silence, to hear. "Can the man no' walk, like other folk? But an upcome craw will aye display his feathers, like a peacock plumed and strutting. Ah, well; a good-day to ye, minister."

William raised his hat for the final time. He was not adept at conversation, and wanted more than anything else to be alone with his own thoughts, once these chattering fools were clear ... It was not, he knew well, that he did not make painstaking efforts to talk with them and their wives; but it was, for all his genuine strivings to the contrary, as if he did folk a slight favour by unbending to talk to them at all. He was not, he knew, despite his intriguing bachelor status, a popular figure even with the ladies; still less held in affection. He had never previously reflected on this and it did not yet trouble him. Folk turned out, in increasing numbers, to hear him preach; he was a good figurehead in the pulpit, always finding something worth while to say there, either culled from original research in books or, as many of the older folk realised, from devout prayer.

But no one except his parents and his brother James loved William. He had always known and accepted this. Now...

How could he think of love so soon? He had no knowledge of the girl he had just seen; she might be a married woman. But he knew, in some way, that she was not.

He turned at last to walk downhill to where his greystone manse stood; Mrs. Prescott would have his tea ready. He did not look back over his shoulder to watch the way the girl had gone, a quarter-hour since. He would see, he knew, nothing but the varied skyline of the Necropolis, where the well-to-do of the city were buried in increasingly opulent mausoleums. By now, there would be nothing more.

Over tea, William reflected that his own knowledge of the married state was limited to the fact that it was, above all, a matter requiring much careful thought. Such thought had preceded the nuptials of his own father and his mother, forty-odd years ago. Nathan Heatherton, having uprooted himself from the no longer rewarding north, had come down out of the place of his ancestors and looked about him for a sensible Lowland wife with a good tocher.* Jean Dyce had been the right choice, being not only well dowered—her folk were long spoken of as canny and hardworking, and Nathan had to prove his own value in this way before they would consider him—but also a noted cook and housekeeper, no longer very young. That they had two sons as a result of the marriage was gratifying to both Nathan and Jean; sons could help in the forge, whereas lasses had to find husbands and be provided for; but early on Jean started to harbour greater designs for her younger boy, William. By the time these were becoming imminent James, the elder, was already in the shipyards, having attracted the notice of his fiery, brilliant cousin, David Heatherton, who had made money in designing ships' hulls and engines. David, a bachelor, had a younger sister, Alicia, whom he had brought up after their parents had died; she was pretty, had been educated at a grand school, could speak French, and played the harp and pianoforte. Nathan and Jean at the cottage frowned on reports they had of James, their foremost stay and hope, hanging about, blushing and hesitating, in a fair-haired laughing lassie's path; as it was, James himself took almost three years to propose, so shy was he. An accomplished daughter-in-law, clad in for ever changing, delicate fashions of silks and lace, unlikely to redden her white hands by baking, or pucker her white brow with mending hose, seemed an unlikely helpmeet for a young man with his way to make in a hard, competitive trade; but Alicia and James were married for all that, and were to this day as happy together as children. Presently, in the small house James had brought himself in the unfashionable city-centre, their own children began to be born; two boys and two girls came, and by then James and his brother-in-law David Heatherton were well started together in the shipyards and were attracting orders from as far off as England, hitherto chary of entrusting contracts to a Scot. But the work of James Heatherton was so meticulous, his mind so thorough, that he bade fair by these days to outstrip brilliant David, who had always been some-

* Dowry

what erratic. David bore his young sister's husband no ill-will, and even James's parents began to soften towards the marriage. Alicia's dowry had been sizeable enough, it was true, but Heathertons never lived on their wives' money; old Jean herself had set aside her own tocher over the years to help make a minister out of Willie.

By now, Jean held both her sons in high regard. It was true that James's wife put on airs, as Jean saw it, and called their evening meal dinner and would have grandeur with it and damask and silver, and the French Mamzelle, hired to teach Maudie and Evangeline foreign manners, bringing them down, at dessert, in frilled useless petticoats to curtsy and eat sugared almonds, then depart. Old Jean sniffed; there'd be less of such stuff, she thought if James himself were not well spoken of at the shipyards as a designer and probable builder of the fastest ships for long-distance travel yet known. Jean was pleased at that; the yards themselves were in her blood, her folk had wrought with iron as long as Nathan's, and she could understand the very dawning of the age of steam. What she could not fathom, simply, was that either of her sons would gladly have had her visit them whenever she chose; but Jean would never do so except by arrangement, and that rarely, such as when the horse-fair was held annually on the Green, and she could come up in any case by water-ferry and hunt for likely bargains among the booths. Wool for knitting Nathan's stout everyday hose, or linen for his shirts which she still smocked by hand, or a round bonnet for him from the famed makers of Stewarton, were the things Jean sought and cherished; she herself had few needs. Her strength lay in her tongue, which was sharp and terse; both her sons still respected it.

William had forced himself to think of his mother after seeing the ivory girl with the fringed shawl and flowers. What would she have said had she known that her son, had it not been for the crowding elders at the door, would have followed straightway an unknown young woman who walked the street alone? The shame of having been brought to so unlikely a pass was stirring in William himself already, even while the desire still lingered in him. The more he thought of his mother the deeper grew his reproach.

He could not remember a time when she had treated him and James alike; he himself, the younger, had been set aside, as Hannah dedicated the infant Samuel, he knew, for temple-service. Nothing Nathan could ever say would divert Jean's firm intention that her younger son should enter the Church. William himself could remember the long, lean form of smith Nathan, his hair already white in the flicker of the wall-lamp, bending over the box bed where William and James slept together, those early days at the riverside cottage when they were boys. "Look at the laddie's big hands," William could remember Nathan saying, while he himself feigned sleep. "There's a born smith for ye. Willie'll make dunts on an anvil yet."

"He'll not, I say. He'll be a minister, a credit to us baith. Ye canna aye bide by an anvil."

"We've been ironworkers since the eleventh Duke's time; maybe before that. Ye canna alter the ways of nature, woman; the Lord meant Willie for a smith."

"If I say he's for the Kirk, he's for the Kirk," repeated Jean stubbornly. All through William's childhood, after that episode, she instilled into him that he was a being whose hands were not for toil; not like James. James, whose tough, lanky frame had been early accustomed to manual work, loved nothing better than to show his own hands' cunning strength, forging and twisting iron; he was happiest when left alone with hammer, nails and the forge-fire blowing cherry-red with the bellows' wind. William was rarely permitted even to blow these for him. He himself liked, when he was very young, to help James; but Jean, who had set her mind against any such fate for Willie, seldom let him stay to see the end of it. As a result of her teaching the boy developed from an early age a dislike of dirt under his fingernails, or callouses on his palms. His spare time was spent in reading, because it led to less trouble than sitting by the forge; and William learned to love books as James loved iron. That his physical strength was almost equal to his brother's was realised by few. Once at school, where William, except for his brother's support, would have been both lonely and unpopular, a bully tormented him. James squared up to the bully at once, and drew blood from his nose; after that no one tried any tricks on the younger brother.

William's self-esteem, had he been permitted to defend himself, might have suffered less insidiously; as it was, anxious to prove himself important, he remained shy and pompous all through his schooldays. He invited affection from nobody except James, who gave it ungrudgingly. Later, when William had made reality out of his mother's dreams, and had passed in his examinations well enough to be admitted to the Faculty of Arts at the University, and from there to study divinity, the pomposity was more in keeping than it had been. It passed by now for a dignified sense of awareness of William's calling, a certainty that he, though a Heatherton, was not as the other men of his race, being set apart, a very Samuel, as his mother had wanted. The fact of physical manhood was not yet troublesome.

In each successive year of the college course William Heatherton was first in his subjects. Books, so long his chief companions, remained so, increasingly after James's happy marriage. Even Greek and Hebrew presented no difficulty. It was beginning to be evident even to old Nathan Heatherton that his wife was right, and that his younger son, as well as the elder, was destined for a brilliant future in his own way. "Ye were maybe right enough," he said, with difficulty for he found it hard to express himself as having been wrong, to Jean one evening, when as so often they sat together over the last of the glowing coals, while the Dyce shovel-tongs Jean's brother had made long ago on their marriage, and which she sanded and cleaned lovingly and often, shone. Her grey head, in its goffered cap—she had always been proud of her laundrywork, her linen and Nathan's were fine as gentlefolk's, summer and winter—her head, with the blunt stubborn features of her race, raised itself and looked at Nathan, whom she respected and loved. "Ay," she said, in answer to his admission. "Ay, I was right about William." Nathan passed a hand over his long-lipped face to hide his rare smile; he must never be caught laughing at her!

"Willie's set for high places, then," he said presently.

"Maybe. How often have I said it? But nobody heeds me," said Jean, without justice. Her face softened. "We'll not need to call him Willie when he's in his bands," she said. "It'll be an affront to him then."

They attended William's graduation, and his reception into the Kirk, and, filled with a grave, delighted pride, his first sermon. The fact that the young man was soon called to Gowanmount was no surprise to Jean.

"It's a fine kirk, they say, fu' o' the best folk," she said, "I couldna ask better for any son o' mine."

Nathan said nothing. He himself was more keenly interested in the progress of James. The elder son had lately been admitted to a select and honourable ironmasters' company, and had wrought a superb hammer for his entry-test. Nathan knew that the tradition of his own folk was safe with James. He did not grudge Jean her lesser triumph over William.

For nobody called the minister Willie any more, except James when he forgot. The profound respect which all accorded to such folk was extended to the Lord's newest elect, young as he might be; time passed and William Heatherton was no longer so young. Unless he chose to visit his parents, which he endeavoured to do each Saturday if his duties did not intervene, they did not trouble him. It was as if they accepted the fact that he had stepped out of their world, and they would not deliberately shame him in his grand new calling.

If they had had an inkling of the experience which had come to William in his student days some years previously, their shock and grief would have been profound.

William himself had not mentioned that earliest matter of all to anyone, even James who was as near to a confidant as his brother had ever attained. At the time it happened, and after, William had spent many hours wrestling with himself in fervent prayer. Shortly he had convinced himself that it had been one more manifestation of God's special choice of him, William Heatherton, as an instrument, that he had been guided unscathed through the fire.

Like a fire indeed it had been, burning and gutting his vitals. Even after his shameful retreat, with the woman's laughter sounding in his ears, he would have gone back, and...

She had been a harlot, that woman. She was no longer young. She was well known in that part of the city near by the river, where a century and more ago tobacco-lords had had their residences, now mainly slums still boasting delicate doorways. They had strutted in powder and velvet along the pavements beneath the arcades, followed by black slaves bearing sunshades fringed with silk, who beat the common folk back with staves in order that the lords might pass by with their grand gear unsullied. Now, the arcades were noisome and their shadows housed folk like Betty Pringle, whose name never passed respectable lips. William, in course of his theological training, had heard her mentioned, as an object of pity, a soul to be saved. On fire with zeal—how convinced he had been that a word, a simple salutary word, from him, the Lord's servant, would recall such a creature from the error of her ways!—he had made his way down to Betty's quarter, the harlots' quarter. It was not possible to visit the place by night ordinarily clad; a man would have his clothes torn from him and sold for whisky-money. So William had gone by day; and had picked his way upstairs to Betty's place past puddled slops and excrement. The yells of filthy, half-naked, barefoot urchins beset him, demanding a penny, a halfpenny, from the big well-set-out young gentleman in the dark suit of clothes, with his brown curly head, and pale shaven face, turned aside with uncontrollable disgust as he mounted the stairway. He gave them nothing. "Be about your business," he said, and they yelled the more, and tried to clutch at William's coat; he elbowed them aside, and at last knocked at a door which hung crazily on one hinge, so that the world could enter.

Betty was in bed. Her voice called to him cheerfully to come in; with his big frame finally blocking such light as entered by the door, she thought he was a customer.

"Come awa' ben, dearie, and tak' aff your coat." Some other children, he remembered afterwards, were playing in a corner by the further wall, on the floor; they had not looked round when he entered. The stench in the room was appalling; a mixture of stale sweat, woman's courses, privies, grease, wall-bugs, strong spirits, cabbage-water. Betty herself lay on straw, with a single blanket half across her; it was warm in the room and she remained naked to the waist. William had never before seen a woman's body. He stared at the great mounds of her breasts, none too clean, the nipples brownish with childbearing. His breath was coming thickly; he told himself it was from climbing the stairs.

Betty Pringle flung off the rest of the blanket. Her hair, cascading untidily down over her naked shoulders, was black. She might once have been beautiful. She had opened her legs, in the usual manner of greeting customers.

"Come on, dearie. I got to go out, after. Ye ha'e the money? A gentleman like you." She had now seen more of William's appearance; a fine young man, the like of which she didn't often get the chance to have dealings with, these days. What ailed him that he didn't get on with it? Perhaps——

"Plenty of my customers is gentlemen. Don't be shy, love. Come on." Perhaps he hadn't done it before. He looked quite young, she now saw, for all he was so big. "I'll show ye how, dear," she said. "Don't you be scared of it." She smiled; that always started them, any of them that were slow. Men didn't like being told they were scared. Men——

William was aware of the confusion of shame. He was aware of something else, a pounding of his blood, a rising desire—so he later owned it to be—that discounted the stinking room and crawling straw, overrode everything but the urge he had to take great strides towards the woman on the bed, mount and possess her. It happened as swiftly, while he stood there, as that; the word of God, his message, forgotten with the swarming urchins and the filth; and Delilah, Jezebel, paramount in his awareness.

Jezebel. The Scarlet Woman. All of them, the whores of the Bible, ranged against him, personified in this one woman, red mouth open, inviting, teeth showing now, and they were black. Even the rotting horror of her teeth did not deter it, this thing which had come upon him.

Come awa' ben, dearie ... take off your coat ...

He had opened his lips to say something. He was trying to remind himself and her that he had come to preach to her of the error of her ways.

Error ... sin ...

William turned. He blundered out of the door, down the foetid stairs, out of the evil place, past the children, the animal hordes of greedy children, hearing laughter. Was it their raucous laughter, or hers, which pursued him out into the street?

For long after that William was afraid of showing himself in the poorer part of the city. He began to achieve the reputation of a young man who had an eye on the better preferments, the residential parishes of the well-to-do. This was understood, even approved; it was from such places that, after all, the money for charity and local mission-work came. And William, as his professors realised, was not a young man who would readily achieve a common touch with the poor. He would give an impression of patronage; they would resent it, and no good would be done.

William alone knew the truth; which was that he was afraid Betty herself, if he met her, or another such, would point at him and call out after him for what he had been, had shown himself to be, in that brief instant, while the devil wrought in him. That he had not succumbed to the devil's wiles was no doubt one more evidence of the finger of God, the sheltering wing of the Almighty, above him, William Heatherton.

But sometimes at night the devil would return and would not leave William alone. He would lie sweating in the night hours, knowing that he must wrestle with his flesh. For long now he had subdued its urgings in the catharsis of prayer, even tried to recognise, in its appearance, a signal by God that He desired verbal and direct communication with William. The devil, as it were, had become a messenger of the Almighty and would in due time, when William's own will should be fully attuned to God's, show the purpose of the temptation he had been strong enough to resist. Resistance, that time . . . and the others, the others that came in the terrible, solitary night hours.

He need not have suffered for as long, he knew. Month after month, year after year, young ladies, and lately the not so young, had been paraded for his inspection at Gowanmount. But William was fastidious; they were all either plain, had raucous, uneducated voices despite their gentility, or stank at the armpits, a state of affairs William could never endure as a daily tribulation. Despite the invaluable mamas or aunts in the congregation, who must not be offended, who must be placated, William continued to attend soirées, tea-parties, musical evenings, prayer-meetings, in difficult and unrelieved shyness and solitude; the final relief was not there.

Not there, nowhere until today, when he had seen the girl in the dove-coloured dress and fringed shawl. Some difference in her had attracted William; he had felt, for the first time in long, that condemnatory flicker of the loins, that unbidden surge of desire, that hitherto had come upon him for no living flesh except a harlot's, and the unnamed creatures of dreams.

William tried desperately to return to the practical world he knew, the practical correct way of proceeding; there, one was on safer ground. After he had, by discreet means, found out who the young lady was and where she lived, and if she were suitable to his purpose, he had more ways than many men of making himself known to her family, her parents ... a guardian, perhaps? There must be some untoward factor; otherwise he would at least have met, or heard of, her in what was after all a limited social circle, the upper middle-class folk of the city. He was certain that the girl herself belonged to such a class. In fact William could readily contemplate no other.

For some reason, for he was not normally self-enquiring, William then saw himself as he was, as the young lady today might have seen him. His facial appearance, his own gait, he knew from daily observance in his shaving-mirror. He was, he liked to think (and Jean had somehow impressed the fact on him) not unhandsome in his gown and bands, mounting the pulpit-steps. He was accordingly certain that, when he met the young lady's relatives as he intended, they would have no objection to him as her suitor. It remained, of course, to ascertain that *they* were suitable. William was strictly mindful of his own position, and of the importance of any marriage he might make. Yet at the same time his blood still pounded, as it might have done in the veins of the strong smiths his ancestors, seeing a bonny barefoot lass come across the heather-clad moors towards the forge, with the Duke's castle shimmering beyond in a haze of late summer, and grouse chirping unseen, and the anvil fire low for lack of tending. All things ceased in the moment of first love, except the beloved's sight; and where was she now?

So William waited, with the cold wind blowing about him, unaware that he had made a slow business of traversing the grey, watchful street between postern and manse; that a dozen curtains might be twitching, and his lack of haste commented on; it was evident, everyone soon knew, that the young minister was thoughtful today, and in no hurry for his excellent tea. Later, he was seen by the same watchers to emerge again, set his hat firmly on his head, and make his way, with measured steps, up towards the Necropolis. There had been time enough now between the girl's earlier walk that way and his own; no connection could make itself evident to the watchers of Gowanmount.

III

Gowanmount Church had been St. Jude the Apostle's in Papist days and it still had empty niches where the images had stood. William passed the great, brooding building later in the day, for once not thinking of his Sunday sermon when, in sober glory, preceded by the beadle bearing a Bible before him, he ascended twice on each Sabbath to preach. Nor was he thinking, as he sometimes made himself do, of the needs of the smoothly gloved, well-shod, grandly clad congregation rustling and stirring below him at intervals in the polished pews. William was for once still face to face with himself; knowing the difference in his everyday talk, his daily manner, from that of other folk, and wondering how to overcome the barrier, as he must, if, when ... For all his desires had, he knew, hitherto been granted. He could, genuinely and from his heart, thank God that the way his mother had predicted for him had been the way he himself would have chosen. Had anyone suggested to William Heatherton that he might have made an actor, that his liking for the eloquent gesture, the telling apt phrase, would have graced the boards of a playhouse as well as it did the pulpit, he would have been horrified and pained. But it was true that that particular day, as if for the first time, he sensed the reality of the barrier between himself and the rest of humankind, and his heart cried out to be acknowledged among them, as one of them.

He could not now conceive how it was that he could have seen the girl pass by, and not have followed instantly, making some excuse to the assembled elders. In his later recollection it was always, when he first saw her, afternoon; the light still steady and pale, with a chill wind blowing and the familiar uphill street, with its Regency-built houses and spaced carriage-blocks of pallid stone, so that the gentry might alight without spoiling their clothing if it should rain, looking placidly as usual. Yet nothing was the same; and by the time William found himself striding uphill in the direction she had already gone it was surely evening, for the shadows were long by then and the light dark golden. It would almost, he knew, be time to shut the great gates which permitted access to the Cathedral by way of the burying-ground.

So he had hurried. It was as if he knew that God would guide his steps in the way that he must take. And on that way he had seen the bright asters lying on a new-dug grave. He could not mistake the asters that she had carried. A sense of triumph filled him, and then he remembered that he was in presence of the newly dead; he removed his hat. He stood there, the wind ruffling his short-cut, curly brown hair, with the architraves and pedestals of pretentious tombs a background for his great height and sober dark clothing. The respectable of the city were buried here, the recent well-to-do; it was a sign of worldly prosperity for one family to outvy the other with the solid addition of carved pillars, Ionic columns, swags of acanthus on small stone urns. The site of the Necropolis was on a hill which sloped to allow the heights of the varied monuments to be displayed to full measure. William looked at none of them; he looked at the flowers. There was nothing to show to whom the grave belonged, nothing.

"A cauld day, minister, for the time o' year."

It was the groundsman, Tom Inches, a veteran of the Napoleonic wars. William had not heard him approach from among the petrified forest of new tombs. He turned, courteously.

"Good-day to you." It was his customary greeting; old Tom, who knew all the clergy in the precincts of the Cathedral, called all of them minister, and watched them come and go. A stubbornness in William made him forbear to ask the identity of the occupant of the new grave. But Tom told him without asking, as the other had hoped he might.

"Ye kenned the Frenchy, minister?"

The red-rimmed eyes squinted up at the big young incumbent of Gowanmount. They said he could fairly preach, that one. The impersonal gaze William turned on the old man now was bland.

"There are not many of that nation buried here," he said coldly. He had an objection to lying outright, and a greater to being questioned as to his reasons; yet without one or other happening it was likely he would get nothing more out of old Tom. He waited, not yet replacing his tall hat.

Fortunately Tom talked. He had a morbid interest in the Frenchman, whose coffin he had seen lowered lately into the ground there; it would be twenty-odd years, maybe, since he last saw a French corpse. They had lain about a Belgian wood like leaves, very young enemies, Marie Louises, he remembered, they'd been known as, after the faithless Empress in those days. Well—"They say *he* hadna been in the Infirmary more nor twa-three hours afore he died," he told William now. "A pity of the young lady, his dochter. A vessel it was, burst they say, in the brain."

"He had no other relatives? Was no one else present at the obsequies?" William felt his customary, professional interest reviving. It was in order, by now, to enquire about the friendless girl. It might be that if he could give help——

"Mr. Urquhart, the builder, came. They say the Frenchman worked for him. He'd pay for the lair, like enough; and saw the puir body laid away himsel'. It's a pity of a young man." All those young men, the Frenchies, at Waterloo, had been the last squeezings of an exhausted nation who'd lost all its eldest sons in the Emperor's earlier wars. Complexions like girls, they'd had, he remembered, the Marie Louises, and the little stout man in the grey coat——

"Mr. Hector Urquhart?"

A small vertical crease, indicative of inward triumph, had made itself evident in the well-nourished flesh between William Heatherton's brows. Dislike suddenly rushed into Tom's awareness. Smug, he was, that big Gowanmount minister, doubtless reared from a bairn to nothing but the best, never knowing discomfort, bitter cold, the sight of blood, while *he*—Ay, they all knew one another, the genteel prosperous of the city; lawyers, doctors, builders! Mr. Urquhart had had a street named after him, this last year; they said he built fine, lasting houses. There wasn't much he, Tom, didn't hear one way and the other. "Ay, the builder," he said shortly. The minister would know everybody who was worth knowing. But he hadn't known the Frenchy.

William, unexpectedly, searched in his pocket and gave the old man a sixpence. Tom looked at it for an instant, then put it carefully away. "If there's a stone, it'll be Mr. Urquhart puts it up, in a wee while," he added. "But it'll not be one of *yon,*" nodding towards the towers of baroque silence on the nearby hill.

"When was the funeral?"

Tom gave value for his sixpence. "Tuesday, it would be; ay, Tuesday. I mind it, for I had another the selfsame day. They come and they go, then none for a while. It's no' this time o' year's the worst, but mid-February; that month goes for auld bones, with the cauld and the damp. But *he* wasna auld."

But the big minister had put on his lum hat and prepared to turn away, and was no longer listening. Once he had gone Tom spat on his sixpence, more from habit than conviction; then peered after the tall figure as it went on down the path, turning in at last to the Infirmary gate. "Now what's he after?" said Tom aloud, and wandered back to his graves.

IV

By the time William Heatherton made his way down the steep Infirmary path he was for some instants cured of his madness; a Frenchwoman, as the young girl must be, would as like as not be a Papist. That rendered her entirely unsuitable for any ambitions he himself might have entertained regarding her. He was now, he told himself, merely pursuing the path of duty and charity, for a forlorn fellow-creature who might well be in need of aid such as he could give. Hector Urquhart himself—William knew of him, everyone in the city did, though Urquhart was not a member of Gowanmount congregation, having for some time now been an elder of Savill's —Urquhart was well-found enough to help the girl financially if her father had indeed been in his employ. William, on his way into the Infirmary entrance, recalled briefly the kenspeckle, tormented face of the Highland builder, looking always as though a fire burned in him from within; his marriage, they said, to a mean and vulgar woman, had been made for money. William recalled again the thick-browed, lean, strong-boned face, resembling that of Urquhart's own sister who was a well-known schoolmistress catering for the education of young ladies in a thorough and exclusive manner. A talented family! The fact disposed of itself neatly at the back of William's professional mind, as being likely to be of use maybe in the future. The errand on which he had initially come here might he helped by the Urquhart connection, or might merely help William himself to become acquainted with the Urquharts. The proper social contacts were never wasted.

The smell of the Infirmary, a mixture compounded of ether and stale pus, recalled him to where he was. The porter, seated in the hall, rose to his feet as William appeared. He was, William noted, a trifle inebriated. As most men would have done, William did not condemn the man; how could he himself stand, day after day, the sickening smell of festering wounds and incontinence, the nearness of ward-fever, with the whisky always used for amputations freely available? No, one had no right to judge such a man. "Rather," thought William, "I must judge myself." He had, he knew well, little taste for visiting and sitting by the wretches in the wards, turning their verminous heads from side to side as they were and moaning; and the helpers, too, were often drunk, and William could remember his own disgust, on one occasion, when the skirl of bagpipes sounded in the wards where men lay dying, and the whisky-sodden nurses leaped about the beds in a reel while a piper played. One came into a hospital only to die...

"Can I direct ye, sir?"

The porter did his best not to stare at young Mr. Heatherton. He wasn't, as everyone knew, given to coming here often; he'd be after something, as like as not; what was it? Coldly, William asked for details about Tuesday's funeral, the burying of the Frenchman.

"A foreigner." He was surprised at the curtness of his own voice and manner. Why had he demeaned himself by coming here, by allowing the brief episode so to weigh with him? The air was foetid, he himself might catch some infection to pass on to his parishioners ... once the required information had been obtained, he could be quit of the business, once and for all. He had never in his whole life met, or encountered anyone who had met, a Papist. The word itself still, with the upbringing he had had, caused a certain adverse stirring in the marrow of William's bones. The unwholesome business could be dispensed with as soon as the porter put his thick finger on the right entry in the book ... if he could still read. Idolatry, the undue mention of Mary, the Gowanmount niches again filled with images instead of, as now, healthily empty...

"Here ye are, sir. Vanneau. Émile-Jean Vanneau, profession architect, age forty-two."

"Religion?"

William's heartbeats had stopped. In a moment verification would come, and he could go back again to his life as it had been. A mercy no one had observed him making a fool of himself! But he had been careful, he knew, to cover his tracks if——

"It doesna say anything here, minister. But it was Dr. Brodie himsel' took the service, and nae priest."

William's expression revealed nothing; his mind was still cold. He knew Dr. Brodie, the Infirmary chaplain, well enough to go and ask, make further enquiries; as well be certain. But so far any facts uncovered had not precluded a further, and separate pursuit...

"Raining, it was," said the porter unexpectedly. "They brocht the French gentleman in as he'd fallen, him having been ta'en ill in the street. The young lady, his dochter, was with him. She came in and sat over there"—he jerked his head—"a long while, till word came that he'd died."

"And then? She would be greatly upset, I have no doubt."

The bloodshot eyes glanced up at him. "Quiet, she sat; and quiet she left, with such folk as came. The lung-rot, the Frenchman had, they say, and it's the haemorrhage that finishes them. He wasna auld."

Tom Inches, the gravetender up on the hill, had said something the same, William remembered. He saw, clearly as though he had been present, the silent figure of the girl in her quiet dress and shawl, seated there alone across the floor's space waiting for news of her father's death. The flowers, later, had been for his grave. Few folk here concerned themselves with flowers, but most wore mourning. *She* hadn't purchased any, save perhaps for the black gloves. Foreigners, William already knew, felt differently about such things; hadn't there been a white dule in France for widows at one time? The Queen of Scots——

Comparison overrode William's turning aside into history; only, there was another aspect of it he should, he realised, have thought of. What had become of the Huguenots after the Edict of Nantes a century and more back? Some, he knew, had come to the south, as weavers. Perhaps—but it was useless to speculate. That it was his clear duty to find out what a French, probably Protestant architect had been doing up here working for Hector Urquhart became evident to William. He must satisfy himself that the young Frenchwoman had, at least, succour in what must be an alien city. He heard himself thanking the porter, asking a few routine questions about the welfare of the other sick; then strode out of the building with the facts in his mind that he needed to know. God's finger had guided him in this matter. The accruing knowledge that other help, feminine help in fact, would be inevitable was not yet clear to William, nor as yet had he thought of almost the only source of such help at present; James's wife, his delectable sister-in-law Alicia, of the fine education, the ringlets, silks, laughter, blue eyes and lace.

V

WILLIAM'S WAS A CAUTIOUS MIND, ACCUSTOMED TO MULLING over each point of argument with itself; accordingly, the notion of Alicia as an aide, perhaps an emissary, had not yet crystallised by the time Sunday itself dawned. All that day, as usual, his duties took up William's entire energies of body and mind. Ascending his pulpit in the morning, he could be conscious of nothing but the sermon and prayers he had conscientiously prepared, and of his responsibility in making these direct messages from God manifest to his congregation. His text on that particular occasion was, he remembered, "The fear of the Lord is the beginning of wisdom." William preached with inspiration, as Elijah might have done, or Amos or Moses. He did not underrate himself in allying his own mind with those notable leaders of men, those recorded as directly inspired of God. The prosperous congregation rustled receptively; in the centrally placed pew, George Howie and his wife and young family sat. Mrs. Howie had on yet another new bonnet; William was less aware of this than of the keen, alert gaze of her close-set grey eyes. Margaret Howie, he knew, was attending every word of his sermon; the notion came to William that he would have liked, afterwards, to ask her opinion on certain points as they applied to everyday life; an intelligent woman! A handsome one also, he noticed even while he preached; the innate notion of the comfort of marriage, of the presence of a wife in the now empty manse pew, assailed him. He would not, such was his dedication to duty, permit himself yet to imagine a slim figure in a fringed shawl already seated there, dark eyes fixed on the ground in wifely submission. Only, after the day was over, late at night, William found himself unable to sleep. Was he still waiting for the Lord to send a sign?

In the morning he got up, donned stout country clothes and

took a walking-cane, and set out, as was not his wont, very early before his housekeeper rose to make his breakfast. He left word that he would need none, and left the city on foot while the streets were still empty, walking westwards.

He knew quite well where the Urquhart house was, and how to find it. The early sun, for it would be a fine day, still shone between the boughs of the apple-orchard included, by the Highland builder, in his late purchase of a farmhouse devoid of its surrounding grazing-land. The blossom was not yet over and its rosy mist, and the discreet murmuring of bees, greeted William as he walked by, unwilling to stop. Why he had come, what he would say if accosted or questioned, he had no real notion; such behaviour was irrational, he knew, not typical of him. He only knew that he had had to come here, that the message derived from his wrestlings with himself in the small hours had been to this effect, that he must come here, to this place, and reassure himself. If he were to meet Urquhart, who knew him by sight, he must trust to the Lord to put words in his mouth. There was after all no reason why a healthy man should not choose to go for a walk in early morning.

There was however no carriage outside the gate, or in the open byre, which served for coach-house as there was no other. The erstwhile farmhouse was long, low, and whitewashed, kept in good repair, exuding an air of prosperity it would not have had in the days when the tenant-farmer lived here. Urquhart himself, evidently, had already left for his office in the city. William accordingly let himself linger by the hawthorn hedge, sheltered by the blossoming apple trees; and saw the girl again.

This second glimpse of her had the quality of a dream, a miracle; and convinced William that his journey hither was indeed sponsored by God, that God had now placed the girl again before him. She was in fact on what must be the upper floor of the low-set farmhouse building, at a window above eye-level. She lay on some kind of low couch or chaise-longue, so that he might watch her as one does a framed portrait. Like a portrait, also, at first she did not move; today, when she wore no bonnet, he had a better view of her dark hair, smoothed evenly down on either side of the sallow oval face. It was echoed by a black cord or ribbon she wore, its ends disappearing inside her dress. Her eyes were closed as if she slept. But she was dressed, and tidy; the silk shawl had slipped aside from one shoulder and in the blossom-filtered light, which gave her flesh a roseate quality, William could see the black cord and, clearly, the cleft between her breasts. These were small; in no way like that other's once seen naked. But his breath began to quicken, as it had done before, and he began to be assailed with an intense fear of discovery. He knew now, certainly, that this young girl aroused a bodily sensation in him that he had not permitted himself to acknowledge since the shameful day in the harlot's lodging, long ago. There had been dreams ... but now the fact that God had sent him here, permitting this further glimpse of the young Frenchwoman, opened the way to another fulfilment than that of wickedness. As if it had been dictated to him, William knew from that moment what he must do; he must have this woman in the eyes of God; he must make her his wife.

In that instant, as past and future came together, the silence was broken. He heard a voice, a child's, from somewhere in the house.

"Marie!" The young shrill cry was sharp, curious, questing; it came from inside the room and William could not see the speaker. "Mama says you must come down now; breakfast is almost over."

"I will come."

He had seen her dark eyes open languidly, noted the shallow, almost oblique quality of the way they were set in the ivory face. She had spoken less to the child who called than to herself, as if she made her own company. He watched while she rose, almost unwillingly, and pulled the shawl back over her shoulders, and went away. When she had gone there were only the white-pointed shutters, staring blankly out towards the orchard; he could not even see the chair, or sofa, where she had sat. He gave up the attempt, closed his eyes briefly, and remembered her voice. It had been low and pleasant, with a kind of overtone of bizarre attraction, unlike any of the women's voices he had ever heard; yet not quite foreign. She knew the language; and he had heard her speak, and knew her name. Marie. Marie.

The sun arched to its accustomed zenith as William made his way back towards town, to the reproaches of his housekeeper. He hardly heard them. He had downed also irrelevant quotations from *King Lear—her voice was ever low and soft, an excellent thing in woman*—and from the Song of Solomon, rashly included among the books of Holy Writ. One must be practical, and proceed without delay; he knew now what the next step must be. On the way home the notion of consulting James's wife Alicia occurred to him for the first time. Alicia knew everybody. It would not have been politic—William's heightened mood hesitated over the unromantic word—to approach his sister-in-law before he himself had made investigation and had finally made up his mind. It was made up now, irrevocably. He had not undertaken a wasted journey. It would have been folly to act in such a way unless God, the eternal and watchful God, had sent him a sign.

VI

Hector Urquhart, by now the foremost builder in the city, had first made the acquaintance of Marie's father, Émile-Jean Vanneau, fourteen years previously outside in a tavern in the Loire valley. Seated on a bench out of the full sun, both young men had been drinking water and watching the small tributary called the river Cher drift by to join the Loire. Beyond the scatter of autumn leaves borne past on the smooth, dark surface lay the Château de Chenonceaux, white and graceful as a reclining woman. Shortly, in the nature of things, the two men fell to talking, Émile-Jean using his halting English once he ascertained that the other was a Scot. They had both, they discovered, travelled far to stare at the château, built by a King of France for his beloved mistress, for the same reason; both were in the building-trade, and wanted to design arches and towers which seemed as though they sprang naturally from the ground of Renaissance France.

Vanneau was in fact a chartered architect; he had had a good education. Urquhart on the other hand had risen by his own effort from misery, half-starvation and near illiteracy to the position he now occupied, that of junior manager in his future father-in-law's firm. His handsome, dark-browed face brooded over the prospect of the near future; this trip, paid for by old Shawfield with intent that his young successor might gain experience, would constitute Hector Urquhart's last days of freedom. Thereafter he would be shackled—it was the price he must pay—to Shawfield's spoilt, unattractive only daughter and heiress, Sophia. The handsome size of Sophia's dowry had not brought in handsomer offers, and since the day she had set eyes on himself, no doubt at a site they were laying ready for a new great house Shawfield's were under contract to build for a pulp-mill owner, nearby the river . . .

He had been working late on the day in question. The

foreman was ill, and Hector Urquhart knew, with the determination that was in him to take advantage of every hour, every chance he had to make money for those sick at home, that he must seize this opportunity, tired as he was after the accustomed work of the day. He had mixed and smoothed the concrete carefully, thinking at the back of his mind that, with Shawfield pleased with him, it might even mean more food for the little sister who was slowly dying of tuberculosis: some delicacies, calf's-foot jelly perhaps; although Flora herself had said that nothing now could save the child. There had been that grim time when there was nothing to eat at all, and they had made do with garbage and raw oatmeal, the latter brought down from the north with them in their bundles. Flora ...

He had been thinking of Flora, the eldest sister, and how her cleverness must find an outlet, must be given a chance; it mattered less about himself, he was meantime their breadwinner, and if he had, on one of their walks together on a Sunday out to the bens, seen a comely Highland girl working in the dairy where they had stopped for a drink of milk, and exchanged a few words with her in the Gaelic, it did not matter. Those of his blood and race knew well that years might pass before marriage could take place, even where there was abiding love. Sheep grazed over the old beloved glens in the north whence they had come. They who remained of the clans had been driven out, and Mary McAlpine of the hill-girt dairy would understand such things, and would wait if he asked her to, but he had not yet done so. But he would see her next Sunday, when he and Flora took a walk out there again ...

A small dog scampered at that moment over the mortar, which Hector had been assiduously smoothing; it left footprints, and the young Highlander cursed it under his breath, and made a threatening gesture with his free wrist. He would not in fact have hurt the beast. It was a black poodle, its combed hair tied up with ribbons and its shaven feet grey with the wet concrete into which it had just run; it stood back yapping at him. Then came a girl's voice.

"Minny, you naughty, naughty little dog, what a mess you have made of yourself, and how am I——" The voice stopped, and young Urquhart continued, grim-lipped, to repair the harm the dog had done to his concrete. The damage maybe hadn't gone too deep; but for the smooth, thorough job he'd made of it to be doubtful in the event angered him. Best say nothing, however; the young woman had an over-genteel Lowland accent, which grated on Hector's ears. Mary MacAlpine's soft lilt would heal them, tomorrow. They'd set out, he and Flora, early; when the sun had just risen.

A parasol prodded him between the shoulder-blades. "What a rude, uncouth creature you are! You make a horrid sight of my dog, and never a word of apology—I'll tell Papa."

Hector looked round, and beheld an overdressed young woman, in a green braid-timmed walking-dress which did not accord with her florid complexion; she had frizzed yellow hair, and bunched satin ribbons in her Dresden hat. She was squawking, still, about her dog. Hector had never to his knowledge seen her before, and did not know or care who she might be. "Keep the beast on its leash, and it will go to other places than into drying concrete," he told the girl evenly. He returned to his careful smoothing, and heard her stamp her foot.

"You shall listen to me—you *shall*! There," and she took her parasol and jabbed with it and viciously stirred the concrete, making a chaotic porridge of it, half dry, half wet. He would have to do it all again. Rising to his feet, Hector towered over the girl with his eyes blazing; he let fly at her in icy, accurate Gaelic.

"May the devil take you for a dirty, mean bitch, and get your ugly face out of my way; what do you know of work, or folk who need money to live on?" What he said could not be understood by her, but his expression held deep rage and contempt; this he knew, but what he could not himself know, being a modest young man, was that the very sight of him, with his lean tall wiry frame and blazing dark eyes, had some time since lit a fire not readily quenched in Sophia Shawfield, his employer's daughter. She tossed her frizzed yellow head now, and told him who she was.

"And so you see," she finished triumphantly, "it is of no use to be insolent, and to forget your manners; for if I say a single word to him about what a rude fellow you are, my Papa will find another man to mix his—concrete." She uttered the final noun with an overtone of disdain, as if no lady should know about it; and minced away with her lips still drawn back over bad teeth, which no amount of care while Miss Sophia was at her school for young ladies, and later, had managed to save. It was not often Sophia showed them; she had been taught to smile with closed lips, which it was thought might perhaps also lend her foxy features some mystery; but just now she had been too angry with the young Highlander, whom she had often furtively watched, going here and there about Papa's business or working in his yards. How handsome he was, or rather would be if he were dressed as a gentleman, in a well-fitting coat and brocade waistcoat, and peg-top trousers! None of the young men she knew—and Sophia, whose mama did her best, had been introduced to a great many without avail—could hold a candle to Hector Urquhart, if only he had suitable clothes.

A social invitation to Shawfield's house followed rapidly. Hector was surprised, not that it was unusual in the north for employees and their employers to mingle in such ways, but he himself was not aware of having even been noticed by Shawfield. The peppery old man, however, had noted Hector already, without any prompting from Sophia; the honesty and reliability of the young Highlander had been made manifest in several unintended ways. Now, with his puss—old Shawfield lacked sons, and must needs make a show of affection for the only child he had, though he was under no illusions—his puss beguiling him, making play upon his knee, after dinner, for him to invite the young man to drink tea one day soon, and procure him a suit of clothes—Shawfield demurred. "They are as proud as the devil, these Highlanders, my dear; they will take money for their work, but they earn it first. Young Urquhart would not accept other clothes than he has on, until he may buy them for himself. And I understand he has a sick sister to keep, or is it a sick mother?"

"Then you must promote him, Papa, so as to enable him to make more money. He is very clever, I am sure; and Shanklin is ill, and you need somebody, do you not, to see to the men?"

"Ye ken overmuch," growled Shawfield, and caught a meaningful glance from his wife, at the far end of the laden mahogany table. That lady had been intending to complain to her spouse concerning his recent improper use of words, mention of the devil, no less, before their virgin daughter, who should not even hear of such things until after she was married. But the difficulty of marrying Sophia at all was becoming manifest to her anxious parent, as season followed season. This Highlander ... what was he like? There was after all no disgrace in having risen from being a mere labourer, provided always that one were not Irish.

The tea-drinking at Shawfield's took place, followed by a subsequent musical evening when Miss Sophia played the pianoforte, and thirdly a dinner. By now Hector was appointed foreman, for Shanklin had conveniently chosen to die of a phlegm. The young Highlander was not lacking in astuteness, and he was early aware that both Miss Sophia and her mamma, in their separate ways, were making a bid for him as husband and son-in-law. He had been silent on the walks with Flora for the last few Sundays; and for some reason had not again chosen the path to the bens. He knew well enough that Sophia would be a *cailleach*, like her mother: there would be no pleasure in his marriage. But there were reasons enough, God knew, for putting his own happiness second to that of others. And when old Shawfield sent for him at last one day to the office, Hector knew very well that the interview would not be about bricks and mortar. He did not go straight there, or in haste; he thought over the matter coldly, for the fourth or fifth time. But perhaps he had known the final answer from the day he had not gone back again to the assignation with Mary MacAlpine at the dairy in the hills. He knew he must sacrifice himself, if only for his remaining sister's sake.

He had walked about the work-yards for a while before going to old Shawfield, as he was in any case early. Besides, he needed solitude to look upon what the rest of his life would be. There was solace in work, in the yards; the men toiling at their tasks, who all knew Hector by sight and name, as he knew them, touched their caps as he went by. This aroused a measure of pride in him; it wouldn't have happened, he knew, five or six years back, when the thin unknown lad from the north who was himself had come among them, glad of the hard ill-paid task for money to buy food. Food had been short, indeed, on that long walk south from the narrow glen where he had been born; there had been seven of them then, his father, already ailing, and his gallant mother who walked with them, and kept them cheerful with songs and prayers, and had baked bannocks of oatmeal to last till they got to a town. There was no money; they had had to sell the horse and cart saved from the wreck of the tenant-farm, with its memory of bitter winters, meagre harvests and a landlord who grudged them the room they kept from the sheep. Thirty miles south they had walked each day, more not being possible for two of the bairns were already sick; he, Hector, had carried one, and his father the other; they buried one boy on the way. The bannocks had lasted out, only just, till they got to the city; then it was a case of finding work, work to pay for the next meal. By then the mother was ill with a lump in her breast, but said nothing; she went to work in a tannery, where the stink of the hides was sickening. Her husband, Hector's father, did not last out the year; his heart lay back in the glens, on his lost farm. None of them liked the city, with its squalid shared lodging which was all they could find or afford, and the unwashed smell of humanity close-packed, and never a green place or a tree to be seen. That was maybe why he and Flora took to their walking of a Sunday, out of the city to see the shapes of the bens in the distance, and breathe the clean air, before it was time to walk back.

Meantime however Hector had found work, here and there, then at last in Shawfield's yards as errand-boy. Soon old Shawfield's foreman noticed the willing, lean, barefoot lad, and recommended him to a better job which would buy him shoes; honest men were hard to come by. But Hector had resolved, before thinking of shoes, to put his sister Flora again to school; she had a fine brain, and the dominie who had schooled them all in the Highlands had wept on parting with her, and would have kept her with him if he could have found enough food to fill his own mouth. Flora worked meantime in the city as a laundry-maid, and the work was hard and the company rough; it angered Hector to see her fineness wasted. He had a fierce resolve that, as soon as he might, he would make amends to Flora for a situation which had not been of her choosing; he starved himself in order to save money for her and for their mother, who by now was dying. After she died, and the rest were dead, all of phthisis, except the last dying girl, Hector was able to put Flora again to part-time school. She laughed, seeing the difference in age between herself—she was a tall creature—and the younger pupils, whom she soon outstripped. She owed it to Hector to work hard, and she did; that the crowded, sordid life of the city had taken its toll of all the rest was in itself sufficient to draw her close to her brother. There were few thoughts they did not share; on the Sunday walks, with a piece of bread and kebbuck between them, they would stride swiftly and far out of the city ways, and discourse on many things; Flora by now was Hector's teacher. She was already proficient in French, and could quote great tracts of Shakespeare, and knew some Italian. "But I love best the old Romans, with their succinct tongue, and their brave deeds; what folk they were!" she would say. Another whom she loved, and often quoted, was the still-censored Robert Burns, whom Flora said would be reckoned as great a man as the Avon Bard, when enough time had passed. "It always takes time after a great man is dead, and then they shed off the things that do not matter, and see the heart beneath; maybe 'twill be the same with yourself, Hector." She turned to watch her brother with the wise, all-seeing hazel eyes which were her only beauty; otherwise she was a lean, raw-boned lass, with features too harsh for a woman. She turned them now towards the rare sun which had risen, and said, "Soon, I'll maybe get a post as governess myself, and take some of the load from your shoulders." She still spoke with the pure, gentle accent of the glens, different in intonation and effect from either the broad or mincing Lowland; this was her chief attraction. It would be an asset, Hector knew, in any application for a post, and her teacher would recommend her; but would Flora be happy as a governess?

"Some bairns can be young devils," he grunted; he was becoming increasingly taciturn. He heard Flora laugh.

"We all have our devils; you, I know, have yours. Some day perhaps I'll have my own little school. That's what I should like, and maybe when things are eased I'll begin setting aside for it. But it'll take time."

He remembered, however; and knew that the thing old

Shawfield would have to say to him today would help, sooner than any of them could have expected, to make Flora's dream come true. Otherwise he might not have entertained it for a moment, now that the mother was gone. Sophia Shawfield, with her blackened teeth and rancid armpit-odour! A shrill-voiced harpy of a wife, instead of the gentle Highland girl he could still remember, with her eyes grey as northern lochs and her hair black and lustrous, not tortured as Sophia wore hers!

But he would never see Mary MacAlpine again. His youngest sister's fleshless skeleton had been lowered into the grave that very summer, and his mother's gnawing pain had latterly needed a doctor to her, and drugs, so that there were debts to be met now she was at last dead. He would meet them ... by means of Sophia. He'd sell himself, but dearly enough.

So he turned his steps and went in outward obedience upstairs to where the master-builder waited to have a word with him. The fact that it was no ordinary interview was made manifest at the start; Richard Shawfield invited Hector to partake of a dram. Both men then, the old and the young, sat drinking their whisky while Shawfield put his proposition in terms that could not be misunderstood.

"Ye ken well, Hector man, what I think of your work; ye have a great capacity for't, and I would trust you as I would myself. Ye ken also that I have no male heir."

The hard, pebble-coloured eyes of the old man had met Urquhart's dark ones. "You are as well aware as I that Sophy's a young bitch," Sophy's father said squarely. "The man who marries her will need a firm hand and a fearless tongue. And she's ta'en a fancy to you, my lad: she's thought of nothing else for a twelvemonth. Will ye take Sophy, and the inheritance of the business with her? I may live five years, maybe more. I wouldna like to think of all I've builded"—he smiled at the pun, the eyes remaining hard—"of all of that going piece by piece to some rival who scamps his duty: you yourself can take the reins from me, and hold them steady. Will you think o't, lad?"

In this way Hector Urquhart had become betrothed to Sophia Shawfield, and the wedding was to be next month. Looking down now into the dark evenly-flowing waters of the alien river, he comforted himself with one thing; he had already found a tall house in a respectable part of the city, where Flora, with a shade of initial help, could start her own school.

Émile-Jean Vanneau's tale was different; nor at that time did he tell it. It was not, in fact, their common bond of misfortune so much as their shared interest in architecture that united the two men, and extracted a promise from Urquhart that if he ever could employ the Frenchman, he would do so. But the longevity of old Shawfield, and other reasons, made it a dozen or more years before Vanneau was sent for by Urquhart, though they had meantime corresponded. By that time Vanneau was consumptive also, and had not long to live.

VII

William chose to call upon his sister-in-law Alicia in the late forenoon, when he knew James would not be at home. Close as the ties had always been between himself and his elder brother, William felt, for reasons which he could hardly make clear even in his own mind, that the matter had best be broached to James by his wife. In other words, if he, William, intended to make a fool of himself it was as well if his brother were not present. William had not the humour to take this view of the question or of himself; he waited, having handed his tall hat and cane in the hallway to the prettily befrilled, capped maidservant, in Alicia's drawing-room in a grave state of mind, not taking in the furbelows of which he knew his parents disapproved; the ornate, inlaid furniture, already somewhat more solid than its Regency forebears in other drawing-rooms; the gilt mirror from Madrid, and a pair of coloured plaster matadors James had brought to please his wife, and which stood facing one another in belligerent anticipation atop the china-cabinet. Inside this was displayed a superb Rockingham dinner-service, enough to make old Jean say crossly to Nathan, last time they had visited here, "What's the use o' a set o' dishes folk canna eat their dinner off? Alicia'll never daur use that fine stuff for fear the servants break it." And, indeed, this and other signs of her elder son's growing prosperity made Jean almost angry, knowing as she did that money should be put by, not used for outward show. But Alicia, very sweetly, had herself explained to the old woman that James must be able to bring home rich clients, and impress them with the fact that he also was doing well. "He's that," Jean admitted grudgingly.

William stationed himself now near by the window, where beyond the velvet drapes—the colour was a pallid vegetable green, so unusual a choice that none of the elder Heathertons would admit it was pleasant, and set off the furniture and the gold-and-white Rockingham, and the elegant chairs upholstered in striped satin—beyond, William could watch the shipyards and the constant coming and going of the ferries. James Heatherton loved the river, and as soon as his fortunes were secure had moved himself and his wife and young family out from the centre of the city, where they had first set up house, to this place, still unusual as a residential choice. But James nowadays could step beyond his own front door, and square green lawn, into a world that was home beyond home, with the constant hum of great ships' engines and knocking of hammers against rivets and anvils; a world of sound, so that his practised ear could tell without seeing what the men were at, and if it went well. For William the preacher, born into such a world but no longer of it, the faint unwearying hum of the shipyards meant nothing, except a lack of quietness and a variety in the changing skyline, as a load was lowered to or hoisted from a wharf, or a ship came in, many still under sail, for it was unsafe to venture farther than the Irish coast under steam. William stared, but as usual saw into his own mind rather than outwardly. He was amazed at his own tenacity in coming here, in persisting so far; already, the walk he had made into the country lately seemed like madness. But he had done it, and had been rewarded by a sign from the Almighty; how could he now turn back?

"It is like the certainty vouchsafed to Gideon," he told himself, again unaware of any levity concerning his own affairs; and before he had bethought himself of a sermon on this head, Alicia Heatherton came in, still wearing her walking-bonnet and veil. She flung the latter back to receive William's formal kiss, and revealed a face bright with beauty and inherent sweetness. The formation of the bones alone would have ravished a sculptor, with the almost Oriental slant of the large blue eyes with their butterfly-brows, and the mobility of the mouth below high-set cheeks. Alicia's beauty would not fade with age. At this time she was verging on thirty; she had been married to James Heatherton now for seven years.

"But what a pleasure to see you, William, and will you not bide for the meal with us? James will like to talk with you after so long a time." She kept hold of William's hand in her own small, elegant one, and led him to a chair: all her actions were designed to make him feel that she liked him better than in fact she did, but Alicia could not have borne, even to herself, the notion that any flesh and blood of James's could be alien to her. All the same, she admitted, William was growing increasingly self-satisfied; the way he sat now on the edge of her striped chair, staring at the wall, was unnecessarily pompous. "I thought you would have been on parish-business all of the week," she said very gently. "It is good of you to spare the time to call here, William."

He had already refused to stay for the meal. "I have come," he said weightily, "on a matter which concerns us, the family; I—I confess I do not know how to proceed." His frown deepened, and Alicia raised a hand to her slight bosom; what new thing was about to be announced? Had something perhaps gone wrong with the old couple, Nathan and Jean, some way down the river as they were, that William needed help from her? Alicia knew that if so, she would respond gladly; she had tried, tactfully and long, to win the difficult love of her mother-in-law; she already had Nathan Heatherton's. Old Jean respected her now, she knew, as the mother of James's sons. "But that is not the same as love," Alicia told herself, and sighed a little; she would have liked nothing between them all but approval, warmth, and love, and now here was William, the unlovable . . . yet was he? What right had she, or anyone, to say so? Yet he had always seemed to her cold, alert chiefly for himself and his own preferment; with none of the shy yet dignified warmth of James, that she herself knew more about than anyone. Refreshing her spirit with the knowledge of her husband's undoubted love for herself, Alicia smiled, and folded her white hands in her mousseline lap, and said clearly,

"How can I help you, William, in a way James cannot? You flatter me by coming to me and not to him. But I will do what I can; tell me what troubles you." For something was indeed troubling the big, formal man; his very shoulders sagged with it.

"I . . . have . . . seen the lady whom I would wish to marry," said William slowly. "But I do not know how such things"—he spoke with difficulty—"are set on foot, apart from matters in my own family; you and my brother were of long acquaintance first, and my father and mother also. Whereas I——" He gave, for him, a small helpless gesture, an almost foreign outspreading of the hands. "I have only seen her at a distance," he continued. "I have never spoken to her. I—I wish to do so, but it should be accomplished without impropriety, I feel. If it were possible for you, as my brother's wife, to act in some introductory capacity between us, I—I should be grateful." He ended lamely, and the pale eyes dropped once more behind their concealing lids. Alicia, who had listened to his speech almost with incredulity, guarded her expression and her reply. This can't be Willie, she was telling herself; the chosen of Israel, the—Oh, but she must not mock at James's brother! She composed her features to a gravity matching William's own. It could happen; even to William, long despaired of as a ladies' man, evidently, it could happen. She herself had first become aware that she loved James, her lanky preoccupied cousin, to distraction on the occasion that she, fresh home from finishing-school, came upon the pair of them, her own elder brother David and James, grown men both, standing in a puddled burn with their breeches rolled up above their knees, like little boys, while they tried out a model of a narrow hull James had thought of that promised, now it was at last made full-scale, to be the fastest ship as yet on any ocean. Ah, but Willie still waited for her reply! She smiled, remembering how on that other day neither of the men had seen her standing there on the bank, with an east wind tugging at her skirts and hair. "Do you know the young lady's name, William?" she asked, hoping the query might not be out of place. Cupid's dart, hitting William Heatherton: and he hadn't even said the lady was young, now she thought of it.

"Her name is Mademoiselle Marie Vanneau. She is a Frenchwoman, a Protestant." William made the latter statement with conviction, going on the evidence he had uncovered in the matter. He went on to relate the circumstances of Marie's stay with the Urquhart family, following the death of her father. He was grateful, he remembered afterwards, to Alicia for not showing surprise that he should consider a Frenchwoman; after all, provided no religious difficulty were present, why not? And Marie spoke some English. He felt the colour mounting in his face as he thought of her name, and remembered the circumstances under which he had heard her speak; better not tell Alicia about the walk. But his cousin's mouth, usually so amiable, had already hardened a little.

"That Mrs. Urquhart—oh, yes, I know of her, William, though we are scarcely well acquainted, it was only through James's business-connections with Urquhart himself, and he's a splendid builder, they say—she is a common, mean kind of a woman, whom I should not care to visit were it not—were it not that you have asked. For you have done so, have you not, William? You would like me to visit Mrs. Urquhart, and find out how to make you known to this young French lady? If it can be done, it shall be; and if not, we must think of some other way." She must, of course, she was telling herself, consult James. Her husband would consider the matter quietly, in his level-headed, kindly way, and tell her what would be the best method of proceeding ... if one must. Suddenly, the picture of a Frenchwoman as daughter-in-law to Jean and Nathan presented itself clearly before Alicia Heatherton's vision. It'd be worse by far than when James, despite all opposition, said, long ago, that he'd marry *her* and no other. But for all that, or perhaps because of it, one must make very sure poor Willie hadn't made the wrong choice, and got himself entangled ... Alicia raised her head, regarding the solid, unalterable form of William on the chair's edge, and suddenly decided that for William to become entangled would be a very good thing; it might take the smugness out of him.

"I will do what I can," she said, extending her hand, "and will inform you immediately." Perhaps a polite invitation to Mrs. Urquhart, to drink tea, would be preferable to a visit, which might after all seem as if one lowered oneself a trifle, put oneself too readily in such a woman's way ...

William departed, gratified, and Alicia remained in much perturbation of mind. On second thoughts, perhaps she had best not say a word to James until she had somehow inspected the young Frenchwoman for herself: though that she could do about it if Willie remained firmly set on his notion was not yet clear. But the matter would clear itself; such things did in the end, and meantime she must go up to the schoolroom to see Evangeline and Maudie's paper theatre, which they had set up for themselves with the help of safe footlights devised by

James, who was so clever about toys and little carriages for the children; when they were tiny there had been one drawn about the field behind the house by a real goat, with a groom to tend him, that they rode in together.

Such things, coupled with her husband's arrival home and the loving greeting they always exchanged, helped to put the problem in perspective in Alicia's mind. That evening she compiled a short list, and sent out invitations for a tea-party. Among those invited was Urquhart's wife. No need, thought Alicia uncharitably, to fear that *she* would decline; nasty, vulgar, mean woman! Perhaps the matter would after all end there.

VIII

Sophia Urquhart, née Shawfield, had been secretly flattered less by Mrs. James Heatherton's tea-party—after all, Papa had made money years before James Heatherton, or the other shipbuilders, had been even heard of in these parts; and Sophia herself, as she said with a toss of the head to young Mademoiselle Vanneau, had had no expense spared in the matter of young ladies' schooling, or extra accomplishments, such as the pianoforte—than by the subsequent appearance of Mrs. Heatherton herself, by arrangement, for a carriage-drive, with picnic-hampers. That there might be a further reason for improving upon the acquaintance did not yet occur to Sophia. It was true that Mrs. James Heatherton—"whom I knew quite well by sight, my dear, but of course she is a little older than I am, so we did not come out as girls together, and I married young"—had hitherto done no more than pass the cool time of day if met, for instance, in a haberdasher's shop, or face to face in respective carriages. Now, the carriage which called for Sophia and her brood was sumptuous, very well sprung, with its varnish clean and sparkling in the spring sunshine, and the horses admirably groomed. Sophia was glad that she herself did the equipage justice, in her India shawl for which Papa had paid a great deal of money at the time, and her new velvet satin-trimmed bonnet. Looking at herself in the mirror prior to departure she couldn't but admit that she had grown a trifle high-coloured and stout of late, but a child every year soon ruined one's complexion and figure; and apart from *that*—Sophia bared regrettable teeth for moments, reflecting that Hector used her as a brood, no more, and hardly spoke a word to her he didn't have to. A woman could hardly be expected to retain her youthful looks and—the appearance at that moment of Marie Vanneau in the doorway, cool, slight, and clad unremarkably as usual, in her drab gown, eternal shawl and unfashionable dark bonnet, irritated Sophia. She had hesitated to include the French girl in today's social outing; it had only been the somewhat insistence of Mrs. Heatherton to know about *all* the inmates of Sophia's family who might come, and it had been cozened out of her, now she thought of it, that the young woman was staying in the house—well, Marie had to come; fortunately she didn't put herself forward on such occasions. As one in supposed mourning it wasn't proper. Sophia had, at the time of the French father's death, mentioned black clothing. "I daresay you can't afford it," she said bluntly, "but I have a gown, left over from when my own poor papa died; I wore it three years; it'd be on the short side for you, but maybe with braid," but the creature hadn't been as much as grateful.

"I thank you, madame, but my father disliked black. He said it made one resemble a crow." And the corners of mademoiselle's ordinarily grave mouth had shown a quirk, just a little, although it was only the day following the death. Foreigners had no feelings such as oneself might have entertained. And now, for today's outing——

"Is Richard ready?" Sophia asked now, fussing over the tying of her bonnet-ribbons. Marie Vanneau helped a good deal with the children, as well she might. The older ones were with their governess, or at school at Aunt Flora's, today, and might not come; and the babies, of course, were with the nurse. Richard, aged five, having lately recovered from measles, was the only one enabled to accompany the party; Mrs. Heatherton had also mentioned the brother of her husband's who was a minister, and would perhaps join them later in the day.

"Richard is waiting downstairs. He is afraid of being sick in carriages."

A gleam shone now in the dark eyes; was the girl being impertinent? In no way did she appear to look on herself as one's inferior, though the man Vanneau had after all been an employee, and that for a short time only, and with all the trouble and expense of the funeral, and the girl's having to stay on, one would have foreseen some gratitude for hospitality, but no, foreigners had none. And if Richard really felt sick ... How hard it was to arrange an outing, even a simple one, without laborious rearrangement! And Sophia's own inside felt queasy; she hoped it wasn't—well, another on the way. *He* wouldn't care, or discuss it; he wanted sons to carry on the business, and had told her so. Heartless, for all she'd raised him from what he'd been, before the marriage. And now——

"I do not think he will remember so much when we start, and he sees the lake. *C'est qu'il se sent maigre un peu, non plus,*" said Marie, and when the hallway was reached she took Richard by the hand; his large golden-brown eyes raised themselves adoringly. Neither of his parents could imagine from whence Richard inherited his appearance, which was that of a dark angel, or his talents, which were clearly musical. Sophia twittered about her own early progress at the pianoforte; but Richard's Aunt Flora, who now ran a flourishing school of her own in the city, said he should have lessons soon from a master, and that his voice was uncommonly sweet and true for so young a child. That Richard's father only grunted, and said a singing voice was useless to a master-builder, disturbed no one as yet. They walked down the path, where Alicia and her young daughters waited in the carriage, with the hamper, a white damask cloth, and a servant up behind.

"Richard will have to sit facing the horses," said Richard's mother. The adjustments were made, and the company bowled off down what soon turned from green hedges to a tree-lined road, increasingly rougher as one drew nearer the small loch where Alicia had proposed they all have luncheon. It lay beneath blue skies today, reflecting whitewashed farmhouses in the distance. "My brother-in-law," said Alicia, "will be waiting, I think; I said we would make our way by noon."

The carriage jolted on, redeemed from discomfort by its well-sprung underparts. Marie Vanneau sat with hands laid in her lap, withdrawn into her usual remoteness, saying nothing. It was almost the first leisure she had had to think of her father lately, and to realise that he was dead. It was less of a grief than everyone supposed it to be; Marie had not known Émile-Jean Vanneau well. People changed, she knew already, and circumstances also. There had been the shock on hearing of Papa's haemorrhage, in the street, and of visiting him in the hospital, and waiting there till his blanched, changed face told everyone he was dead; Marie was glad for him, because he had gone to Maman, as he desired to do. She could remember Maman clearly for herself, though that lady had died when Marie was only four years old; a fairytale personage, lying for ever on a chaise-longue, attended by Papa and others as if she were a queen, with the shawl Marie now wore flung over her delicate shoulders, or else spread to cover her tiny feet. Papa had wept when she died, Marie remembered. It was therefore no surprise to know that men could cry.

She herself had not wept, as was expected, at Papa's funeral. It had been strange and grim, in this grey northern country to which they had travelled together so recently, as soon as Papa received Mr. Urquhart's letter saying he at last needed an architect in his business. Papa had only worked for Mr. Urquhart two months when he began to spit blood, and said nothing. Marie had washed his linen, and had said nothing either. They both knew what was wrong. It was phthisis, of which Maman had long ago died. There was nothing one could do.

Afterwards, Mr. Urquhart had made Marie pack her belongings in the lodging where she and Papa had lived and had brought her home in his carriage to Mrs. Urquhart, who disliked her; Marie was aware of this from the first glance of Sophia's ferret's eyes, no words being needed. She had made herself as useful as she could with the Urquhart children, though their nurse resented interlopers and Marie herself, on the whole, disliked them all except for Richard, who seemed to have strayed into this unlikely flock from another herd, another breed. She and he made as much of one another's company as Sophia and the governess would let them; otherwise, there was enough given Marie to do to prevent either thinking or remembering. At nights, in the room she shared with two of the little girls, she would either sleep for sheer weariness, or else be kept awake with Flossie's toothaches, or Agnes's evil dreams. Marie did her best to comfort them; but had the feeling that they disliked her as much as she them, and by day withdrew into the tight, remote, knotted place where she would remain except when Hector Urquhart himself came home, for she liked the Highland builder and they sometimes spoke French together. "He does not know that I spent my youth in the company of *les anglaises,*" Marie told herself. That in itself had been due to the intervention of Papa.

"Here is my brother-in-law now," said Alicia Heatherton. A large young man in black broadcloth climbed into the carriage, temporarily out of the view of loch and hills; he was sweating slightly with the heat of the day. Marie was introduced, but hardly noticed William Heatherton; she was too much engrossed with her own thoughts and the luxury of being able to think them, and did not even perceive that his eyes were fixed in a constant pale, piercing stare on her face, her clasped hands, and the quality of her silken shawl.

Marie had been remembering Maman again, wondering if, when she and Papa met after death, they could be happy together. Maman had been an aristocrat and Papa had not; so much Marie had known even then, with Papa acting often like a servant, spooning broth tenderly into his wife's mouth when it was known she was ill, combing her long dark hair and washing the bloodstains from her lace-bordered handkerchiefs himself, as Marie was later to do for him. It was later still, when he himself was sick, that Papa had told Marie the whole story of that marriage. It seemed to take one back in time very far, into history.

She recalled it now. Maman's father had been an ageing Comte who had gone into exile at the time of the Revolution. Returning at last with Louis XVIII, he had sought out a young woman of thin though ancient blood, in the hope of providing himself with suitable heirs. After some years of marriage the only living child the young Comtesse bore killed her, and was a girl. Bored and disappointed, the old Comte abandoned further attempts to continue his name. He reopened his house in Paris, and settled down in attendance on the King and his successor, Charles X. In due course, when her convent education was complete, the young girl, his daughter Cathérine, joined him. He took little heed of her, and less heed of how she passed her days, failing to notice that she was gay, beautiful, and at that time still innocent. Gaiety and beauty were wasted at the sterile Court of Charles X: Madame Royale, now Dauphine and barren, made no alteration in the harsh narrow routine of her life, or that of her ladies. Occupied with the remembrance of her own tragic past, with memorial-masses for her murdered parents, Louis XVI and Marie-Antoinette, she failed to notice or to understand that there was a young girl near by such as she herself had once been, and that the child was bored.

It so happened that Émile-Jean Vanneau had just completed his apprenticeship to a company of Paris architects. His employers thought enough of his talents to entrust him with some minor alterations to the domestic quarters of the Tuileries. Near by were the palace-gardens. One day the young man, busied with his work, heard delicious laughter from behind one of the statues among the parterres.

"Vous me semblez trop sérieux, monsieur," said the most beautiful creature he had ever seen, whose elders dozed as always within the palace over prayers, embroidery and bézique.

Émile-Jean had been brought up by a father who had been a revolutionary in the days of the Commune. He was, therefore, indoctrinated with notions not in any case calculated to appease the Comte. The girl was, in addition, by now a little minx; nevertheless when it was discovered, at last, that she was pregnant by Émile-Jean she dared not tell her father. Instead, taking in a small tin trunk her jewellery, pin-money and a few belongings, which included a fringed silk shawl and a crucifix which had belonged to her mother, Cathérine entered a plain closed carriage which was waiting, by arrangement, outside the palace side-gate beyond the Dauphine's croquet-lawn. Inside the carriage was Émile-Jean Vanneau, and thereafter her life was his.

The Comte never forgave his daughter and never saw her again. The expected child miscarried and Cathérine was very ill; another child, a girl, was safely born two years later, by which time the young mother was already ailing. A humbly worded epistle from Émile-Jean—they were by then short of money—brought no word from the Comte; and the years that followed brought increasing hardship. Vanneau found work as a rule, but he was ostracised from any appointment patronised by Court circles. He stinted himself of food in order to buy delicacies for his invalid wife. She still ailed; the stale air of poor lodgings and the cramped conditions of poverty told on her as though she had been a flower left out of water. Her consumption made rapid progress. At her death, Émile-Jean wrote again to his father-in-law, by now living on his country estates. This time the letter was bitterly angry.

No direct word came; blue blood would not sully itself by acknowledging *canaille,* though Charles X had by now been forced out of France to make way for the July monarchy. But some weeks later the Comte himself died. In his will, he left instructions for the education of his grandchild out of a conditional legacy, the condition being that Vanneau must relinquish his daughter and neither write to her nor see her until her education should be complete. The school chosen was that same convent at which Cathérine herself had been educated. Its inmates had returned from exile in England after the Restoration. It catered for young ladies of a station in life superior to Marie's own. There was a clearly worded understanding that the Comte had left his grandchild no other money. Likewise Émile-Jean had access to none.

Marie remembered her father's hard young arms enfolding her, and his tears. "You are all I have of her," he said, "and now you too must go. Do not forget me."

Marie, also crying, had promised that she would not forget. But shortly an unwonted thing happened. Émile-Jean went out and got drunk. In the courage of drunkenness, he went to see the convent's Mother Superior. This lady, whose name when in the world had been one of the most-ancient in France, received him equably, in her enclosed parlour whose windows—Émile-Jean noticed them at once with his artist's eye—were lancet-shaped, with crossed plain inserted windows; the revolutionaries had destroyed the glory of stained glass that had formerly been. He glared at the makeshift panes, then at the Mother Superior.

"You are to take away my daughter. You are to turn her into a thing of prayers and crucifixes, of unmeaning gabble. I, her father, who am a freethinker, am against it. Has a father no rights to his opinion?"

The Superior inclined her head courteously. "Indeed, monsieur, the rights of a parent are paramount. We do not seek to dispute them."

"But you will bring up my daughter as alien to me."

"We will educate your daughter, monsieur, as befits a young lady. That was"—a slow smile came—"the expressed wish of her grandfather, the Comte, whose soul God rest. He said nothing specific concerning religious persuasion—no doubt the question did not cross his mind—and we would not seek to act in such a matter against your own expressed wishes. We would sooner pray for you and for your daughter that both your hearts may be led into the true love of God."

"You are an intelligent person." Émile-Jean glared, somewhat at a loss; he had expected resistance, and this undoubted aristo, with her pale, ageless face calm beneath the mediaeval coif, announced herself after all to be on his side in the matter, unless she was devious.

He fumbled with his hat, which lay between his knees; they sat facing one another across the customary partition of wood and glass. Émile-Jean heard the voice, and unshaken cultured voice, of a great lady. It still did not appear to disagree with him.

"M. Vanneau, we have in our care here several young English ladies who were given in our charge because their parents remember our years in England, where we had a school at the time of the Directory, after we were at least forced to flee from France. We made many friends in England, and it is a frequent happening that one of these young Protestant ladies is sent across to us, with the understanding that we do not instruct her in the Catholic Faith of intent to turn her by force from her own. We cannot but hope that by example and precept—and by love, monsieur, concerning which you do not perhaps know everything"—the nun smiled on—"the truth will make itself evident in a mind which is ready by grace to receive it. One cannot deny truth if it is made plain."

"But if the old—the old——" Vanneau groped for a word which would not, in the presence of this gracious personage, be offensive in describing his late father-in-law, and gave it up. "If *he* said nothing in the wording of the will regarding all of that, you can still take her, and make a lady of her, without making her a Catholic?"

"We will contrive it as I have described, monsieur; but you

must understand that the terms of the will—I have it from the Comte's own lawyers—state clearly that you must not see or write to your daughter again until her time with us here is complete."

As he left she made a small, compassionate movement of one hand. "It is hard choice, M. Vanneau, but you have made it clearly," she told him. "We will return you the little one as a young lady of education, manners and talents, of whom you may be proud as a companion. And you yourself, you have your work, have you not? Work is a great solace."

IX

Marie had been unhappy at the convent. She could remember, even now, seated in this smoothly travelling carriage in another country, the cold, contemptuous faces of certain of the young boarding aristocrats, who had discovered, by some means, that she had been admitted under a charitable, bequest and in any case lacked the requisite prefix *de*. Now, on this clear Scots late spring day, Marie felt the old sensation of fear and choking loneliness again rise, as it had done through almost all of that first year at school and many times since. How she had cried often then in the night, cried for Papa, for familiar things about her, and at the same time stuffed her small fists into her mouth lest Cécilie, or Marie-Ange, or Marguérite de Fleury-Molinet be awakened by any noise she might make; generally they had slumbered on in their curl-papers. The difference between herself and those young ladies, the difference between herself and everyone about her, had in the end caused a veil to drop between Marie and the present world, so that she could best live in one of her own, undisturbed. They had said she was dull at school; she revealed no talents.

There had been one, however, she remembered; drawing had in itself been an extra for which additional fees were charged, and the Comte's allowance had left no room for such. But Marie, a lonely, ostracised child even among the young English ladies—they had taken their cue early on from the French ones, and had treated Marie as befitted a person of no origin and mixed blood—Marie had lived on her own heart for almost ten years; the holidays were solitary, and none of the other boarders ever invited her to go home with them at such times. She had however learned English through her association in separate classes with the Protestant boarders, and one day, patronisingly, a young woman who was the sister of a landowner in Buckinghamshire, and would later become a duchess by marriage, offered Marie some stubs of pencils and charcoal, and the end of a drawing-pad.

"They would only go into the rubbish-box otherwise," the donor had informed her. "You may as well amuse yourself," and she had hurried off for her riding-lesson. Marie had tried, and the first thing she drew was the departing young lady, with the caught-up folds of her habit over her arm. She drew other things, then and later; the nuns in chapel, kneeling in a repetitive row, heads bent, like, Marie told herself fantastically, blinkered horses in their stalls; and tree-tops, which she could see from the convent dormitory above the garden; and the lancet windows Émile-Jean had noticed on his single angry visit long ago. Marie had drawn many things, but soon the stubs wore out and there was no way of obtaining new ones; and after her education was completed and she rejoined Papa, who by then was ill, there had been no time to think any more of such matters. Marie took time to think of them now; how she would like to draw the shining, satin shape of the well-groomed horses here, as their buttocks moved in sleek rhythm to the coachman's urging. But one couldn't draw motion; one couldn't draw smell, the smell of warm gently exercised horse-flesh, the smell of close-pressed bodies. They were kind, the people who had come today with the carriage. They and Richard were the first solace she had had after the death of Papa, with Sophia's added unkindness to redress the balance.

"You are silent," said the big young man in dark clothes who had joined them at the road-fork, blotting out, Marie remembered, the light and the view as he climbed up. She had forgotten him since then, and thought now that he was perhaps offended; it was not polite, she recalled from conversation-classes at the convent, to ignore anybody, to permit anybody to feel left out. How had they reconciled that with the behaviour to herself of most of their boarders? Marie wondered, and forgot it; by now it did not matter. She smiled uncertainly, focussing her eyes on the young man instead of the loch in near distance, which she had been watching. It was difficult to find a reply. Ought one to say "Yes, I am often silent?" She opened her lips; then became aware that Richard, close beside her, was manfully controlling his sickness. "Ought they not soon to stop?" she asked in a whisper, addressing not the young man in particular, but everyone who would listen. Sophia and Alicia, however, were making polite talk one to the other; and William thought Marie's reply practical, delightful and restful. He saw and heard too many chattering women. He was glad that he had come today; he had confirmed, within himself, his as yet undeclared intention regarding Marie; without delay, he would set matters on foot, now that he had seen her closer, observed her quiet ladylike manners; her understanding, also, was excellent.

At a point on the road where there was entry to a field they stopped, and the servant untied Alicia's hamper. For the first time, in handing her down out of the carriage, William saw to it that he touched Marie; the contact sent a tingling of anticipation through him. He occupied himself thereafter with the ordinary courtesies of the little expedition, the handing round of eatables and light wine Alicia had brought, and which were laid out now on the snowy damask cloth: he even made conversation with Urquhart's wife, whom he assessed, from his own congregational experience, as the kind of woman to be avoided as much as possible, except in the due exercise of Christian charity. For her own part Sophia, who had missed nothing of William's scrutiny of Marie Vanneau in the carriage, played her hand well. A solidly-endowed young man of good social connections, who might conceivably rid her of the French nuisance, was an unsolicited heavenly gift. But so personable a young minister would be bound to have unlimited opportunities of meeting girls whose parents were on everyone's card-list, and who would provide a marriage-portion. There was accordingly no time to be lost; Mr. Heatherton must on no account be permitted to find out her dull Marie Vanneau was until he had committed himself irrevocably. And yet, one must hardly appear to rush things. But, as to how it might be brought about...

"I believe friends of my husband's are parishioners of your own, Mr. Heatherton; the Howies," said Sophia genteelly, smiling and showing her discoloured teeth a very little, indicating her own controlled urgency. The matter itself was indeed so urgent, it was practically now or never... "How delicious these sandwiches are, Mrs. Heatherton. May I . . . ah, sir, my warmest thanks! Mrs. Howie came, they say, of very good family in England. One can tell, can one not, from her manners and address?"

There was not, accordingly, much leisure given to William to acquaint himself with Marie directly on this picnic; the restraint thus imposed on him only spurred him on, and by the end he was uncertain whether his strongest sensation was one of irritation with Sophia, or desire for Marie. Alicia, as in his state William failed to notice, was strangely silent; had he known, she was becoming increasingly his ally in the matter of Marie.

She is intelligent, Alicia thought, and has natural courtesy. As the back of her mind a shade of disloyalty, not to James but to the company she herself, as his wife, must generally keep, danced like the shadow of a gleeful, hidden sprite. It would be pleasant to have an occasional companion with whom to discuss matters other than those of everyday, which as a rule seemed all that the heavily-fed wives of shipowners, or the Admiralty delegates who had lately come, at last, to reconsider their immemorial employment of southern marine-engineers only, seemed capable of, or interested in. Nobody since she was at school had discussed water-colours with Alicia, or fashions beyond the ordinary, or music. James's interests were all in his work, and though he loved his family, he was its breadwinner, and Alicia saw less of him day by day than, she hoped, she would do when they had both grown old together. "Shall we sit opposite one another over a low fire, saying nothing, like Uncle Nathan and Aunt Jean?" she thought irrelevantly. For folk to sit together in silence there must either be deep understanding between them, or none. She and James——

"When do you return to France, Mademoiselle Vanneau?" said Alicia to Marie, in praiseworthy French. The girl looked startled, then composed; she glanced quickly round the company, as if to ask their permission to reply in a language foreign to them. Prettily done, thought Alicia; I like the young woman; I shall do all I can for Willie. How astonished James will be!

But Sophia must have her say, and leaned forward to answer Alicia in Marie's stead, spilling cake-crumbs on her gown and shawl in her eagerness; really, a delicious cake! "The children will miss her sadly if she decides to do so over-soon. Is that not so, Richard, my dear boy?"

But Richard had eaten too many sandwiches too quickly, and leaned sideways and was sick upon the Reverend William Heatherton's sleeve. If I had trained him up for it, Sophia thought, he couldn't have managed better. "Oh, sir, sir! You must stop by as we return, and my servants shall wipe your suit of clothes clean. Dear me, what a thing to happen."

By the time the job was done, she was thinking, she could ask him to stay on to supper, no doubt; it would be in the way of ordinary courtesy. One must beware of appearing too pushing ... That French miss was gawping at the loch, as if she had no regard for her own future, as if she were even unaware that she *had* no future, was dependent, as Sophia knew well enough, on Hector's charity, whether or not she chose to return to France. If this plan involving the young minister failed, as well if she did go back: Hector himself and the young woman were already too friendly together for propriety. It would be a relief to be rid of Marie on all counts, wherever she went. And a mean, designing stratum of Sophia's mind, the same which had led her to persuade Papa to inveigle young Hector Urquhart to marry her if only for the business (how humiliating that had been! Nowadays she wondered at herself), was busy. By hook or by crook, Sophia was resolved, the French hussy should be married to the minister, without delay, before he found what a fool he was making of himself, for of course the girl would never truly make the mistress of a manse, she was by far too feckless.

Had Sophia been informed of the genuine state of her own mind, and her reasons, she would have professed herself shocked. She was, she told her inner self now, doing the best she could for the penniless orphan Hector had brought home, without so much as a word to her, his wife, beforehand: and a foreigner at that!

X

Time seemed to spiral for William Heatherton thereafter, so that in retrospect it happened, all of it, on the same evening, which would not have resembled the way he chose to act in other respects; almost improper, the haste which made it seem that it was then, on the same evening he stopped by invitation at the Urquhart house to have his coat cleaned by the servants, that he had a word with Mrs. Urquhart herself about Marie. But in his memory it always happened so; memory played tricks.

He recalled being asked to stay on for supper, and of doing so and then, for reasons he could not explain, regretting it; perhaps it was the self-conscious way in which he, as a minister, was asked to invoke the blessing before meat. It made him, for the first time in such a circumstance, feel theatrical; as if the very silence of the young girl whom he so greatly desired to possess reproached him. Yet what could be improper in saying a grace? William approved such household customs; when he himself married, he thought, he would institute them among his family. His family ... and himself, the head of it, at one end of the great mahogany table where he now sat alone at nights, in his manse, eating a meal cooked by his housekeeper, while at the other...

Miss Vanneau, being a Frenchwoman, would no doubt have a knowledge of cookery. The fact of his almost total ignorance of her race, arising in his mind now for the first time, made William awkward, as though his big hands could not hold his knife and fork correctly. It was, he knew, perhaps directly due to the impossibility of turning to her and saying, "Miss Vanneau, can you cook?" But Sophia Urquhart, chattering without pause from her place at the loaded table's head, and the dour, burning-eyed silence of Hector Urquhart, returned from the day's work at his office at last, affected William strangely.

How had so ill-assorted a couple come to wed? There would, of course, have been the Shawfield money.

He was relieved when Hector Urquhart excused himself, due to pressure of work that must be seen about before morning, and he watched the lean, prematurely bowed and greying figure reach the door and go. Marie, he remembered, had already gone upstairs to see to the children. However it had happened, and on whichever visit—there might have been several—he and Sophia Urquhart were by the end left alone, confronting one another. William was aware that it was to the woman's husband he should speak; and promised himself to do so on the morrow.

Ill at ease as he had already been, how had he begun? "Mrs. Urquhart, ma'am, I have a delicate matter to broach with you, as your good man is occupied for the moment and I want to make the matter of my intentions plain ... Mrs. Urquhart, I desire to be permitted to pay my addresses to Miss Vanneau." That, or in some such way, had been how he'd done it; and the gleam of triumph in the ferret-eyes had been so swiftly concealed that William rebuked himself for fancying he saw it there, but later he knew it had been so. "Mrs. Urquhart, the time is so short, but I feel that with the late sad circumstance of her father's death, and her lack of kindred, my seeming haste may be excused ..." Some such thing.

He remembered only Sophia's coy rejoinder, making him a fellow-conspirator with herself in some plan which seemed already faintly unsavoury, though how it could be so William could not think; he perhaps had overrated the subtlety of the woman. "You young men are so ardent, Mr. Heatherton!" And then "Best see my husband at his drawing-office tomorrow."

By then, Sophia herself would have seen Marie, and dragooned the girl to play her expected part.

She had gone to Marie's room when the latter was half undressed to go to bed, thus catching her at a disadvantage with her hair loose, in her stays and chemise. Sophia held the lamp she was carrying high enough to take in every revealed detail of the young girl's figure; the thin chicken-hollows below the throat, with bones fine-drawn, and the small outward thrust of the negligible breasts against the linen; what a scarecrow for that personable man to want to take to his bed! Jealousy was not the least of Sophia's faults; she hardly recognised it in herself, merely that there was need for haste, if this alien, this useless sallow nonentity, were not to be housed with her for good, for no other gentleman in his sober senses would offer for Marie Vanneau without a dowry. Sophia smiled with closed lips as the flush mounted to Marie's cheeks and throat, and from throat to breast; ay, my foreign gosling, you'll blush hot enough when you find out what it is a man does to you in bed. Innocent, are you? So was I, in such ways, when I married Hector. I wanted him and didn't know why. I'm not so innocent now. However Sophia knew she had known, if only for lack of other offers despite much dangling, that a girl must take herself to market by the best means available. She'd wanted Hector Urquhart, and had got him; and by God she'd keep him by her, even if it meant bearing a child each year in groans and misery. (It was true enough, Sophia had ascertained by now; there was another on the way.)

Briefly, brutally, she told Marie of William Heatherton's offer. "You would do well to accept," she concluded. "What other future is there for you? You have no kin left even in France, and no accomplishments that I've noted."

Marie trembled, and did not reply for some moments; her fingers plaited and unplaited her dark curtain of hair. "Be done with that," said Sophia harshly. "You'd best listen to the advice I'm giving you, and wed Heatherton the first time he asks. It's likely he will come here tomorrow to declare himself." She would leave the pair, she thought, alone together in a place by the downstairs parlour window, where she kept plants in pots. She herself would be available beyond an opened door in the room beyond; there would be no question of impropriety. Mr. Heatherton could make his declaration and be accepted, and Sophia would be in time to come rustling through, in her second-best gown, and congratulate the betrothed pair, thus making it impossible for the suitor to withdraw at a later date. How stupid the Vanneau girl looked now! Her eyes were like a doll's, of opaque dark glass, with nothing behind that could be read by anyone. Sly, Sophia assured herself; such as Marie Vanneau would know very well what she was doing, for all her protestations. It had been no mean feat, when all was said, to capture the Gowanmount minister where so many other, richer women had failed. There need be no explanation ... let Marie find out, if indeed she didn't know, thought Sophia, the facts of married life; the shock, sweat and pain of it, the ingratitude, the constant unfeeling appetites of a man; the resulting agony of bearing children as though one were an animal, year after year ... let Marie Vanneau find out! But meantime it was almost as if Marie herself had heard nothing, as though she didn't understand the singular fortune of this offer of the minister's for herself. Was she perhaps a trifle deaf, or lacking mentally? The manse would bid her welcome all the same, thought Urquhart's wife venomously. She herself would have another new bonnet for the wedding; it'd be like youth come again to have the house to herself once more, without that foreigner in it, surveying Hector in the evenings with those same eyes of unreadable dark glass. Ay, she'd noticed, often enough, but having learnt her own wisdom had kept silent. There'd be an end to all that, Sophia decided, when Marie Vanneau had gone.

XI

William did not present himself at the Urquhart house next day, and the reason was one which he himself could not have foreseen, or, he would have told himself, avoided. In the early afternoon, after a prebendary meeting had kept him occupied all of the morning, a note came round from Mrs. Howie, the session-treasurer's wife; would Mr. Heatherton excuse the haste of an invitation to come to them that same evening, and drink wine? "The matter is a pressing one, or there would have been no such urgency; I hope that you will forgive it," the letter ran, and the bold hand, large for a woman's and written in black ink on hand-made paper, was, William thought, significant of the way things must be in the Howie household; the cock-sparrow of a husband might say to all and sundry that he ruled the roost, but it was his wife who made the decisions, whether or not Howie knew of it. William took a second glance at himself in his shaving-glass before departing, to make certain that his stock was properly tied. To say that he consciously compared himself at that moment with the short-legged, inconsiderable figure of George Howie cut would have been untrue; but it was certain that William left the house well satisfied with his own appearance, and handled his yellow kid gloves with particular care to avoid soiling them.

Margaret Howie received him from her customary seat by a wood fire, high-piled despite the season. "I trust it is not too hot for you, Mr. Heatherton; even after six or seven years in the north I still find your country a cold one." She smiled, and motioned him to be seated and to take the wine which Howie himself, having dispensed with the manservant, was pouring. William accepted and sipped it gravely; despite himself he almost gave way to naïveté at the heartwarming splendour of the finest madeira he had ever tasted. A pretty penny it must have cost! William raised an eyebrow at himself, thinking how still, at times, he could hear the echo of his mother in his own imaginings. He downed it, and permitted himself instead to admire the richness of the room, the handsome attire of Margaret Howie herself, whose delicate black lace shawl concealed what must be a fourth or fifth interesting situation; her gown was of banded violet silk, and became her: she seemed in excellent health. William became aware of the close-set eyes watching him sardonically, beyond the obedient blazing of the applewood logs in the hearth. They gave off a pleasant mild scent.

"You will know well enough that we did not ask you to come at such short notice to discuss the climate, Mr. Heatherton. Pray, my dear, let our guest know why he is here." The voice, and the slight overtones of unfamiliarity in the way she used her vowel-sounds, glossed over the fact that Margaret Howie showed William less humility than an ordinary Scotswoman of his congregation would have done. To one of these, he would have been "the minister", no ordinary guest. But at the same time as his realisation of this infinitesimal lowering of his status—didn't they term a clergyman "parson" in England, and regard such, socially, a trifle below the steward of a great house? He had heard that somewhere. The different histories of church and state in north and south accounted for it.

"Is your brother James in good health, Mr. Heatherton?"

A trifle of shyness, of deviousness even, in little Howie's method of questioning intrigued William. He inclined his head. "He is in good health: I was unaware that you and he had met." Had it been the right thing to say? One did not wish to offend the Howies, and his own reply had perhaps again savoured of patronage. But George Howie gave his customary guffaw of loud laughter.

"We havena; but there is a notion of his that interests me—interests us both—greatly. I refer to a saying of Mr. James Heatherton's which many folk think of as mad; the crossing to America itself being made possible by steam."

William's brows flew up; so engrossed in his own affairs had he been that he had, he realised, failed to follow up James's progress in such matters. Their two lives, and the separate circles in which they moved, were different by reason of the chosen profession of each brother, and he——

George Howie had turned meantime affectionately to his wife. "It was Margaret persuaded me o't; I mysel', minister, like most folk, had doubts concerning it at the first, but Margaret says your brother will be a great man with or without us, and we——"

"Do not speak, my dear, as if I were a gipsy woman with a crystal," broke in Margaret Howie, and William saw that although her whimsical mouth smiled, the eyes were cold as river-water. "It is a family of mettle that can produce a fine preacher on the one hand, and a fine ship's engineer on the other. I have watched your brother's career with interest, especially as regards his recent dealings with the Admiralty"—"A notoriously sticky assignment, sir, for a Scot!" interjected Howie. His wife continued placidly, as if he had not spoken.

"I know some little concerning steamships, and their prototypes, Mr. Heatherton," she said. "I lived for many years among models of them."

"Woman, woman, the minister will not be wanting to hear all of that," Howie broke in again, and William was left with a sense of irritation at the strutting pertinacity of the master of the house. How had such a woman—a well-born, handsome, personable woman with cultivated mind—come in all the world to marry such as George Howie? The man—William fought against his own prejudice—was little more than a jumped-up errand boy who had made the most of his opportunities. That he had a sharp eye for a bargain was evident in his marriage. "I would like indeed——" protested William, anxious to hear more of Margaret Howie from her own lips; but the story of her youth was not yet to be related to him.

"To be brief, minister, would you yoursel', o' your ain knowledge, say that your brother—that—he——" Howie appeared to hesitate, and his wife, ignoring the recent marital rebuff, gently aided him; had William given objective thought to the scene it might have seemed like one which had been perfectly rehearsed, before his entry. "Come, George," said Howie's wife. "Why not tell Mr. Heatherton what the situation is that has caused us to bring him here today? It should not be hard to achieve full understanding among persons of our intelligence," and she smiled, as though smiling at two children. But she spoke like a queen, and William, despite her handsome presence, was reminded by her of what he had heard said of old Queen Charlotte, now a dozen and more years dead. That small, ugly German woman had been respected for her firmly expressed, adhered-to opinions; this woman here, he thought, would grace a throne. What a magnificent creature Margaret Howie was! He himself had not realised, as week followed week and his own glance, from its godlike elevation in the pulpit, surveyed and passed over her bonnets and those of a hundred other women, how superb she was physically, both in manner and movement; with a statuesque quality like the early matrons of Republican Rome. Implacable, like those ladies? It might be; but whatever the business to be decided upon today, William was certain that this woman's mind had fostered and guided it. In any other circumstances, the fact itself would have shocked him.

"It's this, minister,' said George Howie, "and no more, to be plain; am I or am I not to gi'e my vote to the furtherance of this Atlantic venture o' your brother's, that he an' Davie Heatherton swear can be made possible in the ships they've a'maist built for a higher tender than was at first mooted? Folk noted for the canny laying away o' their money, Mr. Heatherton, say it's madness; the distance is overmuch for any other means but sail, and the crossing o' the water to Ireland, which your brother also contrived by steam a year or two back, as much as any engineer may hope for. The Atlantic, Mr. Heatherton, is not the Irish Channel."

"That's manifest, my dear," said Margaret Howie, "but——"

"Dinna hinder me, woman. If I were to put my money, and lead others to put theirs, into a wildcat notion, a dream without substance, sir, I'd—I'd be the laughing-stock o' the city, and maybe ruined forbye."

"My dear George, pray forgive me for interrupting once again," said his wife, "but Mr. James Heatherton is not demanding the whole of your fortune. You can well afford to lose—and I do not think you will—whatever you adventure in this projected enterprise; and, my dear, if the steam-voyage to New York is successfully accomplished, what a rich man you will be then! The shares thereafter will soar."

"Women! What do they ken o' any o't?" said Howie irritably, while William held his peace; when the time came for him to speak he would do so, he knew now, in James's favour.

Howie's wife played them both like fish, lowering and then raising her eyelids. "I may know very little, George," she said evenly, "but you would make a very great deal of money if so, would you not? More than you stand to lose if the venture fails?"

"By far the more, but—ye see, sir, how she cozens me?"

William gave his close-lipped smile, and continued overtly to watch Margaret Howie. Her thin, hooded eyelids had drawn down now over the strangely unnerving, narrow-set eyes; beneath, William intercepted a gleam. The man amuses her, he thought, with a feeling of shock; she's like a cat with a mouse, but he'll never be permitted to know it. Aloud he said, summoning words as best he might in a situation somewhat foreign to him,

"I have small knowledge of finance, Mr. Howie, or of the prospects of how long a distance may be in the end traversed by steam. Yet I know that my brother is a sound man, and would never advertise such a venture were he not certain that it would, with God's help, be possible, given his talents and care. That is as much as I may say, I believe; but I am certain that my brother, if he is indeed fully determined upon this endeavour, will put all that he himself may spare into it for his own part. He will mislead no one, or else himself before everyone."

"Well spoken," said Margaret Howie, and William was aware of her tacit, almost lazy approval; as though a tactical battle had already been fought and was now, and predictably, won. "There is a meeting to be held on Tuesday week, and Mathew Gloag is in the chair, and was on at me to be there, and speak, and cast my vote as I saw fit; he kens I can handle his money, and my own forbye, when we're baith o' us on land." Howie guffawed again, and cast his pudgy, well-tailored arm about his wife's shoulders, fondling her unseen flesh below the lace. "But if it hadna been that Margaret was on at me on the same head—she reads the daily papers, Mr. Heatherton, as we men, and thinks it a' out in her head later, there was never such a woman—if it hadna been for that, and your own estimate o' your brother's character, I'd ha'e been in two minds; and maybe I still am. It's a lot o' money, Mr. Heatherton, I stand to lose, if the venture fails. Four thousand pounds I may spare to offer, if what we ha'e spoken of this day bears fruit; and where I lead, others may follow."

"I can help you no further," said William, and was aware of his own protective innocence about money; he could husband what he had, but seldom ventured it. Such had been his upbringing. What would their mother say, or their father either, if they knew that James was about to launch so grand a venture at so great a cost? A steamship to sail as far as New York ... or to turn back, with at best a tale of ignominious failure?

"We cannot halt progress," he heard Margaret Howie say. "It may well be possible that, one day, man will at last find the means to fly. If a bird can do as much, why should not we? And the sailing-ships of Columbus never credited, I daresay, that they would reach the farther shore. But it was done; and other things will be also. It is better to move with the tide than against it, do you not think, Mr. Heatherton?'

But George Howie had given way to loud spasms of laughter at what he chose to call his Margaret's fancies about men who could fly. "Spare me your havers, woman, or I'll begin to think your advice isna as wise as I'd thought, and ... Ah, but ye're a canny woman, Margaret! A rare, canny, couthie woman!"

And he smiled down with proprietary pride at his wife's goddess-form, almost like a showman in possession of some large, aloof and rare animal. William was aware of a rising of dislike for the commonplace little man, and of admiration of the woman for so coolly enduring his touch. He made his excuses as soon as it was polite to do so, and left.

He visited the Urquhart house on the following day to make his declaration to Marie Vanneau, and found her acceptance, which was made in French—William could not afterwards remember how she had phrased it, and recalled only the little, formal curtsy she made him, as if he had offered her a post as his housekeeper—found it, and everything, a trifle flat. He could not help comparing Marie, so miraculously and swiftly within his grasp, with the proud, besieged woman seen yesterday;

the thought of Margaret again bearing Howie's child—how many children were there already? The man was like a rabbit, breeding incessantly upon her—nauseated him; he found that he could not give his full attention even to the fact that he was now betrothed. He kissed Marie; finding her cheek unresponsive, and thinking that perhaps she preferred meantime that he should act as one of her countrymen would do, he then kissed her hand. It was thin and dry in his grasp, like a papery leaf: there was no life in it. The vulgar woman whom Urquhart the builder had married came bustling out then, and well-wished them both; William was unpleasantly aware of the odour of sweat about Sophia as she moved. Another unsuitable marriage! How had Urquhart, how could such as Urquhart ever endure—ah, well, at any event he himself was engaged suitably, purely! That there was no dowry with Marie he was aware; fortunately that problem would not beset them unduly in the Gowanmount living. William returned home, at length, uplifted in flesh and in spirit. He had followed the pointing finger of God, and had found the wife he desired, who was promised to him as from today. Soon also, though William did not permit such profane approaches to the subject to enter his conscious mind, the burden on his body would be relieved, when he married: it had been agreed that the ceremony, in all the circumstances, should be soon. That night William knelt, as he always did by custom, at the side of his bed in his nightshirt, before climbing in; and prayed longer and more fervently than was usual with him, devout as he was.

The previous day Marie herself had come to Sophia Urquhart, white-faced but resolute.

"I have a plan, madame. I need no longer be a burden to you. M. Urquhart's sister, who has a school, needs a French instructress for her young ladies. I have already written her a letter." And the girl handed Sophia, as if asking her approval, an envelope addressed to Miss Flora Urquhart. There was no address. Sophia lowered her sparse eyelashes in triumph; so like Hector, if he had put this notion in the fool's head, not to provide full direction!

"I will have it delivered for you," she assured Marie; and a little later, returning from a short errand in the carriage into town, she informed the young woman that Miss Flora was, unfortunately, already suited. "She told me so herself," she informed the other, and watched the opaque, familiar mask manifest itself in place of the glow of hope there had briefly been. Strange how the girl's face could lose all expression at will! Afterwards, Sophia was to ask herself why she herself had been so adamant in her intention that Marie should wed William Heatherton whether she would or no. It should come about, Sophia was still resolved, if she herself could make it do so: but by the afternoon, when he hadn't shown up, she was sorry she had not somehow kept the matter of Flora's school in her hand after all. There had, of course, been no delivery as yet of Marie's letter.

Next day however Mr. Heatherton put in his appearance, and Sophia again advised the girl to make no bones about accepting him. "Do you otherwise wish to be a burden to others for the whole of your life? You are not needed here, and it is unlikely that my sister-in-law would ever consider employing you; she told me, when I did my best for you, that all of her staff must have several accomplishments at their finger-ends, and you've none; even a French instructress must teach Italian also." Sophia made up her ready farrago of lies, feeling the more secure in that William Heatherton was already waiting in the parlour. She almost hustled Marie downstairs for the expected proposal. It was, Sophia knew well, unlikely by now that the girl would dare refuse it. Once the knot was tied, that would be one burden the less, Urquhart's wife thought; a gleam of satisfaction showed in her mean eyes at the thought of the almost certain innocence of Marie.

William Heatherton married Marie Vanneau at a time which would permit the wedding-trip to coincide with the annual General Assembly in Edinburgh. He had determined to take his bride east by the river-route, first spending a night in an inn at Stirling after a coach-journey. The wedding-ceremony itself was to be of the quietest order, because of the bride's mourning; only close relatives were invited, and the Urquhart family; Hector Urquhart gave the bride away.

The bridal attendant was Alicia Heatherton, James's wife

had hesitated, unwilling to offend Sophia Urquhart, whom she suggested, explaining the fact in her adequate French, to Marie as a more suitable person to choose for the honour. To her surprise William's betrothed coloured deeply, transforming herself from a mousy little thing—James and Alicia, without unkindness, had seen no great attraction in William's choice of a bride—to something made of fire and colour: and angrily refused even to consider Sophia. Marie would, Alicia thought thereafter, have looked her best accordingly in a warm glowing red or, perhaps, a turquoise gown; but that being impossible, Alicia herself presented the bride with a dress of douce-coloured silk, and had Marie's wedding-bonnet trimmed with the finest black French velvet, in lavish bows. It was, Alicia knew, a fine distinction between remaining inconspicuous enough not to offend the congregational ladies of Gowanmount when Marie should have returned from the honeymoon, and drawing down on herself the fire of old Jean Heatherton, as not being good enough for her son. Jean was already suspicious; there had not been time, with the haste of the wedding-plans, for Marie to visit William's parents as yet at the riverside cottage, and the wedding-day itself was the first occasion Nathan and Jean set eyes on the bride. The old pair had come up by water for this momentous day, Nathan in his best long-hoarded blacks and Jean in her cherished Paisley shawl; but they would not agree to stay overnight with James and Alicia before returning, and there was an ominous tightening of Jean's lips when she saw the bride come in on Hector Urquhart's arm. Papists, all French folk were; nobody could persuade Jean otherwise. She could remember well enough the Napoleonic Wars and the towers they had built, all along the coast, to keep the enemy out; and for her younger son, her miracle and pride, to throw himself away on a penniless Frenchwoman almost broke Jean's tough old heart. But of this she gave no sign, except dour silence; and she would eat no cake with the wine, after the ceremony. Nathan was different; he greeted the bride with the stately, inbred dignity of his blood and calling. No one could tell, from his lean bewhiskered old face, what he thought, or whether or not he were pleased with his son's voice.

Hector Urquhart played his part also, with the grave Highland courtesy that matched Nathan Heatherton's own. But he was thinking, even while he walked down between the small assembly of guests with the bride on his arm, that if Émile-Jean Vanneau had been alive this marriage would not be taking place. In some way, he knew, he himself had failed Vanneau's daughter. What more could he have done? He could not, he admitted, complain of the bridegroom's conduct in any respect; William Heatherton had come to his office in person to ask formally if he might wed Marie, and if he had Hector's permission to speak. "I have no right to order the lass," Hector had grunted, and then wondered if he should have ascertained, before giving his tacit consent, whether or not Sophia had any hand in this affair. He understood, none better, the unpleasant character of his wife; his disgust with her had led him long ago to retreat into a world where only his work mattered, and Flora and her school; but he was also sensible of the position of young Marie, and the lack of any real future for her, penniless and orphaned as she was, unless she perhaps fancied governessing; and his own memories of Flora's youth made it preferable, perhaps, that the minister should have his way, and wed Marie as soon as possible. Why should he himself object to Heatherton, well-found and eligible as the man was? Yet he disliked the minister, he knew; that kind of fleshy, urbane Lowlander had access only to the good things of life, and never would be brought to understand its struggles and difficulties, the hungry incessant ache of poverty, an empty belly and no hope, such as he'd known himself, when he was young ... But why blame Heatherton? Let him have his wife, and keep her in comfort. "Ay, ask her," he barked, and then remembered, as if to explain the matter to his own conscience, that in France marriage was in any case an arranged business, and from all accounts worked out well enough, as a rule.

"I take thee, William ..."

The low, only slightly accented voice of Marie Vanneau recalled Urquhart to himself. He realised that the marriage-service was three parts over. Did Marie know all she should? He'd asked Sophia of that; and had been met by her shallow laughter.

"Hark at the man, as though we women did not think of such matters for ourselves! Trust me, the minx is better instructed than *I* was on my wedding-day."

He left it; it was, he knew, no part of a well-brought-up young lady's upbringing to be aware of certain things before she had to, and no doubt Sophia had seen to all of it. "I have treated her like my own daughter," acceded that lady, bridling, and Hector contented himself with hoping that the young minister would deal gently with Marie, and said no more. There was, in any case, little more to say; as the years passed shyness and taciturnity had enveloped Urquhart like a cloak. He loathed the very begetting of his children on Sophia; the need he still had for her body at times was in itself distasteful to him.

Sophia smoothed the ribbons on her prosperous corsage, and tried not to let her relief and triumph, now the couple were man and wife, show on her face. She'd contrived it, she'd got the French creature out of her house, *her* house, and into William Heatherton's bed. Thoughts of how the newly-wedded pair would fare together tonight were perhaps improper to dwell on, and Sophia turned her attention instead to the splendid forehead and famous spreading beard, giving him an appeaance like a Hebrew prophet of David Heatherton, Alicia's elder brother. She'd heard it rumoured already that David's erratic genius, and the consummate care of his brother-in-law James, had combined forces to evolve some hitherto undreamed-of ship. But no woman could go very far in understanding such things. Perhaps, during the little reception afterwards as they all drank wine, she herself would have the chance of a word with the celebrated Mr. David...

A loving, spontaneous glance passed at that moment between James Heatherton and his wife, and Sophia's shrew's face set in habitual mould of discontent. Old Nathan Heatherton saw it, and the reason. Later, as he and Jean went home after the new-married pair had departed, the smith told his wife that the French lassie had been right enough in not asking that Mrs. Urquhart to be her attendant. "She's given her shelter, maybe, but it would be grudged enough." He remembered the bride's set face, but knew his own wife as Urquhart knew his, and that it was useless to say anything in the young woman's favour to Jean, at this moment. "She's unco plain," said Jean spitefully, watching the familiar passing by of the wide river. Nathan shook his head.

"If she's what Willie wants, why deave at it?"

"It was a grander wife for Willie *I* wanted. That one'll not help him rise." She had forgotten, for the first time in years, not to call her son by his boyhood name; it showed how greatly she was upset.

"Tuts, woman, he's risen high enough. What more were ye hoping for him?"

"Whatever I was hoping, it'll come to nothing now. What's done is done, and there's no sense in dwelling on't."

"Then wish them well," said Nathan, and they both fell silent as the ferry neared the widening river-mouth, and home.

XII

William Heatherton's wedding-night held overtones he did not afterwards care to remember; it was, looking back, on that occasion that the first suspicion, which he would not name as yet, that he had let impulse misguide him in his marriage came. This feeling was in itself brought about by an episode which for William held impropriety rather than strangeness; though had he been a man addicted to fancy, he realised, he would have found it strange.

They had made their journey uneventfully be coach, and William had pointed out to his wife, from his own store of well-read knowledge, the varied and edifying sights on the way. That she did not reply more than by a subdued murmur of acknowledgment pleased him; a wife's part was submission; already, briefly remembering Margaret Howie, he thought of Margaret as a monument, an example, rather than as a woman. The coach drew up at their inn, with a sudden rearing of high mountains near at hand, and the bulk of the sunset-crowned Castle. They must take a walk up there tomorrow, William thought; and then recalled that by tomorrow his wife would be indeed his, they would be one flesh, he would have penetrated her mystery and fulfilled himself; and desire rose in him. He controlled it all through supper, contenting himself with watching Marie's delicate, bird-like handling of knife and fork, and the food they ate. "This inn is famous," he said sententiously. "You find the meal pleasant?"

"It is pleasant. I cannot eat more. It was the journey, I think. How it rocked, that coach!" And she said something more in a low voice, in French, that William could not follow; so he said, seizing the opportunity to disguise his own eagerness in concern for her, that she must be tired; would not she like to go to their room? "I will join you in half an hour," he said, and felt his voice thicken.

Marie was shown up to the room by the inn-maid, and asked if she would like a posset sent up. "No, I thank you, I have everything I require." The girl departed, without interest; so plain was the baggage, and Marie's dress, that they did not look like a new-wedded pair. She had drawn back the bed-curtains already, and turned down the sheet; and there were other customers to see to.

Marie did not undress at once; sudden panic had possessed her. Despite her stay in the Urquhart household, it had not been evident to her that a wife had her husband of necessity beside her in their bed; and William's unrolled valise, William's nightshirt, were in evidence, also his shaving-things, laid out carefully on the washing-cabinet, which was made of rosewood; the curtains, both at window and bed, were of faded Royal Stuart tartan, left over from a fashion prevalent at the time, some years back, of the visit made to Scotland by his late Majesty King George the Fourth.

Marie made herself undress at last, with trembling fingers; she was tired, and the prospect of having Mr. Heatherton beside her in bed was not an inviting one. If she had given any thought to the conditions of her marriage, it was, as William had noted in her curtsy of acceptance, as though she were to become his housekeeper, no more; the probability of something added grew increasingly manifest. She did not know what it might be, and for the first time in her life felt quite alone, and frightened. If Maman had lived, and could have advised her ... but Madame Urquhart surely would have said something, if—if what? The curtained room became suddenly stifling to Marie, and she sought about her for escape, however brief; the tartan curtains at the window drew aside under her hand, and she was rewarded with a breathtaking view of the Castle under a risen moon, with clouds veiling it. The silvery, ghostly radiance filtered down on to a long garden which must surely belong to the inn; there were roses growing in it, all of their daytime colour blanched by the night and the moon. A wind blew, scudding the clouds before the moon: Marie opened the casement, and let the cool breeze stir her thin shift and loosened hair. How pleasant it would be to venture out on to the dew-wet grass, in bare feet! If only——

She had not moved. The movement was in the blowing wind and the curtains, and in the added draught from the door as William came in. He had expected to find his bride in bed, and at first glance the bed was empty; this offended his sense of propriety; frowning, he looked about the room. Then he saw, between the blowing curtains, the slim barefoot figure of a girl, half-naked it seemed with the moonlight shining through her linen; black hair, like a witch's, blew about her, lifted and laid with the inconstant wind from an open window—an open window! And his wife, visible so to any passer-by who might happen to walk along the river path and look ... and look, when ...

"What are you doing there?" he called out to her sharply, his tone already that of the dominant husband; then as she did not move "How dare you stand there? How dare you show yourself? Have you no notion of propriety?" And he strode forward, seeing her at last turn to the swift realisation of his presence in the room; of him, who should have been foremost in her thoughts at such a moment, instead of which——

He seized her. Left to himself, in his ordinary sober senses William would not have behaved so; now, her soft uncorseted flesh felt beneath the shift spurred him on. He had no clear memory of what happened next; he carried her to the bed, he remembered, feeling her resist him: he could also feel her breasts. Then force; then the ultimate of all desired experience, his possession of her, his entry of her body, the deflowering, his fuller satisfaction afterwards ... He took her again, he remembered; and again, before an added circumstance came to him with the coldness of sudden shock like a plunge into water. He had not, he realised, undressed himself at all; Marie had not, after the first wild ignorant struggle, either cried out or done other than permit him to do as he would upon her, as though she were an effigy. The third thing weakened William in his own estimation at this very moment of his strength. For the first time since he could well remember, he had omitted to kneel down at night and say his prayers, by the side of his bed, before climbing in. Tomorrow, and for all the other nights they were together, he must bid Marie kneel down by him, and they would pray side by side as man and wife, before he again demanded of her her nightly duty. He removed his clothes, at length, and put on the nightshirt which, in their first struggle, had fallen unheeded off the bed on to the floor. Then he slept, well satisfied.

XIII

Marie Heatherton eased her silk shawl where it lay on her shoulders, creating an almost intolerable burden in the warm sun. She would have liked to take it off, but a glance, from where she sat on a convenient stone, at her husband's back deterred her. William was absorbed in the prospect of the capital from Calton Hill, with the clear late summer's day enabling his short-sighted eyes to make out the hundreds of smoking chimneys, the incredible rise of the Castle perched on its rock, and the blue Forth beyond. They had walked up here at the suggestion of Mr. and Mrs. Sproule, who according to custom had offered hospitality, at this Assembly season, to the visiting minister and his wife. Among all the events which made up the highlight of the year for every Church of Scotland manse-mistress, Marie found herself alone; knowing nobody, understanding very little of what went on at debates and prayer-meetings, and unable to mix with the other women who, like herself, had accompanied their husbands when family ties would allow.

Marie remembered the Assembly, and Edinburgh, as a concourse of darkly-clad, portentous, self-satisfied folk, seen lifting hats and sketching acknowledgment to one another when they met in the streets of the capital, or at some function much like all the rest, Marie thought; on such occasions she was able to withdraw into herself, be private and alone. But here, now, with William, it was more difficult; and for that reason Marie drew her shawl closer about her, despite the heat that drew enticing scents from the whin-blossoms where she sat. Everything about her marriage tended, she already knew, to make her retreat into some small, hidden place where William, for all his physical thrustings, could not penetrate.

She felt herself flushing. When Sophia Urquhart had urged her to accept William Heatherton she herself had assumed—

with what folly she now saw—that to be a wife was, perhaps, similar to taking charge of a man's house; involving the kind of tasks she had latterly performed for papa, ironing his linen, shopping for and sometimes preparing his meals; something of the kind, although as regarded marriage itself, the arrival of children Marie knew, from having lived in the Urquhart household, to be a probability. That children could be engendered from the robust demands William made nightly on her, had done ever since that first painful and terrible night at the Stirling inn when her ignorance, her innocence, had been lost, Marie's mind would not yet assimilate. Though the agony and fear of the wedding-night had departed, she was perhaps still in a state of shock; she knew now what it was William would be at with her, and the avid eyes of the Sproule couple, who knew well enough the pair were on honeymoon, in the feather-stuffed bed provided upstairs, would furtively survey the bride as she came down to breakfast daily; how had they fared? But, being an Edinburgh woman, Mrs Sproule asked no questions; nor accordingly was she any easier of access for advice than Sophia Urquhart had been. The conspiracy of silence which had accounted for Marie's total lack of information prior to marriage pertained in many a polite household; but few young girls had been without a family upbringing of any kind. One did not speak of such things, they were not proper; but the arrival of younger sisters and brothers was silently accepted and partly understood. Only Marie, night after night with William's assiduous weight upon her in the feather bed, could see no reason in such practices; to her the ways of men were barbarous, unreasonable, her identity was being smothered between yielding mattress and demanding husband, and she could ask no one anything. After the invading, brisk, determined force which was William by night had strained her narrow body to the full and left it wrung, she would lie awake, long after he slept, and remain crouched sullenly away from her husband; the instinct she already had to close her thighs against him she never dared give way to, but her thoughts were her own ... Herself, the person who was unknown to anyone but Marie, had meantime shrunk into the inward space remaining to it, a place as far as possible out of William's physical reach. It had never occurred to him to question her concurrence.

He turned back to her now, on the hill, and in the kindly, unctuous tone he habitually used when instructing his bride, began to point out the details of the symmetrical New Town, spread out in fine Georgian splendour, so that the fleur-de-lys which waved below on a staff above Holyrood Palace seemed unimportant. "It should interest you that the exiled French monarch, Charles X, is in residence here," William said. "It seems unlikely that he will ever return to his native country."

She listened passively, unaware that Madame Royale, exiled also, could perhaps have told her certain things regarding her own mother. But Marie could summon no interest in the Bourbon flag, and in any case William had already turned to other aspects of history with which he was better acquainted than that of the ill-fated Legitimist monarchy already in decline. He stroked his clean-shaven chin as he talked; already, he congratulated himself, he had shown Marie various aspects of the history of Scotland; there had been Stirling Castle, sadly grass-grown and in neglect, and the high windswept balcony where queens had once stood to watch the tilt below; some of the carved wooden portrait-heads of James V's ornate ceilings had been lying about neglected, prey for any dishonest person to purloin. William had dilated on the ancient summer-place of royal Scotland to his bride, and in his enthusiasm had not noticed that she seemed listless; he himself, after that first experience of the marriage-bed, was increasingly active and vigorous, both in body and mind; it was as if a wellspring had been released in him. That Marie should be here, and his in the flesh, had already ceased to be a wonder to William; it was as if he had for the first time found himself in his natural physical state, and now was content. He discoursed on the ferry-journey from the old capital to the new, pointing out here a tower, there a little island or a crag where the King's falcons had used to be reared; he himself was well instructed in history. By the time Edinburgh was reached, and they disembarked and had their baggage conveyed to the Sproules' house by hand-barrow, William could feel his mind sparkle with new energy, a kind of added faculty of absorption; the fresh dry air of Edinburgh, bracing after the gentler west, increased his appetite. He ate the excellent meal of oat-herrings his hosts had prepared, made cheerful conversation with them, and hardly noted his bride pecking at her food. Sproule's wife, having ascertained that Marie was a Frenchwoman, made small effort thereafter to draw her into talk; the town was full of French since the Bourbon invasion, and there was nothing remarkable about any of them; it was by far better to listen to young Mr. Heatherton, and have the benefit of his superior mind. Sproule himself, a devotee of old St. Giles's, droned on at some length about the preachers he had in his day heard there; he himself was an attorney and elder.

After the evening meal there had been tea served, in the old Scots manner; it was only in England that the gentlemen withheld their presence over wine. After that, again, the couple were shown their room.

There was a wash-stand, as by custom, with the ewer and jug decorated with an engraved pattern of dark-green leaves and birds. It had been Mrs. Sproule's mother's; it was put in the room to enhance the honour of the occasion, and watching Marie wash at it revealed, between the cleft of her small breasts under the chemise, a long ribbon, the same William had seen on the morning he had—one day he must tell her of that!—walked out as far as Urquhart's house and orchard. He resisted the impulse to ask Marie, now, what the ribbon held at its end; lust had risen in him at sight of her partly-revealed flesh, and he was anxious again to savour the pleasures of marriage. He turned to ensure the bolting of their door, thereafter laying his fingers about her wrist.

"Come," he said; first, he caused her to kneel by him while he prayed with her. Afterwards, it was again as Marie had known it would be, between them. It was true that she had not expected this of marriage; but it was evident that one must endure it, and shut within herself, she did so, oblivious as William might be of her closed eyes and mutinous mouth. That a woman should enjoy the marital act was not in his reckoning; if Marie had done so, he would have thought it improper in her. He finished, and again felt the surge of well-being envelop him; sufficiently to cause him to forget about the ribbon she always wore.

Now, though, in the afternoon sunlight, on Calton Hill, he turned from his view of the capital at their feet to the sight of her, his wife, easing back her shawl against the heat at last; the ivory tint of shawl and flesh commingled, then separated before William's closely focused sight. He saw the ribbon again clearly; and smiled. "What is that you always wear?" he asked her. He had not yet seen his wife naked, nor would he have expected to do so. He reached out his hand to the ribbon, and pulled it out of her bodice. Marie made no effort to resist; but drew back, startled, at the expression of incredulous anger which came from him.

"This is—is——"

William then used the strength of both hands, and broke the ribbon; taking the small silver crucifix which had revealed itself, and hurling it among the gorse as far as his arm could reach. Marie gave a cry.

"Cela appartenait à ma mère; vous n'avez pas ni raison, ni droite——" She broke off, frightened in some way she did not understand; the cold, icy rage he exhibited made William still more of a stranger to her. She stopped expostulating and began, in silence, to search by herself among the whin-prickled grass. It was impossible; she would never find it again. Behind her, William's voice thundered.

"What other Popish symbols are about you? There must be no more seen of them, you hear me? What do you suppose the congregation, the session, would say if they knew you had even worn such a thing? It might well be the end of my career." That, he knew, was unlikely; it was not possible to dismiss a minister. But there would be raised hands, shocked rumours, whispering...

He gripped both her wrists. "Are you a Papist, Marie?" he asked her, looking down sternly at her withdrawn face. "Answer me truthfully; it is of no avail now to tell lies."

"I am nothing."

"You are a Protestant?" She had, he knew, responded correctly at the wedding-service. That could not have been so if—The nearness of almost physical danger, as he saw it, chilled William both for himself and her. He should have made further enquiries before committing himself; he should not have tied himself irrevocably to—to——

Marie said again, sullenly, "I am nothing. I am whatever you wish." She pulled her hands away and began to walk before him down the path, back to the city. William followed; they had intended, that evening, to join the Sproules in going to hear a preacher William knew of old, who had sometimes lectured to him while he was a student in the Faculty; he himself would enjoy meeting his former professor, and no doubt the reverend Doctor would wish to hear, from William's own lips, how the younger man had progressed as year followed year at Gowanmount.

William felt his own rare anger depart from him. "We will say no more of it, my dear," he told her, and taking her gloved hand firmly in one of his own tucked it into his broadcloth-covered arm. So they regained the level ground; and William resolved that in future no reference should be made to the unfortunate occasion. Marie said nothing.

William was, accordingly, as the days passed, in a parlous state of mind; even the sermon by his erstwhile professor, replete with the edicts he had understood all his life, failed to comfort him. So early to doubt the state of his wife's soul and the according wisdom of his own marriage, seemed so terrible a thing that by night he would possess Marie the more ruthlessly, as though determined by such a means to make her his own and not the devil's. At the same time conviction grew in him, aided by his bodily release in marriage, that he was more than ever by right the elect of God; he had been chosen from among others to preach God's Word, and had not God himself guided him to Marie, perhaps to save her?

Looking back, William would never know at what moment of their joint lives Marie ceased to be a person to him, if indeed she had ever achieved personality in his reckoning. To say that she was a physical convenience would have shocked him; but he considered her state of mind not at all. He had, in his life, met only such women, even young ones, as were set in their ways, with a certain life's pattern mapped out by careful, purse-proud guardians of morality. No such haphazard upbringing as Marie's had been would have been available to William's understanding. Nor could he ever, in after years, recall a single memorable remark of hers to him, or try to; the fate of a wife, when all was said, was submission. By the honeymoon's end William had fashioned of Marie, at least, an outwardly humbled wife.

One event occurred to vary their days, and lift his mind from the episode of the lost crucifix, and his wife's passive silence. One day, as they were returning from an afternoon function addressed by the Moderator, Sproule hastened out of his house to meet William with a letter.

"It was handed in as ye left, minister, and I was near coming after ye with it." The handwriting was James's, spiky and precise. William opened and read the letter, and his rare smile enlightened his face, spreading even to the pale eyes.

Sproule was alerted. "It's good news, then, minister?"

"The best." William pocketed the letter, and said no more; as Mrs. Sproule remarked to her husband afterwards, he hadn't as much as shown the bride the news; a shilpit thing, she was, for such a fine man, and as likely as not would not have been able to follow it; no doubt that would be why he'd kept it to himself. The Sproules nodded, and withdrew a trifle disappointed with the choice impersonally handed them by the Assembly's guest-list; young Mr. Heatherton was clever enough, but he didn't have much to say to everyday folk; too formal, too ponderous for such a young man.

But the name of Heatherton would ring up and down the country by the week's end, when the gazettes had news from the south. William's letter had informed him that James's Atlantic steam venture, invested in by the Howies, other shareholders, and to a small extent William himself, had been successful. The long crossing, which had hitherto, it was claimed, been too far for any man-made engine to take without running into trouble, had been achieved in fourteen and a half days, making as much as two hundred and forty knots in the best day's steaming. James Heatherton by now was famous as far away as London and New York, his Atlantic greyhound destined to go down in history. William's troubled mind took solace; he'd been right enough, his name and James's had substance, even genius, behind it; the garnered inheritance of generations of craftsmen could manifest itself in devious ways. He himself also shared that inheritance.

XIV

James Heatherton's success and international fame, made almost overnight, had greatly lengthened the subscription-list of the Gowanmount congregation; an acquaintance with the brother of so notable a man being in itself desirable. The initial aim, which had been to present a small brass timepiece to the minister and his bride on their return, was expanded to include a silver one, rotating visibly on engraved wheels beneath a thick glass oblong. The wedding ceremony itself having been so quiet that few had attended it, it was more than ever gratifying when no less a person than Mrs. George Howie offered to lend her drawing-room for the later presentation to young Mr. and Mrs. Heatherton on their return. Many who had thought, as Joe Craik's wife assured him, never to see the inside of her hall-door flocked to Margaret's house that day, as curious to behold the Howie abode as they were to set eyes on the minister's young foreign bride; it was already rumoured that she was very plain.

The Howies had, of course, done well out of the Atlantic venture; it was proper that they should show gratitude, in however devious a form, to the Heatherton family. Like the advice to invest, the incentive for the invitation had again come from Margaret; but like the clever woman she was, George Howie was left thinking that it was his own idea. "Ye'd maybe best cultivate the young French bride a wee bit," he told his wife condescendingly, from his small stance, while Margaret smiled and got on with her embroidery. George bridled, and said then, "Willie Heatherton'll go his own gait, I doubt, married or single. But a man's better to have a wife." His small, salacious eyes roved over his lady's goddess-form; it had, though he would be the last to admit it, never ceased to be a miracle to him that Margaret headed his table, mothered his bairns, and supported him—advice was never the name

George would allow himself—in such gambles as the Atlantic steam venture. Man, he'd made a packet out of that! The pun was so good that he repeated it to Margaret. Her smile never wavered, nor did she raise her head.

"Pray, my dear, do you like the presentation clock?" she said. "It is very fine, is it not?" And George strutted and declaimed the title of the famous maker to whom Margaret, he recalled later, had herself recommended that they go. The minister was lucky to have so fine a clock; he himself was lucky in owning so fine a wife. The latest addition to the Howie family had been born, took nourishment, and showed signs of being well able to live; he was a son. George beamed with pride. It was all that he had lacked, so far, in this marriage; an heir to inherit all that he himself had gained through hard work and, at times, a flair for business; again, Margaret had aided him there. A magnificent woman! The whey-faced creature they said the minister had married could never hold a candle to her. She had borne his son with ease, with hardly a murmur; and now sat embroidering baby-caps. George Howie basked in his fill of contentment, warming himself before his summer fire.

The clock was duly presented, as the words of the polite invitation-card made clear, at the house of Mrs. George Howie at half-past four o'clock. Tea would be served after the speeches. Into a street lined with elegant carriages there walked, accordingly, at the proper time, the new-wedded pair. The manse was at no great distance, and they did not keep a conveyance. William, in his familiar sober broadcloth and high stock, looked well and walked proudly; in his waistcoat-pocket was a note of the speech of thanks he intended making, and as he went he surveyed the points of it in his own mind, making sure there was nothing that should be said and had been left out; it was otherwise easy in such ways to offend some dowager, who had maybe given more than her neighbour. William was punctilious in such ways, and he reviewed his speech seriously.

His wife walked by him, her hand on his arm; it was impossible to guess that she hardly let her gloved fingers touch it. She wore for the occasion the gown purchased for her wedding, a plain straw bonnet without trimming, and suitable gloves. The face beneath the bonnet's brim seemed to have sharpened and receded, as though Marie herself were already completely passive, or else in some way removed from everyday. As she entered on her husband's arm the dark eyes, staring out towards the concourse of people, held no light either of shyness or of pleasure: they were expressionless, as though the rich room, crowded with well-dressed people, did not exist for Marie. She spoke so little that as a result of that afternoon many members of Gowanmount assumed that French was her only tongue, and made no effort to address her beyond the first, shouted courtesies invariably directed at foreigners in such circles. Subsequently they ignored her; it was easier, and somehow more proper, to be able still to turn to the large, personable and fleshy presence of their minister, no longer feeling any rival present for his attention. There were reviewed compliments about his preaching. "My word, minister, it'll maybe not be long before ye sustain a higher call, and leave us," quavered one old lady. Craik, who was by, quipped in. "Why, were ye wishing the minister in heaven already?" and there was some laughter. Behind, others were pursing their lips. The new wife would be no help, was the common thought; predictably, they could foresee Marie Heatherton stitching obedient calico at ladies' meetings, saying nothing; that was maybe as it should be. But the young woman had no presence at all, and the French had a bad history. It would have been better for the minister to have married someone of his own nationality and class; but the thing was done.

Marie began to receive impressions of colours and forms; she had been in a dream, but now, as she would sometimes do, absorbed near images. The Howies' front door had shone with prosperity, brass fittings and green paint. After the heat and dust of the summer street the maid who had opened the door, in starched frilled headgear and apron, seemed cool, like foam bobbing on a busy river, away into the dim unknown interior. Marie knew little likewise of maids. There were two servants—if one dared call Mrs. Prescott, who was leaving soon, a servant—at the manse. The other was a cook-maid, and Marie had been told she must direct her, and also find and employ a scrubbing-woman. She did not know who to ask about such things; Alicia Heatherton, who had been kind, was away with her husband in London, meeting famous folk. Marie already felt the servants' collective contempt of herself; Mrs. Prescott had always ordered everything as it should be done, but the bride was already afraid of displeasing William. There was a great deal to be seen to, some of it new to Marie; the house-linen and furnishings and silver to tend, and William's special laundering, his shirts and nightshirts and caps and Sunday bands. Then the food to buy ... Marie felt a shade of sickness, which was growing familiar, rise at thought of the kinds of food they ate here; it was always rich, for ever too heavy and greasy, starting with mutton, finishing with apple-pie. Marie recalled the terrifying visit they had made, before James and Alicia's recent departure south, to the old parents at the river-side cottage. All together, after being driven down, they had drawn in chairs to a table laden with Jean's proudly served, home-grown, wholesome food; lifted covers revealed great mounds of potatoes, roasted and boiled, and meat with rich gravy, and red-currant jelly made the previous summer from Jean's own fruit in the garden. Before she was halfway through the first course Marie felt sick; she had pushed away the food on her plate, sitting with lowered eyelids lest the old woman in the frilled cap who was William's mother and who, Marie already knew, disliked her, burst out with, "Why are ye not eating the good food?" or some such thing. But Jean had said nothing; her lips had folded together in the way they had, and she had borne Marie's plate away without saying a word. James and Nathan, meantime, were making grave interested talk with one another about a building-site on which was a small cottage James had lately bought, for his family when they took seasonal holidays. "It will need to be made bigger, father," said James with his lean face intent, and Alicia laughed and said, "Oh, he wants it to be a palace, to hold the models of all his ships," upon which James turned to her and said, "Why, my dear, there will be room for you and the bairns as well, and a guest or two." They smiled at one another, and Marie felt the closeness of the pair, and the devotion of the family of which she was now, or should be, a part; but she felt shut out. She and William ... it was not, could never be, a marriage like that of Alicia and James. Even today she had felt, again, like a small obedient pinnace following in the wake of a large, handsome, all-conquering schooner. At least where there were ships there would be the wind and the sea . . . but, again now, Marie could see the familiar, overtly curious stares of the women in William's congregation. They had nodded on introduction, and she had nodded back. That was all she knew of them. The closeness of the crowd began to have a frightening effect on her; it was as if she would die if she could not win out to the air.

The speeches droned on. When the gift was handed over William made his reply eloquently, without a flaw; Marie stared at the clock's costly ugliness and hated it. For all of her life now it must repose on the mantelpiece, and be dusted and wound; the moments and the hours would tick away, until . . . until what? Until one was dead?

The cost of the clock was, discreetly, a matter for congratulation. "Mind ye, minister, marriage doesna happen every day!" That was George Howie, whose own wife was more expensive than the clock; a murmur of approving laughter came. William himself was flushed with his own importance, the heat of the day and the well-wishing crowd; he unbent a little. The well-appointed house, the rich room, filled with persons of standing and some wealth—he saw an elder of Savill's present, here by invitation as a friend of the Howies; this was his element. The thought flashed through his mind that perhaps, having heard of his preaching, the man had come today to sound matters out about his own consideration for that vacancy when old Dr. Turnbull should retire next year. Savill's Old! That would indeed be a plume in the cap of a relatively young minister, and he would have stiff competition, he knew, when other preachers rivalled him for such a call. The congregation at Savill's was the most distinguished in the city; professors, lawyers, doctors from the teaching-hospitals, and their wives. Nothing must be said, even hinted, yet: the vacancy might well in any case go to an older man. William contented himself with his present state for the moment, knowing that it was comfortable enough; George Howie's expansive flattery, the echoing approval of the well-dressed wives in the congregation, was subtly different from their treatment of him before his marriage. Now, he was an asset, a preacher who would mature year by year like vintage wine. No more hopeful daughters and nieces; thank God his pastoral work, with the close confrontations William in any case found difficult, could proceed without embarrassments of that kind! The Lord's hand had led him to a wife who ... where was Marie?

William looked about for her, and realised a fear in himself that she might again behave in the strange way she had done on their honeymoon: as though she were only half attending. Now, in Howie's house, she ought to be here, by his side, minding her place, or else walking discreetly about with a word here and there among the ladies of the congregation. But she was neither. She was not in the room.

The frown Marie already knew and feared manifested itself in a vertical crease on William's fleshy forehead. The polished grate with its heavy andirons had no fire lit today; even Margaret Howie could not complain of the lack of August heat. She—he could not, come to think of it, see Margaret Howie either—she had received them with the air of a duchess today, her white shoulders again draped discreetly in lace, her manner gracious. If she were with Marie, all was well. William ceased to let the matter trouble him, and turned to listen instead to the men's talk which, now that the presentation was itself over, still centred almost exclusively round James Heatherton's recent marvellous achievement of an Atlantic crossing by steam.

Marie had backed out of a further door some moments earlier, oppressed by the heat, the unending overt stares of the chattering women, and William's near presence, which as usual caused her discomfort. Standing at first for moments in the passage she could still see, as if it were a magnetic focus, his broad back, the well-fleshed, well-kept hands gesturing expansively. "It is as though he were in his pulpit," she told herself wearily, indoctrinated enough, as she was by now, to be aware of the near-blasphemy of equating the glorious figure of William, the cynosure, with William in a nightshirt as a constant, assiduous presence in her bed. By now, as Marie herself realised, she had no personal privacy at all except, oddly, when she sat twice on each Sunday in the boxed manse pew. There, enclosed by mahogany sides and an inward latch, they might stare at her across the width of the church from their own appointed places, and did; but they could not reach her. William would by then be, also, in his own place; he would have mounted his carpeted steps with dignity and be giving forth of himself, his face grave as the austere paraphrases he announced, his voice duly sonorous. They had a precentor at Gowanmount, who would start on the correct note, leading the risen congregation through the lengthy sung verses, after which they would seat themselves once more. Marie had found it difficult, at first, to know when to stand and sit, but soon learnt to follow the Scots form of service. By now, she no longer heeded it.

She was, she found, so very tired. It was already as though William, in his extension of himself, had engulfed her, and swallowed her up. At nights before he lay with her she no longer felt any rebellious surge when he caused her to kneel by the bed's edge with him, while he said an impromptu prayer aloud. She no longer had feeling or interest in any matter concerning herself and William; not even the fact that her monthly periods had stopped. One of *les anglaises* at the convent, Marie remembered, had instructed her, briefly and contemptuously, when her own first attack of bleeding had terrified Marie at the age of fourteen. It would stop when one married, the young lady had said. Well, it had stopped; Marie thought no more about it. She leaned back against the coolness of the wall beyond the door through which she had lately come, and closed her eyes. How blessed peace was, and solitude, a little! If only she had a room of her own——

"Are you unwell, Mrs. Heatherton? Shall I have them fetch you a glass of water, or a little madeira, perhaps? Should you care to lie down?"

It was not one of the prying, furtively curious women of the congregation who had followed her outside; this voice was deeper, and accented differently. Marie opened her eyes and beheld the tall fine lady she had already seen at Gowanmount, and who she knew was her hostess at today's function. Mrs. Howie wore an unsubstantial lace scarf over her shoulders and lilac-coloured gown; she looked very elegant. Marie heard herself stammering, discomfited by the discreet regard of the close-set eyes. "I was too hot, and the food we ate at midday was heavy, and I came out for air." It sounded lame, and unconvincing; the young woman dropped her eyelids, seeing as she did so that Geroge Howie's wife wore also, on her white forearm, a heavy gold bracelet set about with amethysts. How fortunate to be a woman so rich, poised and charming, who despite being married to a ridiculous little man like George Howie retained a portion of herself!

"Let us go upstairs, where it is cooler," said Margaret then. "Court will see to the tea-cups." She made, with the jewelled forearm, the slightest of commanding gestures to where the maid in the frilled starched cap, whom Marie had already noted, was waiting beside a loaded tea-tray whose cups were in fine white and gold china; and preceded Marie upstairs, past a first landing, not pausing till they reached a second.

"Do you prefer to lie down?" said Mrs. Howie again.

"No, madame, I feel better." It was true; she was well out of reach of the crowd, the heat, the stares, and William: and the elegant whiff of verbena from Margaret's ascending skirts had refreshed her. She saw the other smile benignly, her eyes nevertheless remaining cool and wary. "I will show you my children, in that case," said Margaret, and opened a white-painted door.

Marie was first shown Master John Howie asleep in his cradle, an embroidered baby-cap on his head; and then Miss Georgy Howie, clad in dimity because it was summer, and seated with her wax doll by her upon a fluffy lambskin rug. A paper fan was in the hearth in lieu of a fire. The nursemaid, starched and respectful, rose, bobbed a curtsy, and withdrew to see to her other charges, leaving the two women together. Marie thought she had never seen so full a nursery. The other children, girls of different ages, crawled about the floor playing or shaking an ivory rattle they had; the dry foreign sound made a background to the two women's talk. Marie was trying to overcome her own timidity. If she could ask this easy, unselfconscious woman how children came, where they came from, what happened!

Margaret was already amusing herself with the antics of small Molly, who bit at the ivory with teeth that were just coming through. "Children do not divert one always," she said, "and I do not believe that an intelligent woman should have their company solely. But our lot is, of course, laid down; there is no escape from it, if we marry."

"What does she mean?" Marie thought, and stumbled out her query; instantly a veiled look came into the grey eyes, like the third eyelid of a cat or reptile, brought down swiftly against possible danger. "It is your husband's duty to instruct you," said the alien voice coldly. "You are happy at Gowanmount? You have made friends among the members' wives?"

But Marie, rebuffed, had already flushed deeply, and returned her gaze to Georgy on the rug. It was as it had been when Sophia Urquhart had betrayed and sold her; never again would she ask for advice or, for that matter, give the appearance of requiring it. The mask drew over her own face again. "She is very pretty, the eldest Miss Howie," she said, smiling. It was true; Georgy's fat legs boasted tiny boots of milk-white kid, done up with many buttons at the sides. She was somewhat like a small red-cheeked apple; her black hair, freed from its nightly curl-papers, was lustrous and obedient. The large dark eyes surveyed Marie wordlessly, then returned to survey their owner's wax doll. The latter was sumptuously, if unseasonably, dressed in red velvet, trimmed with lace.

"You must curtsy to our guest, my darling." Margaret Howie had removed her gaze from Marie also; the moment's embarrassment was surmounted. She had guessed that, by now—it was natural and to be expected, but not proper to be discussed between persons of short acquaintance—that William Heatherton's wife had commenced a pregnancy. It did not yet show, as the young woman had a customary pallor. Later, when she grew thick—"I myself always wear a pelisse or scarf in the last months, it can be managed to great advantage," Margaret reminded herself. But she did not say this aloud, nor add that many people had, on the occasions she herself gave birth, been surprised, as they had no notion another child was on the way at some recent meeting with her. Good health and endurance were blessings given only to some, however, and George——

At this point Margaret Howie switched her thoughts' direction quickly; she did not care to admit to herself that to have a fine, heavy man like William Heatherton as her own children's father would by no means have displeased her, nor would she have behaved like this poor creature who felt faint, for such a cause, in the midst of a small gathering of ordinary people for tea. As Georgy achieved her wobbling curtsy, her mother smiled down at her. "I believe," said the light, dry voice to Marie, "in instilling correct manners into them while young. When she is a grown young lady, Georgy will cursty faultlessly, and without hesitation, when it is required of her."

When they regained the drawing-room the company was beginning to take its leave; everyone flocked to Margaret Howie. Marie was left standing beside her husband, who seemed displeased.

"Where have you been?" he asked, frowning down at her. "It was discourteous not to be present throughout the speeches. The gift is one for which we ought indeed to show gratitude. What became of you?"

"The fault is mine, Mr. Heatherton," said Margaret, making an urbane reappearance. "I invited your wife upstairs to see my babies; have we been absent so long?"

William was gratified, and a great flood of relief possessed Marie, noting the instant change in him. Mrs. Howie was a kind woman, after all, in her own strange way. One must merely take care not to assume familiarity with her. Otherwise, she would take one's part—she had taken hers, Marie's, unhesitatingly—as if she were not afraid of William, or of anything.

XV

The news of the Atlantic steam-crossing was forgotten by most of the Gowanmount congregation as winter passed, favoured by unusually mild weather, so that there was not even the customary skating-holiday for children at school. Their elders indulged in the usual sociable exchanges which made the darker days tolerable; tea-parties, soirées, sewing and prayer meetings, foreign mission speakers, and a Punch and Judy show in the public street. The city had also become thronged with beggars, who sang cap in hand or played instruments; some were in fact veterans from the Napoleonic wars, others said they were. Christmas came and passed unnoticed, for in the north it was still frowned on as part Papist; Hogmanay was a different matter, with many folk hopelessly drunk in the streets about the town-cross and Tolbooth steeple.

William and his wife had driven down with James and Alicia to the clay cottage to bring in the New Year, and Jean had brought out her famous black bun, matured round cheeses and Hogmanay bannocks, as well as the traditional roasted fowl with bread sauce and onion stuffing. The family were merry, especially in view of James's continuing success: the steam-voyages were now an established novelty, with further contracts promised. David Heatherton, who had come down, made a speech in his memorable voice, and then everyone drank James's health in whisky; his long face was flushed with pleasure, and he got to his feet and made some sort of a reply, mumbling half of it, about his new great house which was already building, and how they would be welcome there before next Hogmanay. James would never have the ready oratory of his brother; he seldom spoke either in public or in private unless it were strictly necessary. He was a devil to think, old Nathan said; but Jean pursed her lips; the thinker in the family, both personal and professional, must be William. It was William's task, therefore, to ask a blessing on the meal, and afterwards to invoke a prayer bringing in the New Year. Her performed both tasks with reverent ease; Jean's eyes were hard with pride as she looked at him. No matter what wonders lay in her elder son's brain and might be transferred therefrom to steel and iron, the greatest achievement of all her life stood here, in black coat and snowy stock, over the table with its laden glories. She had given a minister to the Kirk as she had dreamed: "And he's not done yet," she told herself. "He'll preach in the finest kirk of all before he's grey-headit; maybe St. Giles's." But the latter, which she had never seen, was beyond Jean's reckoning; she didn't know but what she would as soon William stayed in the west, where her own folk had lived and died. Iron men they had been, she recalled, working it as other men tilled earth: she herself, no doubt, was a hard woman enough. But where her heart was given she never wavered; only she could not like or trust William's foreign wife, sitting there douce as a hen on its nest; last summer Jean had already suspected the young woman was breeding. Now there was still no outward sign of pregnancy, but William's mother knew it was unlikely she had been mistaken. The foreign creature was darker and thinner than Christian folk. No one could tell, in any case, what went on beneath that shawl, with her corset-laces no doubt drawn tighter than was customary. "If it sits far enough back for folk not to jalouse it, it'll be a girl," Jean told herself, with some stirring of interest. She herself had never borne a daughter.

It was early morning when the carriage set out to return home; James drove the horses himself as the coachman had a holiday for Hogmanay. Alicia sat close beside James, wrapped in her furs; the two little girls were asleep, cuddled against her. William and Marie sat in the opposite seat, not touching, not speaking; William because he had already said what he considered important, Marie because, as usual, she had nothing to say. A thin drift of rain fell as they neared the city, making a dazzle of the many lit candles and lamps in wakeful households. Nobody, even the youngest bairns, would be in bed before one or two in the morning; the hardened roysterers would go on all night. A man stumbled in the path of the carriage now, drunken and singing; James's careful hands steered the horses' heads aside, so that he and they escaped uninjured. Alicia watched her husband with devotion; how knowledgeable, how precise James was in everything he did! Her own life was like a safe ship, well guided by a pilot who would avoid storms and whirlpools. She spared no time, in the contemplation of her own happiness, to conjecture about the couple in the other seat. She had thought, in fact, little enough about William's wife since the marriage; it seemed to be proceeding uneventfully enough, and her own engrossed Alicia. She yawned, delicately, behind a gloved hand drawn meantime out of her muff. There should be a good enough fire left to warm them all when they reached the house; perhaps William and Marie would join them in a final glass of toddy? She would ask, presently.

But William declined. Tomorrow, or rather today, was the Sabbath; he had to be in the pulpit by eleven of the morning, and they had best go straight home. Marie obeyed him like an unquestioning shadow; as usual she expressed no preferences, and allowed James to drop them at their own front door before he turned the horses about and drove home.

The happenings of that New Year's morning were for once to eclipse William's sermon, which concerned the text commencing the Book of Genesis. In the act of making all things, as it were, now, he failed to notice that Marie, below in her pew, was suffering discomfort. She made no sound, and stood up for the psalms and paraphrases with the rest of the congregation; but by the time the rustling silence for William's sermon commenced, she was biting her lips with pain; beads of sweat stood out on her brow beneath the bonnet.

Above, William's voice declaimed concerning God, moving on the face of the waters; God Who had made life out of nothing, the world out of a void. While half the congregation listened with rapt interest to his words, the other half were looking at Marie. It began to be evident that something was very far wrong with Mrs. Heatherton. Could it be——? "But never a sign of anything that any of us could see," murmured one matron to another, as soon as it was practicable; others counted on their fingers that it was only eight months since the marriage. Altogether it was a memorable occasion; but nobody did anything about it until, with a quiet stirring of silks, her very gloves pulled on again unwrinkled, Margaret Howie rose up from her place, walked towards the manse pew, bent over and unlatched the entry-door, and to everyone's amazement scooped up, as it were, the small dun-coloured figure of the minister's wife and swept her out of church by the side aisle, while the beadle hastily remembered himself and opened the door for them. Above, William's voice never faltered; it was not clear whether he had even noticed what had happened, so taken up was he with the rounding of his phrases and the theory he had that Moses, from whom the Book of Genesis of course came, had made good use of his knowledge of the ancient secrets of the priest-Pharaohs with whom his early up-bringing had been associated. It was unnecessary to ascribe everything to a vision on Mount Sinai; but William was careful not to offend his listeners. He finished one of the sermons he would afterwards make fuller notes of, with a view to eventual publication privately; and again bowed his head on his hands and said, "Let us pray."

The two women had not come back, the matrons noted. It must either be a question of serious illness, or one of—let it be whispered—labour. The minds of Gowanmount congregation were, perhaps for the first time, not on William's well-rounded prayer, and the New Year greetings on the church steps afterwards were unduly prolonged, as though everyone hoped for some scrap of further news. But George Howie himself said nothing except to wish everyone a happy Ne'erday, and depart on foot with the elder children, his lady having already commandeered the carriage. It must indeed be an occasion of some weight, as the wags said when they reached home. But before that, naturally, most tongues remained discreet.

Marie, aware only of the memory and recurrent presence of pain, felt herself directed, supervised, warmed, at last stripped of her clothing and compressing whalebone stays and laid in a cool bed. Strange that the linen should be so cool and fine ... and then the agony began again, only now she could no longer bite it back and must cry out against it, to try to make it stop...

"Cry out as loud as you wish," said a woman's voice. "The

house-servants are away; no one will hear. I will fetch a hot brick to your feet; while I'm gone, pull hard on the curtain: it will not come down."

The curtain—it was of thick stuff—was left in Marie's hand; presently the pains began again, and struck sharply and regularly, like turning knives in the back and belly; she screamed repeatedly with the pain. What had become of her? What would the end be? Would she die?

"I do not care if death comes," she thought. She must have said it aloud, because shortly there was the warmth of a brick at her feet, and a sane, level voice replying cheerfully; the voice of the woman who'd brought her away, who had undressed her, put her in this bed. Whoever she might have been, Marie would have been grateful; then the pain began again, and she heard her own voice screaming. When she had done there was the woman's voice once more, and through what seemed like ensuing hours there were the two sounds, her own recurrent cries and the woman's voice; Marie remembered now, as if she were far off, Mrs. Howie, who sat in church in a central pew and wore rich clothes, and smelled of verbena. Marie sobbed aloud; there would be no more elegant sights and smells, no more of life, for her. She was going to die.

"No, no, my dear——" Mrs. Howie's voice was kind now, as though she had been Marie's own mother. "Why should you die? You are going to have a child, that is all; we've all lived through it; I have five of my own, upstairs in the nursery with their attendant, and I live still."

To have a child! Of course, she'd wondered about it; but why had there been no one she could ask, never anyone who would tell her? And before she could frame an answer to her questions there came the pain again, searing, unending; as though she were no longer in charge of her own body, as though it were inhabited by a demon who forced its way out.

"A-ah . . ." The voice was her own; and the pain, unbearable now; yet she must endure it. It was easier now that she knew the reason. Why had no one told her before?

"Bear down, my fear. Do not trouble yourself, I know what must be done. When Court comes back from church, she shall bring up hot water; and by then, you yourself will want a little warm milk, or perhaps some broth. No, don't keep saying any more that you will die; that's foolish talk. We women are worth more than that."

Margaret held the straining creature in her arms while the child came to be born; when its head showed, she laid the mother back on the pillow.

"The worst is over now." She pressed on the baby's head, encouraging the straining movement. "Only a little more effort and it will be done ... there, now, there." The poor thing was like a child herself, with no control, Margaret Howie was thinking. Even her own first time, when Georgy had been born, she'd shown more fortitude than this. She extracted the baby at last thankfully; it was a girl, small with its insufficient eight months' gestation, and had dark hair.

"You have a fine little daughter," she said cheerfully, on her own account as well as Marie's; by now she could hear the returned footsteps of Sarah Court hurrying upstairs. Presently the woman knocked and entered, still in her Sunday cloak and bonnet.

"I would have followed you out, ma'am, but I thought you would maybe not want——" Then she saw the baby, held between her mistress's hands. "I've the kettle on again already, ma'am, I filled it as I came upstairs. Soon as may be I'll bring what's needed; would it be in order, ma'am, maybe to use a binder of Master John's?"

Margaret sent Sarah Court round to the manse to apprise William Heatherton of the fact that he was the father of a daughter, and to see his normal creature comforts in the way of serving his food. Sarah was of greater intelligence than the average serving-maid, and had her own reasons for carrying out Margaret Howie's lightest wish. She came back to say that the minister seemed bewildered ("as well he might, poor man; it didn't show in her at all", thought Margaret); but pleased, and had offered to come round at once; but Sarah had taken it upon herself to tell him that he would be sent for when it was time to see Mrs. Heatherton, who had had a trying ordeal. "He was sorry then, ma'am, and said I was to ask you to ask her, Mrs. Heatherton, that is, what she would like the baby called. Like enough as it isn't a boy, he'll not have the same interest in naming it," added Sarah. She went on to say that the minister had been served with an adequate meal, and that she had left him drinking his coffee.

Margaret went up to the bedroom some time later, when Marie was awake. "What would you like to call the baby, my dear?" she asked; she had placed the wizened, yellowish bundle, wrapped now in John's snowy binder and shawl, by the mother's side, in bed. Now she lifted it and placed it in Marie's arms. To be sure, it looked as if the foreign colouring would persist . . . a pity for a girl to be so sallow.

"What was your mother's name?" she suggested, as Marie showed no interest in the choice of a name. Had the creature no notion at all of what was afoot? She herself had determined, as soon as she first knew she was pregnant, on John for a boy, or Georgina if it should be a girl. But this poor soul . . .

"Cathérine." Marie Heatherton stirred, and looked down at her new-born daughter. I will keep her, Margaret was thinking, with me for a few days, in case she's feverish. "Cathérine Heatherton will be a grand name for such a small lady," she said, preserving the briskly cheerful tone she had used, like a nurse, to Marie from the outset. Very likely she won't know how to feed a child, that is if she has milk . . . I'll have to tell her.

When Sarah came up with the sherry-whey Margaret had bespoken for the invalid her mistress sent round a further message to William Heatherton. He might call tomorrow; his first child was to be christened Cathérine, after her maternal grandmother; and his wife might well be away till the end of a fortnight, perhaps even three weeks.

XVI

Before her marriage Margaret Howie had lived in the north of England, where her father had been a clergyman. So much was known by the ladies of Gowanmount congregation, for those enquiring souls had been agog to familiarise themselves with the origins of someone who gave herself what would certainly have been airs in anyone else, who dressed more richly and with better taste than they did, and whose conversation had a unique flavour of dryness. The ignorance prevailing about conditions south of the Border made England a foreign country, whose customs would undoubtedly differ from those pertaining at Gowanmount. Far from showing any wish to be instructed, however, Mrs. Howie had from the beginning preserved a detached amusement; and this, naturally, inflamed the ladies to bursting-point inside their whalebone stays. They would have done anything conceivable to get themselves on familair terms with Mrs. Howie, but it was not to be achieved beyond a nod and a smile on Sundays; and except for the occasion of the minister's wedding-presentation, not a single one of the matrons had so much as seen the inside of Margaret's house. Yet she was to be observed at all the best assemblies, as they read enviously in the newspapers, or, worse, had the fact pointed out by their husbands at those breakfast-tables where women were still not permitted to read or discuss the daily news for themselves. Much was the speculation that raged round Margaret Howie, and the discovery, made somehow, that her maiden name had been one of the most ancient in the northern English shires. Mrs. Howie was, in fact, an aristocrat; and was thus regarded as a very rare bird indeed by those who warily eyed her from their pew on Sundays, and if feasible copied her bonnets.

In fact Margaret had narrowly escaped being born out of wedlock, for her father, the younger scion of a famous house, who was in orders, had seduced the cook. The affair would in the usual way have been shelved by a few guineas changing hands from the reluctant purse of the Squire, who had already had reason to deplore his younger brother's few capacities. It was, however, the year of Trafalgar, and the cook's brother, a stalwart able-seaman in Nelson's navy, came home filled with glory and rum and, it was reported, met the Reverend Alfred and threatened to beat his aristocratic head to a jelly if his sister were not promptly made an honest woman of. As a result of this, an addition to the noble house was born, with as much privacy as possible in the circumstances, at Bonsam Rectory on a spring morning in 1806. By the time the small Margaret was running about everybody had accepted the situation, the able-seaman had taken himself back to sea, and the course of events saw to it that he was conveniently drowned within the year, off Teneriffe.

Margaret remembered her mother as a tight-lipped person in a linen apron, who still cooked and, by now, served the meals for the parson's household. Her single lapse and its consequence had annealed her soul against further incursions of the devil, and Margaret from an early age was reared to believe in this personage and his capacity to do harm. The cook's family had belonged to a sect of Nonconformist origin which closely resembled the bitter Calvinists of the north. Predestination, denial of joy of any kind and a certainty of eternal damnation for the unrighteous, or those who were not of the elect, figured largely in their creed. Margaret's mother knew herself to be a damned soul; how else had she succumbed to the Reverend Alfred? Repining was useless; but she could at least set her child's feet in the narrow way. She succeeded so well that to the end of her life Margaret was to feel guilt at the sound of any musical instrument and to find difficulty in making frivolous talk.

This state of mind, which was formed in her by the time she was seven, would be enlivened by the occasional crash of broken bottles from the rectory study, and the resulting diatribe of the Reverend Alfred against his lot. Friends shunned him, less on account of his forced misalliance—though to the end of his life he blamed this—than because he had grown increasingly objectionable with his growing intake of wine and spirits. As his liver hardened, Alfred would now and again still feel a maudlin affection for the child his own act had brought into the world, and would send for her to his study and overwhelm her with kisses flavoured with whisky or port. Margaret endured it. Sometimes, if he were himself and had remembered to buy any, her father would stuff sugared sweetmeats or cherries into her mouth, and tell her confidences of a nature no child should know. She kept them to herself; she did not even tell them to her mother.

When Margaret was twelve years old her mother died. By that time the girl had acquired a certain education, part of it deliberate and part not. She had read all of her father's books on the classics and theology; sometimes he could be persuaded to discuss them with her. She had at one time been sent to the village school, but held aloof from the other children. She made no friends of her own age except her cousins, John and Augusta, who lived at Bonsam Hall. Their situation was like her own, peculiar; their mother played at being an invalid because she had been used to hunt, and the nearest hunting-country was forty miles distant. So my lady would lie on her sofa giving herself interesting airs which she could not now abandon: Margaret noted these, and decided which to copy and which not. She also noted, with some envy as she herself was shabby, the way Cousin Augusta (who was later to go crazy) was dressed, in embroidered muslins and tiny kid slippers, and a fur pelisse in winter: a rector's daughter had nothing of that kind. Already there was a division in the girl's mind between the life she had, and that her father could have given her had he behaved differently, and married as he should. The kind ladies of the parish were to thank for this information; they had from time to time taken the poor child up, for she was kin to the Squire, and had asked her to tea or to the entertainments given at Christmas for the village children. But as Margaret grew older, these invitations ceased; she was growing handsome, and the good ladies would not have considered her as a match for their sons; blood was blood on one side only. Also, by now, the Reverend Alfred had become a byword with his drinking and his tumbling of maidservants and farm-girls; there had even been efforts to have him removed from the living, but the Squire, while he survived, would have none of it.

Margaret's aristocratic uncle and aunt had themselves tried to do their duty; some time after her mother's death, they had asked that their young niece might be permitted to come and make her home with them; they had been pleased with what they had seen of Margaret's manners and poise. The Reverend Alfred refused; he still had intermittent bursts of affection for his daughter, and she was the only being he could be sure of recognising at sight. "Don't think it's to turn you into a fine lady they want you up there, Meg," he mumbled. "Worse than a governess, it'd be; and no pay either. Stay here with y'father, though when all's said there's precious little, lass ... damned if I can even find a dowry." And he stumbled off, asking himself aloud who was to be found to marry Margaret anyway? They'd cut the daughter as they cut the father; food and drink, in the end, was all that mattered: what was to be for dinner?

Margaret already knew what a governess was; she had had one, in the days before things grew so bad no decent woman would stay overnight in the rectory. The governess, who had looked like a stork with soiled plumage and knew a little French, had been used to play a harpsichord which still stood in a corner of the rectory drawing-room, though by now damp had got at most of the keys and rendered them dumb. The voice in which the governess sang had been stork-like also, but out of the shrill recollection Margaret extracted one or two Scots ballads. Imbued with the ungodliness of all music as she was, it was difficult to remember every verse; but one song stood out clearly, about a proud girl walking in a wood and asking a robin when she should be married. The governess, here; had poised her wrists, so that the soiled lace on them preened up like a bird's feathers. *When six braw gentlemen kirkward shall carry ye ..., who makes the bridal bed, birdie, say truly?* Damned if I can find a dowry for the cook's daughter. She herself was different from the village folk.

She could cook and sew neatly; when she had to, she could make her own clothes. Often with the cut-down stuff given her she would copy Cousin Augusta's as best she might, or the elegant drapes affected by Augusta's invalid mother, lying on her sofa. Margaret's own mother had taught her something of household management; and while Waterloo was being fought, the child had sat and stitched a sampler, which later the Reverend Alfred, with rare generosity, had had framed and hung in the passage between the study and the hall. Underneath was Margaret's name and the date, in cross-stitch; and the text she had chosen was sufficiently edifying.

Who lives to follow nature
Never shall be poor.
Who lives to follow fancy
Never shall be rich.

Her association with her father came to an end soon after her fifteenth birthday. It happened at early morning church. It was the last Sunday in Lent. The pews were filled with soberly-clad folk, less conscious of their dress than the Scots congregations Margaret would meet later: but they preserved the age-old hierarchy of place, the county to the right front, the village to the centre back. Margaret herself occupied, as always, the rectory pew, which faced the rest of the worshippers. The girl was alone today, as the sole remaining housemaid had gone home with pains in her belly. Dressed in her customary round-gown, bonnet and cape, sad-coloured in deference to the season, Margaret still managed to look distinguished. She was tall and already mature, with well-shaped hands and feet: her corn-coloured hair lay in smooth wings on either side of a face in which the complexion was fresh, the eyes set perhaps a thought too narrowly. She was worth looking at; several of the county had already looked, as Sunday followed Sunday and Margaret's bosom filled out to be a woman's. "Fine filly that's turned out of the Rector's," murmured one noble lord to his spouse, who replied "Yes, a pity," and continued to turn over the leaves of her prayer-book, to find the appropriate place. Everyone was wondering if the Rector would be sober enough to preach today; he did not always attempt it, contenting himself merely with finding his way through the maze of the Liturgy if at all possible.

He appeared at the head of the aisle that day, and lurched down it; it was evident to everyone that the Reverend Alfred was quite unusually drunk. The reason, if they had known, was the death of Napoleon, which had already been celebrated in a seemly manner by such of those present as had cared to take notice of what was no longer front page news. But the Reverend Alfred had worshipped Napoleon Bonaparte more than he had ever loved a woman or a bottle. He had deplored the Emperor's imprisonment on St. Helena and his forced isolation from his family; he had held forth on these subjects to an extent that merely added to his own considerable unpopularity in the neighbourhood.

Margaret had never discussed the matter with her father. She saw now that her difficulty in getting him out of the house that morning, and into his proper array, had been pointless; he had been imbibing in the vestry afterwards, drinking to the shade of the vanished Emperor and to the confusion of those who had caused his six years' martyrdom on St. Helena. He began to mumble through the General Confession, botching it but helped by the replies of those present.

When he came to the Communion proper, the Reverend Alfred's hands shook so much that he could not hold the chalice steady. At the crucial point, he dropped it. A red stain spread over the alter-cloth Margaret had laundered, dripping down so that its presence was fully visible to everyone in church. The Rector's figure swayed unsteadily as he attempted to proceed. There was a murmur of protest from the pews.

Margaret rose in her place then, gathered her skirts aside in one hand and walked down the aisle and out of the church. After a pause most people followed. When they came out into the porch they found the Rector's daughter still waiting there, pale-faced but otherwise calm. She ignored everyone but the Squire and his family, whose carriage waited beyond the lychgate. Margaret walked towards them.

"Once you invited me to come and live with you all at Bonsam. The invitation was refused. May I, now that I am old enough to decide for myself, accept it?"

That was all, and the avid parishioners heard nothing of any reply, seeing only the courteous inclination of the old Squire's head, and his lady's feathers bobbing. Master John, and young Miss Augusta who was already spoken of as a bit queer, goggled hopefully at their tall cousin; then all of them, Squire, lady and family, walked to where the Hall carriage stood and climbed in together and drove off. It was noted with approval that Miss Margaret had stood aside to go in last, as was her place, but that the Squire, being a gentleman born, had handed her in. And so the cook's daughter went up to the Hall to live there as a fine lady, for all anyone knew to the contrary. The fate of the Reverend Alfred followed within two years, and it was many years before folk in those parts could speak of it without shuddering, or fail to blame his daughter who had left him, even while they glossed over his faults. When all was said, a daughter's duty lay with her father, and had she been by him he might have lived longer; but to what purpose? He had never been a God-fearing man.

There was a lack of social life at Bonsam Hall. The Squire's prompt action in agreeing to Margaret's suggestion that she stay with them there had not been solely dictated by charity. He had hoped on the earlier occasion, and perhaps still hoped on this one, that his sane niece might stay the insane maunderings of his daughter Augusta, which were becoming more noticeable with puberty. Later the poor creature would be confined to an upper room at Bonsam from which she seldom emerged, and then only with a keeper; but when Margaret first joined the family Augusta was still at large, already drooling somewhat over her meals and having to be cozened into coming for a walk with the pug; this persuasion was Margaret's first duty. Other times, when it was not possible to take Augusta in one of her fits, Margaret would be sent to exercise the pug by herself. He was black, stout and elderly, and resented the thought of putting one elegant foot before another except for food: Margaret grew used to the sound of his protesting snuffles before his fat, stubborn frame would finally seat itself at some point in the woods, and have to be carried home.

Other company, apart from the family, there was none: Cousin John was indolent, taking in this way after his mother. It was perhaps inevitable that, as time passed and the pattern of her dull days established itself, the girl should feel some interest in the only young man she knew. Sometimes, whether by accident or not, John would meet her with Augusta on their walks, ambling up to them mounted on his bay hack. He would dismount and, still with the horse's reins in one hand, take hold of poor Augusta by an arm while she, Margaret, led her by the other, with the pug bringing up an unwilling rear. They would walk through the wooded estate; the pattern of tall trees arching to make a cathedral-aisle against the sky became familiar to Margaret, and the changing colours of their leaves as the year changed also. Sometimes John would come when she and the dog were alone, and such days were happy; later she was to recall that they had in fact held bliss. They said little together; Margaret was slightly taller than John, and together they would stride, if Augusta should be absent, farther afield, to where hay-ricks and hedges were; and over a stone wall which, John said, the Romans had once made, and over there was their bridge. "It's not safe to walk across," he told her, stealing a glance at her from his long-lashed hazel eyes. That had been the first time Margaret knew he admired her; she hadn't known then what to do about it, with herself hardly better than an unpaid servant at Bonsam, and John, as everyone knew, half promised already to a substantial heiress somewhere in Yorkshire, to carry on the name. The money also was needed at Bonsam; but John was in no hurry. Margaret felt her heart beat more quickly thereafter when he came, and once there was a memorable day when the high wind tore her hair from its pins, and it tumbled down in a whirl of ripe corn-gold before she pinned it up again, with Augusta whimpering and laughing crazily amid a swither of dry autumn leaves. Yes, it had been already autumn by then; and she'd been at Bonsam two years. It was then, in October, that the thing happened to her father.

"The news didn't come that day, or the next," Margaret would tell herself, later. John had been fond of her for days, for weeks, and she knew at last what it was to feel happy, to know that each waking moment would bring its particular magic, that suddenly for no reason they would meet, and draw breath and smile at one another. "We were young," she would remember. John had been not yet twenty, she herself just past seventeen. They'd had candles and a cake for her birthday at Bonsam last April, to cheer Augusta.

But the news came one day, that day in October. There had been nothing to warn Margaret of it; nothing that anyone could foresee, or of course it wouldn't have happened. No one would have wanted her father to die, like that; not her father or indeed anyone. The flames of hell were hot enough, her dead mother had always said; but it was the Reverend Alfred who felt them before the end, and Alfred's charred remains that they'd found still lying on the twisted fragments of his bed, later when the ashes had cooled, and among them green puddled glass from bottles that had melted nearby and set again. His candle had caught the bedclothes, they supposed, and him in his bed dead drunk at the time; too far gone perhaps to feel very much of what happened. If his daughter had stayed at home, he wouldn't have died.

To the end of her life Margaret never spoke again of her father's death. It was perhaps about that time that folk began to realise that they did not know her, that no one had ever really known the Rector's daughter. But when the appalling news came to Bonsam, it was John who went to her. John, who so seldom bestirred himself, had chosen to break the news of the tragedy to his cousin, whom he admired and, at times, almost feared; she was so tall and golden, so forthright, with firmly set notions of right and wrong. John, content as a rule to let the world drift idly by, not to attempt to alter or break the rules of the strict caste he knew, might have felt a fiercer sword-thrust of a different love, a love that would take him beyond his feudal limits into a strange, uncertain place. But now, with this news, he could feel only tenderness and deep pity; he could have put his arms round Margaret, let her weep into his coat.

He went to tell her; she was in Augusta's room, sewing, while the daughter of the house mumbled happily on the floor amid yellow and white halma-figures. When John appeared at the door Margaret rose. Her calm face and eyes, the still tall beauty she had, the beauty of Ceres, unmanned him. He blurted out his tidings as though he, not she, had been the sufferer; as though it had been his own father who was horribly, grotesquely dead.

What would she say? He moved nearer, as if even yet half hoping that she would burst out crying, and run to him; as Augusta, a year or two ago before she got quite so bad, would have run, if she'd cut her finger or burned herself . . . burned. God knew, God had seen the flames rising round the iron bed, spreading so that the house itself now was a ruin with blackened roof-beams naked to the sky. They'd come running from the village and tried to put it out, that fire, and called and called aloud the Rector's name.

"It is God's judgment on him. He sinned; he has paid his debt."

At the first John could not credit that it was Margaret speaking. Then he saw, when his frightened glance could at last survey her, that her dry eyes glittered with some inner certainty, almost madness. Of the two, Augusta playing with wood figures on the floor was the more sane . . .

John turned and blundered from the room. Augusta, sensing that some strange thing was afoot, upset her game and started to whimper and cry. Outside it had begun to rain, sousing the remaining glow from the Reverend Alfred's bottle-decked ashes.

John rode into Yorkshire as soon as the charred remains of his uncle had been decently interred, and arrangements made for a monument to be inscribed and, later, erected. He returned with the news of his betrothal to the heiress; his father and mother were greatly pleased and, secretly, relieved. They had worried lest news of Augusta's madness, without doubt hereditary, might have reached the questing ears of rival suitors for the heiress's hand, and thence to her family: it had not occurred to them to regard Margaret as a cause for alarm. But the name was in any case ancient enough for the marriage to take place without hesitation, on the day John came of age in the new year. The bride was a plain, undemanding creature who did not expect even to ride to hounds, only to be left eating sweetmeats and reading somewhat lighter novels even than Miss Austen's or Sir Walter Scott's. Her young husband bore her company at first; he was a dutiful creature, and it was hoped for a long time that there would be an heir.

So Margaret was once again alone.

It was Cousin Hubert who, indirectly, brought her out of what Bonsam had now become; a place of despondent bitterness, of weary day following day. But Margaret had nowhere else to go; and saw herself as the years passed—she was by now twenty-five—falling into the neglected pattern of a poor relation, a spinster aunt; though John's wife had not even yet borne the expected heir. Perhaps there would be children made between them in the end; but Margaret cared no longer, and continued her walks with Augusta and the pug, which latter lived on to an incredibly old age; and cribbage with her aunt in the evenings, and repairing of the church-linen now a new rector had come to Bonsam. He was sixty-two, and had been twice married. There were no younger men.

There was at the Hall, had always been, Cousin Hubert. Cousin Hubert was confined in a back room in much the same way as Augusta, later, was to be confined abovestairs; but his madness took a particular form; he modelled ships. He did not even attend meals. He pottered among the models all day, and at one time they had been permitted to grace the great hall of Bonsam, until there grew too many in their glass cases for anyone comfortably to pass by; then Cousin Hubert, to his immense hurt, had been caused to remove them all to the wing above the kitchen-quarters, where there was a large unused room. Here he would still be found, vaguely peering from among his stuffed cases like a lost hobgoblin; the models themselves were exquisite, ranging in variety from the *Great Harry* and *Great Michael* to the latest ships of the line, scaled down. Cousin Hubert had a working table on which he made the parts, variously littered with shapes of sawn wood, screws, bolts, nails and hardened glue-pots, tools and a brazier. Margaret won the old gentleman's approval early because she brought him mutton-sandwiches from belowstairs, and, later, scraps of fallen twigs and branches from her walks, to be sawn in due course into deck-planks.

It was the model ships which brought George Howie to Bonsam in time; their fame having spread somehow, as such things will, to the north.

Everybody else was out, attending a village christening, when he came. Margaret was sent for from where she had been combing out Augusta's hair, briefly smoothed her own and went down. The Scottish gentleman had arrived with suitable introductions; he presented these to Margaret, thinking her the lady of the house. "It's a fine place ye have here," he told her. He was a cocky, stoutening little man with a balding scalp across which strands of hair, suspiciously black, were sparsely plastered at intervals; he had side-whiskers, which of late years had become fashionable. Margaret was at once diverted by and wary of him. She had never met such a person before.

She denied her mistaken status, explaining who she in fact was; and at once Howie's manner changed. He straddled before the cautious wood fire the Hall servants had lit, causing it to wink on ruby studs and gold fob-watch chain. From his conversation Margaret found that he was a man of business, a financier, a shipowner—"for the future, my dear; a wheen o' us is interested in certain engines run by steam. Ye'll ken naught o't; 'tis not a lady's matter." But Margaret, educated by Cousin Hubert, held her own; and afterwards George Howie was to confess that it was her intelligence and grasp of matters, as much as her looks—"and a fine handsome woman ye were, Maggie, even in those days, and better now I've dressed ye as befits the wife o' a man o' substance"—that had led him, as soon as the inspection of the models was at length concluded, to ask the Squire's permission to pay his addresses to his niece. He made it clear to that astonished gentleman that he had little time to waste; he must return north in a few days' time, he said, as his affairs were pressing.

When he did return, Margaret went with him. She had no idea why she had accepted without hesitation the offer which the Squire had wryly referred to herself, saying she was of age and her own mistress. Her uncle, doubtless, had expected her to refuse an alliance with a person of so inferior a social connection, though it seemed true enough that George Howie had money. But Margaret had seen a sudden way out of the dreary, endless tunnel of her way of living, into a daylight perhaps alien and too bright, but tolerable. She married George Howie in church before they left a week later: he had, and flourished it with pardonable pride, paid the sum demanded for a special licence.

Howie had married Margaret for one reason only; he wanted to be one of the nobs. That the young woman was comely enough he could see for himself, but he had over the years protected a number of other such comely women who catered, in the most private capacity possible, for George's fleshly needs. To say that he had fallen in love, at his age, would have been ridiculous. But Margaret had breeding; the way her finely turned wrists and bosom moved, her graceful pouring of wine on that first evening, with the firelight shining on her hair and gown—such a plain gown, he'd buy her a better! As a wife who could bring George Howie the worldly recognition he craved, now that he had risen by his own efforts from the lowest to the highest, except that the nobs still ignored him ... well, they shouldn't, once *she* was by his side to show them who was who! "Shouldn't be surprised if she was at home with a duke," Howie told himself, dazzled that this creature, who would make so presentable a hostess to all the best folk, and on whose fine flesh he also hoped to breed sons to inherit all he'd gained, sat by him in their homeward carriage. They hadn't, on that first night, had much to say to one another; but he'd shown her, as he put it, to himself, who was master. With such a wife it would be only a matter of time before the nobs—who'd made full use of his knowledge of business, his engineering connections—would accept him, perhaps ask both of them to dinner, who knew? They'd stop a night or two on the way, and furbish Margaret with a few gowns and other matters: she must make her impact on the critical city society fully feathered as George Howie's lady-wife. Bonnets, pelisses, furbelows—what didn't he know about all of that? Best say naught, however ... and he himself wouldn't be surprised if, other nights being like last night, he didn't give the other little lady her notice to quit, and cleave solely to his wife.

So Margaret drove away from Bonsam with few regrets, and no illusions. She found, in the nights they spent together in four-posters at the various changing-inns, that she could endure Howie's demands on her with equanimity; life with the Reverend Alfred had long opened her eyes to what men were. As she satisfied George, he would grow, with her tactful handling, less brash as time went by. His shirt-studs began to shout less loudly, his stocks and his manners improved, and he no longer openly flourished his wealth in newcomers' faces; it was discreetly reflected in the richly furnished house to which William Heatherton, and his wretched foreign bride, came for their wedding-presentation some years afterwards. By that time the Howie nursery was increasing its inmates yearly, only one ambition remaining to be fulfilled; all the children born had been till now young ladies, and Margaret, as much as George, had longed for a son. When he was at last born, his mother insisted on calling him John, after her cousin at Bonsam. She would not be gainsaid in this, and George Howie, who by this time doted on her, gave in to this wish of hers as he now did, unknown to himself, in all others. The unofficial ladies had long gone their way: and upstairs in the nursery there was, after all, a bonny wee lass with shining black hair and rosy cheeks, bearing the feminine version of his own name: Georgina.

XVII

Sarah Court re-entered Margaret's life in the fourth year of the marriage. When the shabby, tight-lipped creature was announced as waiting in the hall Margaret was about to go out, drawing on her gloves preparatory to entering the carriage. The woman waited in silence, hands in her lap. She had the unmistakable manner of the born servant, yet Margaret could not at first recall ever having seen her before. Being in haste, she asked the woman somewhat sharply what she wanted. "I have no vacant places here," she told the other, thinking that the woman might have come to ask about the possibility of work in the Howie household. There was however no lack of domestic help in the city, though of a rough nature: most of the girls Margaret had already hired were Highland, and required some patience in training, particularly for the serving up of food suitably at table. Margaret had begun to give discreet dinner-parties to such of George Howie's business acquaintances as he sought to impress; and she insisted on a high standard both in the cooking and the serving of the food, and the setting out beforehand of shining crystal and silver. Having had much to do with the management both of the rectory and Bonsam in latter years, she knew how to go about training servants. This woman, from the look of her, was not as young as most applicants. "Why are you without a place?" said Margaret, containing her own impatience to be gone. The woman gave her close-lipped smile, and Margaret was aware of an increasing certainty that they had after all encountered one another previously. But she could not say where it had been, till Sarah herself reminded her.

"I was with you and the Rector, ma'am, in the year or two before he died. I was laundry-maid eight month: do you mind of me now?"

"You were——" Amazement, followed by a kind of belated

recognition, struggled in Margaret; the laundry-maid, whom she recalled well enough, had been a fresh-faced, strapping thing, with dark hair and a trim figure. This woman's hair was lifeless and greying, and she had lost her teeth. Her hands, which despite the cold autumn day were without gloves even of cotton, were red and raw. Could it be—what had that girl's name been? Sarah. Sarah Court.

"You left us, I remember, with——"

Sarah's smile grew grim. "Pains in the belly, ma'am; would you know the cause? Maybe not then, for you were a young maid such as I was; but now I can tell it all; I should have done it then. My father laid about me with a hide belt when I'd walked home twenty mile, and next day the pains began again. I doubt me if the boy 'ud have been other than he became, if I hadn't had that belting then, but we don't know, do we? Anyways, it was the Rector was to blame for't. I can say it all now, when they're both of them dead."

Margaret looked hurriedly behind her; none of the servants were in the hall, and the children, whom she would not have wanted even to witness such talk, were with their nurse upstairs. Georgy at three was retentive enough to have remembered, and perhaps repeated what she might hear. "Come into the small parlour, and say what you must," Margaret said calmly to the woman. And so she heard the rest of Sarah Court's tale.

The boy Sarah bore the Reverend Alfred prematurely had been an idiot, harmless enough; "But my father said 'twas a judgment on me for the sin. How was I to know, no one having told me how such things happen, and I an innocent maid? I didn't rightly know what it was the Reverend would be at, the first time; after that I was frightened, for I knew I wasn't as I should be. But I didn't even know, ma'am, why it was I was getting big. We never did speak of such matters at home, my father being a strict man, and a member of the sect." Sarah's people and Margaret's mother had belonged to the same nonconformist group; their language was such as Margaret understood and, in her own way, condoned; the Scots church which she now attended weekly with her husband presented no difficulty to her in the way of worship, with its similar stern creed and emphasis on direct revelation and strict morality: Mr.

Heatherton, although he was so young, impressed Margaret by his preaching, and she followed his words from her pew each week with close attention. She looked at Sarah now with her direct, narrow gaze.

"We will not speak of such things here either, Sarah; I do not wish it in my house. Why have you come to me?" She did not ask how Sarah had found her; anyone at Bonsam could have directed the woman, but why had she waited so many years before coming north?

"Because he's dead now, my boy, of a fit: they got worse over the past year, and in the end went on and on and——" Sarah's face hardened spasmodically; she had loved her helpless bastard boy and had been his sole bulwark against a harsh, unfeeling world. "I'd take him with me, ma'am, whenever I looked for work, 'cause I wouldn't have him parted from me; unkind, they'd have been to him, maybe, with me not there, and him not able to answer for himself, or know what 'twas about. But mostly folk wouldn't take me when they saw the way he was; I took all kinds of work, ma'am, mostly in the dairy; sometimes I'd scrub, and again sometimes I'd launder, the way I used to do for you. Do you mind the way I used to starch the church-linen? Maybe, ma'am, if you were to give me a place ... seeing as we both know one about the other ... I'd serve you well, ma'am, you know that."

The woman passed her tongue quickly over her thin pale lips, with a flicker like a snake's. Margaret was aware of a moment's revulsion, an instant's foreseeing wariness. Was she in fact being coerced into taking Sarah Court into her household? Could this poor ill-used woman, knowing whence Margaret herself had come and what her true status had been, do her harm in the influential circle she was beginning to draw about her now, among the people who had taken George's word for it that she had been of high degree in her English birthplace? What would they do if Sarah told them her former mistress's mother had been the cook, and that mistress herself a poor relation, unpaid and clad in cast-offs till George Howie came? And Cousin Augusta——

Margaret shivered inwardly. It hadn't been the beating Sarah had had which caused her to give birth to an idiot. It was the madness that tainted all the Reverend Alfred's family, the same as had produced Augusta. She herself, Alfred's own daughter, carried the seeds of that madness. Any of her children might, at any time, be born insane; have fits, drool pitifully like the poor creature back at Bonsam now, locked in her upper room with a keeper. And there were those in the south who still said that she, Margaret Howie, had caused the death of her own father.

She made her face a mask and said cheerfully, "It will be pleasant for us both, Sarah, if you stay with me now that you are alone. I'll be glad of expert laundrywork, and you will be a help, I know, in keeping the Highland girls at their tasks; they are often impractical."

"I'll serve you all my life, ma'am," said Sarah. The flicker of doubt Margaret had had about the matter soon passed; why should she cavil at having acquired a trained, faithful servant?

So Sarah stayed.

Sarah Court wordlessly included in her other duties the welfare of young Mrs. Heatherton and her baby, and when both were returned home she told her mistress, with whom she was at times in danger of becoming over-cordial, "I don't like that Scotch minister." William had visited his wife each afternoon. Margaret looked up from her sewing; a reproof started to form itself on her lips, then she thought better of it. Nothing would ever prevent Sarah from being outspoken with her; better so than that the woman should go and spread gossip outside, and she was a good worker, for which reason Margaret had ceased to regret acquiring her.

Margaret merely smiled, therefore, and put in a stitch before saying idly, to give the matter its minimal importance, "Why, Sarah? They say Mr. Heatherton is very faithful in his pastoral duties, and he preaches a fine sermon. What more can one ask?" She found herself, for the first time as a result of this converse, surveying William Heatherton as a person, a man rather than a preacher. She reserved her own judgment on this head till later, when she should be alone. She had not, truth to tell, had any considered opinion of the man hitherto one way or the other; Sarah's dislike had forced her now to take sides, and this in its turn made her angry. But she said nothing.

"There isn't always a reason for such things," replied Sarah to her late question. "Shall you be wanting the mutton for today, ma'am? I said I'd go out, straight down to the market, for it; that way it keeps fresher in these towns."

Her mistress nodded, and having seen the woman go out felt a lingering trace of wistfulness for Bonsam overcome her. There, they had had a deep well lined with brick, in which the winter's snow could be packed hard down and keep frozen all the year, except perhaps in an excessively hot summer. She had no way here of keeping such things as meat fresh, and the milk turned in July month even though it was bought daily, for the children, from a peddler who came the rounds with it fresh from his own cows, which he kept at graze just beyond the boundary of the city. Georgy loved to be taken to visit the cows and have a draught of sweet, creamy milk served to her by the dairy-maid. How pretty the child was growing!

Margaret went on in course of this contemplation to assess her own happiness; and decided that, when all was said, it was reasonably complete. She was more contented by far than William Heatherton's young foolish wife, who also had had a difficulty and straining in her labour that Margaret never experienced. A pity that such a fine man had chosen so puling a wife, but perhaps it would not hinder his career if Marie Heatherton applied herself now to the promotion of her husband's well-being as others did. At the moment the young woman seemed to think exclusively of herself, and no doubt, her baby.

But Marie did not consider the baby greatly as yet; she had too recent a memory of the pain endured in bearing Catherine. There was also the question of Catherine's father. Since first returning with the small creature in a shawl on her arm, installing her where she now was in the new nursery in a curtained cradle, Marie had spent her own nights near by on a truckle-bed in order to get up and feed the baby according to Margaret Howie's strict instructions. Marie had obeyed these, and hoped in time to become a suitable mother to Catherine such as Margaret was to her own brood; but the baby's pulling at and nourishing of itself from her flesh afflicted her with a strange, unnatural discomfort. It was as though William's child, like William himself, was and could be no part of her; as though its late habitation of her body had been itself an intrusion. She would feed the child adequately, replace it in its cradle, wipe its mouth and see to its needs; but she could not feel love for it. It was a good baby, affording the minimum of inconvenience after its first unheralded entry into the world. Its dark hair would remain straight, fine and somewhat lank, like Marie's own; its eyes were dark like hers also, but its temperament was William's. Marie was already a trifle in awe of it, climbing back to her own low pallet with relief when the night's tasks were done.

The appearance of William himself in his tasselled night-cap, on the fifth night, afflicted Marie with rebellion. Had she not done her full duty in lately bearing his child? She knew now what marriage meant; had she known in the first place, she would never have married William Heatherton. She struggled with her natural timidity and dislike of addressing William at any time unbidden. In the end she forced out speech; clutching her robe about herself, hair and eyes wild, speech rapid and reproachful.

"You are irresponsible," he said in reply. He had noticed that she spoke for the most part in French; undoubtedly women grew hysterical at such times. William reminded himself of the now discredited mediaeval belief concerning the womb as the seat of imbalance, and smiled placidly; but in spite of this toleration he was angry with Marie. To say, as she continued to do that she wished to sleep alone, to cease to be his wife in any physical sense was—again the only word recurred that would serve—hysteria. Such fancies were to be sternly discouraged; a show of firmness at the outset should perhaps be enough. William therefore addressed his wife firmly and, as he saw it, kindly; and this despite some awareness of his own lack of dignity in nightshirt and cap. His sight, without the glasses he had taken to wearing lately, was inclining to blur nowadays for near objects; the dimly outlined, ghostly figure of his wife was as out of keeping as her behaviour on the wedding-night had been. Despite his own resolve annoyance mounted in William. He flushed slightly.

"Women are compelled to suffer in this world as daughters of Eve, my dear. Pain is a part of the price to be paid for the sin of our first mother, and——"

"But you, you do not suffer. It is only I."

"Do not interrupt me, Marie. We must abide by the will of God, before Whom we made our vows of marriage, and are one flesh." Still employing his determined kindness, he laid hold of her and guided her, by now browbeaten into passivity, back to their mutual bedside, and made her kneel down by him there while he prayed aloud for some minutes. Then he placed her in the bed and, without further resistance from her, re-established the physical relationship which he had lacked since the birth. The interim had strained William's continence, and his possession of her tonight was the more urgent and insistent. It was, he told himself, every man's need he felt; how, looking back, had he contrived before marriage? "For years I was celibate," he thought. At the end, his good-humour restored, he kissed Marie with affectionate forgiveness. The situation of her mutiny should not recur, he promised himself; for her own sake he must continue to subdue the devil in her.

Marie had been lying still in weariness and resentment; why must she suffer for the sin of Eve? "*C'est la folie, ça,*" she told herself, and drew away from William in the bed. What did he know of suffering such as she had already endured? And suffer she had, and would again if another child, other children, came. Margaret Howie had given birth five, six times; the sweat broke out on Marie's body at thought of it. Whatever Mrs. Howie chose to forget, it had not been granted to herself to have the memory of the recent labour pains dulled; she could still recall every moment of their sharpness and agony. Was William to fill her with children every year, like Mrs. Howie, perhaps like Urquhart's wife who, when she saw Marie last, had looked at her with furtive triumph as if she herself had gained some victory? "I was not her enemy," Marie thought, and began to cry. She continued her crying in silence; for William to hear her, to wake again, would be intolerable. She would perhaps die next time a baby came. She would tell William so if she were less afraid of him. She would tell him ... and perhaps would in any case be better dead, out of misery, out of servitude. Not a single moment of her life now was her own. She should never have been married, and now there was no escape from William, unctuously kind, for ever physically about and within her; and William's children, who would increasingly demand attention from her of a kind she already disliked; she would never be alone again. Why had it sometimes troubled her that she was ostracised, an outcast, at the convent school? One's own company was enough, if only women were allowed to know it in time, in time...

It was perhaps at that moment that Marie resolved to look for a place which she could call her own; an unknown, unsought place, where nobody would think of looking for her. It would be a relief even to hide behind a curtain and hear William calling and calling for her, and to know that she need only not answer to be left sometimes alone. She could draw again, perhaps. She would take paper and pencils with her where she went; there was certain to be somewhere in all the great rambling, half-tenanted house that William's church folk made him live in.

But it was not to be at the Gowanmount manse that Marie at last found such a place as she sought. It would not be long now till William received the coveted call to Savill's, obtaining it over the heads of five older men who preached to the best of their notable ability. William's physical well-being continued to contribute to the power of his preaching. The night before the decisive sermon, he had got Marie with child again.

XVIII

It was no doubt as a result of William and Marie's mild social elevation that they were bidden, very shortly after William's sustaining of the Savill call, to drink tea with Mrs. Howie at her house on a named afternoon. Few were ever so invited, Margaret Howie being a personage who somewhat limited her closer acquaintance; and William at least was conscious enough of the implied flattery of the invitation to tell his wife that she might meantime purchase a new gown.

"Not unbecoming," he instructed her, and Marie knew well enough that this only meant, as always, a sufficiently subdued manner of dress in order that the ladies of the congregation might not be outshone in their Sunday finery, or their husbands' attention perhaps even diverted from the sermon. She went, accordingly, to a modiste Alicia had told her of, who might be relied upon to provide what was wanted and—James's wife being tactful in such ways—not overcharge for it. But as it happened Madame Mirabelle herself had a slight indisposition on that day, and it was her assistant who served Marie. This young woman did not, as William would have put it, know what was proper; she brought out a taffetas walking-gown with flounces, in a reckless combination of the new brought colours lately made possible by the discovery of coal-tar dyes.

"I do not think——" stammered Marie, who was nevertheless filled with a sudden hunger at sight of the brilliant, surely improper gown. If only she were permitted ... if only she might ever wear such things! It would not be unbecoming to her sallow skin. It would make her—as the dull shades she had hitherto worn did not—stand out in any assembly. But that was the last thing William would permit her to do.

The assistant's enthusiasm was, perhaps, partly caused by fellow-feeling for this poor brown wren. How the bright new plumage would become her! The girl held the dress up before Marie, exclaiming at the bold aniline colours which still, until folk grew used to them, dazzled the eye. "Not everybody could wear it," she said, "but *you* could. Try it on, ma'am."

She aided Marie in the unfastening of her unpretentious gown and bonnet. The flamboyant, rustling garment slid at last over Marie's shoulders.

"Ma'am is transformed! It fits like a glove, would need hardly any altering. The price——"

Marie was no longer listening; she was seeing herself in the mirror. There, revealed as though from the chrysalis, stood a being who was no longer the crushed, colourless, inevitably pregnant helpmeet of the rising young minister of Savill's. Here was herself, as she should somehow have become; as she could still become, if——

If what? For there was, she knew, no escape. Even death, should William die, could not free her; she would be a widow then, condemned to mourning, perhaps later to half-colours, possibly to a certain circumscribed social existence. And William would not die; how could she have supposed that he would? Already her confidence ebbed as she remembered William in his vitality and, no doubt, his anger if, with his money, she unthinkably bought this unsuitable, garish gown. She must remember—how often she had been told of it, had it hinted and dinned into her!—that she was the wife, the partner for life and the hereafter, of a respected public figure, a preacher in direct daily contact with the Almighty who might, one often thought, almost be the Almighty himself; someone who would never, never abate one jot of his pretensions to indulge any whim of hers; and why should she need such a gown? She was a woman, a lesser creature fashioned from man's rib; women must do as their husbands bade them, bear children, see to the housekeeping, speak little, remain in the background, never flaunt themselves, never show what they felt . . .

Marie turned away from the bright temptation in the mirror, her metamorphosis, herself as she might have been; but even at this moment, with, again, William's child firmly implanted in her womb, she grew confused, less certain of herself than a moment ago. By the time *he* died—if he ever did—she'd be an old worn-out woman, and there were the girls; no doubt they, too, one day must also marry.

"Take it off," she said to the assistant. For instants they gazed at one another, as equals might; the initial sharp intent of the saleswoman still shot through with that brief, mysterious compassion. She hadn't for a moment thought ma'am would buy the gown; she only ... Madame Mirabelle didn't pay much in wages, and there was an old sick mother at home; everybody had their troubles. "As you say, ma'am." She undid, in a kind of lassitude, the flamboyant walking-dress, and took it off and away; its exotic rustling sounded for moments behind a plain holland curtain where the goods hung, and then was stilled. The assistant came out with others, dully.

"These may perhaps suit ma'am better." They might, no doubt; two unremarkable gowns, one of which Marie chose because it fitted her, and saved the cost of alterations. It was the accustomed colour of dead leaves, and was—Marie winced—respectable enough to satisfy the standards demanded by William and William's world, in particular George Howie's wife on the occasion of her tea-drinking *en famille*.

The tea-drinking took place as predicted, with Margaret Howie presiding over an embossed silver tea-pot, plates of scones and cakes, and the white-and-gold china. Small Catherine had been taken upstairs, for nursery tea with the young Howies: the room was quiet, elegant and adult. Margaret replaced the heavy pot with some contentment on its tray. Unlike Scotswomen, she did not use a cosy; nor did she tell the guests how George had brought back, from one of his visits to London, the complete tea-service with its cream-jug and two bowls, and the tray. He had beaten the old silversmith down, he told her. "Georgian, he said it was; that didna matter to me, I said, provided the wife liked it. If he kept to his fancy price, I said, I'd go elsewhere. The business was winding up, my dear, after a century in the one family, as owners; it's possible to drive a good bargain at such times. What d'ye think on't, Mag?" And she had praised it, and him, while all the time he watched her with his shrewd, salacious dark eyes; he'd grown unusually demanding lately. She had explained to

George what Georgian meant, in process of his social education; but it was a pleasure to sit here and know that she need not do the same for William Heatherton. Margaret knew, for she had taken especial pains today with her appearance, that she herself looked well, more so perhaps than usual, in her new grape-purple bombazine, for she favoured dark colours. How delightful that, at last, she was pouring tea for William Heatherton—George was not present—and, of course, his dull young wife, who sat there sipping her tea without a word and staring down, but evidently without appreciation, at the Turkey carpet. Truth to tell, for such a splendid man it was more than ever a pity that——But Margaret downed her thought, smiled, and remembered how she'd persuaded George, against his initial inclinations, to desert Gowanmount, where he'd been on the Session for many years, and follow Mr. Heatherton to his new charge of Savill's. "All of the very best people will be met with there, I give you my word," she had said, and her word in the end, as he always nowadays did, George Howie had taken. He was finally won over when Margaret reminded him how valuable the right connections might be for their children's futures.

So now the three of them, William, herself and Marie, sat in the drawing-room where the fire in the grate leaped cleanly, showing whitewashed hearth-bricks. The Queen had her coals whitewashed when she was about to travel by her new private train, they said, as otherwise the smoke was dirty and soiled one on the journey. The power of steam...

They discussed that, James, his prosperity, and thence the royal news, which was gazetted daily in the papers. Presently the conversation turned to theology, out of a desire on the part of the hostess to make Mr. Heatherton feel at home. To have him actually here, on her sofa! One must not, of course, give any inkling that the favour was sought rather than given ... He was handsomer than ever, one would think, now that the Saville's vacancy was secured, with its added stipend and reputation. He had put on flesh a little, and his well-kept hands manipulated his tea-cup, plate and saucer creditably.

"Will you not try a ratafia biscuit, Mrs. Heatherton? They are a speciality of my own cook." It was not yet, despite the aid given in that first labour, a matter of Christian names between

Margaret and Marie: nor would it ever be; the formalities must be preserved. Marie having declined a biscuit, the gold-and-white plate was passed to her husband. That young woman, Margaret immediately realised, must be in an interesting situation once more; she herself was aware of a sudden sharp pang of envy. A mercy one could control one's thoughts ... Leaving William's wife suppressing her faint, familiar nausea, Margaret turned again to the man with whom, when all was said, she could properly enjoy an intellectual gallop for this intimate half-hour. "Mr. Heatherton," she said, still smiling, "may a member of the weaker sex be forgiven for posing a question on a point of doctrine?"

She was forgiven; she posed the question; Marie never afterwards remembered what it was. Freewill and predestination, two words she did not understand, battled with one another presently across the Turkey carpet; for herself, it was enough discipline to control the tendency its pattern had to grow nearer, then melt further away. She could not, for a second time, in this house ... in this house ... what were they saying? For how much longer must she endure ... endure what? To return home was, she knew, no cure.

"Certain souls are set aside from the beginning for eternal damnation."

"No, no, my dear madam, that is not according to the benevolent dispensations of Providence, which ..."

William launched forth on his convictions concerning the possibility of redemption for all men. "How can we, before we know even what we are, and what we may do, be so rejected? No, Mrs. Howie, a soul may work out the will of God, or else its self-will ..."

"I do not agree. The inability to feel within oneself what used to be named as original sin, surely argues a predisposition ..."

"If we were too certain of our own state of ultimate damnation or of blessedness, that in itself would be pride, which in itself, in turn, is sin. One cannot so order Providence."

"But you are saying, sir, that Providence cannot order us. I myself believe that we are so ordered."

"One must not judge rashly——"

"Some must surely be damned by their very nature, and

cannot escape eternal punishment. If God will not have mercy on such at the Day of Judgment, how can we do so?"

During the weighty pauses, the reasoned cross-arguments, William noted, as he was perhaps intended to note, the broad, white, unfurrowed brow beneath Margaret's smoothly parted hair. Behind it such thoughts surged as he would have thought unwomanly in any other woman. Where had she learnt so stern a creed? Her forebears——

But William would never know of Margaret's sectarian mother, the cook. He expatiated again on the nature of God's gift of freewill; both women appeared to be listening. But Marie, ignorant of that narrow sect whose creed had finally cast Margaret's mother out, was in the grip of an older, harsher aspect of terror. From long ago, as they talked, she remembered it; from long, long ago; it was as if it were in the very marrow of her bones, not only from the brief encounters, accidental as they had been, that she had had with the teachings of the Catholic Church during her time in the convent. Papa had expressed a wish that she should not be reared as a Papist, and his wish had been respected. But one still heard things ... and remembered them, in words and images.

"De poenis inferni, et de profundo lacu; libera eas de ore leonis, ne absorbat eas Tartarus, ne cadant in obscurum ..."

Why was she so frightened? Why was the sweat trickling down between her breasts, beneath her dress, to where the stays caught her, to where the unborn child already lay? Though she could not remember the words all in order she was assailed by a creeping sensation of horror, here in this rich unaware room; that nobody except herself was informed of it she knew. The two figures sitting here with her in the room, whom the horror consumed, were meantime placidly drinking tea from white-and-gold cups; the glimmer of the fire shone on Margaret's embossed tea-service, nothing had changed, yet, yet ... The uttermost pit, the abyss of hell, the place of the damned, the lion's very mouth; it was to receive them, perhaps not herself, and yet there was still the horror ...

Margaret Howie returned her narrow gaze to survey William's wife. The dull creature was even yet gazing down at the carpet as though it held some matter for intelligent comment, but she had contributed nothing to the conversation.

What an instructive, what an enjoyable battle of wits she herself had had with William Heatherton concerning what, in fact, Margaret herself felt to be most deeply true! No doubt in the future they could cross swords again, after today's progression of acquaintance towards a somewhat closer friendship. What a scholarly, handsome man! Yet he had not quite bested her. Margaret nursed her triumph, glossing over any desire she might have to submit mentally, perhaps even physically, to William. Such a conclusion would not have been proper; yet it was, as she again reminded herself, a pity so fine a man had so unresponsive and dull a wife.

II

I

Paul Henri Lucien Chantal had made his way north after a period of, for him, expensive advertising in the weekly gazettes. One, perused mostly by the genteel of the city, carried a column of London news, where the briefly described charity-concerts, celebrities and fashions made mouth-watering reading to such as Sophia Urquhart the builder's wife, who had never been farther south than Carlisle. It had been Sophia, in fact, who first noted the modest insertion concerning a young French gentleman, anxious to improve his acquaintance with any part of the British Isles and, as if in afterthought, to give lessons in French for a fee. Sophia had brought the notice to the attention of her husband's sister Flora, by now a lady of some local fame for her successful, expanding, and elegant girls' school. To have the young ladies tutored in what stated itself to be the best accent of Paris appealed, as Sophia had known it would, to Miss Flora. She sent for the young gentleman to appear for an interview, liked his modest manners and engaged him.

That had been some weeks ago; and it accounted for the fact that Paul, who was a freethinker, was escorting Miss Flora and her flock now to church, after which he had been invited to partake of Sunday dinner. As the alternative was a snatched poor meal in his draughty, inadequate lodging, Paul had accepted gladly; it was a few hours' *ennui* in order to look forward to a full stomach. Miss Flora, who could remember enough of her own pinched youth to have sympathy with Paul's lot, was nevertheless unable, for she had expenses to meet, to pay him more salary than he was worth to her. Despite his dapper appearance, accordingly, one of Paul's shoes had a hole in the sole, and his cuffs were frayed and carefully trimmed with scissors. Nevertheless, he was of pleasing appearance; his brown eyes had the appeal of a lost spaniel's, and his brown silky side-whiskers added somewhat to his resemblance of that lovable animal. However, he taught the schoolgirls strictly, and corrected their essays thoroughly; any doubts Flora might have entertained about employing a Monsieur, instead of a Mademoiselle—the last had retired with bronchitis—were laid at rest after the first few days she had employed Paul Chantal at the school. His manner with the girls was perfect; never pompous, but distinctly not familiar, or encouraging familiarity from certain of the more forward young hussies who, regrettably, included Flora's own niece and godchild, Flossie Urquhart, a minx if ever there was one. She took, Miss Flora was sadly aware, despite all that education and precept could do, after her mother; in other words, no expense could turn Flossie, and even less her sister Ag, into young ladies. Flora's conscience rebuked her for failing her brother Hector in such a matter, but Hector's interests, as his perceptive sister soon came to realise, were centred exclusively on his sons, especially Richard, who was by now both steady and handsome; the younger Hector inclined already to be unbiddable, and Alexander was extravagant with his pocket-money, and sometimes told untruths.

Such thoughts flitted through Miss Flora's relaxed mind now, when she could see from her place her brother himself, grown grey-haired, and Sophia by him in a very vulgar bonnet, seated as usual well to the front of Savill's. The professors, occupying on the whole the remaining body of the church, were digesting every word uttered by the Reverend William Heatherton with profound intellectual analysis and, in general, approval; William had been with them now for years. So—and this had caused no little gossip at the time, though such things were known to happen sometimes—had the Howies, who by now filled a handsome pew each Sunday at Savill's, as they had begun to do at Gowanmount before they left it. Margaret Howie it was who had insisted that they follow when William Heatherton left Gowanmount to take up his new charge; it was true that the Howie house was of equal distance from both Gowanmount and Savill's, but several of the former congregation had thought, and had not kept their thoughts to themselves, that George Howie by now was completely dominated by his wife. To have so rich a source of support removed from its midst left Gowanmount, no doubt, worldly the poorer; and Savill's was already well endowed enough.

But there it was, and the Howies duly sat in state in their central pew. The stylish bonnets of Mrs. Howie, and the way she dressed her daughters, were perhaps less outstanding here than they had been in their last, less competitive place of worship. Georgy, by this time almost eight years old, wore crimson velvet, with a little squirrel muff; she looked like Red Riding Hood, and was a foil for her handsome mother, clad today in discreet dove-grey taffetas with a Paris veil. The heads of the other children scarcely reached, when they were seated all together, above the back of the solid oak pew; and Sophia Urquhart removed her somewhat soured gaze from contemplation of the Howie family, and quickly passed by her own, seated nearby Flora. There was little to cheer Sophia in the sight of her girls; Flossie was lumpish, still with too much puppy-fat at fifteen, and Ruth and Agnes already had pimples; their clothes, on which no expense and trouble had been spared, looked garish today, nor was their demeanour anything to boast of. Sophia's lips tightened as she saw Ag ogle the young French tutor seated on everyone's right; oddly, it was M. Chantal's possible feelings in the matter which concerned Sophia, for having, as she told herself, been responsible for his appointment at her sister-in-law's school, she desired him to be comfortable there. Such elegant, perfect courtesy as he always displayed, in particular to a lady! And his appearance was, while not perhaps of the first tone, elegant also, despite unavoidable shabbiness; how was it that foreigners contrived such a combination? Sophia's eyes narrowed. She had already, on an occasion when they had asked him to partake of tea one day last week, pumped Paul shamelessly about his past life, without satisfaction; no matter how she prodded, he remained politely evasive. "But always so *polite*!" acceded Sophia. It made what must from any other person have been a rebuke seem almost like a compliment. There must, Sophia was now sure, be aristocratic breeding in the young man to enable him to confront situations so faultlessly; perhaps he was the heir to confiscated lands and titles, a descendant of the *émigrés* of last century? She had suggested as much to Hector; and he, of course, being a man and her husband, had merely grunted and told her to mind her own business and not be a fool. But it *was* her business to know who had access to her girls. Sophia had continued to take an interest in Paul Chantal. After church today, he and Flora were invited out again to the Urquhart house, this time to eat luncheon; Sophia had taken no denial. She jabbed now with her parasol at Agnes's near side, to make that young lady conform, and behave herself. Ag suppressed a squeal, and giggled instead; several persons looked round, and Flora frowned sternly at her niece, which achieved the desired quietus. Sophia contained her own annoyance, consoling herself with remembering the prosperous manner of their arrival today, in the carriage. She herself, and the girls too, all had new spring outfits; she fancied she, on Hector's arm, for once looked as well as that Howie woman, sweeping in always so pleased with herself, as though she were a duchess despite the absurd little husband by her side: and not at all easy to get to know. The bells of Savills's Old had almost ceased their clangour as Sophia and Hector entered, at precisely the right time, with everyone in their pews ready to spectate as they entered their own, which was located in exactly the right part, in the body of the church, where one could be both central and observed. It was, also, an indication that one paid more pew-rent than the people who had merely reserved a place at the side aisle. Sophia subsided, pleased, not having heard one word of William Heatherton's sermon. Neither, if she had known, had Paul Chantal.

Paul was in a strange state of mind. At first he had contented himself, even with some degree of amusement, with gazing at the architecture the denizens of Savill's considered very fine; Paul thought it vulgar, and he was not yet accustomed to a total absence even of any place for statues, or stained glass. The windows here were fan-shaped, with ugly yellow panes which made, he decided, those seated below them seem bilious. How different from the last time ... yes, the last time he had been inside a church, as a boy! The Abbey of St.-Denis. Paul closed his eyes for instants, feeling the pain flood behind them, even now he had thought himself hardened, unable any longer to feel either pain or surprise.

He no longer believed in God. Perhaps he had never done so; his upbringing had not encouraged it. He and Papa, boon-companions ever since Paul could remember, had discussed all things, sometimes talking together far into the night. Paul had not been made to keep to a little boy's bedtimes. Always Papa had treated him as a man. Maman was never mentioned; she had gone off, he knew, with someone else long ago. Papa, Henri Chantal, was nevertheless a gay, young-seeming man. It did not even yet seem possible that he was dead, had been dead for over a year. The hopes with which he and Paul had finally launched their freethinking newspaper, into which they had put all of their small capital, were shattered when the July Monarchy banned a free press in France. "In any case Papa is dead," said Paul uselessly to himself again. Papa had been the life-blood of the enterprise, he himself hardly more than type-setter and reporter. But it had given him an insight into people, many of them like the overdressed, self-conscious hypocrites among whom he sat now. Miss Flora, she was different. But that sister-in-law, who looked at him with avid eyes and sweated lamentably beneath the arms ... and her daughters who would also be like that when they were grown ...

Perhaps he could soon obtain employment in some journal. The school task was all very well, but not for the rest of one's life. He himself, young as he was, had already seen and heard too much to tolerate so narrow a compass, though Miss Flora seemed to let it satisfy her. "But she is a remarkable woman," thought Paul. He enjoyed talking to the clever, plain head-mistress when either he or she had time. The school was, however, Miss Flora's enterprise, as the paper had been Papa's. That fact would make one endure narrowness, impertinence perhaps. And Miss Flora had not lived in France, where so many changes had come in the span of an ordinary lifetime that anyone not of that nation would grow confused by them. From old régime to republican, republican to Bonapartist, then with the Empire gone for ever one endured the Bourbons again for a time, then Louis Philippe had ridden in on the July triumph some years back and was now, it seemed, heading for downfall, but that had not been in time to save Papa or the paper. One knew nothing, except that one could predict nothing. Perhaps, in that case, it was as well he, Paul, was following the career briefly pursued, at one time in youth, by King Louis Philippe himself; that of schoolmaster. To have to think for oneself, let alone write what one thought, was unsafe anywhere, even in this country which boasted of itself as free. Let a single one of these well-found Philistines read what he, Paul, thought, and out he'd go, even Miss Flora not daring to protect him, in her position; she'd lose every girl in her school.

But how appalling these people were! It seemed that they were here, as Paul's father would have said, not to worship a God for whose expressed preferences they would have had little time; they came to be seen in the right place, to compare one another's wardrobes. If one were to try to discuss with them what one had heard from this preacher who was said to be on the way to achieving fame, they would not do it. It would be like asking a sheep to turn in a different direction from its herd. It would——

An enviable fate, to be about to become famous! Paul looked again at the preacher. William Heatherton was praying now, his bespectacled head with its well-ordered curls, sprinkled of late years with some grey, bowed on his hands. Their gestures, and the sonorous voice, afflicted Paul with dislike; the man was unctuous. He suited his congregation. He earned every penny of his stipend merely by being what he was. And I, thought Paul, do less; I have to be what I am not, to pretend an interest in correcting the exercises of young ladies who are too stupid even to appreciate their own tongue, let alone mine. The English language is itself flexible, but they will not use it. They know perhaps thirty-eight words which they use regularly. Yet each Sunday they hear this minister, who is to be famous, preach. Why cannot I listen?

An enviable fate ... to climb steadily, prosperously; to arrive duly heralded at the utmost height, whatever it might be. Not, for it was not respectable, to fall suddenly from a great height afterwards like Ixion, in torment for having attained the highest prize. Not to have known hunger and cold, or servitude. To hearken unto this preacher, take a leaf out of his Old Testament, must no doubt be one's own cue.

He had already noted the arrival of William himself at the commencement of the long morning service. All other sounds had ceased, the rustling of the congregation, the whispers of the women in round hats and fur pelisses. No one stood up as William entered; he was accorded no deference not entered in the statute-book, as befitted an adoptive son of John Knox. But it was as if, in a sudden fuss and rearrangement of silk skirts and flounces, the preacher approached with pomp down his aisle, preceded by his beadle, the latter carrying a large Bible with markers. William Heatherton however scattered no drops of holy water, swung no censer; the implied incense was for himself. He had made his way with gowned dignity from vestry to pulpit, mounting its twined steps now magnificently, robes falling about him like the prophets' in their time. He had bowed in brief silent prayer, then announced the opening psalm.

A precentor intoned. During the singing of the metrical version which followed, Paul, who disliked psalms in this form, let his thoughts dwell briefly on this preacher who had lately come in. A large fleshly man; no doubt he dined well, had his creature comforts; was there a wife? Undoubtedly; a feminine version, perhaps, in puce bombazine, with a body of corseted stoutness appropriate to the matching of her bedfellow's massive physique, and its satisfaction. And children? Did Jehovah beget, his wife conceive, regularly? Undoubtedly, even as unto Sarah and unto Abraham, in the end, there had been vouchsafed the sands of the sea, the stars of heaven ... where had he himself got to, in his own thoughts, to remember parts of the Old Testament so clearly? Ah, if good Miss Flora knew what a convinced heathen he was, she would never have allowed him into her school; he had had to pretend he was of Protestant descent and conviction. He himself, accordingly, was as much of a hypocrite as William Heatherton, perhaps more so if this were possible. That personage, in any case, was about to give utterance. Paul settled himself more comfortably in the pew. Pehaps, if he could learn to become a hypocrite in comfort, he would feel it less as time went by. What measure of time? Months, perhaps years?

He found he could not endure the thought of it, or of the difficulty there had been hitherto in obtaining a situation at all. Everyone had been suspicious because he had no references ... he must stay long enough to obtain at least a reference from Miss Flora. How long did that take? A year, perhaps? And then?

He looked at the congregation. It was easier to watch the flock than the shepherd; less challenging, if less rewarding. The more prosperous, it was evident, sat in the centre, where he himself was, not by choice but because Miss Flora had joined her brother and his family, in their appointed place. Paul would rather have been with the lesser lights, partly obscured by pillars and able to eat, at the least, the occasional peppermint; he saw a matron surreptitiously pass one to her companion, a middle-aged stout widow in black. Beyond them again was a separate, isolated pew, with a boxed door, placed below the high pulpit's very shadow. Paul realised with shock that he was looking at William Heatherton's wife.

She was not, not at all, as he had so briefly imagined her; that heresy was the first to deny itself in Paul's mind. His next incredulity was that he had not noticed her before, had not even seen her come in: perhaps she had been early. She was heavily pregnant, and sat with two young children, girls both, and a servant behind. Her separation seemed somehow enforced and barbarous; in those clothes, revealing such a pregnancy. Already big with it, and the two children mere infants, the elder scarcely older than two years! Barbarous; and not more than a year, perhaps less, between the two ugly little creatures with their sallow faces and dark understated clothes. Yet *her* face was sallow; she was, Paul thought, more like a Frenchwoman than a Scot, with the thin sinews of her body stretched and weighted by the expected third child already distorting her plain *feuille morte* gown. It was savage to have forced her to sit there, there in front where she must be stared at by everyone, in this country where they treated an *enceinte* woman not as someone to congratulate, as in his own land, but as one whose condition must never be spoken of, must remain a thing unmentionable. The monster in the pulpit might at least have bought her a pelisse. In her position, no doubt, clothes must be unremarkable, not fashionable: the dark hair itself was smoothly parted under a dull bonnet. At that moment, as Paul stared at Marie, he felt her gaze briefly fasten on him; and for that instant felt that in all of his life he had never seen such passive unhappiness as was revealed in the dark eyes. Her gaze then became self-conscious, the lids dropped at once and she looked away: Paul knew she had seen him. He spent the rest of the time unashamedly gazing at her, and guessed that she was aware of this for she did not look in his direction again. She stared thenceforth at the floor; presently the husband came forward in his pulpit to preach. The wife still did not look up.

It was monstrous, monstrous! That animal ... unctuous, successful, inexorable; eating up, as year followed year, the poor little mouse in her *feuille morte* dress, filling her with children to satisfy his damnable needs.

Paul did not note the sermon. Afterwards he learned that it had concerned the choice of Gideon, when men went to drink at a stream. Some were taken by him, those who flung themselves down at once, and drank. "It was excellently delivered," said Miss Flora, "do you not agree, M. Chantal?" Paul's command of English, she knew, was good. He smiled. "As madame says." He did not, at Flora's age, think of her as mademoiselle; her position alone demanded the definitive title. He saw her smile echo his, and her shrewd hazel eyes twinkled.

"Mr. Heatherton is married to a young French lady. We must perhaps arrange ... a compatriot ..." But Miss Flora had meantime grown flustered. Sophia, always available, smiled enough to show her remaining stumps of teeth.

"It is ... not convenient ... for Mrs. Heatherton to see company just now , my dear Flora." And the smile tightened, the triumphant ineradicable smile of the ever superior, the properly married woman who knows everything such things entail, who is no longer in any sense a mademoiselle. Paul said nothing. If he showed eagerness to meet young Mrs. Heatherton, this bitch would fasten on it and deny him: he had early been sensible of the evil which focused itself in Sophia Urquhart. The talk turned to other things over their late luncheon; but Paul found his thoughts unable to leave the young Frenchwoman for long. She must shop and keep house for the brute, launder his linen, keep him fed; listen to his admonitions, bear his stolid children; another child put in her each year, and every night ...

Paul was, from his liberal experience, long ago aware of the outlook of certain biassed persons regarding the lot of women, and the due pain they must endure uncomplainingly in payment for the sin of Eve. That Eve's act could have resulted in other compensations, making up almost for the loss of paradise, occurred to Paul flippantly on some occasions, lightly as he took women, and as lightly left them. Henri Chantal had seen to it that his son was properly and sensibly educated to equip himself in life. Paul had had his first young harlot at the age of seventeen, and they had discussed it together afterwards, he and Papa. Paul's bride, when he could find one with a dowry, would have no cause to complain. But now he was too greatly filled with protective anger on behalf of the suffering woman he had seen to contemplate even what she might become to him in such a way. Briefly he was St. George, or the Chevalier Roland perhaps, riding to rescue a heroine in distress; but in which direction? What in reality could he do for young Mrs. Heatherton? Next Sunday, he knew, he would make some excuse not to come to church with Miss Flora. And by then, with the press of everyday things, the whole question would have retreated to the back of his mind. If one day, after her child was safely born, he ever met Marie Heatherton in person, it would be different. For a woman to have borne three children and never have known love was abominable. And Paul had seen from the quality of Marie's glance that she had never known in such a way what love was or might become. In all but the technical sense, she was a virgin. He made himself forget her for the present; the real fact was that he could not afford to remember, and Paul was above all a realist.

II

It was half-past ten at night. William Heatherton was lying with his wife. Surrounding him in the darkness beyond the drawn bed-curtains were the solid, familiar things which he particularly liked to feel about him at this time, with the day's duties done and the fulfilment of his body imminent. Many of them had been purchased in his student days or, a little later, when he was adding to the scanty furnishings of his first, bachelor-inhabited manse; the extinguished culza-lamp, its translucent shade giving a ghostly symmetry in the room's outer dark; the framed crayon portraits of his father and mother, Jean in her goffered cap, Nathan in his high stock and best coat; they hung together on the wall, and James had had paintings in oils copied later, but William himself preferred the sketches and had asked to have them ... The Regency chairs, a trifle unsubstantial for present-day taste but agreeable enough, he had picked up at an auction; the fire which still smouldered in the bedroom grate would flicker now and again upon their rosewood silhouettes. The patina of daily care, of prosperity, was all about William as he lay; he had seen to it that Marie minded her housewifely duties. The rich smell of applied beeswax, the clean aroma of shaving-soap from his ewer and jug which would be ritually filled by Phemie, the maid, tomorrow at seven from a hot brass can to make ready for which she would have been up since four, cleaning out the fires; the Turkey carpet, with its fashionably bright colours, innocent of any fluff or dust. And his own clothes, the good black broadcloth coat he wore on weekdays, the narrow trousers and discreet waistcoat and stock, lay carefully folded, brushed, ready for William's morning rising. His slippers and dressing-gown were to hand and ready by the bed; his nightshirt freshly laundered and ironed. The awareness of all these things aroused no surprise, far less gratitude in William, for he expected no less; but they made a concious background for his sense of well-being, of continuity.

Continuity; the bodily function, indispensable to him now as he had found, both after the first child's birth and the second. He proceeded with it, wordlessly; his wife's body lay obedient beneath his own, the thickened belly and small turgid breasts accommodating to the tensed, active curves of William's buttocks and abdomen. It was still three months before the third child should be born. William contemplated, with approval, his own closeness at this moment to his unborn child; he had been informed by his old mother lately that, when a pregnancy sat well forward, it would be a son. "I could tell that the other twain would be lasses," she had said. William felt communion with his unborn son, here, now, in this occupation; his relaxed mind considered, in logical appreciation, an extension of himself, that gifted and eloquent being who had, earlier today, twice mounted the pulpit-steps with dignity. Particularly, at this time, he felt that he had rendered a good account of the wishes of Providence, as vouchsafed to himself, in his official position as interpreter. "Many are called, but few are chosen," drifted through William's mind, the latter being clarified by the body's final expression; this in itself was familiar by now. He thought of the late text as adjustable to continue his first sermon today about the choice of Gideon at the stream's edge. It was almost, had propriety not intervened, as if he could set out the points of next week's sermon on the table of his wife's obedient body. William forbade the thought in himself as he would have done, had he known of or suspected it, in Marie; and recalling himself to the comfort of his present surroundings, thanked God for his prosperity and, properly, for his marriage. It was not, he was now aware, that Marie made the best possible of wives; had he been less hasty he might have found one who would be more of a companion to him, appreciate him more. That he now realised that Marie was not of either calibre showed, after all was said, a new maturity in himself; and for that one must be, likewise, thankful.

The firelight gave a sudden spurt and light filtered for an instant between the space separating the half-drawn curtains. In this light William saw Marie's face familiarly outlined by the frilled cap she wore in bed, her closed eyes, the shape of the pillow behind her head, the shadows beyond. William would have expected nothing else; the notion that a woman could enjoy the marital act would still have shocked and alienated him. Marie was in a state of properly induced submission; presently he spoke to her and she answered, passively: the matter of which they had spoken concerned Catherine and Alicia, the two little girls upstairs, and her reply soon slipped from William's mind. Presently he withdrew from her, and turned on his back to pursue the line of thought which had come to him while he was within her, about the called and the chosen; and presently, with the sense of well-being still enfolding him like a blanket, a benison, slept well, as was his custom.

Marie lay quite still in the renewed darkness, subduing the stirring of the blood that came, as so often, too late for William's invasion of her secret places. She did not understand this, and had long ago learned that there was a haven of further withdrawal, an almost completely separate abode where oneself waited, enduring without deep feeling whatever was being done to the body. Without this refuge, life would have been intolerable; from it, she was able to reply courteously enough to William, if he should speak to her. She could also remember later what they had said; it was as though she made notes in a little, separate private book, for reference at any time. But there were other places, other things; hitherto not including anyone except herself. Today, this morning, her private place had been invaded; not as William would do it, but publicly, almost insolently. That young man with the familiar look, whose clothes had been shabby and who had stared at her; he had been with the Urquharts; he wore side-whiskers, golden-brown like his smooth hair, which shone like silk; who was he?

Foreign, perhaps. She herself, married to a respectable figure, a minister, was or had been a foreigner, an alien: the women of the congregation never let her forget it, or that it had been a condescension in them to appoint William when his wife was a member of a nation with whom, in the memory of many, they had been long at war. Why must she feel, as she had today, that the prison-bars had been opened, prised open a little, for a moment only, while those gay appraising eyes in church had assessed her, both as a woman and as a person; in such a way as she had never before in her life been assessed? Why had that moment still the power to make her forget, as she had just now, that her life here, circumscribed as a coffin, and William upon her, and the child again in her womb whom she had not wanted to bear, were unimportant? If she could only believe that; if only the closing in once more could be delayed, and the return of fear to her, for it hardly ever now left, of the coming pain of childbirth, of an agony no one could describe who had not endured it, as she would have done soon three times ... Three times. Why were men made as they were? There was no one of whom she could speak of it, not even Alicia who had been kind at the second birth, as though the history of that unheralded first, in Margaret Howie's house, had shocked her into vigilance. But Alicia was married to a man she loved and it pleased her to bear his children.

Marie turned her head away from her own children's father. She was a prey to the misery of what must be wickedness in herself that made her, even after all this time, still dislike and resent her lot as William's wife, still be thankful when William, at last, slept after his nightly transports. She forced herself, as always, to lie still so as not to wake her husband; and recalled the second baby Alicia's birth, and knew more fear. They had had to use instruments then, at last, after a labour of many hours, during which she had strained and moaned; all of it was useless; the child was lying transversely. The doctor had, at last, come; Marie recalled his grey spade beard, bent over her, the smell of tobacco, and his dry uncaring voice. He cared nothing; no man cared, or could do. But he had had knowledgeable hands, that doctor. She remembered feeling at last that he was in control of the child, that it would after all be born; and so it was, a long sallow ugly baby, another girl, with the red weals of forceps-marks on either cheek, so that at first they had thought it must be disfigured for life, but later the marks had gone away.

When they had shown her the child at last she had turned her head away and said sullenly, "I did not ask for it." She had spoken in French and only Alicia, who understood, was shocked. How shocked she had been, her pink mouth—a trifle less pink and full-lipped perhaps this last while as she grew older—like a round O in her face! And the doctor, smiling into his beard now everything was over, and he would get his fee; a little steamed fish, perhaps, for the invalid tomorrow...

It was then Marie herself had cried out like a madwoman and asked him for God's sake to free her from her husband. "I want him to leave me alone," she had sobbed, and the doctor had said, "There, there, Mrs. Heatherton," and later, "Now, now; there is no need to behave like a spoilt young woman, my dear," and said she would be as right as a trivet in a week. What was a trivet? And, a week later, William had been back in her bed again.

There hadn't been any milk in her for small Alicia; they'd had to find a wet-nurse. Was it because she hadn't been able to nurse Lissy that William got her pregnant, the third time, almost without any delay? Old women said—Alicia had already told her—that a nursing mother didn't conceive. But James would never force himself upon Alicia while she was still nursing. James would be kind to his wife, consider her, always, before himself.

But she, Marie, was again pregnant, as was customary. She had long ago settled down into a kind of apathy, no longer either rebellious or fearful; when it was time for her to die, she would die, and William could wear out another wife. He was busy all day on his sermons which he thought of editing to publish, and left her with the children; the revising of his notes had caused him to suffer from eyestrain, and the heavy glasses he wore made him vanish daily behind them, unmet with as a person except perhaps in bed, in the firelit dark. But what did she know of William even then, except as a demanding force which possessed her to his satisfaction, never hers, then slept? What more was there for her to know of him, or anyone?

The young man in church today had had a sensitive face. When she found a half-hour to spare in her attic room she would try to draw the features, before she forgot them. She would draw the curve of lower lip against upper, the way the eyes were set somewhat mockingly in the head beneath peaked thin brows, the way the silken whiskers curled invitingly; it was a face like Pan might have, perhaps, that she could remember always if she had the likeness ...

She slept. The fire had died down meantime to ashes.

III

It was some time after the removal to Savill's manse that Marie had found out about the attic room.

To say that she was consciously searching for a refuge by then was untrue; all of her days and hours were occupied. The manse itself was on a far grander scale than the one they had left behind at Gowanmount. The latter had been a Regency-built small house of cream-coloured stone, greying by now as all others were from the contact of city grime and factory-chimneys. The dull tinge of Savill's manse was however a far older, nobler thing; it had been built in the eighteenth century, and was attached on one side to a similar house, its mirror-image, inhabited by an old spinster who, Sunday after Sunday, rain or shine, limped into her place in the pew she somehow contrived to rent at Savill's. Miss Eustacia Hyslop had been one of a family of eleven, all of whom had been daughters except one son, who became a physician and died too early at thirty-four. His memory still hung about the echoing Hyslop house, and the beechwood staircase was ascended and descended by his ghost. Savill's manse next door had a corresponding staircase, but of mahogany; installed in the days of the nabobs, its intricate balustrades, its deep pile carpet and brass stair-rods required brushing and polishing daily. There were few domestics allowed by William's stipend: it took, accordingly, some little time for Marie to do more than note the fact that there was a further, uncarpeted stair. There were attics, no doubt, to which it led; that it was not immediately ascended by Marie was due to the fact that she made a painstaking effort, during all of that first year, to fulfil her duties cheerfully as mistress of William's house. Perhaps the love between his brother James and James's wife Alicia, who after the first child's birth endeavoured to reopen their early friendship, was responsible for this attempt. Alicia loves her husband,

Marie would reflect; why cannot I love his brother? It was, no doubt, due to some obstructive fault in herself; and, allowing for this, she tried to be a good and loving wife to William. She was sufficiently practical by nature when not constantly reprimanded, ordered and supervised. During the daytime while William was at his books, or out on his parochial duties, which he carried out as usual conscientiously, Marie had leisure enough to decide where things should be stored, and to plan the shopping and meals. She grew familiar with the arduous frequent climb from the basement, where the food was cooked, to the dining-room where it must be served, having been meantime kept hot. Water was heated and delivered in brass cans by Phemie, drawn from a pump in the rear of the house, and the fire, lit well before dawn, must be stoked and never allowed to die down. Food—this included the awesome ceremony of Sunday dinner, when William, fresh from the pulpit, would say a particularly long and sonorous grace—was always broth, made from scraped beef; roast meat to follow, two vegetables, a pudding for themselves, milk gruel sent up to the nursery, where Catherine's and Lissy's young nursemaid must be trained to her duty also, for experienced children's nurses were far beyond William's allowance to procure—and, at the last, coffee, made in a machine invented by a forebear of David Heatherton, Alicia's brother, and obligatory on all of his family to use. All the food was cooked, transported in covered dishes to the sideboard in the dining-room, and there served by Fletcher, the parlour-maid who lived out. Among the patina of daily applied beeswax, silver épergnes, the coffee-machine, whorled gravy-spoon warmers, carvers and the like, Fletcher herself moved in majesty: Marie was a trifle in awe of her. Even Fletcher, however, could not ensure hot food in winter, and William disliked congealing grease on his plate during the long grace. Marie tried to tax herself about such things, partly because she was timid in presence of William and partly because, by blood, she was after all a Frenchwoman; this alone would have been sufficient to prevent her endurance of badly served food. Given the choice, she herself would have substituted lighter, more varied meals than those William ordained: she would have used other sauces, omelettes, varied herbs and wine. But both William and his guests, who generally consisted of the family, preferred as always the traditional, heavy Scottish dishes. Their appetites did not correspond to Marie's own; more and more she felt herself unconsidered and inconsiderable. Instead of being the mistress of William's house, she was its servant; never more so, never made more strongly to feel so, than when his parents at last came to dine and sleep.

This was a departure from tradition, and arose from a need Nathan had discovered in himself; he must see a doctor. The old one who had delivered baby Alicia had taken a partner, and it was to this young man that, to his wife Jean's disgust, Nathan was induced to bare himself. "A laddie like that!" the old woman would repeat, her porcelain teeth chumbling. "He'll ken naught o't; I could ha'e done as muckle for my ain man as to turse him o'er the sic a chiel." For in her deeper moments Jean, like most folk, returned to the vernacular of her youth. Marie found it impossible to understand all of what she said; all she herself knew was that her mother-in-law still disliked her. Nothing was said of that; but without even watching the old woman's narrow, suspicious glance, Marie knew. Jean pried into the kitchens, and examined the cooking-pots and the state of Phemie's finger-nails; Marie felt anger rise, but could not bring herself directly to criticise William's mother. As for mentioning the matter to William himself, such a thing would have been beyond expectation. He still lay with her nightly, but any confidence between them was no longer to be expressed in words or otherwise. Marie had found herself, soon after Alicia's birth, pregnant yet a third time; and fear and terror preyed on her to an extent which made her now ignore, as far as she might, the feeding and maintenance of the household. It must have been about then that, seeking escape, she mounted the attic stair.

It ascended at an angle. By contrast to the prosperity of the lower reaches its treads were lean and worn; from below, a smell of burnt meat floated up. "The poor would ha'e been glad o't," old Jean would no doubt have said, grimly; they had gone back by now to their riverside cottage, and Marie felt something of the pressure abate, now Nathan was eased and his old wife amenable, or at least less anxious. "The poor would ha'e been glad o't." With her still light step on the topmost stair, it occurred to Marie, in rebellion, now, to wonder how Jean got her information about the poor. The old woman had not, in her careful and thrifty life amid well-found, upcoming folk, ever encountered real poverty; it was doubtful if she ever would. Would she, Marie, ever dare say so to her mother-in-law?

Marie was to remember, afterwards, a particular day when she had climbed to the attic. This itself was small and encumbered, as such places are, with things listed among household furnishings but not in constant use, and readily forgotten; a chaise-longue belonging to the late incumbent, its dark-red satin covers nibbled at by moth. There was a violin-stand, left over from no one knew what forgotten music-lessons; and a children's nursery screen, half begun, with scraps glued on of cherubs, Little Red Riding Hood, a huntsman in full pursuit, other things. Marie had toyed with the notion of finishing the screen, of bringing it down to the nursery for the delight of her own children, when they should be a little older. But she had done nothing about it. There was a door, flush with the farther wall, leading no doubt to a cupboard. She had not taken time to open it, intriguing herself merely with the luxury of at last, for a little while, being alone; William had come in early that day and she could hear his voice calling for her belowstairs, and did not answer.

He called again. It was a customary thing for him to call for her for a while, in case she should be down in the basement supervising the cooking, or supposedly instructing Phemie. Marie could picture the way her husband must look, standing by the opened study-door so that the light, filtered red and blue from its passage through the garish painted glass in the hallway, fell on his big figure in its well-brushed black suit of clothes, turning it to that of a harlequin. William's features would, as usual, be bland behind their spectacles, betraying nothing of what he really wanted. Perhaps he had mislaid something, or wanted to give her some message from those women in the congregation, who held weekly meetings at which she must attend and sew. It might be some such thing; or to tell her, perhaps, that James and Alicia, or the old parents, or all four, would come again to dine on a date already determined, and she must accept the arrangement, and later prepare the meal. Her fists clenched. Nobody consulted her, Marie's, preference in any matter. If she did not wish to entertain his parents on the day he and they had chosen, if she stayed upstairs in her bed, and said she was ill...

The feeling grew in her that she could not endure to go down to William at this moment, could not, for the present, tolerate the sound of his voice, the fact that his body was again even near her. During the daylight hours he seldom in fact touched her; she had begun already to feel that she was no longer, had perhaps never been, a person to him. He had wanted a woman in his bed, that was all; and few personalities could survive the full onslaught of William's notable self-esteem, mental and physical. For all her ignorance, Marie realised something of this, phrasing it to herself in such terms as she could frame, here alone. How had the realisation first come to her? Had it been when she said some ordinary thing to William and realised that, though he replied blandly enough, he had not been listening to her, had perhaps never listened from the beginning? That first time, when he said he had seen her walking by herself uphill, to Papa's grave with asters she had bought, he had made an image for himself. A graven image. She smiled a little at the sad pun. If she remembered nothing else of William's sermons, she remembered that; one must not make images or bow down to them. The jealous God of William's understanding had him, no doubt, in thrall. And she, his wife, must suffer for it.

William had called again, finally; the voice showed a trace of impatience. "He cannot understand that I am not always there when he wants me," Marie thought, and withdrew, picking up her skirts to hush their rustling, farther into the attic. If William came up here after her she could pretend she had not heard. There was such privacy here, she thought she would come here often; over there, where the light was good from the high window, she could perhaps put a small table, and draw.

There was silence now from belowstairs; Marie listened, and heard her own heartbeats thudding fast. There was no other sound; it was her first victory over William. Thereafter she often escaped from him, and from her life with him, by day, in the new place she had made; the servants did not suspect anything, she never ordered Phemie up here to dust, and the terrible Fletcher went out shopping by the door to the back lane, and need know nothing. No, this was her own place; when had she ever had such before? Never even in Maman's time, never since the womb itself had held her; the long ago desecrated womb of an aristo, who lost caste and fortune for bearing her, Marie.

On that first day, with William at last silent, she felt relief flood her till she trembled with it, standing hard against the door she had shut for herself, staring at that other, which opened to some cupboard in the wall . . .

It was William himself, no other, who at length suggested that Paul Chantal, the French instructor at Miss Urquhart's school, might lodge with old Miss Hyslop, next door to the manse. William, his mouth lately filled with roast mutton and potatoes, fastidiously wiping the gravy from lips afterwards with a laundered napkin; William, who always did his best for his parishioners when they were in straitened circumstances; William, the elect of God. Marie listened; there was nobody there except themselves, dining together. As always, William talked, and answered himself. As always . . . and elsewhere in the great house, small Catherine dined upstairs with the aid of her young nurse, and smaller Alicia slept. And the third, the unborn, swelled Marie already so that her chair, when it was placed at table near enough to eat, caused her thickened body almost to compress itself against the unyielding, polished mahogany. Everything was highlighted; the silver, the table-top; William's signet ring he wore nowadays on a finger of his left hand; the late sun shining between the lattices. Everything shone; and she, Marie, was deadly tired. It seemed a long time since she had risen this morning from William's bed, and had gone downstairs to see that Phemie was doing her duty with the fires. A long time . . . and tonight again, she thought, he will lie with me.

"Old Miss Hyslop," William was saying now. She focused her mind to attend to him. Was she ill, this old Miss Hyslop? One saw her sometimes, going to and fro along the street with crippled, arthritic gait to buy herself food. She could no longer, she had said one day to Marie, climb the stairs of her own house, so that the top floors were neglected. What was William saying now about old Miss Hyslop?

"I wish you will attend me, my dear. I believe her circumstances are pitiful; she has the house, which was left her. I understand, by her father, apportioned among the sisters. They are long since dead."

"And so?" Marie felt further weariness assail her; why should she care for Miss Hyslop, she who, herself, today, for the first time, had felt a heavy unwillingness even to ascend to her attic room? Up there, the drawings she had made would be gathering dust. There was one of a young man's head, the silken quality of the brown hair shown without colour, the features surprisingly clear ...

"I think that she may be persuaded to take a lodger." William smiled, with closed, satisfied lips. "That young Frenchman whom Miss Urquhart has lately employed in her school seems genteel, and would not seek advantages. At Miss Hyslop's age she cannot be excepted to go up and down stairs; such a young man could fend for himself. I shall suggest it to her. His lodging, I believe, is at present unsuitable. If he were to rent the upper floor of her dwelling, and come and go without trouble to her ... an increase in her income ..."

William droned on, and Marie felt a trembling, as if of sickness, assail her. Paul Chantal, that young man whom she had lately portrayed, to come here? Paul Chantal to be, perhaps, through the wall from her, while she sat upstairs alone in her secret place, sketching, drawing: drawing chimney-pots, pavements, faces ... His face. She felt deathly sick. It was too soon for the labour to start, it was only seven months, but even so ...

"Please," she said aloud, and instantly William was aware of her state. "Marie ... my dear, you are certain it is not ...?"

The matter of Paul was forgotten, but recalled later when William Heatherton had an hour to himself, to regret his bitterest loss, his ultimate disappointment. Marie was brought too early to labour, and delivered at last of a stillborn son. It was the will of God, William told himself. He did not connect the mishap with any habitual action of his own, any inconsiderate treatment of Marie. When the new young doctor told him the situation things were in, must be in for a certain time from now on, William was astounded ... To rid his mind of the unpleasant reality, as it were, he went to call, next day, upon Miss Hyslop next door. She professed herself, after a certain initial recoil—taking lodgers was a thought unladylike—willing to consider any young gentleman the minister might recommend. It was to be understood that she herself could not climb the upper staircase to what had once, long ago, been her brother's room. The dust was thick on the few things left there and she ... the young gentleman, maybe ...

"I myself will ensure that everything is made ready," said William Heatherton; and he sent his own servants to dust the room. So kindly and considerate of old folk, the new Savill's minister!

IV

When James and Alicia Heatherton celebrated the tenth anniversary of their marriage, they gave a dinner-party; not solely to the family, for Jean would not let Nathan go abroad so late, even though his recent complaint was to a great extent eased by the new doctor, who had also delivered Marie of her stillborn son. Other guests were asked to the town-house which the couple still inhabited although they were also building in the country, beside the loch, where a fantastic near-palace, mostly of James's own design, was rising. The Howies, whose support had made all the difference between success and failure for what had, at the time, been considered that madcap scheme of James's to make the Atlantic crossing by steam, came. Now, the steam-voyage was accepted and acceptable, and so indeed was James; he was spoken of far further off than the canny shipbuilders and ironmasters here and in the south. After many years, solid contracts with the English shipowners had come, and at the last, an Admiralty summons for James Heatherton for estimates for hulls. He could, he knew, build these well and cheaply, not stinting my lords of whatever might be necessary to keep their ships afloat. Nelson in his day had been grudged anything but rotting hulks which could hardly have sailed the Mediterranean, or won Trafalgar, without the genius of the man in command. Some of this genius might have been, folk already said, transmitted in some way to James Heatherton, who of late years had begun to seem as if nothing were impossible to him. It was partly to celebrate this triumph, as well as a decade of happy marriage, that the dinner was bidden at James's town-house by the riverside, with conveyances for six of the evening.

The evening, as fate would have it, held fog. A closed carriage had been sent by James himself to convey his brother William and his wife, for they owned no means of transport and, as everyone knew, Marie since the still-birth had been poorly; this was in fact her first venture out of doors. The coachman handed them in, therefore, from what had already become a yellow, unfamiliar world, without accustomed landmarks; a ring of many-coloured lights round the brass carriage-lantern flung itself back as though from a wall ahead, on the road. "We'll be late, I doubt, I doubt," said the old coachman Josiah McQueen, turning his head so that the folk in the interior could hear. He had served James Heatherton by now nine years, progressing from the foundry, where he had lost the fingers of one hand, to James's own stables and coach-house, where the quarters were snug and the employers considerate. He need not, he knew, accordingly, show undue awe of Mr. James's brother, the minister, and his shilpit foreign wife. They had nothing like the living that Mr. James himself enjoyed now, having done it all from the beginning with his own hands. "Fine I mind the days when he'd come hame to his bride in their wee city house nearby the foundry, and now he's bigging a better still by far than was meant when they started, down on the loch shores, and coming to and fro each day from there by water," thought the coachman as he tried, unsuccessfully, to guide the horses through the fog. "Fegs! The dinner'll burn; but we are maybe not the last." Miss Flora Urquhart, the schoolmistress, and some young man, and Mr. and Mrs. George Howie, were to come. Till all were present, the company no doubt would drink sherry-wine, and wait. Josiah tugged at the reins as the air cleared somewhat beyond the inner city, and the horses broke into an obedient trot which in twenty minutes, now that the way was somewhat to be seen, brought them to James Heatherton's square stone riverside house, with its lawn in front.

The sound of their wheels had been heard; yellow lamplight spilled already down the steps from the opened door. Alicia's slender, pretty figure, unaltered over the years, showed itself in the hallway, beyond that of the lace-capped maidservant. "I did not think you could come out, on such a night," she called; as always, Alicia contrived to be informal while never for one instant losing dignity or grace, or forgetting the niceties which so greatly impressed James's clients. She kissed Marie affectionately on the cheek, holding the other back to admire her dress. The gesture was spontaneous and, in its way, sincere; although, as Marie knew well, there was nothing in the dress to admire, and Alicia had seen it before many times.

"How cold you must be," said James's wife. "Come to the fire, and drink some wine; it will bring colour to your cheeks, you're by far too pale." She fussed about Marie, remembering she had lately risen from a sad childbed. "I doubt that young man of Flora's will be wishing himself back in his native country," she said. "The Howies are delayed as well, naturally; it will take them a while to get here with the fog so thick. Margaret would certainly have sent word, though, if they found themselves unable to come out."

Trivia; accompanied by a warm, firelit room where the curtains banished the cold outer night. On the walls hung paintings of James's ships, and a new half-length portrait of James himself, painted by a local artist after being commissioned by the shareholders. The painted face looked almost as stern as old Nathan's, with a slight frown between the brows; there was none of James's kindly personality shown on the canvas. Paint could deceive ... Marie turned her head away from it, and from contemplation of the engraving of the narrow ship which years ago had successfully crossed to Ireland in a record of hours. She still felt the cold in her bones; her flesh was weak with too much giving birth, her mind weary.

William had made her come out tonight; she must not, he said, give way to self-pity; her duty was with her husband's family on so auspicious an occasion. Marie had allowed herself to be brought; it did not matter, she would eat her dinner and then be taken home, and then, and then sleep alone ... Alone! The luxury of it, of her narrow attic room, chosen by her as a place to lie by day, to sleep by night, after that young doctor, who understood her cries and tears as the old one had not, made it clear to William that after this, she must be left alone, there could be no more births or she would die. And William had listened, almost incredulously, to the young doctor, who talked to him as surely no man, young or old, had ever dared address William Heatherton before, and the end had been that Marie was allowed her way; there was no more of William meantime in her bed, no more living or dead babies. The fact that her body was her own again had not yet, with the feverish illness she had subsequently had, grown fully clear until tonight, when she sat here among them, among all these Heathertons. James and Alicia were happy together, as always; they loved one another, had been meant for one another, all through the decade of their marriage as through their lives. Although they had both grown older, it was with gaiety and grace; Alicia's face showed hollows under the cheekbones, which added to her distinction, and James's hair was grey.

David Heatherton, Alicia's brother, the bearded erratic genius for whom James was fuel to fire, entered with the host now, the pair with their heads close together. They could never stop talking of ships; there was no place for any woman, even for Alicia herself, in this man's talk, which dealt with knots and hulls and pressures and pipe-bores. David Heatherton was still a giant of a man, of a physique which would have made of him the centre of any gathering, even without his bizarre personality and sudden statements, which made many convention-ridden folk shy. But Alicia Heatherton looked at the pair, her brother and her husband, with love in her eyes; the one had been almost as a father to her when their parents died, whereas James, the only man for her, had never changed in heart or ways from the day she'd come upon the pair of them in the burn, measuring hull-speeds. Dear kind reliable, quietly brilliant, secretly ambitious James! He spoke now sometimes of this palatial house for them in the country, hardly recognisable as being built on the foundations of the little cottage at Imrie they'd bought for holidays some years back. Country air would be good for the children; and James could, as he said, travel up and down daily to the city by water: that had been the initial plan, but by now it had grown much grander, and Hector Urquhart and the architect often came here over plans.

Alicia jerked her mind away from James and his ambitions to the awareness of her own duties as his hostess; and openly lamented the necessary delay of dinner. "How late the Howies are!" she said aloud. "It's not like Margaret."

Her voice broke off, even as a stir of arrival in the hall glossed over the fact that, nowadays, when one spoke of the Howie couple one named Margaret, not George, as the responsible party. It had shocked even Alicia a little that the Englishwoman's husband had made her an actual partner in his firm, and that, it was rumoured, he had left her as sole executrix in his will, leaving all of his considerable fortune to Margaret direct, to be at her disposal while she lived and, no doubt, when she should die; discounting their only son John except as his mother might will it. It was, folk said, unfair to the boy when he should be a young man, and have to feel beholden to his mother for every sixpence. Besides, no woman should have so firm a grasp of affairs as, it was clear, Margaret Howie had of George's. The fact that it was his wife who had persuaded the little man to give the lead in investing in James's plans for the Atlantic crossing recurred to Alicia, and she tried to feel gratitude; but succeeded only in feeling some irritation. As though James were not good enough to stand on his own feet, through hard work and talent only! And with her brilliant brother's support——

James himself re-entered from the hall now, looking grave. The sound of wheels had come from the driveway, then ceased as the outlying fog again smothered them. "They have not arrived," thought Alicia, and then, as James turned to her and she saw his pale stern face "There is some mishap, maybe due to the fog." She went to her husband; so tall was he that her still-bright head did not reach his broad shoulder.

"What is it, James? What is wrong, my dear?" He found it, as she knew, difficult to express himself easily in words, when there was a matter of any moment not bearing on his work. The terse speeches he would make at shareholders' meetings concerned only facts with which James could deal. He turned now to her, making a small helpless gesture with his big skilled hands.

"It's poor George Howie," he said. "He——"

"He is ill?" Then as he did not answer, she said, "Is it worse than that, Jamie?" She seldom used the diminutive, the boyhood name they had both known as cousins. He turned and spoke as if to her alone, but the whole room heard it.

"Poor Howie is dead. He has met with an accident. A horse, in his own office-lane, in the fog, backed against a wall; he was about to enter the carriage, and he . . ."

"Poor Margaret," said Alicia, "is she—shall I——" Her delicate hands fluttered helplessly for a little, so that the rings she wore shimmered in the lamplight. How could she—with a dinner-party—leave here? Marie, had she been well enough, could perhaps have gone. There was no word, no offer, however, from Marie; how passive she seemed, as though nothing could touch her heart! Alicia Heatherton was aware of a coldness in the room, an emanation perhaps from the fog outside. She had not hitherto troubled about the almost constant silence of William's wife. But William himself stepped forward.

"I will go to Mrs. Howie; it is my duty. You will excuse me?" he said, addressing his brother and his wife. Marie half rose then; it was as though she were a puppet, pulled on invisible strings after William's broad tall figure in its black coat. Everyone dissuaded her; it was too cold a night, she was not yet well enough! But it was William who, as always, had the final word.

"You are under the physician's care, my dear," he said, "best stay. I will send a carriage later; in the meantime, perhaps——" And James and Alicia hastened to offer their own carriage again, and their coachman; pressed with invitations to cover every necessity of the new-made widow. William departed, leaving wreaths of fog behind him in the hall from the briefly opened door. Moments after he had gone, there was the sound of yet another carriage; Miss Flora Urquhart, with her French tutor in attendance. Alicia's hands fluttered again for instants, like moth's wings, then were still; the Urquhart carriage, after all, could take Marie home later with the returning guests. There would be no need to send out old Joey, and the horses, on a third and fourth journey on this foggy, bitter night. What weather for their anniversary ... and now, to mar it, the news of the tragedy! Alicia chided herself for thoughtlessness; one ought to be filled with sympathy for Margaret Howie, who had so practically remembered even to send word why they were not coming ... Could she herself, if she ever lost James, remember anything of the kind for grief?

At last, though, the rest of the guests were here; Miss Flora, with her grey hair daringly in ringlets tonight, and an aigrette; apologising for her lateness, but the driver had been unable to see a yard ahead. "And Paul, of course, did not know the way." Then she introduced to the company the dapper little man, with hair and brushed whiskers like shining brown silk, whom Marie Heatherton knew at once, as he knew her.

How was it that they had this certainty they had met before that other, now distant encounter at Savill's? Then, she'd been pregnant; he would remember that; perhaps tonight, despite her dull dress, he found her more attractive. Certainly he never took his eyes from her, while all the time discreetly dancing attendance on Miss Flora, his employer, who tonight was determinedly gay; diversions for her were rare enough. The shy, understated talents of the clever Highland headmistress showed themselves to advantage here, in congenial company, with Sophia for once absent; Miss Urquhart's sister-in-law cast a blight on most social gatherings the spinster attended, seldom allowing the latter to forget her inferior state. But tonight the talk over dinner was both witty and grave, too much laughter being out of place because of the news of poor Geroge Howie. "Flossie and Agnes will be absent from school tomorrow," said Miss Flora conversationally to the young Frenchman, who responded with a smile somewhat out of keeping with the grief of the occasion, as if to say "Thank heaven for it!" But he did not say it, or anything as tactless; only looking at Marie Heatherton beneath his lashes with a combined drollery and helplessness, impossible to resist. During the course of the evening she found herself, often, laughing. How long was it since she had laughed even to herself? She would not have done so, she knew, in William's presence; and once found her sister-in-law Alicia watching her with an expression impossible to read. How much did Alicia guess of what went on in anyone's mind? No doubt she was shrewd enough, having helped James attain his pre-eminence in her own way; she always knew the right things to say to the right people, and said a very little, charmingly, now to M. Paul Chantal. It was not necessary to speak French.

Dinner itself was excellent. The fog outside was once again excluded by the rich, close-shut curtains of that surprising vegetable green. A good fire was lit, and winked on much crystal and silver, the fine crested china James had had specially made in Staffordshire, and the carefully ironed frilled cap and apron of the maid, with ribbons of tartan James had lately had registered as pertaining to his family. A manservant moved about discreetly filling glasses, the former replacing, at last, the good viands with tiny silver dishes made in the shape of hearts, holding almonds and raisins, small sugared biscuits and marchpane. For the dessert, young Maudie and Evangeline, and the even younger Jonathan, were permitted to come downstairs, to make their rounds of the guests and be briefly petted. The little girls' hair, newly released from curlpapers, was silvery fair like their mother's had been in childhood: they wore layer upon layer of starched petticoats below their velvet dresses, and long frilled drawers above flat crosstied slippers. They made their curtsies, and presently the nurse took them again upstairs; and as the eyes of everyone else in the room were upon the retreating children, the eyes of Marie and Paul Chantal met again...

Afterwards, she could remember that they had talked, but not what they had said to one another: it had been, no doubt, the customary polite exchanges.

"You are here. I can think of nothing and no one else, now and later, when there will of course be singing." It was as though he said the words aloud to her; as though the hot colour flooded visibly over her face and neck. Yet all they spoke of together, even yet, was trivial; how he liked living in this country, how he liked teaching in Miss Flora's school.

"The school is a success." Already they were speaking in their own tongue, in low voices. Yet always one must be careful, must keep up pretence, though there was no spiteful Sophia here to listen and spy, only kind Alicia, only William's brother James, and Alicia's brother David who could think and talk only of ships, and Miss Flora beside him, her aigrette flashing a trifle desperately in the befogged light, as she tried to listen intelligently about pressure-boilers and the unleashed power of steam.

"But is it not dangerous, so much explosive power? Could it not do harm, if it grew to a state where it was beyond control?" Miss Flora's question, that of a scholarly woman, caused David Heatherton to become pompous. "You may rely upon it, my dear lady, such matters are not left lightly in the hands of any except experts, and though I myself say..." He droned on, and began the description of a great new boiler whose plans he had lately drafted; and Alicia said what a pity it was that William had missed his dinner, but he had, of course, gone at once; perhaps Mrs. Howie would give him a glass of wine if, poor thing, she were in a state to do so. "They always seemed a devoted couple, do you not think so, Miss Urquhart?" Tactfully, drawing poor Flora away from David Heatherton's steam-anecdotes, Alicia exercised her duty; tactfully, equally so, provided for Marie's safe journey home, in the other carriage. "We will have a song, not too gay, perhaps, and then, in case the fog thickens ... dear me, I hope everyone will get safely home! Could we not, Miss Flora, Marie ... a bed? Perhaps tomorrow it will have cleared." But neither lady would hear of it; Miss Flora must be present for the opening school-lesson, Paul Chantal of necessity by her side; and so it was resolved that they should all three travel back together. The empty carriage returning without William Heatherton could go to its stable, Josiah McQueen to his slumbers: already the hour was growing late.

Even then, with the presence of Miss Flora in the carriage, they could not, the two of them, have speech together alone. But it was still as though through the humdrum nature of the talk, clear colours shone; as though he said to her, "I would not dress you in that dead-leaf tone, which does not flatter your skin; but in the colour of geraniums, with a flower in your hair." And when they came to say goodbye, at the fog-girdled manse lamp by the door, and he leaped out to assist her up the steps, ahead of the old coachman, and kissed her hand, it was as though his kisses imprinted themselves on the bare flesh of her inner arm at palm, wrist, elbow.

She felt herself enter William's house in a daze, as though her body were already separated from her mind. She was moreover certain that that young man, who was perhaps not so young, did likewise; that after escorting his employer home, and returning perhaps on foot through the fog—ah, how cold it would be for him in those patched shoes!—he ascended to his lonely room, as she did to hers, and thought of their first evening together, and perhaps realised soon that between them lay only a thin wall.

Marie was in love, accordingly, and did not yet know it for what it was. But she knew enough to keep any mention of Paul Chantal's name from William. It was as though her heart sang over the bare knowledge of the name. She locked it away within her, and carried the secret always. It did not occur to her to wonder if Paul had seduced other women.

Later that same night she heard William come up to her room. It did not occur to Marie to think of the long sad hours he must have spent with the new-made widow, and the fact that he had had no dinner. She feared only lest he invade her secret place, force his way again into a bed they no longer nightly shared. She lay, accordingly, with closed eyes, quite still, feigning sleep. She resented William's coming, his thrusting of himself into what was already a personal dream; a dream of what, shortly, would perhaps become reality. Had reality and dreams already become intermingled, so that Paul lay here in the attic room with her? She did not say it, even to herself; the dark lashes lay in stubborn crescents on her unchanging cheeks. She felt William enter by the door, holding a candle shaded by one hand, so that the light would not shine directly on her face. She made no sign; and heard him nevertheless speak.

"Marie, are you awake? You know, do you not, that George Howie is dead?"

Fool, she told herself; they said that before dinner; why come up and tell me again now? "I have been with his widow," William told her then, as though she had admitted she was awake. Presently, as there was no sign from Marie, and with a dragging step which showed his weariness, William went, closing the door quietly behind him.

His going filled Marie with joy; the sound of his footsteps retreating down the wooden stairs was like a further victory won in battle, a signal for progress to other things than she had ever been aware of or imagined. Her life had suddenly blossomed and flowered from a bud she had not known existed; what would happen next, and how soon would it happen?

She hugged the thought, the expectancy to her; and slept.

It could not have been many days before Paul came to her, insidiously forcing open the boarded-up door. In her own mind, thinking of it later, there was confusion as to which of them had done it first; had she, finding out that the cupboard-door opened into a large brick-lined attic space between the two houses, and seeing a further door no longer blocked up, gone further; into a man's room, seeing the ordinary things Paul had daily, nightly about him; his jacket hanging with its worn sleeves, a patch on one; a pipe filled with tobacco, lying by the bed; the bed itself, where he and she would soon lie in delight, with the curtains close-drawn even though Miss Hyslop never came up here? No one else came. But how had she, Marie, braved the locked door? Had Paul opened it first? Had there been that time when, having left, for some sudden every-day task downstairs, the drawing she had made of his head exposed, she had come back later and found, lying on it, what nobody in the whole Savill's manse could have left there; a budding early rose? And when they had met again publicly after that, how her heart had thudded, but Paul gave no sign except a little smile ... And then he was with her; with her, there, in the doorway, the two intervening doors open between them, so that there was nothing to say or do, after that matter of the rose, and perhaps also of a dropped handkerchief, but to run into his arms ...

And she had so run; she, Marie, the shy, the unwanted one, for the first time infinitely desirable and desired: William was forgotten, all that he had ever meant discounted, as though she herself came virgin to Paul. And virgin she had seemed, that first time, in her uncertainty and, later, in her gratitude; gratitude; gratitude sufficient to make her want to kiss his hands and feet, as though she were a disciple of a teacher, who taught reciprocal passion. So few men knew of that, or heeded it; so few women were alive as she, Marie, was now, being infinitely aware of each drop of settling dew in a dawn that followed such a night as had never surely been lived through before, even by Abélard and Héloïse. It was Paul who told her of that pair of lovers.

Outwardly, by day, she was still the minister's wife, a trifle hampered in her duties by a threatened consumption, so that she must lie most hours of the day upstairs and dream, alone

. . . For Paul had to earn his bread. Poor Paul, driven out of France and unable to return, had no money, no means of making more than would support him alone in poverty; and she herself had none any more than he.

But all that came to its full realisation gradually, not in the first ecstasy they knew together. By imperceptible degrees it became hard to believe that there could ever have been a time when they were not physical lovers. But, as Marie was to remind herself repeatedly, she could never remember how it first began, in his room or hers . . .

Below the stairs' flight from them, William Heatherton wrestled with himself nightly in prayer. The desires of the flesh were so strong in him with denial that it seemed, on certain nights, that there was no course open but to go upstairs to his wife where she lay on her sickbed, and forcibly endanger her health. Poor Marie. The doctor had been explicit, however, and he, William, must control his own desires as best he might. Prayer helped him, and, he found, time after time, deterred him from acting selfishly, and indulging himself in such a way. William often still prayed on his knees as night changed to dawn, the moon the size of a sixpence in the sky, the chimneys black and thrusting across the street; and sometimes, for no reason, thought of Margaret Howie, like himself left quite alone: and in that thought found comfort.

V

JEAN HEATHERTON HAD PUT OFF HER ANNUAL TRIP TO TOWN till her husband Nathan should be feeling somewhat better. When the doctor ceased visiting him, she felt at last that she could go; and left instructions with a neighbour to cosset Nathan, see to his fire, and serve the midday meal Jean had left ready to warm in the oven. "Woman, anybody'd think I never in my life fared for myself, till I married," said the old man, with his rare, long-lipped smile. Jean did not return such a frivolity, nor did she kiss Nathan farewell; relations between them, in public and in private, had always been dignified, restrained and proper. She put on her second-best bonnet, covering as it did the goffered cap which, like many old folk, she still wore to conceal her thistledown-fine white hair; and at the expected hour climbed into the post-coach, which would set her down near the city's booths by afternoon. She hoped above all to buy a warm round-bonnet for Nathan, to protect him against next winter's chills. The fact that winter might come and find her without Nathan had already occurred to the old woman, and was endured stoutly. Things should continue as they always had; the rest was the Lord's provision.

She found her own way among the familiar booths, whose pattern changed so little from year to year that the same folk were to be found stocking the same wares, hose, bonnets, rolls of stout woven cloth and finely graded linen. Jean bought, counting out her shillings carefully, Nathan's winter bonnet, some linen for making shirts—she still made, and, if there was leisure, smocked by hand those Nathan wore, and had done it also for her sons when they were bachelors—and a pair of Jersey hose for herself, to be worn in the damp season. Then she decided to make her way across the Green to see her grandchildren.

She walked determinedly, using the familiar compromise between a countrywoman's stride, for which Jean was too old and too genteelly bred, and the mincing gait of town ladies, which she despised; and presently paused for breath, which she would not admit was growing short, by the water, which still ran doucely between willows. The leaves dipped in the flowing stream, fouled by the nearness of laundresses who trod and wrung their washing here by ancient right, and spread it out to dry on the grass afterwards. Nearby, intent on one another, sat a pair of lovers; a courting couple, as Jean called them to herself. They were a small, narrow-built pair, the man's cheek revealing a shadow of brown silk whisker, laid close to the woman's who wore an everyday plaid gown: then a movement of the latter enabled Jean to glimpse the face beneath the straw bonnet and recognise, to her dismay and suspicion, William's wife, her own daughter-in-law. It had always been Jean's fixed opinion that the Frenchwoman could be up to no good when she was alone, and now here she was, as near red-handed as made no matter. To seat herself in a public place, alone with a strange young man! Jean, who lacked no variety of courage, went straight up to where the couple sat. Paul leapt to his feet, and bowed.

Jean nodded grimly. "I thought I kenned ye." She could not pronounce Marie's name adequately and seldom tried to. She sat down in the place Paul had vacated. "I was passing," she said, "and on my way to visit ye, but I see ye're occupied at the present."

The speech with its flavour of malice gave Marie time to collect her wits. Colouring deeply, she presented Paul to her mother-in-law. "This is M. Chantal, who teaches French at Miss Flora Urquhart's school." The introduction sounded respectable. Jean Heatherton was, perhaps, even half reassured; but being Jean gave no sign of it.

She ignored Paul, and turned to address some remark of humdrum nature to William's wife. "And where is my son?" was implicit, if not stated; Marie replied that William today was conducting a wedding-service. "It is to be quiet, and there are few guests," she added, as if to explain why she herself was not present. The undeceived eyes of her mother-in-law regarded her with candour. "I heard tell ye were on a bed of sickness," said Jean. Marie bowed her head. How could one be rid of so terrible an old woman? Nothing one said, could think of to say, would be of any value; she herself would never be believed in any case. "She has never liked me," the younger woman thought. If William's mother had indeed had an affection for her, would it have made any difference to the marriage? None, Marie knew now; things of that sort did not signify. She did not even care, by this time, whether or not Jean told her son William of their meeting by arrangement here today, which was a Saturday, and meant that Paul was free.

In the end, Jean did exactly that: later encountering William in his study before awaiting her homeward coach. "They were having a grand long crack together, your wife and the Frenchy," she told him, watching closely to anticipate his reply. "It isna a proper thing for a young married woman to consort with a strange man in open places. When I was her age I would not have considered such a thing without telling Nathan of it; not that he——"

"Mother, mother, times are changed since you were my wife's age, and she is glad of an acquaintance who can speak her language," replied William equably. On the surface, during the remainder of his mother's visit and after she had gone, he remained unruffled; but the barb had entered, particularly as, on speaking to Marie on her return of how she had spent her day, she made no mention of having encountered young Chantel. "My mother was here, and said she saw you with the French tutor," he told her, allowing her a chance, unnamed by himself as such, to defend her innocence; but Marie made no such attempt, merely agreeing with what William had said. It might mean anything or nothing. Marie had not, that day, which was fine, no doubt, considered it necessary to spend the entire afternoon on her sofa. This was his real grievance, William told himself: she had made no effort to attend the wedding at Savill's with him, saying she felt too ill. Perhaps it was the first implanting of suspicion in William's mind; but he dismissed it at the time, having other matters to attend to with regard to his arduous pastoral work as minister of Savill's.

VI

MARGARET HOWIE HAD UNDERGONE THE PRESCRIBED PERIOD OF dule for her husband, George, whose funeral was attended by an impressive number of mourners; even his widow, from her shuttered carriage, was startled and flattered at the turnout of black-garbed men of business from the city and the near-by shipyard-offices and foundries. Since their marriage, she knew, George Howie had begun to be taken seriously as a force to reckon with, and his acquaintance had widened to include many of note; the number of carriages was Margaret's own accolade as well as the dead man's; she had, discreetly, improved George's social standing as year followed year. She stared at his short coffin which the horses drew ahead, without much except pretended feeling. Affection, no doubt, of a kind, she had known for George, as one might feel such an emotion for a dependent, ubiquitous spaniel. Of George's physical demands, however, Margaret was glad to be free.

As the cortège jogged towards the Necropolis she reflected on her own now enviable state, as a free woman, still almost young, and of more than independent means. The gossips had been correct in saying that George had trusted his widow enough to leave her in sole management of the fortune they had, jointly, acquired and added to: its disposal would be Margaret's affair and no one else's. She forbore to smile behind her screening widow's veil, but told herself, though no doubt it was a thought unbecoming at this moment, that she would by no means squander the money on the first fortune-hunter who came shortly seeking her hand. Margaret had few illusions. She knew herself infinitely more desirable, even after having borne six children, than the penniless young woman of half-noble blood who had, as the only means of escape available, married George Howie after a single day's acquaintance. She could, when the mourning-period was over, take her own pick from the highest in the land; but was not at all sure that she intended to.

There had been a letter today from John, her cousin at Bonsam, condoling on George's death which he had read of in the gazettes. John's own wife had died, he added, three years since. He would gladly welcome his cousin back to Bonsam after this sad time should be over. Could she spare the leisure for a visit? "You will find us little enough changed here," John wrote, "still the same daily round; the weather has of late been rainy." The rain, as Margaret remembered well, would be making puddled clods of the many rutted ways to Bonsam woods; among the trees last year's fallen leaves would lie rotting. There would be no Cousin Hubert nowadays to accept retrieved twigs of chestnut and beech, for his ship's museum; there would only be poor Augusta left, and John. John. How her own heart had bled, in silence and for a long, long while, after his marriage! It was certain by now that, with John's added maturity and her own capital, they could make a match of it, the pair of them, as soon as propriety might allow. "But I am older, and less of a fool," Margaret told herself. She'd not dance, now, to John's piping; it would be herself, if anyone, who called the tune, if tune there should be. At the same time, she thought to herself, when the mourning-days were over, she would take a private trip to see Bonsam again, and John; but she'd stay at an inn, and maybe would not say she was coming. To put the clock back was hardly possible; she'd changed, even if Bonsam had not. For Bonsam would never change, or the life there; a far cry from this bustling, oncoming city, where fortunes were still made overnight.

Margaret found that thought of Bonsam had sustained her all through George's funeral-service, which was suitably conducted by the Reverend William Heatherton. Perhaps this fact aided her own composure; folk said afterwards that Margaret Howie had remained cool, collected and uncommunicative as usual during her late husband's obsequies. Only the men, of course, went afterwards to the graveside; and on the return journey, with poor George's body safely interred, Margaret found her thoughts dwell on him, perhaps for the last time; it seemed already as if he had never been part of her life.

A few weeks later, leaving the children in charge of their nurse, Margaret took herself privately south, with only Sarah in attendance and a single hamper of luggage to last their stay. Sarah she found growing closer, almost despite Margaret's own resolve, as time passed and the Reverend Alfred retreated into the further shades of buried memory. At no time had Sarah drawn attention to her own powers of revelation, which Margaret had at first feared as much as she could in fact fear anything. The woman and she were silent companions, riding side by side together in the common coach across the Border. Few folk would have known the elegant, kenspeckle Mrs. Howie in the classless, nameless traveller in plain mourning-bonnet and untrimmed cloak, who spoke little to anyone in the vehicle during the journey. Margaret in fact did not take overmuch note of the other travellers; she was, as she sometimes did, surveying her own motives with detached amusement. It had come to her that she must at all events see Bonsam again, if only to lay the young ghost of herself rather than resurrecting it; that latter could best be decided when she saw John, and what the years had made of him. Had he been a provident squire, as his father had? She would be able to tell, when she saw the house and grounds. She would walk there, early tomorrow, unaccompanied even by Sarah, up to a high place she remembered in the woods, and look down on the manor and kitchen-garden. She would do that even before visiting the churchyard, and her parents' grave, where a monument to the Reverend Alfred gave nothing of his life away. A faint yellowing over of lichen above strange names, no more, it would be; she had almost forgotten her father and mother. The living mattered more. What did John, for whom she had named her only son, look like now?

Next day Margaret put on a pair of stout walking-shoes and tied a kerchief over her hair. The folk at the inn were new since her girlhood days, and did not know who she might be. She looked enough like a countrywoman, she knew, to discount comment, but found that, with the years of soft living and riding in carriages, her muscles felt their lack of use, at first; but soon she was back into the old, familiar striding up the woodland paths. She felt her strong body respond to the challenging wind, which blew her dark skirts back against her moving thighs; there was the smell of damp leaves and dead wood, as she'd foreseen, borne on it, and the occasional sounds of small animals scurrying in the grass; once she saw a hare, ears pricked, waiting, then scenting her on the wind it vanished on its habitual wide circular, loping run. Margaret walked on for almost an hour, then turned and looked back.

Bonsam already sprawled below; there was the medley of chimneys she remembered, some of them made of carved ornate brick from Tudor days. There was the rebuilt part with the high-pitched roofs, and a portico done in Regency times, and an old dovecote of long before, which they'd let stay in the garden. There were no doves flying about it; everything had an abandoned air, no longer expectant but dying. The walled kitchen-garden, which even in John's father's day he held cabbages and kale, was overgrown, what remained of the gooseberries a wildly straggling hedge, beyond which a couple walked slowly up and down; the keeper, with Augusta. Margaret stared beyond the imbecile's lolling head to where former fruit-trees had been espaliered at one time against the wall; they sagged now, and the box paths were untrimmed. Money was needed at Bonsam, and a mistress with some pith and energy; she herself, no doubt, could resurrect Bonsam as she'd done George's failing credit in the busy city in the north. But in the city there was the stimulation of diverse humanity, other struggles to match one's own. Here at Bonsam the struggle had been given up long, long ago; perhaps when John's mother first lay down on a day-bed because there was no hunting near by, and did not trouble to rise again. No, she herself, were she to re-enter Bonsam as mistress, would soon enough shrink back to its size, her mind become like a cabbage, no solace for boredom but once more to walk, and walk. "As Augusta walks now," she thought. What went on in Cousin Augusta's crazed head, or ever had?

It was her contemplation of the thing Augusta had become that made Margaret decide against returning to Bonsam. She would not even stay to see what time had done to John. There was no need for him, in his turn, to know that she had been here. She would write from the north to say she was unable to come.

She walked back to the inn. "We are returning tomorrow," she told Sarah. The servant said nothing. Margaret had directed her own thoughts meantime to the future. The country air had refreshed her today; it would be good, she thought, now and again, for the children. As soon as might be, she herself would purchase a small country cottage, perhaps on the shores of the Solway looking across to England. She would accustom Georgy and young John and the rest to the dancing sun on leaves, reeds and water, and teach them birds' names and the names of wild flowers. That would be for a month, maybe even two, each summer, perhaps also in spring for a time. There was no need to dispense with the great beating heart of city life for longer, or lose what she had gained and come to need over the years as George Howie's wife.

VII

To own a great deal of money is a passport to swift fulfilment of one's desires; and no sooner had Margaret made known her wish to obtain a small cottage on the Solway than the opportunity to purchase one was found for her by her lawyer. It was in good repair, and had been till lately lived in by a careful couple; the farmer nearby who owned it was willing to sell outright now that the old labourer had died, and the old woman gone back to her own people in Westmorland. The price was not exorbitant; and that same summer Margaret, this time with Georgy by her, was able to go down for a few days, taking with her cooking-utensils, old clothes and some linen. Having put certain things in order in the house, she bethought herself of the space available, and whether or not they could have guests this year. "Would you like the little Heatherton girls to come to stay, dear, with their mama?" she asked Georgy. The child's face composed itself obediently, no more; Georgy never showed strong preferences, being guided in all things by her own mother. "If it is what you wish, mama," she replied, as a copybook daughter should. Margaret laughed; alone here, it was already possible to forget that she must comport herself with gravity, mourning for poor George, for at least a year. But the country permitted leeway; and she mocked Georgy a little.

"Come, you must say whether it will make you very glad or very sad; there is no need for them to come, if you would as soon not have them. But poor Mrs. Heatherton has been very ill, and a holiday would do her good. Do you think that we should have them?"

"If it will do good, Mama, why, yes."

Georgy was well taught, reflected Margaret wryly; she herself would have welcomed a greater display of spirit in her own child whom she loved most dearly. The reason why she loved Georgy more than John, the longed-for son, was not clear to Margaret, and the lack of clarity in itself irritated her; she strove to spoil John a little accordingly, in order that he might not feel himself less loved. Georgy watched and said nothing, and did not resent the treats and presents given to John. It was as though, Margaret thought, the child were complete within herself, and that was not yet quite desirable. She was, therefore, pleased with the notion of having the Heatherton children to stay; it would draw Georgy out of herself. "You must teach them to play your games, and be a little mother to them," she told Georgy, without thinking; and Georgy quietly replied, "But, mama, they will have their own mother with them." Margaret smiled, and said nothing; but reflected on the fact that, as all the congregation knew, Marie Heatherton was no more a mother to her children nowadays than a wife to her husband. How this information had filtered from the servants to their employers was a matter for conjecture; but everyone knew that the Frenchwoman occupied a separate room in the manse of Savill's, though where it actually was no one seemed to know. Pity for William Heatherton had been expressed, and also the hope that matters might mend soon. It was perhaps, Margaret told herself, in an effort to restore a more laudable state of affairs that she posted the invitation to William Heatherton on behalf of his wife and two small daughters. The minister's permission in such a matter went without saying as a first necessity; and no doubt Mr. Heatherton himself would be glad to have his spouse restored to full health. Town was sultry in summer, "and here she will have the fresh air, and river breezes," Margaret thought. She awaited the reply impatiently; it was an acceptance, in Marie's handwriting. The passive creature had, evidently, been induced by her husband to write her own reply. That she herself was disappointed not to receive a missive in William's hand struck Margaret briefly, and astonished her. Perhaps she was more of a hypocrite than she had known, and the relationship with William, and not his wife's health, was her own primary cause in writing. That must be put firmly in its place; and Margaret, an adept, schooled herself to think of every possible comfort for Marie in the somewhat primitive conditions which were all the cottage could offer, with its box beds built into the wall, and all water having to be carried up from the river, and boiled on the fire.

William had made Marie write the letter of acceptance, impressing on her that it was important both to accept, and to behave herself acceptably, in order that so desirable a social connection might be kept up and improved upon. He had no notion that it almost broke Marie's heart to leave town at this moment, and Paul.

Paul likewise was at a loss. After Marie and the two little girls, both in broad-brimmed hats and pantalettes, had driven away —he had watched them go from his place in the street, that early morning, on his way to Miss Flora's school—he felt the town empty. He no longer cared to roam in his old haunts, among the busy streets where he had enjoyed watching humanity pass, including the rich city merchants on their way to a meeting-house from which Paul was of course excluded, but wherein all the daily gossip was exchanged, and business done. He wandered alone, at the end of the long school day, to the place of willows and water where he had lately sat with Marie, under the jealous eye of old Jean Heatherton who followed thm. He then went home, back to his lodging where all he possessed, in itself so little, served only to remind him of Marie; and knew himself at last, after so many idle heartless conquests, completely in love; any doubt he might have permitted to linger in himself was resolved in those first nights alone, when no white-clad figure could glide barefooted across the intervening space into his bed, and leave in the dawn's light after repeated passion. He missed Marie's body, that yielding entity which bore, in its very surrender, no resemblance to the submissive flesh her husband knew, or had ever known; to picture William and Marie together was now, to Paul, an impossibility, sacrilege. They had vowed, he and she between them, that it must never be so again; but for lack of money had devised no means of going away together, and so in such ways the months had passed, and now there was still no definite or possible plan ... But Heatherton must never have his rights again as a husband; of that Paul was resolved. She had been ill, his love; though not as ill as she made out to those whose concern it was not, should never be any more, now that he and she, Paul and Marie, loved nightly together. He had never in his life given himself to a woman so utterly as to Marie, in body and mind; ordinarily when a woman passed from his sight she was forgotten, but Marie ate into his soul, like a loving cancer, a devouring, growing thing. He found that he could no longer sleep at nights for lack of her; his days at school after this sleeplessness were a torment; his teaching deteriorated. Miss Flora noticed, as Paul had feared she would, that there was something wrong with him; and questioned him concerning it. Paul lied to her; what else could he do?

"I lack sleep, madame, because of my cough which troubles me." And Flora had purchased a syrup for him; then said that, as he grew no better, he should take a short holiday. "I will pay your salary," said the kind woman, seeing the brief alarm in Paul's eyes; he had only just enough to live on, and she herself could afford no more if the school were to continue to pay without troubling Hector, whom she had by now repaid.

So it was arranged, and Paul thanked Miss Flora Urquhart for her kindness. "Where will you go, M. Chantal?" asked the headmistress. "To the north, madame," answered Paul, with every intention of going south to Solwayside. He would make up some tale of the mountains he had seen, afterwards.

Katie and Lissy saw a change in their mama, after they had all driven down to the cottage owned by Mrs. Howie, who was kind but of whom they stood in some awe, as they did of her daughter Georgy. Miss Georgy was, their own nurse had told them, perfect in every way, her dress, her mind, her manners; they must model theirs on hers. At first the two silent, lonely younger children drew together against the Howie brood, then as the days passed the Georgy remembered her mama's instructions to her regarding them, were brought out and made to play children's games and fashion sand-castles, with the rest, and make pebble-gardens. Georgy's gardens were neat and tidy, and Kate set herself to do her best also, but always in her own way; Lissy could not, and only made a mess of trailing weed and unbalanced stones which drew silent criticism from Georgy; it was always silent, and she never put a foot wrong, which was no doubt why the Heatherton children could not feel at home with her. To escape from the glossy-haired, rosy-cheeked demon in her carefully ironed gingham aprons, they sought out their own mama more than they would have done at home; and so noticed the change in Marie. At the outset of their holiday the young woman had lain in a chair, as she lay forever on the chaise-longue at home; but one day a letter came. After that—the children did not consciously think of the letter, only noticed the improvement in Marie—she got up, went for walks, played with them sometimes, brushed out her own dark hair and even laughed and sang; though not if Mrs. Howie should be present. When that was the case, their own mama and Georgy's sat quietly together, talking or sewing, while the green reeds stirred in the light wind that came from the water.

Margaret became aware of the differences between her own nature and Marie Heatherton's in the time the latter spent at the Solway cottage. The weather continued brilliant enough to pass a great part of the day out of doors; this pleased Margaret, who was an active and energetic walker. Accompanied by her elder children she was used to cover many miles daily, clad in stout shoes and with a kerchief over her hair as she had done at Bonsam. There were few parts of the shore on which she had not by now ventured, and she was already a familiar sight to the sparse human life of the region, the fisherfolk and farm-hands, and the postman. But Marie Heatherton seemed too indolent to walk far, and too withdrawn into herself for much conversation of any interest. Margaret's feelings altered from the initial sympathy with which she had issued the invitation, to a positive reaction in favour of William Heatherton; so brilliant a preacher deserved a less dull wife! Further than this reiterative statement Margaret's thoughts did not go, for that would still not have been proper. She never consciously considered herself as the potentially ideal partner for William; someone who would help him actively on the social side of his parochial duties, an organiser who could appreciate company while—this Margaret knew concerning herself—never at any time objecting to solitude. She was already coming to realise that the latter was, for any woman, a privilege; either one had no independent existence, being tied to the whims of a husband, or if not, one was a spinster such as Flora Urquhart, who worked for her living incessantly though no doubt, by now, somewhat rewardingly; or again such as Margaret had once herself been, an unpaid poor relation in others' houses; or like Sarah Court, a servant.

Court had not come on this holiday. The rough work was done by two country-girls Margaret had hired, and she herself had time on her hands and would have cultivated Marie had there, she now decided, been anything to cultivate. Idle young woman! "She will not help herself, so others have to help her," Margaret told herself, sententiously.

Georgy had been given a box of water-colours for her birthday, and Marie had evinced a stirring of interest in these; once she painted, with the careful exploratory manner of a prospector finding gold, a small head of Georgy herself, which Margaret considered a good likeness. "You have talent," she told the younger woman positively, and thereafter tried to interest Marie in a certain view, a scene with artistic possibilities, or the light on the changing water. But Marie did not paint again meantime. She seemed to have lost the energy she still possessed before leaving town, and to be in worse health, rather than better, for her holiday. Margaret, tired of watching her guest sit day after day doing nothing, spoke to her, without acerbity, on the merits of using such gifts as Providence had seen fit to bestow on her, and to gratify others. "It is told to us that we should not hide our light under a bushel," said Margaret. "You, my dear, have given nobody the notion that you might paint so well as you do. Why will you not continue with it?" But Marie shook her head.

"I am too tired," was all she would say. So Margaret turned from William Heatherton's unrewarding wife to his two small daughters, already benefiting from the clean silken air of the south-west, and its sunshine. Their mother kept them, Margaret admitted, neat and well-clad enough; the two maids looked after them together with Margaret's children. Kate was strong-minded, Lissy tentative; the elder girl always made the decisions. Both were plain children, and beside Georgy looked like sparrows beside a brilliant kingfisher. But Margaret hid her pride in the beauty of her own eldest daughter; such things, she told herself, were temporal. Georgy's character also was without flaw, as far as one might judge at her tender age. It was surprising that the two little Heatherton girls did not love her, but they kept to themselves, as much as they might in so crowded an establishment; all the children slept together in two box beds.

Then one day a letter came for Marie and she lost her dullness and become almost glorious; and she took Georgy's paint-box and made a coloured sketch of tall emerald reeds shimmering in sun along the Solway. It was pleasing, Margaret thought, but seemed unfinished.

"Will you not continue with it tomorrow?" she heard herself saying. She had begun already to treat the other woman almost as a child. She heard Marie's answer, with the dark head turned away.

"Tomorrow the light may be different. And . . . other things may happen." As she said this, her face illumined itself like that of a saint in a stained-glass window. Margaret saw the flush of colour, and congratulated herself that, at last, William Heatherton's wife was beginning to feel the good of her holiday.

Next day, again, was fine. To Margaret's surprise, Marie made the announcement that she would take her two daughters a little way along the shore. "It is safe there?" she asked. The sands in certain places were treacherous; Margaret had Georgy well drilled as to the parts where they might, or might not, play.

"It is safe enough as far as——" and she mentioned a place. "But may not Georgy come with you? She knows the sands well." Margaret was, she herself realised, showing tact in not offering to accompany Marie. It was perhaps too confined a space for two women to live in constantly without irritating one another on occasion.

To her somewhat offence, Marie refused. "No. I want only my own." Then she put a quick, slender hand out to the other. "You have been good," she said. "I must sound—ungrateful. But I know that you are a good woman, better than I."

Margaret smiled, mollified. "Nonsense, my dear; no one of us can assess any other's worth in such ways. We follow the rules as they are laid down for us, and——"

"*I* do not," said Marie, defiantly. She went over to the small dark glass that hung in the room, and put on her bonnet. "Katie, Lissy, come." The two little girls went obediently to her, and she took charge of them, one in each hand. Before going out she nodded to the painting of the Solway reeds, which lay on the table.

"You may have it," she said, "if you would like it, and the one of Georgy also." It was the longest sentence Margaret had ever heard her utter. She seemed a changed being there in the doorway, as though her mind as well as her body were about to emerge into light. Margaret demurred a little.

"You must frame them for yourself," she said, "and hang them up in the parlour at the manse." But Marie shook her head in the new positive manner that had come to her.

"They are not important to me now that they are done," she said, and went out down the short path that led to the shore. Margaret stared after her. Her own thoughts were in chaos, and she was brought back from a glimpse of a strange, unknown world by Georgy, immaculate in blue-and-white gingham, with the sand showing between her bare toes.

"What shall we do today, Mama?" The perfectly formed little face was expressionless. It was impossible to tell whether or not she had been hurt at being left out when the Heatherton children went off; Margaret decided against asking her. "Why, my darling, whatever you would best like," she said suddenly. It had occurred to her that she did not know her daughter any better than she knew William Heatherton's wife. No doubt knowledge of another human being was possible only to a limited extent, but as a mother——

"I would like best whatever you would like, mama," replied Georgy, her large dark eyes without expression.

Marie Heatherton returned four hours later, her hair unbound. She was in a strange, exalted state; the two little girls, unchanged from their customary selves, trailed after her, Lissy carrying sea-shells carefully in both hands. They were intent on the shells, and had forgotten their mother.

"May I speak with you?" said Marie to Margaret Howie. The other, puzzled, nodded. Marie flung back her hair.

"Let us go into the parlour," said Margaret, shocked at the

other woman's dishevelment. That room, as in all such cottages, was unused except for formal occasions; an aroma of old damp clung to it, as if air and nature were not allowed to enter.

Marie looked about her wildly. "I am going to have a child," she said. "We have no money, either of us, to go away. Will you, who have been so good——?"

Margaret afterwards made herself forget the request, the whole episode: except to question the pliant Lissy, later. She could not even remember how she and Marie Heatherton had ended the conversation. Later that evening, when all of the rest were in bed, she at last lit a lamp, seldom used in summer months at the cottage, and took pen and paper and wrote to William Heatherton. She did not repeat Marie's statement to her; she would never in her life tell it to anyone; but she said, as Lissy had been persuaded to verify, that the young French tutor employed by Flora Urquhart had been down that day, and had been for some time alone with Mrs. Heatherton while the children played on the beach. She, Margaret, did not feel that she could longer be responsible for the situation that had arisen, and while he could trust her discretion on this matter, she thought William himself should take his wife home; the holiday had benefited her and she seemed very well.

Margaret then laid down the pen with a feeling of inadequacy. What else was there to do but pray?

VIII

Marie would afterwards remember the day in question as one of perfect happiness. It did not hold the former ecstasy she had known with Paul. The children were with her; she had taken them deliberately, as though to lay emphasis on the fact, to herself, that they were half her flesh, that she was French, and a Frenchwoman never forgets that she is a mother. But they had played, in the end, William Heatherton's children, alone by the sea, collecting shells, while she and Paul . . .

What had they been to one another then, she and Paul Chantal? A perfect complement, partnering one another in thought, their bodies close. They had moved towards one another like two streams, inevitably meeting in the sand to become one before joining the sea. They had not even spoken aloud at first, not uttering the conventional explanations; why he came to be here, how he had contrived to get away. It did not matter. She had been standing barefoot by the tide's edge with her wild hair blowing, and a child in either hand, having guided Lissy's still uncertain steps towards the sea. It was possible to see all things clearly; the way Kate's pink toes, like small starfish, closed over the pebbles the tide stirred; the way the light summer wind blew about the little girls' plaid dresses. They had taken off their shoes and stockings and left them further up on the sand; they had run, all three, like children together down to the water. Now Kate was the grown-up; William's daughter, already strong-minded and somewhat suspicious of levity, seeing her mother dishevelled in front of a stranger.

"We have got our skirts wet," she said, "and, Mama, your hair has come out of its pins. And there is a man watching us."

Paul was watching. She saw him smile. She could remember the light on his brown head, and the way the sun itself had already warmed his skin a little. He did not have enough of sunshine, did not eat nourishing food. He was so poor it tore at her heart; he might even have walked here. But he had come, by whatever means. He had come, and from then till eternity it was theirs, this moment in time. Nothing could ever take it away.

Marie was laughing. She could remember how she had laughed, and the sound of Kate's prim voice, and the way she herself, from habit, had put an uncertain hand up to her dark hair blowing loose, and felt glad she still had pretty feet. Then she was with Paul, and nothing else was of significance; they sat together, in the shade of the sparse trees that blew here in winter so that they drifted sideways, forever shaped by the wind. Kate and Lissy had gone to make sea-shell gardens; the hour was their own.

"You are here. Nothing else matters to me." She did not ask by what means he had travelled, when he would have to return. She let him run his hands through her dark hair. William's stolid children played on, unheedingly. The air was full of contentment, as though the sun and wind made their completeness in one another eternal rather than transient, as though he need never go back again. She had begun to think of it, the return, already, while Paul was still by her.

"You are so beautiful, Marie; now, when I see I see you without the trappings, the solemnity." They spoke in French. She laughed. It seemed now that she had not had enough laughter in all of her life. "I am ugly," she said. "No one has noticed me before." It was true; William was as if he had never been. This moment, this, was all of living. If I die now, she thought, I shall have lived; with Paul, for this hour.

"I have always noticed you, from the beginning." He fell silent; and, from between the silken strands of her hair, thought how at the beginning it had been with him as always, and he had perhaps diverted himself by seducing Marie, by seeing her as someone to be won, as other women were. Now, it was different. "We must go away," he said. "I will arrange it." He did not know yet how it was to be arranged. Even this sojourn, with its necessity of two nights at an inn, had exhausted his small resources. Paul had never saved money; he thought of it as a thing to spend. Now, protective towards

Marie, he berated himself. Fool, vagabond, not to be able to remove her now, today, from the house where she was! To have come here, to have escaped, the pair of them, from the bondage that held them both, and then to have to return ... But she must never return to Heatherton. That determination held Paul Chantal. "You are mine," he said, "and no other's. It has seemed very long since you went away." And he took her hand and turned it palm outwards and kissed it, seeing the inner colour like that of a shell, the fine small fingers with their clever talent hidden among narrow bones. "I do not know," he said, "what is to become of us. You will say I am foolish. Do you say so, Marie?"

"It may be so. Today I do not care." She had determined not to tell him the thing that still, in her mind and below her heart, lay hidden; it was too early. "Today we are happy. There are few moments in one's life when one is completely happy, completely at peace." She spoke haltingly, unused to express her inner feeling in words. There was no need for her even to touch him. "While you are here, I am happy," she said. "When you have gone, there will be nothing."

"Foolish one, do you think I would go far?" he said, and played with her hair.

Lissy brought shells, and they admired the pearly cowries together. Everything today was texture and light; the sun still picked out the gold in Paul's brown hair, his sun-warmed skin. When he grew old he would make, she realised, a fat little man, like Napoleon. The prospect of this weakness aroused in her tender laughter: he asked her its cause, and Marie told him.

"Napoleon was not old," he said. A shadow seemed to cross the sun. Marie feverishly tried to return to their former state of happiness, forcing herself to remember the thought that had come moments before, that in true love one did not regard the beloved as Adonis but saw him as he was; slim small bones like a chicken's, covering fast, like that bird, with pale malnourished flesh; the places behind the ears baby-fine, intimate, so that she must, at the last, touch them. She caressed the places, thinking again how she was almost sure she carried Paul's child. A drowsy peace had overcome her, postponing the necessity for action, preparation. She would write, perhaps, to

Paul concerning it after he had gone back. That was easier; a strange reluctance persisted in her as regarded telling him now, and perhaps spoiling the day with reminders of responsibility, the money needed for a birth, for baby-clothes, a place to live. Where could they live? As though he sensed her thoughts, Paul's golden eyes raised themselves to her face.

"Qu'est-ce que tu as, ma chérie?" She smiled; the phrase was apt.

"I said nothing." She traced with a finger the design wrought on his watch, of dark metal on a chain slung from one to the other pocket. The colour of guns, of war; Marie knew it well by now, and that it had come to Paul from his father Henri Chantal. Dipping into his pockets like an exploring child she drew the watch towards her, and listened to its steady tick; trite to think of time passing never to be recaptured, but these moments had been, for both of them, real ... The watch-hands moved inexorably. Neither Paul nor Marie spoke. Then Marie turned the watch over on its face, and troked the initials, H.C., and the date, 1818.

"The metal was taken from one of Napoleon's gun-batteries at Leipzig," he said. His hand closed over hers; almost with an unthinking gesture, he returned the watch to his own pocket. Marie gave a little, uncertain laugh.

"And Napoleon was not old," she said, adding hastily, "one does not think of him as either old or young. You loved your father."

"He was the finest man I have ever known. Until I met you I have never felt deeply for anyone else. This is all I have left of him, but now there is you, and——"

"That, and memory." She had interrupted; she could not bear the nearing of their separation. Paul caught her mood; his next remark was almost flippant. "If one were without memories, one would be dead," he said lightly. Suddenly he took her in his arms and, regardless of the playing children, kissed her on the mouth. They clung together. By the time they had done with gazing one at the other, the two little girls were carefully exploring the further sand, Kate's mindful hand in small Lissy's. Overhead the sun descended from its zenith, so that the sky seemed dark before they turned away. Marie did not watch Paul depart. She occupied her thoughts on the journey back to the cottage with a notion which, she realised, had come to her while Paul still lay in her arms, and she saw the poverty of his clothing. She would tell Margaret Howie, who seemed kind, of their plight, and Margaret would lend them money to go away together for the child's coming birth. "She is so *comme il faut* that she will not want Paul's child to be born among the congregation," Marie thought, with the facile gaiety which had so strangely sat on her all day, and made her, Paul had noticed, beautiful.

Now Margaret Howie would not lend the money. It had not gone as it should, any of it; she herself should not have trusted this woman, with her narrow-eyed prosperous face swiftly white with shock, and her mouth a line of grim silence. Marie, likewise, could not recall the end of that conversation, which like another of long ago had embarrassed them both; nor could she recall how she got into the cottage box-bed she shared with Margaret, for lack of space, and later they lay back to back, as strangers. Marie already had to down a trembling of fear that had no open reason. It did not occur to her that Margaret, before she came to bed, had already written the letter to William that was to leave in the morning. She herself lay awake, not daring to gaze at the unheeding stars.

William set his hand on the latch, and entered the attic room. It was plain and almost bare; Marie's needs were still as simple as when she had been in the convent. The bed, a chaise-longue, a pinewood stand with jug and ewer patterned with ferns and primroses, and a row of green-painted hooks where her few clothes hung; the room might have been a servant's. There was a tin trunk, which William recalled as having accompanied them on the wedding-trip; and some papers piled up on a table near the window. William thumbed through these; to his surprise, they were drawings. Why had Marie never told him that she could draw?

He was not intrinsically interested; as an aspect of possessiveness, he looked at the subjects she had chosen; chimney-pots, the street below, with houses in sharp perspective and a single figure, it might have been her own, seen far beneath on the pavements. There were some sketches of her children, and one of a young man who—William could not but recall his mother's warning to him on that subject—could be none other than young Chantal. William pursed his lips. Some instinct made him withdraw the sketch from the bundle, and presently tear it through and through.

He looked about the small room, the fragments of the drawing still in his hand. Marie had, without doubt, behaved improperly. William sought in his mind for suitable subjects with which she should have chosen to occupy her time, if it must be done in such a way; matters suitable to an invalid's leisure, the making of shell-pictures perhaps, or if she must sketch, flowers; such things were pleasing and readily understood, and the likenesses of his children he could also approve of; from the brief glance he had taken, Marie had captured, presumably from memory, Kate's resolute calm expression, small Alicia's plain, uncertain face, the too-long nose balancing the still plump cheeks of childhood. That was a charming sketch, and should be hung framed in the parlour downstairs, or perhaps in his own study.

He continued to look about him. Marie's silk shawl, which she had not taken with her to Solwayside, hung by itself on a hook in the further wall, beneath her winter bonnet. Assailed by memory, William went across and fingered the silk fringes. He had had, for good or ill, his wish first expressed on that long-ago day: sentiment flooded him, recalling how Marie, the first time he ever set eyes on her, had been wearing that selfsame shawl and carrying asters. Had she ever been back to visit her father's grave? There was, now he took leisure to consider, much he did not know about Marie ... the anomaly disturbed William.

The stuff of the shawl was rich; he pulled at and fondled it, almost as though it were her flesh, her body, for months now denied him. Soon, perhaps, if she were recovered after this holiday ... The stuff was rich, with a raised embroidered pattern on it of birds, flowers, leaves. William held up the embroidery to survey it at close range with his myopic eyes, and found that the folds were caught in a door.

How much of a fool had he been? How long, after the discovery of Chantal's sketched portrait, did it take him to discover, even in his own mind, what she had been at, a matter he would never have credited even after his mother's expressed warning? How soon thereafter had Margaret Howie's letter come? It must have come about then, when he was still embroiled with the matter of the portrait and the caught shawl.

Later, he went up to the room again. He must have gone away alone, perhaps to deny to himself the thing that had happened, must have happened time and again without his knowledge, while he himself wrought with his fleshly longings belowstairs and for her sake, her sake! did not attempt to slake them.

He ascended the stairs again. He walked straight across the room and opened the further door.

To his surprise the space between the two attic rooms was large, larger than he had expected. Did she traverse this space lustfully after night? It was large, lined with the bricks that made the filling between the adjoining houses, with the sunlight filtering in on cobwebs which neither of the pair had thought to brush off as they came and went ... there was other light; a door, the door beyond to the man's room itself, was open. William could see the everyday belongings and furnishings, and a bed. As he watched, the outer door opened and Paul Cantal came in, hat in hand. In the other hand was a letter.

The two men saw one another; for a moment in time both stood motionless, staring across the space that still separated them. Then Chantral, with a cool deliberate movement, bestowed the letter carefully in an inner pocket. As though the movement itself had released his own powers to think afresh, William knew, with a faculty beyond all reasoning, that the letter came from Marie. Marie was all about them; the silk shawl, caught where it by custom hung as she had closed the door behind her, and the pair of them thinking themselves so safe that she had not even turned to look if all were concealed, if the room were as she should have left it ordinarily. Marie: of nights, while he himself suffered and prayed below, stealing across that brick space to her lover, or had the lover by custom come offenest to her? Had what had been between them taken place, perhaps, also in *his* house, on his very couch, or on the narrow invalid's bed, from which he, the husband, was by fiat barred? And had the dawn crept up before the guilty couple parted?

Marie. She had been looking well, almost in bloom, lately; he had never seen her look so well, had thought perhaps it was the delicate colour of a consumptive, while this fellow ... this foreigner, he ... standing there now, concealing Marie's letter ...

William did not remember crossing the brick-lined space. He only knew that he found himself in Chantal's room, with the Frenchman before him; so puny a little weasel of a man, to steal into another's wife's bed and cuckold him, cuckold *him* ... William was as certain already as if he had seen it happen; by now, he knew it was true.

"I must ask you ..." His own voice, he heard, was hoarse; it seemed as though he laboured under great emotion. Yet the matter was paltry enough. "I must ask you for my wife's letter," said William clearly. He held his right hand out; his strong, well-fleshed hand, with the nails cut clean and square. He clearly remembered seeing the hand, and the nails. On Sundays, in the pulpit, gesturing, he had reason to be proud of them ...

Paul did not deny the matter. He smiled, and made a little bow. "My letters, monsieur, are my personal property. This room also"—he made a slight, embracing gesture with one hand—"is mine, for the moment. I do not recall inviting monsieur to enter it."

He turned away, and laid down his hat. It was the smile that enraged William. So cool, the smile, as though to take another man's wife by stealth were an amusing thing ... the French, notoriously light in their estimate of marriage. Marie was French. Marie ... his wife, *his* wife! "I enter where I choose," William heard himself say. "It was I who obtained you these lodgings." What did that matter? Lame Eustacia Hyslop, who could no longer climb the stairs ... the room, William had time to note, was again somewhat dusty. There was more in the way of furnishing here than in the room next door; a curtained bed, a satin-striped couch the worse for wear, and——

It was then that William saw Marie's slipper. There was only one; then and afterwards, he never found where the other was. They were brown worn flat morocco slippers, such as she often had on about the house. The simple slipper lay on its shabby side, half hidden by the frills of the bed. She must often have lain in there, behind the curtains, with her lover. Adultery ... and for his wife, for Caesar's; no less, for the mistress of the manse should be a pattern to the congregation.

He did not know what, if anything, he had been saying meantime to Paul Chantal. He saw the man now through a mist; at one time, he was sure, they shouted at one another. William recalled it afterwards, thinking also how it was seldom that he himself lost his temper. They had squared up to one another, the big man and the small, the Frenchman and the blackmith's son with soft, powerful, unused hands.

"She never loved you. What do you know of love? You took her as though she were a possession, a chattel. Such a woman can know passion like a harp with strings, and yet all you did was cause her to bear a child yearly, and cook your potatoes and your mutton." The small French tutor was red in the face with emotion and rage; William heard the blood drumming in his own ears. "She is not your possession," said Paul Chantal, suddenly cool. "I will take her away to where she can learn to be happy. She has never in her life known happiness except with me, you comprehend? Perhaps you cannot do so, you who preach always of misery and sin and the fire to come. Pah! You are your own god, in your pulpit, in your bed; a woman made of marble would be all the same to you. Get out of my room now, and I will leave tonight; I will go away with Marie and we will make love together always, you hear me? She loves me in such a way——"

It was then that the red mist descended before William's eyes. He could remember, afterwards, only the recollection of his boyhood's sight of the fully-fired anvil, the flames cherry-red beneath, and the one occasion his mother had permitted him to use the great air-forced bellows of leather and brass. The air hissed out of the bellows' mouth and made the fire glow brighter. It took a strong man's hands to squeeze and work the bellows, to elicit that long final hiss of expired air.

Afterwards William looked at Paul's small crumbled body

lying on the worn carpet and thought "They must not find it. They must not know by any means that I was even here." And then it was as though all things descended in their respective order of importance until after he had cleared away all traces of Paul's entry today, even to removing Paul's hat from the table, and his gloves from where they lay. Then it was a matter of conveying Paul himself out of the room, out of the adjoining house, and Paul as a dead body was light, so light that it was almost as though he, William Heatherton, carried a child. The French had brittle bones, a chicken's bones. There must be, somewhere, something that would contain so small a body, some receptacle that he himself could use until at last he got rid of it ... but how to do that? Throw the body by night in the river, bury it in the country, beneath last year's fallen leaves? There was danger that such a thing might be traced to him. William, if anyone saw him engage in either unusual activity; he, the minister of Savill's Old, journeying laden across bridges after dark, carrying a spade like a labourer through the far woods. No, it must be in a hiding-place nearer than that; a space lined with brick, a near place, here beyond the very door, and that other door built up so that it would no longer open from the further side. Generations of foundry-workers in his blood made William, in such matters, quick.

But the body would rot even between the bricks, and perhaps stain the ceiling beneath, though there was no blood. No blood ... and the painted tin trunk in Marie's room could hold it and quicklime, which destroyed and dried remains swiftly. They had used it, William remembered hearing, for the mass murders in the French Revolution, so that afterwards it had been almost impossible to identify the headless remains of Queen Marie Antoinette. "But they searched diligently, for they knew she was there," he told himself. If no one knew a body was there, if the very wall were closed and sealed, it would be different.

A ticking noise beset him; Paul's watch. For some reason he could not ascertain it did not seem right to William that the watch should be let run down, and he wound it, feeling the chill of the metal strike his fingers. A good watch, telling the time accurately, was worth preserving...

He could not recall putting the watch away, with its attached chain, into his own pocket. Later its ticking sounded as loudly as the beating of the dead man's heart, and William put it away, together with the letter from Marie, in a drawer of his desk, but meantime there were other things to be done...

It proved impossible, in the event, to place Paul's body in the trunk so that the lid would close altogether. It was left, in the end, with one booted foot sticking out. It was the best that could be done without breaking the bones, or distorting the body unpardonably.

When this was all done the reaction had set in and William had begun to tremble. He trembled in the manner strong men will, with the sweat running down his forehead and behind his spectacles in great beads. Behind the sweat his mind, cool always, worked separately; he knew that it was essential to be quick, and remove all traces, not only of the murder—he called it by no other name, but as though some other man, not himself, had done it—but of other things, everyday things such as the arrival of letter which could not be answered. He must remove all such traces, then call round, from his own side, to old Miss Hyslop to say her lodger had received an unexpected summons home to France and had asked him, William, as a neighbour to see to the packing and despatch of his goods, and to leave word with her and also a month's rent. The prospect of leaving the poor old woman with additional money cheered William; it was a little, a very little, he could do in reparation.

For some reason he could not ascertain he had also, with the watch, left Marie's letter still unopened, as it had come from Paul's inner pocket. It would be unmerciful in him, he now felt, to open the letter and read it, though most husbands would without hesitation have done so. The fact that Chantal had not had leisure to read it either gave William, even now, a certain satisfaction.

At some point he told himself that no one must ever again have access to the space between the two houses, where Paul's body now lay stiffening in the trunk. He thought of the things he must do; he must, for instance, move his study at once to the room on the topmost floor that had been Marie's barring the entry on both sides so surely that no casual observer would ever know doors had been there. After all *he,* until lately, had not known ... had not known many things.

He himself would never again look beyond the wall, once having secured the two doors each with hammer and nails. The book-cases he would set against his own side, filled with his books in constant use, and this would be his protection ... nobody should ever use that room again but himself ...

That booted foot ... surely the quicklime, in time, would reduce it unrecognisably?

"You will return Mrs. Heatherton's things to the downstairs bedroom," he said to the servants, having handed them Marie's few clothes; her gowns, the shawl. It slithered through his hands like a living thing, a cold thing, a snake perhaps, though one must not lack charity, poor misled Marie ...

"Oh, sir, when does the mistress come back?" enquired Phemie, round-eyed below him on the stairs, her arms full of the humble gowns. The sight of the master carrying a book-case up on his shoulders had been queer, and all the books to put back again. "It's only on account of the marketing," she explained to the big revered figure above her, the light behind the head making it featureless. "I wouldn't like any of the meals to go short, sir." What was the matter with the minister? He generally showed an interest in his food.

William had been thinking that he himself must go to Hector Urquhart's yards, to bring home quicklime. "You are a good girl, Phemie," he said absently. "See to the marketing yourself: here is money. I shall be fetching Mrs. Heatherton home the day after tomorrow."

He would have to say the quicklime was for rats.

IX

THE POST CAME LATE EACH DAY TO THE SOLWAYSIDE COTTAGE, having travelled meantime in a leather bag, borne on the hunched shoulders of a very old postman who had walked the long daily round for forty years. By the time he had traversed the winding lanes and fields, stopping at farm-steadings for a gossip and head-shake concerning the weather, it was early afternoon before tidings could reach the place where Margaret and Marie were staying. They were in fact drinking tea, made on a wood fire, while Katie and Lissy, with Georgy and her younger sisters and John, played a round-game within sight of their elders, not too near the water. The sunlight still shone between shimmering reeds on the one hand, and on the other revealed the postman's white-bearded figure, dark now against the sky above the rise. Marie trembled. Surely, surely by today, there must be word from Paul? It was four days, no, five since she had written to him. The phrasing of her letter had burned into her memory, and she saw it now, as though it were in Paul's very hand. What would he do, what could any man do, on receiving such tidings?

I am quite certain now, my dear love, that I am to have your child. I could not even bring myself to tell you when you were here, lest there be disappointment. Disappointment; denial of the joy it brought to her, and must surely also do to him, to know that they had fashioned this fruit of their loving together? Was this the truth? She herself could still not down the joy the discovery had given her, though anxiety grew daily when no answer came, and none again, and now—— Would Paul be angry, perhaps, with the unpredictable anger of men in certain circumstances embarrassing to themselves? Would he be—this, she knew, was more like Paul's response to situations—lightly amused, perhaps with a single shrug of the shoulder dismissing responsibility, letting her suffer? It was not impossible, being a man, that he might naturally act so. Men, from her knowledge, took their pleasure, and thereafter were heedlessly cruel. William——

She downed any thought of William, in the surge of now familiar nausea that came; and noticed, not for the first time, her hostess looking at her strangely. How much Margaret's narrow gaze saw, or guessed, was not manifest; the old postman arrived, and Margaret herself rose coolly, disentangling a fold of her grey cotton gown from the clutching summer brambles, and took the letters. There were only two, both addressed to Mrs. Howie; one was in William's handwriting. Margaret slit open the envelope of the other letter; it contained some matter of no importance. Lastly she opened the first letter William Heatherton had ever written to her. She had deliberately delayed feeling the pleasure she knew it would give her to read it and see his hand: at the same time she was curiously aware of the strangeness of William's having written to her rather than direct to his wife, despite Margaret's own earlier warning.

She looked up shortly; the letter was very brief. It thanked her for her hospitality to Marie. "I have a piece of news for you, my dear, which I know will be welcome," she told William's wife, smiling resolutely into the pale, almost witless face. Whatever ailed the young woman was no longer Margaret's concern. "Your husband is taking a few days' holiday, and will come to fetch you home with him—why, this very day! What a time they take, to be sure, with their mail in country parts: this was sent four days since. I shan't be sorry, in a while, to come back to town: everything there is more convenient. But your husband asks that, as the weather is so fine, the children may stay on with me here for a day or two; they may as well return in the carriage with the rest of us, perhaps at the month's end."

Small Catherine had meantime left the round-game and crept up to her mother's skirts. "I want to go home with Mama," she said, her dark eyes inscrutable. At such times, she seemed almost adult, and afraid of nobody. Margaret rebuked her gently, as her own mother remained silent and unmoving. "I believe that you must do as your Papa bids you, Kate," she said. "Run back now and play with the others; Mama and I wish to speak alone together for a little while."

Marie might have heard none of it, or seen Catherine turn disappointed away, her dark hair hanging lank with the river-damp. She wore, all the children constantly wore, plaid gingham, easily washed and laundered. John's golden head caught the sunlight as they all moved about the clear, boggy flats; he resembled his mother, except that the set of his eyes reminded one of Howie. He would be a handsome boy.

Paul has not written, Marie was saying to herself again and again. He has not written to me; yet he must have my letter by now, unless——

"There is one other thing," Margaret was announcing lightly, brightly, as though joining in some game of words with her children in their nursery at home. "Your husband—I don't presume to call him William, my dear, remembering his cloth—Mr. Heatherton says that I am to tell you, by way of news, that that young French tutor who was with Flora Urquhart for some time has packed his bags in a great hurry, and left for France. Evidently some word reached him that he must go back; the poor minister has had to finish packing all his remaining belongings, at the Frenchman's request, and send them after him post-haste. Otherwise he himself would have been here sooner. It's hot still in town, he goes on to say; there, you may read the letter for yourself. I believe Mr. Heatherton intends having a few days' holiday on the way home with you, staying at inns; that way you need not leave the summer country quite as soon; a pity there's no room for him here, but I doubt if it could be contrived, with so many of us, and so few beds."

She thrust the letter into Marie Heatherton's hand, while Marie herself stood still as marble; a chill wind had begun to blow in from the water, and the shadows were growing longer; it would soon be night. "Come in, children," Margaret Howie called, to her youngsters and Marie's, as their own mother took no heed of them. "Come in before dark falls."

He had gone, Marie was thinking. He had not even packed all his baggage on receipt of her letter, but had hastened away with a valise, no one knew whither. Marie knew that as a banned journalist Paul could not enter France. No, he had gone elsewhere, to find another tutoring situation, perhaps another mistress. Why should she care now what had become of Paul Chantal? He had amused himself with her and got her with child, and at news of that had then fled, unworthily. He had been unworthy of all her love. Yet love there had surely been between them, and great happiness. Her duty now—how long it was since she had considered the word duty, and how often she had endured it then—was to provide for the creature made by her happiness, however brief; to give her own fatherless child a father; to return, in short, to William. William would never know that he was not the father of this child. His conceit, which Marie at times understood, would prevent his recognition of any other possibility. She found herself looking at William in her mind across a great distance, as if he were living and she already dead.

William arrived, as promised, on the evening of that same day, when dark had almost fallen; and after taking Margaret gravely by the hand, and thanking her for her continued hospitality to his family, he said clearly, "Now that Marie has regained her health, we have the more reason to be grateful, have we not, my dear?"

Marie did not answer; in her travelling-clothes again, and plain bonnet, she looked like a thin brown bird, with dropped eyelids. No one could tell what she was thinking, or if she thought at all; she gave her usual appearance of complete passivity, preceded William into the carriage he had hired, and they drove off, with the light luggage roped at the back. Turning to wave farewell, the last of the sunset light glinted on William's glasses, turning him for instants in Margaret Howie's sight into a flame-lit devil, all fire within. She downed the infrequent access of imagination, as she turned calmly, efficiently back to the assembled children, who had waved farewell together from the doorway. Poor William Heatherton, more sinned against than sinning; a man who in every way did his utmost for good! "May my own conscience have guided me duly to act as I did," she told herself, almost fiercely suppressing any quaver of jealousy; that spiritless thing, conveyed away by so fine-looking and upright a man, while *she*, who could have matched him in all ways, must stay on here in solitude, but one must school oneself to accept the ways of Providence!

At that moment, alone with a pack of children and an empty sky, Margaret Howie was aware of a second curious sensation. It was not the thought of George, but the fact that, since his death, she had hardly once thought of him as he had been when living. It was impossible to picture George in the hereafter; but at this point Margaret deliberately closed her mind. Such flippant fancies were the result, no doubt, of being too much in her own company. She must busy herself with some useful work, and in due course return, a trifle early, perhaps, to town.

William had arranged to stay overnight with Marie at an inn about twenty miles distant; it was a sad echo of the conditions of their wedding-trip, when as now they had sat and eaten supper in silence, having in fact no words to say. Afterwards she went upstairs to their room and in a quarter-hour or so William, clad in cap and night-shirt, came to her; it was between them thereafter as it had been on innumerable occasions. William satisfied his long-suppressed physical urges, perhaps punishing his wife somewhat for keeping him waiting, as it were, over so many months; the matter of Paul Chantal was by now sealed and walled up at the back of his mind, with other things that must be forgotten. It was as much as to say that, all things being made new, any child in Marie's womb could only be William's own. He did not ignore her lapse so much as having deliberately suppressed all knowledge of it; it had not been; he, the elect, the interpreter of God, could have in no way any substitute; and the fellow was gone. Almost, William found he could think of Paul Chantal as on his way, at this moment, to France. A feature which was not in accord with his other sensations for a moment troubled him. Marie was crying, silently, while he lay here with her; he could feel her cheek and the pillow wet with tears, but she made no sound. William consoled himself, and finally forgave her; she was, no doubt, regretting her deception of him. "You are restored to health," he said, and when no reply came answered for her. "Yes, you are quite recovered; we were right to thank God together. God will guide us henceforth in all our ways."

He had as usual made Marie, before he renewed himself upon her, kneel down by the bedside with him tonight, and pray; it was a ceremony which had been omitted only on the wedding-night, and now all things were fully restored between them. William slept, in satisfaction with his fleshly lot. He would not permit himself to allow memory to defile his mind.

X

THE SUMMER HAD GONE, AND AUTUMN AND WINTER; IT WAS still dark in the mornings. Marie Heatherton had gone downstairs to measure the culza-oil into its jug before coming up again to fill and then clean the collected lamps. It was a task which Phemie the servant did not ever perform properly; Marie spent more than an hour each day on the blackened wicks. She was no longer conscious of strong enough feeling to make her loathe the dirty task; by now, nothing mattered. It was, moreover, important to have a good light in the evenings, not only for William's sight but her own, which had begun to blur a little, making sewing and mending difficult. Her headaches sprang no doubt from this cause; but the puffy swelling of her slender ankles had not occurred in any former pregnancy, nor had she ever felt so ill. All her movements, even with the culza, seemed low and clumsy now.

It was an additional burden today to find, having carried the jug down the basement stairs, that the oil-cupboard was locked. Phemie, enquired of, had no idea where the key might be. The minister, she said, could have taken it with him; he had been downstairs earlier, looking about the cupboard for a boot-jack.

Marie toiled upstairs again. If William had gone out with the key still in his possession, there was nothing to be done but send out for more oil. But it was possible that he might have placed it, absentmindedly, in his desk drawer. He would not be back quite yet; it gave her time to look.

She made herself rest on the landing, then dragged herself up the last flight of stairs to the attic, once her own room, now William's study. His action in taking away her privacy was evident to Marie; but she thought, wryly, that the choice of a place for his books and work must be inconvenient. It did not matter now ... the desk had been moved upstairs by this time, with everything else, since the return from that holiday with Margaret Howie on Solwayside, when she, Marie, had been brought back to the Savill's manse to find rearrangements already made, and her own submissive place again established. She closed her eyes for an instant at the thought of William, and their shared bed; then opened them. The key might be on his ring in the drawer, with others; or again it might not.

She opened one drawer after another, timidly, fearful that by some means William himself might enter unexpectedly, find her prying among his things, and be angry. That she rarely entered his study at all nowadays made such an offence no less heinous; Phemie herself had been bundled downstairs, weeping, one day when she had been trying to dust the books, removing them one by one from their shelves against the wall. The minister had been angry, she sobbed; and her own experience of William's cold, majestic rage made clear to Marie what she must expect if, as a wife found searching in the forbidden sanctum, he should come upon her. But it was the same with anger as with household toil; she had no feelings left. She had none, no, not even for the attic room, so near to where she had once known ecstasy. The room itself held William daily, and its very appearance had undergone change. She would be glad to close the door again behind her, and go back downstairs.

The key was there, with others, in a small side drawer, one not usually open, and beneath...

There was enough morning light. The gleam of gun-metal came to Marie. She drew out Paul's watch. The hands had stopped. They had stopped at a quarter past three.

Why did she notice that first? Why were there, so slowly, other things she noticed; a letter, in a flat sealed envelope, addressed to Paul, in her own handwriting?

Why...?

Suddenly, reality was with her; and present also Paul's voice, heard again as if it were yesterday. "He was the finest man I ever knew. I never again experienced feeling of such a kind for anyone, until..."

Paul would not have left his father's watch behind when he returned to France. And her letter...

Paul had never received her letter.

Strangely, her feeling was one of joy. He hadn't abandoned her, slinking away like a rat when he found she was with child. He hadn't ever known she was with child. Perhaps William had intercepted her letter. But then in the ordinary way if that had happened, Paul would have been waiting when she came back. He would have had no reason to go away, or tell lies about returning to France. Tell lies to William. William.

Her hand closed over the watch's flat cool surface. It was William who lied. William, the righteous, the conventionally demanding husband. William, with the deadly sins of lust, lies and covetousness hidden under his respected broadcloth. For he had perhaps coveted Paul's watch, and had hidden it in a drawer. "But that is ridiculous," Marie heard herself say. And where, if so, was Paul?

Her blurring eyes stared down at the envelope, and the leaden cast of the metal forged for Leipzig. Then she lifted the watch close to her ear, and began to wind it; the light, even tick of the sprung wheels came to her again, a voice from the dead; a voice from the dead.

Marie stayed there for what might have been a long time, her cheek against the slowly warming metal of the watch. Her mind had begun to turn again, like the resuscitated wheels. It ground slowly at first, then gained momentum, turned faster, faster, in an inexorable pattern, becoming certain, manifesting itself in her understanding, burning into her brain.

Paul had not left here alive. She was certain of it. And still the overriding feeling, through the horror, was gladness; he hadn't abandoned her; he hadn't gone away. *But where was his body?*

A shadow darkened the doorway. Marie knew that it was William, the enemy, and that she need no longer feel any fear. She turned and faced him, with the letter and Paul's watch in her hand. The watch had been in good order. Its ticking heartened her. It was as though Paul's heartbeats lay in her very hand, for her to revive or still them. Aloud she said, looking the enemy full in the face, "Where is Paul?" And an echo, as though her voice had been that of a trumpet or organ, sounded in her brain. He did not answer. She could not hear him speak. She asked the same thing again, more loudly; it seemed now that she must shout to make even herself hear.

"Where is Paul? What have you done with him? *Where is he?*"

A shadow moved. It was William, reduced to nothing, only a shadow, going to lay its tall hat down on the desk. Marie smiled a little; he was afraid, was he? He had been so much afraid that he had hurried upstairs, not even remembering to leave his hat in the hall. She heard his answer now, the man in fear; calm outwardly as always, and pompous, and cold. "It is not for me to answer such questions, or for you, my dear, to ask them."

She saw more clearly now; saw the pale eyes, behind thick glasses, focus on the letter in her hand. "What——" he said; and then reached out his hand for the letter. "It was improper," he stated, "for my wife to write to a foreign young man, a stranger. You will have seen that I did not open the letter; not many husbands would have maintained as much reserve." He took the letter from her, and without opening it tore the envelope across. "There, my dear," he said. "That is the end of that episode, is it not? I trust that, in recollecting my position, there will be no recurrence. I was most grieved to learn of your indiscretion in being left alone with young Chantal on the beach; Mrs. Howie did right to inform me of it."

He is defending himself, thought Marie; himself and all he stands for. She was assailed by a sudden desire to laugh; he was making as little of it as possible, was William, for his own sake; because he would not, in his position, allow that she could have done more than spend an hour on the beach with Paul Chantal. An hour! An eternity, like the lovers in Eden . . . and so long ago, and the flesh now perhaps fallen from his bones, while the watch still ticked . . .

She heard it, through a rising bedlam of unnameable things; she heard the meticulous tearing of her letter into small shreds of paper, which William would then bestow in his basket, shreds too small for a servant to read. It was as though he tore at the last shreds of Marie's reason; in her brain, something snapped. The glory that had been hers, the discovery that Paul had not after all left her because of the child, was swallowed up; she began to hit out and beat with her fists at William, fending off with him the other things she dared not name. But William was strong enough to kill a man, and his grip held her back. He advanced, and Marie began to scream, voicing the thing that was in her mind while she could still express thought in sanity.

"You killed Paul. You killed him, and hid his body and took the watch, the watch from Leipzig..."

And then "Do not touch me. Murderer! Murderer!"

William placed one of his hands across her mouth; the other arm held her. She bit his hand; foam and blood appeared at the corners of her lips. She still screamed, the sounds making a bubbling noise against the pressure of William's hand; he began to strike her, to silence her being the only thing paramount in his mind, and shortly she slid to the floor, making no more sound. A dribble of saliva trailed from her mouth to the carpet he had had placed in the room. William began to pray aloud.

"O Lord, let not her blood be on my hands also. Let not her blood be on my hands..."

There was the sound of running footsteps; Phemie, the maid. She saw Marie, began to cry and wail as Highland women will, and made no effort to help; William silenced her, beside the other. He bade her go down and prepare a sick-bed for her mistress. He himself carried Marie's inert body down the slope of the stairs and back to their shared room. By now he was trembling like an old man and the sweat ran down into his eyes again behind the spectacles. Later, he thought, he would go upstairs to the attic room and take the fragments of Marie's letter, which he had never read, and burn it in the downstairs grate so that the servant might not see it. He would have to find some excuse to dismiss Phemie from service in the manse; she might already have seen and heard too much. He must think of that, but first fetch a doctor for Marie ... If only Margaret Howie were here! She was so cool, competent, able to take complete control, to understand the needs of a deranged woman and be discreet, repeating nothing, nothing...

Afterwards, he would go to Margaret. It was a ministerial call, a part of his parish duty, nothing to be misconstrued in any way. But he needed her.

Marie Heatherton spent the last few months of her life under the constant care of her doctor, her husband, and Margaret's servant Sarah Court. The sick woman never left her bed again or uttered an intelligible phrase, being kept under sedation. Every task, even the most menial, was performed for her by one of the above three persons. The laudanum and opium prescribed for her would be less dangerous to the child, her physician said, than the fact that, were she moved, the child might die. It was, in his opinion, preferable to save it than to save the mother, who would continue, he already knew from such cases as he had seen, hopelessly insane. The swelling which had already begun in the sick woman's legs increased till it pervaded her whole body; within weeks she was an inanimate vegetable, puffed and pallid in the darkened room, her breaths coming in snoring sounds from between cracked lips the attendants moistened constantly with water. Marie knew no one, though occasionally the eyes between their distended lids would open; they did not focus, nor did she try, in the last months, to speak. William himself, who at first would hardly leave the sickroom, as if to guard her speech, half lost his fear. He began to be persuaded, under Margaret Howie's guidance, to take up, as the time went by, his normal duties again, and make a partial life for himself among his books.

For Margaret was of prompt, efficient help, as William had known she would be. At the beginning she herself often came, sitting for many hours in the sickroom, knitting or sewing, watchful of the torpid woman on the bed and her needs, as they arose. Sometimes she would feed Marie with a drinking-cup in which was a little warm milk, with the opiates. But the demands of her own young family had still to be met, and the remaining unease of William—what might she not overhear, and understand?—at her constant presence by his sick wife ended in the advent of Sarah, latterly. "Court will nurse her," said Margaret in her calm way; and William, unable to think of any objection, ended by feeling gratitude for Sarah, still mixed with some fear; fear of the silent plodding of the strange-eyed English servant, who said so little, and did so much; bringing her own gear with her in a small, neatly packed valise, and staying. Day and night Sarah Court stayed, inexhaustibly, by the stricken woman carrying out instructions from the doctor as to increased sedation, when the time drew near at which the labour might be allowed to start. It was to be induced prematurely, to avoid undue strain on the mother and jeopardy to the unborn child.

On a night of storm in early February, Marie Heatherton gave birth for the last time. Unlike her earlier labours, this caused her little suffering. It was probable, the doctor assured them, that she knew nothing, felt nothing any more. This child also was extracted by instruments, applied by way of entry to the narrow pelvis; like the rest it was a girl, with dark hair. William Heatherton nodded when he was told of it: strangely, the doctor thought, he appeared relieved. William ordered that this third daughter be called after his own mother, Jean. Later this became altered in daily use to Jenny; the other two girls, sharing Margaret Howie's nursery for the time, were told of her arrival, sparingly, by the nurse.

"You have a baby sister; is that not good news?" For much interest had been shown in the Howie household, among the servants, about the events at Savill's manse; it was ten to one, they were saying already, that Mrs. Howie and the minister made a match of it if the poor young wife died, though it would not be proper maybe for a year.

But any interest in the child's name, or sex, or remarrying, were superseded, in the last instance of all, by Marie Heatherton herself. Doctor, drugs, husband, the conspiracy of silence, all were defeated; she gave at the last one sane, loud, piercing cry which could be heard by all in the sickroom, and out into the street beyond.

"Paul! Paul! Paul!"

But it sounded like the crying of a sea-bird outside among the carriage-blocks of the prosperous, and no one heeded it. Then Marie died. William Heatherton shut himself in for a long time alone, as was proper, after looking down on her dead face. Later, the servant who had been chosen to replace Phemie said she heard him groaning in his attic study, as if with unbearable grief. But that was put down to the possession of too ardent a female imagination; and like other servants who spoke out of turn, the girl left soon afterwards. Sarah Court had by now left also, returning to the Howie house unobtrusively with her valise, and turning a deaf ear to the occasional quest for gossip of the other servants. Nobody ever got much out of Sarah. The child's birth was entered, as all births and deaths of William's children were, on the flyleaf of the great leather-bound Bible which lay on his desk.

III

I

THE RE-MARRIAGE, IN DUE COURSE, OF THE WIDOWED MINISTER of Savill's and the well-endowed relict of George Howie passed without adverse comment by the congregation. It was known that the late Mrs. Heatherton had been in poor health—the matrons still whispered regarding it beneath their feather-decked bonnets—for some time, and things had not been quite as they should be regarding the marriage, at least, of so eminent a person. For William Heatherton by now was of national note as a preacher; it was said that his fame had spread as far as London, and certainly to Edinburgh, were he was asked to hold a responsible position at the current year's General Assembly. Altogether it seemed most suitable that he should in the end marry a lady so well-dowered, well-born and moreover a trifle difficult to know. She must be very capable, the matrons murmured enviously; repeating the already known fact that Margaret's first husband had left her in full control of his fortune and had made her his executrix, thus giving her power even over their only son, now growing up into such a handsome boy! The good ladies then, as hopeful mothers will, measured young John Howie's protentialities against those of their own growing daughters; time and Providence would, no doubt, dispose for the best on behalf of all parties, and in the meantime the minister and his new wife had waited doucely for the required year's mourning before being married, very quietly, at a ceremony where only a few close friends and relatives were present. Among these, of course, was the bridegroom's brother James Heatherton, making rapid strides on his own account into fame. Since George Howie's backing of his Atlantic venture some years back, James had gone from strength to strength, emerging finally as the victor in a tussle against entrenched English companies for the continued patronage of the Admiralty. He had, it was rumoured, built himself a palatial house in the country down-river to which Royalty were invited: and no doubt his example had fired his brother William, upon the sudden demise of old Miss Eustacia Hyslop in the house adjoining Savill's manse, to purchase that also out of his own pocket, perhaps aided by shares supervised on the part of James. William Heatherton had made a condition—Heathertons were always practical gentlemen, the ladies thought admiringly—that he should, during his lifetime, continue to occupy the present manse also. So the additional room needed for his newly acquired step-family would be forthcoming, and the appearance of the Church's property moreover enhanced. Everyone was happy.

Happiness, or rather contentment, at last embraced William also. During the year in which convention had forced him to wait to make Margaret his wife he had been physically deprived, unable even to suggest to such a woman that they might, meantime, become lovers. There had been an occasion just after Marie's death when he, famished in soul and body, had laid his head in weariness on Margaret's shoulder, and she had not drawn away. But then she had said, in the firm voice he had come to know and look for, "William, my dear friend, we must wait," and he had waited; waited through bleak nights and empty days, his bed barren, his strong body by force again a monk's, till the mourning-period should be over. That Margaret would accept his proposal of marriage neither of them had ever doubted. But the time had seemed very long. What William and Margaret did not foresee was that, for her also, who had never yet known pleasure in her marital relations, who had bowed to duty only, the waiting would become interminable. She knew of no reason for this: she did not expect any joy of her body when William Heatherton at last became her husband. That it came, and to them both, was a delightful discovery; they rejoiced in each other, in the rhythm of their bodies fitting as though by a design of nature herself. When he kissed her, on their first night together after passion, it was with the pleasure of a man himself initiated into new mystery. Yet she was not, by then, mysterious to him; she was sane, whole, long-awaited, welcome; Margaret, who had been his helpmeet in truth before she might become so in law; Margaret, whom he respected, relied on, loved as he had never truly loved any woman. The frail ghost of a girl walking in a fringed shawl uphill long ago was, for the time, forgotten. Too much pain lay buried with her memory. William immersed himself fully in the pleasure of his second marriage, letting the bodily satisfaction it brought him flower in new, thought-provoking, almost baroque phrases in the pulpit. His finest sermons were preached in that year.

Other flowering came. Four months after the marriage Margaret informed William joyfully that she was with child. She had never found childbearing difficult; she was at that time like Ceres, goddess of fruit, corn and harvest, bearing always. "But I thought we two old folk would never contrive it," she laughed, mocking him and herself. He took her in his arms and kissed her, filled with delight at the news; a child of his, of Margaret's! If she should bear a son, a son for his old age!

But Margaret herself must have had some premonition concerning the sex of their only child, for she said tenderly, "If it is a girl, we will call her Wilhelmine."

II

William had taken his two eldest daughters down to visit James and Alicia at Imrie, their country-house which by now had the proportions of a noble mansion, for the day. They had left early in the morning, intending to make the journey by river, the two little girls in their accustomed broad-brimmed hats and dresses showing frilly pantalettes. Margaret bade them goodbye, in company with a disconsolate Jenny who had been considered too young to go; in addition, she became seasick with the lightest tidal swell.

"John shall play with you," said Margaret, kindly enough; she had welcomed and, in fact, contrived the absence of her husband for the whole of one spring day, for the house needed cleaning. Clad in a linen cap and apron, she herself instructed the maids as to their several duties; one was to see to the carpets and house-linen: another to dissemble the iron parts of the grate, wash, polish and replace them, leaving them shining black and free from rust. A new boiler had lately been installed, of which Margaret was proud; the thought of such an innovation in her kitchen pleased her in proportion to the irritation William's presence, dear though it was, brought today; a man in the house meant constant attendance, and the full setting out of luncheon at noon, whereas now ... Margaret smiled to herself; it was she who had written to Alicia Heatherton asking her sister-in-law if she could conveniently, in some manner, rid the manse of its master for the whole of one day, stating the reason. Generous Alicia had wanted the whole manse-party, all the young Howies, all the young Heathertons, to come to her and spend the day at Imrie with their father. But such an imposition, Margaret thought, was unnecessary; and Georgy, always a help to her mama, would in any case see to things and mind the younger children; she was already a second mother to little Wilhelmine, who seemed backward a trifle. For the rest, John might have an eye to young Jenny Heatherton, who ran about behind him always like a curly-haired shadow. Margaret tightened her lips. There should not, when he grew older, she resolved, be any intimacy permitted between her son and that ill-gotten brat; not that Jenny was anything but William's daughter now, as that was what William wished. Dear man, so deserving and, till her own advent, so ill-requited! But Margaret curbed her daydreaming, and returned to her brushing of curtains once the steamboat, safely caught, was puffing with its freight down the calm river.

"What would you most like to do," said Jenny adoringly to John Howie. It was a Saturday, and he home for the day from Miss Flora Urquhart's which now catered for very young gentlemen also. Soon, in the autumn, he was to be sent to a grander one in England, to be turned into a fine fellow. Jenny felt that she could not bear to see that day dawn. John was her god; now, against the somewhat confused horizon of her daily life since the advent, so early in it, of all the Howie family, he shone like Apollo; the sun on his hair seemed to make it bright as gold; he wore a blue coat, with flat brass buttons, and nankeen trousers, and a shirt with a white ironed frill. "Court ironed the frill herself," thought Jenny, awed. She herself was already sufficiently aware of the hierarchy in the house to be impressed by Sarah's condescending to iron any individual's linen; but John was the only boy, just as Papa was the only man. Jenny loved Papa, but, perceptively, felt sorry for him. She lowered her long eyelashes, and thought briefly of her stepmother. "I don't love her, because she whipped me on Tuesday," Jenny reminded herself. She had already forgotten what the whipping had been for; but certainly her stepmama was stricter with her than with either Lissy or Kate. "But Kate is always good, and so is Georgy," the child told herself. "I don't like Georgy," and the latter, in its flagrant heresy, was whispered even to herself. Everyone else said Georgy Howie was exquisite, a perfect young lady, a little angel. "I don't like her," muttered Jenny again, and beyond the rise and whirl of vague rebel thoughts, like windswept leaves, saw John's eyes staring at her. They were amused eyes, dark under heavy lids.

John was handsome. Everyone said so.

"Didn't you hear me?" he said now. "You were dreaming again. You're an odd child, Jenny." He met her defiant glance, and said, "I told you minutes ago that it has to be what you want to do, not me, because you're a female. Females always get asked first." John did not add "worse luck" as the words struck him as ungallant. He continued to stare at Jenny's plain, heart-shaped, vivid little face; how different she was from her horse-faced sisters, Lissy and Kate Heatherton! One would think she was from some strange place, a changeling, perhaps, like the ones his nurse had used to tell him about when they were small. But he, John, was past all that kind of thing now. It didn't always suit him, either, to have Jenny tagging along after him. Even in a house as full of girls as this, a fellow had to have some time to himself. But Mama had particularly asked him today to keep an eye on the little devil, and see she came to no mischief. So he would.

A dimple showed; John Howie could be charming when he chose. "Come, now, Jenny, tell me whatever it is you'd like best to do," he said. "Whatever you choose, I'll join in."

"You wouldn't do what I want to do. You'd be too afraid. You'd tell your mama."

"Jenny——" How to explain to this perverse creature that Mama was now *her* mother, and to be addressed as such? Jenny couldn't possibly remember her own mother, who had died when she was born. John pondered the small store of knowledge he had acquired about such events, and increased his patronage. "No, I won't," he said. "How ridiculous you are! I promised, and I'll do it." What would she want? Some girls' game, most likely; he'd play it with her; the other fellows at Miss Urquhart's weren't here to see him make a fool of himself. "Anything," he coaxed.

"Then let's go and look at the books in Papa's study."

"I don't think——"

John bit his lip. They weren't permitted, it was true, to go into Papa Heatherton's study upstairs when he was at home, but today he was out all day at Imrie, and couldn't possibly get back till night. "You *are* a little devil," he said admiringly. "You only want to do it because you know we're supposed not to. Come on, then." He tickled her, and made her run laughing upstairs, in a whirl of plaid and pantalettes, curls flying.

The study door was locked. John knew where to find the key.

Afterwards John felt queer; they *had* seen it. It had been there behind a volume in the works of Shakespeare, seen through a hole in the wall made by a knot lately fallen out of the wood. It looked like a man's boot, with a foot in it. Not a foot, that was; drier, fleshless. A skeleton.

It was queer. Something wasn't as it ought to be, John knew; even Jenny had been frightened, seeing it first as she had. He recalled her voice, shrilling suddenly in his ears, and her face had grown white, poor little thing; suddenly, after seeing it, he'd put an arm round her. But she hadn't cried, as most girls would; and had looked up at him with that white strained face, the face of a grown woman all of a sudden. He found himself seeing Jenny herself as she might be when she *was* a woman. Yet he couldn't forget the—the thing, though he'd laughed at her.

"Nonsense, you silly little creature, it's cobwebs, I tell you; there's only a space or cupboard in there, you imagined it."

"It was a person's foot, with a boot on it. A yellow boot." Jenny's face was still white, her voice determined. She wriggled out of John's embrace and fled through the door.

John gave it up. He'd best tell Mama. She would know what to do, although he'd be in trouble for having taken the key from Papa Heatherton's downstairs desk. If only, meantime, he could catch the little nuisance and make her be quiet...

"Nonsense, you cannot have seen what you say you saw. Go and read quietly in the schoolroom and take Miss Jenny with you; I shall go up to Papa's study presently, where the pair of you had in any case no business to be or take the key belonging to Papa. That was wickedness, which must be punished." Margaret, cross, efficient, in her close linen cap, had been disturbed in the midst of curtain-brushing. The memory was fading already in John's mind. If Mama went up to the study, and looked through the place in the wall, and said there was nothing, all would be well. Mama somehow, by her very competence, made horror retreat. It was possible for a fellow to have been mistaken, perhaps . . .

"Did you hear me, Master John? Away with the pair of you; children who do naughty actions are punished by their own minds, doubtless. Look at Georgy, who is always so good, and take example from her; she will tell you it was no such thing, I know."

John hesitated; ought he to take Georgy up to the study? He asked his mother, hesitantly. "Yes," she snapped. "Take her and she'll teach you sense. Mama is busy now, do as you're bid."

So John took Georgy up, himself still quivering with unacknowledged fear. When she put her eye to the hole he waited for a cry, such as Jenny had given. But Georgy had listened to the voice of her mama, who had told her briefly to put a stop to John and Jenny's nonsense, as they were imagining things. Her beautiful, short-sighted eyes contained no expression when she withdrew from the place at the wall.

"There is nothing of the kind there, as Mama said," she told her brother. "Jenny makes you tell bad stories, I'm afraid, John. Come downstairs now; you know we are not permitted to be in Papa Heatherton's study when he is out."

Later Margaret herself, tired but conscientious where her son was concerned, went upstairs. She removed the leather-bound book of Shakespeare and looked through the hole in the wall. Presently her fingers let drop the book. It fell open to the floor, revealing a crazed Ophelia wreathed in plucked grasses and flowers, finger pulling at her lower lip to make a grimace of madness. Presently Margaret straightened and bent again, replacing the book automatically.

It was some moments later that Sarah heard her mistress's voice. She put down what she was doing and hurried upstairs at once.

III

WHEN SARAH HEARD HER MISTRESS CALL SHE KNEW INSTINCTIVELY that something was wrong; badly, irrevocably wrong. For some reason the woman looked at the clock which stood above the newly-blacked kitchen range, flanked by the bright new boiler with its copper sheen as yet unspoiled. She noted the time, left what she was doing, wiped her hands on a cloth and hurried upstairs. As she did so she heard the clear, familiar voice again, sounding unerringly above and beyond the other, lesser sounds of the busy house. It was, thought Sarah without glimmer of humour, like the Lord calling Samuel in the night, while Eli slept near by; there was the rustle of the temple's inner curtain, the unheeding wind beyond the door.

"Court." The hurrying woman saw her mistress's tall figure outlined against the light from the window on the upper staircase, where she stood. The light left Margaret's face in darkness, accentuating, at the height on which she appeared, the somehow majestic quality of her stance. She was like a statue, a goddess both awesome and strange; someone quite unknown. Sarah felt the heart in her own breast beat suddenly faster, fearfully. It was the climb, she told herself; she wasn't as young as she had been; it was the climb.

Margaret Heatherton moved one of her hands then, as if to bring herself back to everyday living. "You will go downstairs, Court, and instruct the nurse to take all the children, even Master John and Miss Georgy, out of the house into the streets, and walk them there. If there is time they may go to the Green. They must not return until..."

The hand strayed to Margaret's breast, "Until tea-time," she said calmly. "When you have done that, Court, come upstairs here to me again, without delay; and bring a pail and a shovel."

When Sarah returned from doing her mistress's bidding Margaret was once again in the study room. Sarah saw that the bookcases had been disturbed, emptied heedlessly and pulled out from the wall. She downed an exclamation of surprise; what would the master say? He didn't like their even being disturbed, his precious books; had sent one of the maids about her business, when she tried to dust them, the other day. The girl had been quite upset about it. And now! Sarah stared at her mistress. "Whatever she does, she'll do as it pleases her, not as it pleases *him*," she thought suddenly. The discovery cheered her. Who were men to think they ordered everyone?

"Court——" It was then, as she turned to the full light, that Sarah fully saw her mistress's face. It was white as wax, grimed with what seemed like cobwebs and pale dust. What had she been at? "Mrs. Heatherton, ma'am——"

"How long have you been with me?" The voice, her mistress's who, Sarah now realised, she loved, came from a long way off. It'd been true, Sarah thought, that when she first came she'd had the notion, God forgive her, of using what she knew to obtain a place with Mrs. Howie, as she'd been then. But now there was nothing she wouldn't do, to—"Fifteen years, ma'am," she said, "that is if you were to count the time at the Rectory."

Margaret might not have heard, or known where the Rectory was. "Will you swear," she said slowly, "to keep what I am about to show you secret, and never speak of it to a living soul?"

"Why, yes—yes, surely, ma'am." In her turmoil Sarah had gone back to the southern, impersonal form of address. But within herself she felt a personal alliance with her mistress. She's in grievous trouble, she told herself; worse than I was when the Reverend Alfred got me pregnant. It seemed, now, that there were worse things; things without name. "Will you swear it," Margaret said again, "on the Bible?"

"Why, yes, ma'am, if it pleases you." Sarah spoke gently now, and evenly; the poor soul should know, she felt, that no Bible made any difference; if she was asked not to speak, she wouldn't speak, and that was that. But she let Margaret fetch the great clasped Bible that lay, with its markers in place, on William's desk. She took Sarah's hand and placed it on the leather. Sarah swore her oath.

"Come now," said Margaret. She drew the servant with her past the disordered books, thrust anyhow in piles about the floor, and the altered furniture. Only the Bible, replaced on William's desk, revealed a faint smear of dust on its surface; the rest were clean. A door Sarah could not formerly remember seeing yawned in the wall.

"Go in," said Margaret. Beads of sweat stood out on her brow beneath the linen-covered hair. Sarah made her way in through a shadowed passage to where a brick-lined space revealed itself in sparse light, filtered through cobwebs. On the floor lay a trunk, its contents visible. Sarah did not scream.

"Why, ma'am, it's—it's a——"

"You have sworn," said William Heatherton's wife. And paradoxically, gazing down at the horror that the years, and quicklime, had left of Paul Chantal, the words she had just spoken sounded in the servant's mind, like echoes flung back from a wall.

"I, Sarah Court, swear by God's Word as revealed in this Book that I will never repeat what I am about to see to a living soul; that I will do as I am bid in silence concerning a matter about to be undertaken; that thereafter it shall be as if it had never been. And may God punish me, now and hereafter, if I break my word as long as I shall live."

"We will start clearing now," Margaret said. "I think that presently we should be able to close the trunk. When this is done, we will carry it downstairs between us."

"To the boiler, ma'am?" Sarah spoke between taut lips. It was no worse, after all, than shovelling ordure. It was the dust we all returned to, high and low.

"To the boiler," said her mistress. She might have been speaking of firewood or coal.

It was four o'clock by the time it was all done, and no trace remaining, and the emptied trunk returned to its cleansed place. It had taken four separate journeys, in the end, up and down stairs, the pair of them; stacking everything in heaps so that the maids would not see traces on the stairs, brushing the stairs, scrubbing the trunk and brick-space clean, restoring the books on shelves again in their places. Downstairs, the new furnace had been stoked high so that every last thing which had been put in it must be consumed. The rest, charred fragments of bone, the latchets that had held the shoes, Sarah would stamp and hammer later to unidentifiable fragments. Scrubber and pail, strong soda and vinegar to hide the stench, applied to floor and walls, and the inside of the copper-lined trunk which they had decided would be unsafe to leave outside the house; it might still be recognised. Finally it was put back in its former place, the lid left open to aid drying and reduce corrosion, or any tell-tale marks on the copper; empty, scrubbed, cleared, Paul's erstwhile coffin, replaced and the little-known door shut on it again, screws and nails put back in the wood that barred and concealed, the very knot-hole later to be filled up. Presently the study was again as it had outwardly been. The two women had worked for many hours without rest or food; their faces and clothing were filthy with blackened ash and disturbed lime-dust, the sweat lying on the skin in clean runnels in the places where lines would come when they had both grown old. On two occasions someone had rung at the door, unanswered as the servants other than Sarah had all been sent out with the children; going down to the hallway later, Sarah found visiting-cards left. She put them on the tray in silence, then went to heat water to wash herself and her mistress. Later she persuaded Margaret to eat a little food and drink some wine.

"I shall go and lie down on my bed," Margaret said presently. "You will move a pallet in, Court, and be with me at nights; see that it's done before evening, but leave me now. I must be alone."

Sarah obeyed, her knowledge already making her lips set in a morose line, which was to grow habitual with the years. That day, with its imposition of terrible silence, was to mark what amounted to renewed birth-pangs on the part of Sarah Court; from then on, Margaret Heatherton was her child.

She left William's wife lying in the darkness, the curtains of the bed close-drawn. Sarah knew that, in her mistress's mind, the marriage, except for appearances, was done with. She could read her darling, her child, like a book, she told herself; and never, for in part she shared its onset, pondered on what day, and in what hour, Margaret could finally be spoken of as having run mad. It was a silent, insidious madness, engendered as it had been by silence. One could perhaps foretell it now from looking at her eyes.

Presently the children and the young servants returned from their long outing, and were given tea by themselves. Margaret did not come down; nor did she do so when William, in the evening, returned with Kate and young Lissy from his day at James and Alicia's, filled with admiration for the showy, ornate palace his brother was unendingly building over the years on the site of his former country cottage down-river at Imrie.

IV

Georgy Howie adored her mother. From as far back as she could remember, it had always been Mama who made the decisions; her late Papa was a cipher, cleverly induced to continue in his outward struttings, his rooster-like importance to himself. But Georgy's adult mind—it had never been that of a child, although, like all other children, she continued to behave as was expected of a little girl too good to be really true, too quiet and obedient to be natural—Georgy's mind could meet, survey and assess that of other adults; she had already summed up and dismissed her stepfather. Paradoxically, she had an adoration of baby Wilhelmine. It was as though the little girl were, all of her, Mama's flesh, none of that other's; as though, in short, she were an echo of Georgy herself, an as yet powerless, speechless and lace-robed echo, lying in a cradle. So Georgy had from the beginning played the part of Wilhelmine's little mother, well aware of how pretty she herself must look, nursing the baby in her velvet-clad, ribbon-tied lap; but at the same time feeling love for the little creature, such love as she could only ever give to three persons in the whole world; herself, Wilhelmine and Mama. The day they were all of them sent out of the house to walk endlessly with the nursemaid and servants would retain itself in Georgy's memory; it was the day when something went wrong. What it might be Georgy did not know, or greatly care; to speculate was not her business, only to feel in limited fashion, and to obey. When, after their return that day, Sarah Court sent word that Georgy was to come up to Mama's room, the child felt no surprise. Something out of the ordinary was about to happen, as she knew. She evinced no excitement; Mama would make as much known as was suitable. Georgy allowed her hair to be combed out till it resembled dark satin, and her face and hands to be washed till her cheeks shone like ripe apples. She mounted the stairs composedly; a little lady, the servants would be saying behind her. She remembered to knock before entering Mama's room, and to wait outside the door until permission came for her to enter.

When she did so, Margaret was lying on her bed; the curtains were partly drawn so that the child could not see her mother's face. There was only a shadow where the face would be, a shadow framed by a pillow; and Margaret's large, fine hands lay idle on the coverlet. She was, the child thought with rare imagination, like someone dead. Georgy stood still, waiting politely on the patterned carpet. It had been one which had been brought from their own house they had had when Papa himself was alive. A great many things had come, making the manse now appear like a rich man's dwelling. Whoever married Mama would have been as fortunate. The small, cold mind reckoned such matters, like items in an account-book. At the same time she spoke to her mother.

"You are not ill, dearest Mama?" If Mama had a headache, she, Georgy, would sometimes fetch lavender-water and bathe her temples gently, using a finely stitched handkerchief edged with Honiton lace. It made her happy to do such things for Mama. Now, however, the matter was more serious than a headache; nothing lavender-water could cure. Georgy was sure of this when Margaret spoke, oddly echoing her own late thoughts.

"There is nothing you would not do for your Mama, is there, my darling?"

She hadn't said she was not ill, Georgy thought. Into her awareness came the realisation of an illness of the mind. The world swung wildly beneath her feet for instants. Mama, who represented sanity, security, was not ... could not be ... Georgy searched for a word, and did not find it. She answered Margaret's question. "Nothing, dearest Mama." It was true; she would go through fire for Mama. Fortunately there would be no need to do so. The dark eyes fixed themselves on the unmoving shadow on the bed. How still Mama lay! One night, when life had left her, she might look so; and then, Georgy thought, my heart will break. "Nothing," she said again loudly, as if to fight back some denial in herself. Margaret's hand moved a little. "You are my own good child," she said. "I am going to make you a present, and you will, in return, make me a promise. It is an oath, Georgy. You must swear it on the Bible."

The hand gestured towards Sarah Court, who had not left the two of them alone. Why, thought Georgy suddenly, is there the feeling that she has done this before? The Bible lay ready, waiting. Georgy placed her small hand on it. The flesh of the hand was the colour and texture of creamy milk, with dimples at the knuckles, the nails tapering delicately, well-scrubbed, well-tended.

"You must swear that you will never marry anyone. I will give you a little daughter for yourself: Wilhelmine."

Something, a shade of rebellion perhaps, stirred in Georgy, "Why must I not marry, Mama?" She forbore to mention that Margaret had herself done so twice; such a remark would savour of impertinence. "And Wilhelmine is yours, Mama, not mine."

"No; she is mine no longer. You love Wilhelmine, do you not?"

"Why, yes, Mama; very much, but——"

"Then she is yours; you are her mother. You must counsel her and play with her. She shall be yours, all her life. There will be the three of us, my darling; and your sisters, and John. None of you must ever marry; marriage is a great sin, the one our first parents committed, so that we are born carrying it always." The woman's head on the bed moved; both Georgy and Sarah caught the sudden insane glitter of the eyes. It's taken her so, my poor mistress, thought Sarah. Poor Mama, Georgy thought; she is very ill, after all. I will do as she asks me.

After the child had sworn her oath and gone upstairs to the nursery for tea, Sarah permitted herself grimly to wonder about Mr. Heatherton. What would *she*, in the bed there, have to say to him when he came home?

And again, as though she could gaze into others' minds, Margaret answered the unspoken thought. "You will bring the pallet bed into my room, Sarah, as I told you, and sleep on it tonight, and every night thereafter. I do not desire ever to be left alone again."

"Shall I fetch it now, ma'am?" asked Sarah without expression. Whatever happens, she was thinking, I know my duty. Never to leave her alone with him, whatever *he* says, is what I'm to do. She's master in this house, as she was in the last. She'll get the better of him, in the way he likes least; I know it.

And some bitter thing concealed in her from her own narrow childhood, and the later time when she had been betrayed by the Reverend Alfred, rejoiced silently. The victory and the fruits are now, Sarah thought; now and hereafter.

V

It seemed afterwards as if all of the events which followed could not have taken place in a space of only part of a single day, a few hours. That morning, Margaret Heatherton had awakened a happy, sane woman; there had been the horror then to be rid of. That had changed her, irrevocably; now, returning out of her private shadows, she roused herself to go up once more to the children, after tea; to make them cluster round her, perhaps herself feel again in their accustomed presence a return, even if only for moments, to the normal world of daylight she had once inhabited, and would never know again. She mounted the stairs. In the way she had unerringly, ruthlessly dealt with Paul Chantal's remains she treated his memory; it must be erased, and with it any lingering doubt as to what had been seen, from all the children's minds. The fact that she had lately caused Georgy to swear an adult oath did not perturb Margaret, deep in her other perturbations. Georgy could be relied upon to be in all things her second self, her obedient shadow. Her eldest daughter would never betray her; but the rest ... what had John, her own son, and that sharp-eyed little monkey Jenny Heatherton, told them already of what had been discovered earlier in the day, behind the study bookcases? She should have thought of that before sending them out to walk with the maids, up and down, up and down the streets, but there had been that other thing to do and her mind was tired.

The children came to her obediently, curtsying in the polite way they had been taught. Margaret looked at them for an instant with pride, this comely covey she had borne George Howie. There were the four little girls, Georgy shepherding her younger sisters to greet their mama; and John. Jenny Heatherton trailed behind, her eyes always on the back of John's coat. It must be made a part of her policy to separate those two soon, Margaret decided; and returned to other decisions.

"You have been good children today?" That was always the initial question; any badnesses, reported by Georgy, dealt with, gently but effectively. But today there was nothing apart from John's theft of the key: he did not again mention it. Otherwise they had all been good, with a quick, intuitive solemnity because something, they knew not what, was wrong. It would never do to ask Mama, their awe-inspiring, recurrent vision, always grandly dressed; even today she had thrown a lace shawl over her queenly gown, and not a hair of her head was disarranged beneath the evening-cap; she had smoothed herself before her mirror on rising from the bed where she had lain for that while, alone. The narrow eyes surveyed the children. "I must make it clear to you," she heard herself saying, then felt her wits wander; what was she able to make clear? That there had never been a dead man behind the bookcase and the wall, with one mortified foot sticking out of an opened boot, still visible? The dried and changing body would have emitted matter which would rot the thread with which the soles were sewn to the uppers, and made the boot burst open so. She reviewed it in her mind, calmly. It was better to face such things.

But what was she to make clear to these children? That they must forget what they might not have heard, or—in the case of Jenny and John—forget the evidence of their own eyes, persuade themselves that reality was fancy, by her advice who had always taught them to credit their sober senses and never indulge in fantasy, in daylight dreams? It was enough to drive one mad. Sternly, forcing her own mind in the direction it would not willingly take, she instructed the children, disguising the work in questions. Let them answer, she thought, and entrap themselves; then, she'd issue commands.

Georgy replied first, and predictably. No, dearest Mama was quite right; there had been nothing to be seen behind any bookcase. "And, you know, Mama, Jenny and John should not have been up there at all." Splendid Georgy! Her eyes were downcast, the creamy lids discreet, the red mouth buttoned. How pretty she was! The mother's sick mind, shuddering aside from the day's memories, permitted itself an instant's renewed pleasure on the beauty Margaret had herself brought forth. Her hand reached out, caressing Georgy's smooth, plump arm beneath the short puffed sleeve. Elizabeth and Ann, two of the other Howie daughters, had let their attention wander to their young sister Molly's rag-doll; there was no danger there. The mother's eyes turned to John, her only son, the longed-for heir, standing by her chair uncertainly, a lock of straight dark-gold hair falling over his white forehead. John must feel out of place among all the girls; it was time he was sent away to school. With his father's fine dark eyes, her own hair and her height, John Howie should grow into a personable man. But he should never——

"John," she was beginning; but Jenny Heatherton's pipe cut in. Thank God, Margaret was thinking, that sharp-eyed Kate and slow, yet stubborn Lissy were away for the whole day with their father, and had seen nothing! Young Jenny, swinging a small slipper-clad foot in its white stocking to and fro, stood idly; balancing on one leg only, in a disrespectful attitude, her hair in unkempt ringlets about her unremarkable, pert face. Jenny, the only danger. As the stepmother told herself this, the child spoke.

"There was something there, there was." The foot still swung. "A boot, open at the toe. I saw it. It was yellow, and——"

"Be silent," said Margaret, and the child's bright, alien eyes raised themselves to her face. "I have told you there was nothing to be seen," Margaret said then, "and the others have agreed with me. So you are being foolish, are you not?" A prickle of sweat, felt as cold fear, came in the uncorseted places of Margaret's body, the armpits, groin, between the breasts. She frowned deeply, hoping to frighten the child into silence. But Jenny would not be quelled. I shall have to whip her, thought Margaret. The resolve calmed her, enabling her to hear Jenny's next words with equanimity. Young miss would find out soon, with her drawers down, when it was advisable to keep silent.

"John saw the boot too," Jenny said clearly. "Didn't you, Johnny? Tell them you saw." Her eyes sought John Howie's in somewhat scared appeal, but he had looked away. One couldn't argue with Mama. And it was just possible that it *had* been cobwebs, as Georgy said. Anyway it was advisable to shut up. A fellow knew when a storm was brewing, and in a week's time he'd be out of it all, and away south, to the grand school. John Howie was tired of girls. Once he was in the south——

Margaret had turned to her son. "John, you will be a good boy and do as Mama bids, will you not? Little girls are frightened easily, and imagine things they do not see." She made her lips smile, closing them over her teeth; it was a conspiratorial smile to make her at one with John, one with the fellows against all little girls, who were fanciful.

John struggled with himself a moment; there *had* been—and Jenny would be for it ... She didn't seem to know, or care; standing there swinging her foot, ridiculing as well as endangering him. And there was still the business of the key. If only she'd held her tongue, the little fool! She'd always talked too much, there had been the time the other day when he'd hidden white mice in his bedroom and made Jenny promise not to tell, and she'd been caught by cook stealing cake for them from the larder, and it was all discovered ...

"He did see it," said Jenny. "He *did*."

Harmful, Margaret knew, to make a further issue of it, to insist again on an avowal from her boy; but the sight of the victorious child standing there, insouciant as any wrecker, angered the woman beyond caution, beyond endurance. "Be silent, miss, until you are addressed," she snapped at Jenny. Then turning to her son again she said, "Well, John?"

He understood the tone, and that it was a command: no more, perhaps, would be said about the key if he obeyed. "There was nothing," he muttered, blushing and shamefaced. He couldn't look at Jenny. "Nothing at all," came his mother's voice triumphantly. "You may come with me now, all of you, and look at the place." She made them march before her across the nursery landing, up the attic stairs, and survey, from the removed Shakespeare volume in the bookcase, the knot-hole, not yet filled up. She'd do that at the first opportunity, after William ...

Her mind could not yet contemplate William, or what her greeting to him must be on his return. The day already seemed endless.

"There was a boot," muttered Jenny. Something snapped

then in Margaret's mind. She turned on the child and ordered her up to her own room. "And once there you will take down your drawers, miss, and kneel on your stool till I come. Insolence does not pay, as you will find; and you shall have no supper."

Jenny's wail rose in the study, sounding down the passages as she fled to the opposite stairs. John, her god, had failed her. He'd left her to be whipped, because she told the truth and he told lies, lies. Papa was always saying one mustn't be a hypocrite like the scribes and Pharisees, and tell the truth always, even if it made one suffer. Jenny suddenly yelled the truth as she knew it above all the other sounds in the house, even as her mother, in dying, had cried aloud the name of the man she loved, who was dead. "There *was* something, there was. A boot, a yellow boot with someone's foot in it, I saw. I saw the boot, split open at the toe."

But the last word prolonged itself into a child's sobbing cry, as if she knew that Margaret Heatherton, at that moment, had risen from her chair and gone to find the birch-rod, which hung in the schoolroom, and would shortly come and administer a punishment Jenny in her short life knew already far too well; it was less than a week since she had been birched for stealing cake-crumbs.

Margaret herself had no clear memory afterwards of the last time she chastised her stepchild—if Jenny was such. Clear under the day's incredulous layered horror was the fact, sure as stone, deep buried in her own mind, that this was Paul Chantal's daughter, never William's. The lime-dried silt she had shovelled from the attic only this morning, aeons ago, had once sired this rebellious flesh which still lived to try her, to question her authority. Outwardly she did not abate this; her manner, when she mounted the stairs to Jenny's room, was calm, and she even gave the child an opportunity to withdraw by questioning her again.

"You were lying, were you not? You are a little liar?'

"I *saw* it, I *saw* it." The phrase had become a meaningless refrain behind Jenny's clenched hands; pressed hard against her chubby cheeks and shut eyes, they might prevent her from crying when the rod began to fall. She hated more than anything that her stepmother should see her cry, or exhibit any weakness. Fault was difficult; John's mother was always finding fault. Jenny's thoughts shied away from John, who had betrayed her, towards the fact of the birch, brought hard down now upon her bared flesh. If she recited a poem, over and over, three times over, by the time it got to the end, the whipping would be finished. But it hurt so much that midway through the poem Jenny abandoned it and began to howl, like a small tormented dog. This was the hardest she'd ever been given; why should John's mother be so angry over a boot, a boot, a boot?

Bared bottom, enduring it all. Indignity, redness, pain; she saw and felt them, knowing what she must look like to that other, who stood above her with arm rising and falling, beating, tormenting. But clinging to her own straw of certainty which was, Jenny knew, victory of a kind, it didn't at present matter; the rest, who'd told lies as ordered, who had no battle to win, needn't sleep on their stomachs tonight after no supper.

"I saw it. A yellow boot..."

Sanity left Margaret then. Afterwards, even given the other happenings of the day, she was unable in retrospect to credit her own behaviour; that she, the cool, amused, sophisticated, unknown second Mrs. Heatherton, who was widely read and had a cultivated mind, and could converse on any subjects from foreign missions to Paris bonnets—that she should have taken a rod and with all her strength (and she was strong) beaten and beaten at a child's stubborn flesh till the blood came, at last, and the flailing birch brought up drops with it that darkly sprayed the wallpaper of the small room with its careful pattern of roses and ivy, roses and ivy, repeated in narrow bands. She no longer, by then, knew or cared how often or hard she hit the child, who had become an obstacle in her way, the ancient enemy. The devil, to be exorcised with whips.

Margaret's arm rose and fell rhythmically for some minutes. She had ceased to feel tiredness, or anything save a kind of exaltation.

Suddenly the child rolled over and fell sideways off the stool where she had been put to kneel. Her cheek was disfigured with a weal that stretched from eye to mouth. She lay still.

Margaret let the birch clatter down out of her hand; she heard it fall. Then, firstly, she herself pressed both fists hard into her eyes, as the child had done at the beginning. Red and green, red and green, the patterns clouded rhythmically, progressively behind her mind's eyelids, like the disintegrating roses and ivy on the wall. The woman began to whimper to herself, as though she were the one to have been struck.

"O God, I've killed her, I've killed Jenny. O God, O merciful God."

Staggering, she bent and lifted the child's inert body from the floor and laid it on the bed, dragging the quilt over it. A great weariness had come over her, convincing her that from now on, for the rest of her life, she must be alone with God. No one, not even Georgy, could come between her and that Presence. She heard feet trailing on their way back to her own room as if they belonged to a sloven, a drunken woman; but they were her own, she could feel and hear them dragging. Thou hast counted all my bones ... who had said that? William himself had read it out as a text one day from his pulpit, William who was a murderer.

If the child had been badly hurt, if she also were to die ...

But Margaret Heatherton could no longer think of Jenny.

VI

THE FATES OF ALL THE MANSE INMATES WERE DECIDED THAT day; the three families, Howie, Heatherton and even the baby Wilhelmine, asleep in her cot, were catered for; it was then the decision was made that Wilhelmine should never grow up, still playing with a doll's house into middle age. Other decisions were made. William, returning home at last, sent his two daughters upstairs to their schoolroom supper, and himself entered an empty dining-room. The meal was set out, and was cold, as he had expected; the only sound was the ticking of the ornate clock Margaret had brought with her from the Howie house, and which had superseded his own presentation-clock on the mantelpiece; of Margaret herself there was no sign. This did not unduly disturb William, who sat down and began to eat his meal, having helped himself from the sideboard. No doubt, as he was later than expected, Margaret had gone up to her room. He would visit her later, hear her enquiries concerning the day's visit, while he himself, perhaps, would strive to remember the fact that his wife had spent the whole of the day cleaning and dusting the great house, and would be tired. William poured his own coffee, at last, from the silver machine James had given him and Margaret as a marriage-gift, having mastered the initial mysteries of the spirit-lamp; the machine was a cause of great envy among their friends. He stirred the fragrant fluid with satisfaction, then drew a sudden breath; he had not heard her enter, but the servant Sarah Court stood there, respectful enough in her familiar blacks and starched apron and cap.

Imagination, which rarely troubled him, came in that moment to William Heatherton; what did one know of servants? Using the heavy, half-jocular tone he adoped with her, he asked Sarah if her mistress were well. In the instant before she answered him, in which her face, like a smooth mask beneath the greying hair, told him nothing, disquiet stirred in William; it had seemed, for a fraction of time, that some alien thing showed in the quickly lowered eyes; what it was he could not name. He heard himself speak again, louder than before.

"Your mistress is well? There's naught amiss?"

"What should there be, sir?" said the woman smoothly. Compunction rose at his own bidding in William, directing his trained mind to exercise charity and understanding, remembering the tireless and devoted watch Sarah had kept, over all those last months, over Marie. She should be accounted something more than a servant by now, he thought, for that alone; and yet——

He made himself speak again, not answering her query. "You are happy in your place here?" he said. "Your living quarters—they're comfortable?" Some houses, he'd heard his mother say, had disgraceful accommodation even for honoured servants of many years' standing: a tiny garret under a roof, open to leaking rain, with nowhere to keep even the few belongings such folk had. "Your room is good enough? You have everything you require?"

"Mrs. Heatherton sees to that, sir."

William rose, dusting the front of his black waistcoat with his napkin. It was useless, his inner mind told him, to attempt talk with Sarah; she would answer yes to everything, yet he could not rid himself, tonight, of the notion that she was his enemy. "Your mistress is well?" he said again. It was as though he could find no other way of bridging the gap that lay between them. Sarah curtsied, and removed the coffee-tray.

"She has had a tiring day, sir. She had her supper served her in her room, and she says——" For the first time, the woman's voice faltered; but he realised that the hesitation was not due to uncertainty, but triumph. "She says she wishes to sleep, and is not to be disturbed tonight, sir; she will see you in the morning."

William stared incredulously, his mind recording one item out of all that churned beneath it; the woman's red, well-scrubbed hands, carrying James's lamp. "Have a care how you handle that," he said testily.

"Yes, sir." Sarah bobbed again. As if to follow up his tactical victory, William said, "You may inform your mistress that I shall look in on my way upstairs tonight; I am anxious lest she be unwell." It wasn't like Margaret, now he thought of it, to be absent on his return, or to fail to come in after the meal and pour his coffee for him. Even at the time of the child's birth she had stayed downstairs almost till the commencement of labour, and during that had suffered less than many women, less than Marie. Marie ... He jerked his thoughts back to the woman who still stood here, scrubbed hands grasping the tray.

"She is well enough, sir, but there was a good deal to be done today; and Miss Jenny was troublesome, and ma'am whipped her."

"Is that so, indeed?" Jenny, he thought, was proving a difficult child to rear; not like her sisters, placid Kate and docile Lissy, Heathertons both, while this last, this changeling ... William's thoughts swerved away.

"I will come in to bid her good night, then." His voice was firm, his smile kindly. There must be no mistaken inference in his conversations with Sarah about who was master, now, of the combined household.

Some moments later, he ascended to Margaret's room.

He was, he noted with amusement while mounting the stairs, beginning to feel his age. To refresh himself, before he went to his wife, he'd look in upon the sleeping child she'd borne him: Wilhelmine. Leaning, ever so little more heavily than before, on the polished balustrade, he ascended the carpeted treads. James in his fine new house today had talked of putting down Persian stair-carpets; and had designed a winter-garden, and a study for himself panelled in solid mahogany at the end of a short corridor leading off from his great hall of model glass-cased ships. He, William, had no taste for such grandeur; but it was as well if a smith's son had risen to the heights of James Heatherton. Unforgotten in a century, James would be, with his Admiralty contracts and his endeavours in the history of steam, and his great hall with its Gothic arches beyond the cases, and his clock that ticked in the tower.

Wilhelmine was asleep. Her father could not see the flower-like cheek on the muslin pillow for a shadow that covered it; Georgy sat by her half-sister, in nightgown and curl-papers. William chaffed her, not liking to acknowledge the expression in the dark eyes. It reminded him, in a certain mulish enmity it held, of Sarah Court, the servant; ridiculous, such fancies! "You need not guard your baby sister so late, my dear," he told Georgy gently. "The nurse is nearby; and you yourself should long since be asleep."

"Mama says I am to look after Wilhelmine, for all her life." The placidity of the tone deceived William; he laughed, it was only a child after all, not the implacable hatred he had felt everywhere, seeping towards him, like damp spreading over a floor.

"To be sure, you shall; but go to bed now, or Mama will not be pleased. I will tell her how good you are with the baby. Will you kiss your Papa?" He bent down to her, but Georgy turned her head away; it might have been a child's natural shyness, and William decided to treat it as such, and pinched her cheek.

"Kiss Wilhelmine for me, then; I would not wake her." He went out of the nursery softly, passing by Jenny's door. If Jenny had been troublesome today, he'd not condone it by visiting her; Margaret had full charge of his house and children.

But Margaret's door was locked.

VII

He did not see his wife until the following day. She did not join him at breakfast; by now William knew that there must be something seriously wrong. He bethought him of his children; there had been some word, he recalled, of Jenny's disobedience yesterday. He must send for the child, and admonish her, make her beg her stepmother's pardon. He sent the maidservant up to the schoolroom, to give instructions to the governess who had lately taken charge of Margaret's daughters and his own. The young woman came down presently, ashen-faced.

"She—sir—oh, sir, she is not in her room, sir, and I've looked in all the places she goes and hides." The governess came in by the day; this post was a well-paid one, even if its mistress was particular sometimes. It'd be better not to speak of the queer things she'd seen today, in Miss Jenny's room; splashes of blood on the walls and ceiling, and the coverlet lying rumpled although the bed had not been slept in. There was a shed below the window on to which the child could have climbed out, and she—"Oh, sir, what are we to do? She may be in the river," and the governess broke down into unseemly sobs; she'd never been in a situation like this before, and with the minister standing there so tall and pale, anyone would think—"Shall I inform Mrs. Heatherton, sir?" ventured the governess timidly. There had been, the nursemaid said, a fair turn-up last night, and the poor little soul thrashed till her howls could be heard in the basement. It was perhaps true, what they wrote about wicked stepmothers. But Mrs. Heatherton——

"I will inform her myself," said the minister majestically, and made his exit from the room.

He had to knock thrice on Margaret's door, though he knew

she never slept late. She must have breakfasted; he had seen the tray borne downstairs by one of the maidservants; what was wrong with her? Impatiently, he rapped louder, and demanded admittance.

"It is I, William. I demand that you let me in. Open the door, if you please."

He had never addressed her thus before; and knew what he recognised as trepidation on hearing steps cross the carpet, and the lock being unbarred. Was he afraid of Margaret? The supposition amused him, even at this moment; but it was Court who stood there. Her expression told him nothing, and he brushed past the woman and went in.

The room was in half-dark, with the heavy velvet curtains blotting out the daylight. "Why do you keep your curtains closed?" he asked, and striding over would have jerked them apart; but Sarah forestalled him.

"She wants them left," the woman said, and incredulously William heard her, and noted that Margaret did not, as should have been done, rebuke her maid for speaking so to her master. "I believe——" he was beginning, determined to administer his own crushing rebuke; then he caught sight of his wife's figure, seated near the fire.

The coals were red, the ash already piled high in the grate; it must have been lit all night. Had she sat by it so long? Her face was averted, the fitful firelight illumining, now and again, the outlines of her cheek; it seemed to him that her features were swollen.

"Margaret——" he was beginning, and once more turned to the waiting-woman to bid her begone; how dared she stay on, with the two of them, here, a witness, an eavesdropper? He spoke to her, harshly; and this time his wife's voice came, suddenly, almost idly, as if the matter were of no moment; what she said shocked him.

"Court has my instructions never to leave me alone with you again." She took a handkerchief then, and wiped her lips. She still had not looked at William. He felt unbelief rise in him to a level when the whole scene, the three of them as characters in it, had become ridiculous; Margaret could not have spoken thus; in seriousness! If it were a jest, it was in bad taste; he endeavoured to match it, saying jocularly, knowing now the servant was against him,

"No one can come between a man and his wife, my dear; not even the most faithful of servants. I prefer that you ask Sarah to leave." He had never mastered the upper-class habit of addressing a female servant by her surname. It was one of the few links he still possessed with the boy he had once been, the blacksmith's son.

"I am no longer your wife, or you my husband. I renounce the marriage."

Suddenly, in the astonished silence which was his reply, she rose to her full height and faced him, the satin of which her gown was made rustling and falling richly about her magnificent breasts and thighs. She wore, as was her custom, he saw, a small lace cap on her head; the hair beneath, as always, was smooth, but by a trick of the firelight seemed to have lost its own colour overnight, and to be endowed only with warm reflections from the flames, on whiteness. A sense of terror, both echo and forerunner of what had been in his own time felt, and would be again, beset William. Had his wife run mad? This fine woman, whose company and solace he had sought, and now—her face, now that he saw it full in the strange light, had the quality and glister of wax; her narrow eyes gleamed like a deranged woman's, and were dry.

"Margaret——" It seemed all he could contrive, to say over her name; to try, by the repetition of that familiar word, to bring her nearer him; she was, he now saw, far, far away; she was a stranger. He grew jocose again in his terror. "Draw up your chair to the fire, Margaret; let us talk together a little. Send your woman away." It was like talking to a child, repeating, coaxing; for the first time since entering her room, he recalled that he had not yet informed her of Jenny's disappearance. What had happened here while he had been away with James?

"I will not sit by a fire with you again. Nor will I share your bed again. What is it but lust, the state of marriage? I sinned in letting you take me; you shall never do so any more. I must ask you to leave my room now, and never enter it again till I am dead, when you may do as you will."

Sarah Court stood firm; he sustained the nightmare that she was like a chorus in a Greek play, unmoving, occasionally chanting repetitive words, to heighten the tragedy. If only she would go! But he himself was helpless now as a swimmer lost in a great undercurrent whose source and direction he has not time to think of. As though she knew his very thoughts, Margaret herself turned to him, and spoke slowly.

"I know you, and what you are and have been. I know it all, you see, William."

"My dear——" He was, at this blackest moment of all, curiously, without feeling. If she knew *that* ... but if she knew, then they ... what had she found, heard, seen? It could not be——

He knew a desire, stronger even than the one to remain and reason with his wife, to go upstairs and examine the study bookcases. Instead he said aloud, as if to try once more to recall her to herself,

"Alicia and James sent their best love to you." But she only brought up her large fine hands to cover her face, and said nothing. He tried sternness then. "Marriages are made by God," he told her. "You blaspheme in acting so." He would have spoken thus in the pulpit; almost, his voice had acquired its customary overtones of oratory. She began to laugh, keeping her hands in front of her face like a child; presently the narrow eyes looked out again between her fingers.

"I have my own messages from God. Who are you to think of yourself as a chosen vessel? Who are you to know the mind of God, after what has befallen? I tell you, for He has told me, that marriage is a sin. No single one of my children shall ever marry."

She began to move restlessly, and presently went and sat down again. "I shall continue to stay in your house, for to leave it would cause scandal," she told him. "On Sundays, never fear, I'll turn out in my carriage, and grace your pew; and listen to such words as you may utter; you're a notable preacher, William. Who among your congregation would ever suspect that you are not what you seem, or that it is a mockery, all of it, from now till the end? Court knows that. Come here, Court, to me."

As the woman moved nearer again William rose and fled from the room. As he left it he heard Margaret's voice, seemingly sane and pleasant, say didactically,

"The sin of Eden, Court. We both know about it now, do we not? The sin of Eden; tonight again, and every other, you will sleep on the pallet bed in here, and *he* will not come in."

But William had already gone upstairs to his study. Unlocking the door with sweating fingers, he looked and could discover no disturbed thing on the shelves, the locked and hidden further door, the wall behind. He had no knowledge of the knot-hole. Each book was again in place, dust-free as always. Perhaps it was not after all true that Margaret——

But if she had found nothing, what had crazed her? For that his wife was now a madwoman William never doubted; or would do, as the days passed, and by day she continued to make a handsome figurehead for his table, his manse pew, the carriage, social occasions. But a stranger to him Margaret had become, and remained; and he dared not ask more either of her or the servant. For the present he was able to occupy himself with the search for little Jenny, gone now for many hours, and there was still no word of her.

VIII

Jenny had awakened in the end to unfamiliar things; the incessant nagging of pain through her small body, and the light of dawn creeping in at the window. She lay and watched the greyness change to pallor. It wasn't raining.

She was uncertain how long it took, remembering it all afterwards, for her to appreciate that if she got out of the window, she would not get wet. The knowledge that she must leave here, almost with the urgency of danger, was with her, as certainly as the awareness had come to her in sleep that she couldn't lie on her back, because it hurt. She moved gingerly; all of her limbs were stiff and sore, and her upper lip was tender where the birch had caught it. A glimpse of herself in the small, wood-framed swing mirror upon the dressing-table intrigued rather than shocked Jenny. Her mouth and one eye were swollen, and there were streaks of blood on her cheek. Jenny lifted a corner of her apron to wipe it off, spitting and rubbing. If anyone saw her in the street like that, they'd ask questions, she knew; whereas if she could get out of the house looking like an ordinary little girl, perhaps no one would notice. It did not occur to her to think where she might be going. Once free of the manse, and its high back-yard wall, she could decide.

First there was the window to negotiate; it was tiny and narrow, and small as Jenny was for her age she had to squeeze her bruised hips and pelvis through in bunched petticoats. In the pocket of her apron was all the money she had; fourpence, but it would be enough to travel quite some way on the river steamboat, far enough for nobody to come after her. She had tied a shawl over her hair; she looked, she knew, no longer like a young lady, the daughter of the manse, but like a servant's child, less likely to be questioned. Kate and Lissy, who were so proper, had often told her it wasn't seemly to be seen alone in the streets if one were a lady. The others could do as they liked.

Kate and Lissy would still be asleep, tired after yesterday. They hadn't come in to kiss her, Jenny, good night; Mrs. Heatherton would have forbidden them. Jenny, poised between the sill and the convenient wash-house slates below, pondered her state between sky and ground; in the end, she jumped. The jump was longer than she expected and, instead of landing neatly on the slates, as a boy would have done, she found herself slithering foolishly down the grey slope, unable to stop herself when the edge was reached; the ground, with its grass and dockens, came up at her terrifyingly, and she landed in a heap, with a wrenched ankle.

She picked herself up, and still resolute not to cry—it had been painful, and she was limping—hurried to the farther wall. This had to be negotiated, taking hold of its rough places and setting one's foot in the crevices; she'd always known it could be done, but with a twisted ankle, which swelled already, it was more difficult; but she'd gone too far now to stop. Perched at last on the top of the wall, she was in time to see a retreating tall hat; the constable, on his rounds, and if he'd seen her! But he had not, and continued on his majestic way, baton in hand, buttons shining at his tail-coat back. Perhaps God had made her sprain her ankle in order to save her from the constable. It was as well; he would have taken her straight back to Papa, or to Mrs. Heatherton.

Jenny shut her eyes, and once more resolutely jumped, petticoats billowing out as the air filled them. This time her landing was more successful, and without losing a moment—the policeman would be back, she knew, within minutes, on his beat, which went back and forth and back and forth, looking for wrongdoers—she picked herself up and hobbled, with smoothed, adjusted skirts, round the near corner and away, in which direction she no longer knew. There were few persons about yet; Jenny had never been out so early before, and in the ghost-city, peopled by no one except herself, the constable, a cat which galloped from a by-way, and the vagrants who had no home, she felt at once strangely powerful and quite free. It did not occur to her that never in her life had she known freedom before; she simply sensed the presence of it, and was not afraid. As a minister's child, also, it occurred to her that, as she had been taught, God looked after children who said their prayers. So Jenny said, "Please God, let me not have to go back to Mrs. Heatherton, and bless Papa," and then, as she could think of nothing else for the moment, began to recite the lines lately learned in the schoolroom, to the effect that man hath perfect blessedness who walketh not astray. Jenny's sore foot, swelling rapidly until it slowed her pace, and her sore backside, manifested themselves to her awareness more strongly now that the excitement of escape had worn off. She had, it was true, escaped; but where to?

"Or sitteth in the scorner's chair," sobbed Jenny; and at that moment, proving that God in fact did look after mindful children, Jenny saw a carriage in the street, which she recognised. The horses had of course been led away to stable, and the equipage itself was well covered over with tarpaulin to keep it dry; but that it was Uncle James's carriage the child had no doubt; it would have been sent back last night with Papa and Kate and Lissy, and, rather than have to return to Imrie at so late an hour, the coachman had taken a bed with the servants at Uncle James's former house, still used by him as riverside offices.

Josiah would not be out again for many hours; dared she risk remaining unseen, undiscovered till then? But she was weary, and God had let her find the carriage. Jenny took a quick look round, unable to tell if she were perceived from behind the shuttered windows of the house, or other houses. It might seem odd for a little girl to climb in and hide herself, under the tarpaulin. She must find a place where the coachman wouldn't find her when he came to take the covers off, and would take her with him when he returned with the carriage to bring Uncle James to the city.

Jenny was fortunate. During the hours she spent cowering hidden beneath the well-sprung seat of James Heatherton's carriage—there was a space there which contained room for luggage, or a lady's necessaries which might be required too often to be placed outside—during that time, the sun rose high towards noon, so that the child, stifled, hungry and sore, wept sometimes, and at other times dozed. She was too much afraid to go out again into the now populated streets, and too stiff; the impetus of escape had long worn off, and all she was now was a lost creature without a home, like the vagrants. For go home, if the manse was home, Jenny still would not. By now, she knew, they must be aware of her disappearance, perhaps looking for her. Papa might be sad; he took her on his knee sometimes, and heard her say her prayers, and was kind. But Jenny knew, with the intuition she had which was not childish, that Papa loved Wilhelmine best of all his children. "He is fond of Kate and Lissy, and fond of me," the little girl told herself. "But he loves Wilhelmine." The difference between fondness and love did not explain themselves further; the facts were there, and Jenny from the beginning had known them.

She began to think of other things; and presently the horror of yesterday, the dried human foot in its curled-up boot, floated upwards in her mind. She tried to down a nausea of sheer physical terror: one mustn't be sick in Uncle James's coach, with its smells of varnish, well-tended leather, horseflesh, and straw. Jenny shut her eyes, again and again, to tell herself that perhaps before she opened them, the carriage would have moved off. But it was well into the afternoon when Josiah, who had been given various foot-errands to do for his master, brought round the horses to harness, so that they could set off. It was not every day James Heatherton used his carriage; four days out of five he would travel up and down from Imrie by river-boat, liking to see the progress of the great ships lying in their yards, and the new hulls rearing to the skyline. It was accordingly well towards evening when the carriage, bearing its unacknowledged occupant, jogged down the familiar way to Imrie stables.

When Jenny awoke it was night, and the weariness which had made her, at last, fall asleep on a journey which seemed interminable had given place to great fear. Fear was in the dark, and the strange place in which she now lay; for the first time, she longed for her own warm familiar bed at home. Here, she shivered; it was as though she were too hot and too cold at once, and her teeth chattered together as though she had no control over them. Monstrous sounds, the champing and munching of James's released horses in their stalls, came to Jenny; it was dark and she could hardly see, except for the faint shine of starlight above and far off, beyond the stable. How far away the stars were, and how far home was! Even the perfidy of Johnny, his betrayal of her, would have been forgiven now, she knew, if John himself were near, and would comfort her. But there was no one; and presently she heard the sound of her own dreary, hopeless sobbing. She lay there crying alone in the night; and as time passed it seemed as if it were all a dream, a dream also the lantern-light which shone at last into her face, making her eyes blink open.

The face beyond the lantern was Josiah's, but Jenny would hardly have known him without his grand livery and his grander porcelain teeth; now he was in his nightshirt, and a pair of breeches he had hastily pulled on to come down to investigate the sound of crying his wife said she'd heard, although the coachman himself thought it was nothing but a woman's imaginings, being as it chanced a trifle deaf; but now—The beam shone on the child's bruised face, filthy with its sojourn among the trodden floor-straw of the carriage. Her cheeks were flushed and she raved, he thought; easy to see she was in a delirium, but who, and why, had brought the little lass from the manse here in such a state?

Meantime, Josiah's habit of exclaiming aloud held fast, to an extent that the child herself heard it; through her fevered dreams, between one horror and the next, sanity sounded for the last time in some weeks for her, and she remembered it all her life. "The Lord bless us," Joey's voice said, "it's never Miss Jenny?"

Before Jenny was discovered in Imrie stables the news of her disappearance had reached James himself at his office, discreetly as no open scandal must be allowed to touch Savill's. He had immediately offered all possible help, including the use of his coachman who by that time, as it happened, was well on the way home; after Jenny had been found, carried up to the house, given a posset, and placed in a warm bed, Josiah was sent again to the city with word to William Heatherton that his daughter was found safe, though chilled, hungry and, perhaps, fevered. Worse symptoms relating to her physical state were related, in hushed tones, to Alicia Heatherton by her own daughters' nurse, who had undressed the new arrival.

"The like of the marks I never saw, 'm, in any place I've been yet; it looks as though someone'd run mad." And the nurse, who was a straight-spoken woman from the nearby village and knew her place, pointed an accusing finger at the swellings on Jenny's lip, and on her cheek and eye.

"You must say nothing of this," said Alicia Heatherton, and bade the woman go; she herself sat that night in cap and shawl by the child's bed, listening to her ravings until a physician was at last fetched; they concerned what Alicia took to be nightmares, with a tale of a boot, and a foot in it; and other things. "Have no fear, darling, you are safe now," said Alicia soothingly; and glanced with thankfulness over at the dimity-hung beds in which Maudie and Evangeline slept peacefully, their hair in curl-papers. As she often did, Alicia thanked God for her children, the boys grave and reliable like their father, the girls pretty and marriageable, if ordinary: there had never been anything like this before, they had always been safe and happy together ... Fear, seen not as a personal threat but as something which might creep in, and upset her bairns' lives, made Alicia, the tender of heart, hesitate in the act of decision to offer Jenny Heatherton a home. It would be like bringing a changeling into her ordered nursery, a dark unruly little hobgoblin, perhaps disobedient, or a liar who made up fairy-stories. Then Alicia told herself that even if things were as bad as that, she could not send this poor, frightened, sick and beaten child back to her stepmother. For that Margaret was responsible Alicia would have known without being told, or hearing Jenny talk in her delirium.

IX

James Heatherton thought his brother William had aged twenty years in the brief space since they had last met; the man who clambered stiffly down from the carriage at Imrie had hair that seemed more white than grey, and deeply etched lines on his face; he fumbled as though behind the thick glasses he were blind.

"Josiah will assist him," said Alicia, standing by her husband's side; a new, cold Alicia, shocked by the sight of Jenny's weals and fever out of any affection she might ever have had for the brother of her much-loved James. "And that unnatural woman, to use the little creature so!" She almost said it aloud; in the closeness of sympathy they had, James felt her fingers tighten on his sleeve. He said nothing, but stood by his wife's side and watched gravely while his brother was aided by the coachman on his way towards the new porch steps.

They exchanged formal greetings, suitable for the formal great house James had now built himself, with its recesses and statuary gracing the outer walls, a clock-tower, and a mediaeval turret every quarter-mile. The loch beyond glittered today in the sunshine, but the brothers were impervious to the beauty of the bright metallic stretch of water. Their talk was halting and uneasy, as though they were strangers. "It has been so since the second marriage," Alicia thought, tightening her lips; the upper of these had lengthened somewhat with the years, and now showed a whimsical pucker when its owner smiled, or thought of some witty thing to say. But Alicia was all sternness now.

"She cannot go back to that house, William," she said, and repeated the statement when William himself, with customary dignity, said that the child was his own flesh and blood, and must return to her home. "It's no home to Jenny; did you see the weals on her?" his sister-in-law said, dispensing with polite manners in such an instance. "Anyone who would use a child so does not love her; it matters not how naughty she has been. A prison convict never had such marks," said Alicia fiercely, and at this point her husband's strained face smiled, and he said, "When did you have the opportunity of observing any, my love? But if the child was unhappy enough to run to us, I think we should keep her for a little, William; at least until she is cured of her present feverish chill."

"Yes, indeed, and may it not have developed into an inflammation of the lungs, with such an exposure, and no food," said Alicia, the sun striking a gleam again from her faded hair. William, badgered on all sides, and with the memory of Margaret's estranged face as he left, had no option but to thank his brother and sister-in-law, and guarantee a sum to cover Jenny's keep. The last offer Alicia waved aside. "No, she will be company for Maudie and Eva, and can wear their gowns; they have too many, and there's enough room here, to be sure."

So it was arranged, and before parting William was taken up to the sick-room where Jenny by now lay drowsing in the sleep of recovery; her flushed cheek still showed marks. William grew pale, and put a hand to the bed's edge as if to support himself; after he had gone Alicia herself broke down and wept, clinging to her husband.

"I did not want poor Willie to feel that I hated him," she said, "but, oh, that woman! There has been something not right about that marriage that I could never name, but I never liked her, Jamie, though of course I pretended to; one has to, has one not?" She smoothed James's ruffled shirt-frill. "How natural and right our own marriage seems; you and I are part of one another, and it will be so, I hope, while we grow old together." She smiled, with an expression of sudden radiance breaking through rain; he, always short of easy words, bent and kissed her. If they could have foreseen it, they would indeed go on together, that pair, into extreme old age, happy in one another, their deaths divided only by a summer's length. But all of that was still far off, and in the meantime there was still some perturbation to be caused them by Miss Jenny Heatherton.

William had begged the favour of James's carriage for a further hour in order that he might go and visit his parents nearby; it was some weeks since he had seen the old pair. Nathan now sat all day in his ingle-nook, still upright but no longer able either to understand or speak. Old age had, by contrast, made Jean nippier. She tended her man like an old baby, and bustled to greet her younger son with pleasure, but without surprise; it was after all a son's duty to visit his parents and see that they lacked for nothing. William's grand second marriage, which Jean had thoroughly approved, had stood him in good stead, she knew; he'd been named, a whisper had lately told her, for a doctorate in the autumn, an unusual honour. "We'll both of us be there, maybe, if Nathan can travel, to see ye don the braw scarlet gown," she told William proudly. She took no heed of her son's unresponsive mood, standing as he did with his back to the window, so that the light was behind his head. A fine head, William had, she'd always thought: a scholar's, and the better now it was grey. Some of his sermons were in printed books. She was proud of him.

"Was I not right, Nathan, to gar him read his Latin, and stay away from the anvil, though you'd hardly have it so?" she asked the old man, expecting no answer from him, and receiving none. But one came now from William; it startled the old woman not a little.

"You have made me what you wished, mother, and now I am set in the pattern, and must follow the appointed way," he told her. "If what you see is a respected man, I am glad for you. Myself, I know my inner heart," and he suddenly gave a great sound like a sob, and groped for his tall hat at last and set it on his head, hardly taking leave of them on going. The old woman peered after the departing carriage curiously, her face puckered with doubt beneath the creamy, goffered cap; what had Willie meant by such a saying? "He's respected enough," she grumbled, as she went back to her work. "Is he not, Nathan? There's no finer preacher in all the west than our Willie."

Then she pricked her finger with her needle, and tutted with vexation for that, and for the slip of the tongue that, after thirty-odd years, made her again call her son Willie, and him a minister. Old Nathan, imprisoned in his silence, perhaps understood more.

X

THEREAFTER WILLIAM HEATHERTON HAD A LIFE HE HAD KEPT secret from the world. The world saw him, approvingly, as a man who had made his way in it by the power of his oratory, the flawless nature of his scholarship which had in the end, before old Jean died, allotted him the coveted doctorate and bright gown. His sermons, selected and edited, were in every pious household; with the engraving made of him, at about the age of sixty, showing a stern long-lipped face above the carved pulpit, the eyes behind their glasses seeming to predict, like a pointing finger, the unavoidable wrath of God. God's forgiveness, God's love, became increasingly less heralded by William as the years passed, and even his public life became embittered by the Disruption and its effects, which rocked Savill's as other churches. Certain of the congregation complained of William accordingly as too withdrawn, too formal, not amenable enough to trouble-racked souls who came to him for comfortable discourse, or even—and this was a growing source of gossip and speculation—to those who would have met Dr. Heatherton socially, improving on their personal knowledge of a man whose brother would, after all, be remembered among the great of all time. But to say one had met William Heatherton in fact meant little; one might as well have met a granite statue, unyielding, neither friendly nor rancorous, simply never approachable. It was rumoured that within his family circle, he unbent sometimes; but Mrs. Heatherton herself became increasingly eccentric, and by now recognised few even among the congregation of Savill's.

She would be seen each Sunday, exquisitely attired and veiled—she took, even at her age, to wearing frivolous light headdresses, made of veiling embroidered with flowers, beneath which her smooth, now entirely silver hair showed, and her gloves and shoes were always elegant, made of the finest kid procurable—emerging from her carriage, and going up the aisle on the arm of her only son, John. Then she would be ushered into her pew, and the door firmly latched upon her and her son and many daughters. Miss Georgy, at nineteen, had been of such glowing beauty that a baronet, no less, from England, having seen her, in a grey velvet gown and matching hat with curled pink feathers, would not rest till he received an introduction: and, it was rumoured, later asked for her hand, braving the fear everyone had of old Mrs. Heatherton. It was even said that after the first rebuff this nobleman went back a second, even a third time; after which no self-respecting lover could do anything but take himself off. Sir James did so, accordingly, and went by ship to Sardinia, and on that savage and little-known island procured himself some rare wild tulip-bulbs, which he brought home at last and grew successfully in his famed Sussex garden. But the other blossom he would have planted there remained, to pursue the analogy, firmly attached to its parent bulb. Georgy matured finely, and kept her glossy dark hair and peerless complexion. She attended her mother constantly, conducted herself obediently, and—as the congregation were not put in a position to know—took up her place as adopted mother to Wilhelmine. Perhaps it consoled Georgina for the loss of her baronet; nobody ever heard the subject pass her lips.

William's own daughters were less amenable than Georgy. Among the new arrivals at Savill's, though he had known it briefly as a boy, was a man of about thirty-three, very handsome, with a pair of fine dark eyes and shining whiskers which rivalled Prince Albert's own, as did his whole bearing. He was a foreign merchant, as those importing and exporting goods to and from the city were called; he was much to be seen in mercantile circles, and was greatly in demand at private parties as a singer, for he had a fine tenor voice. His name was Richard Urquhart. He lived alone with his old father in a house near the city's centre, Sophia herself by now being dead. The building yard which had once been owned by Shawfield had been sold profitably; the Urquhart daughters were married, the other Urquhart sons—who had not had a good reputation—gone, it was said, to India and Canada, where nothing more was ever heard of them. Certainly Richard more than atoned to his father for any disappointments his wife and remaining family may have caused the old man. It was thought most suitable that, when the former precentor of Savill's died, Richard Urquhart should be invited weekly to intone, and set the note for the singing of the congregational psalms and paraphrases. Such a fine figure of a man roused a flutter in all the young ladies' hearts, especially when they learned that Mr. Urquhart was unmarried. Various attempts were made to secure him, as had been done, in his own young days, to William Heatherton himself. The reverend doctor grew fond of young Urquhart, and soon asked him to luncheon. Having weathered this terrible ordeal of assembled Howies and Heathertons, with its family silver and formality, Richard emerged unscathed; and as to the thoughts of plain, unassuming Miss Catherine Heatherton, who had sat opposite him at table, they were not recorded. It was not, in any case, advisable to show any excitement or interest over young gentlemen; marriage was forbidden by Catherine's stepmama. Kate pondered the silent rejection of Sir James by Georgina in the previous years, and said nothing. She was a practically-minded young woman, and unlike her sister Alicia feared Margaret Heatherton not at all. It would take time, all of it, she thought; and in any case, Richard Urquhart might not, after all, propose. But the dark eyes had shone upon her across the mahogany table with a kindly and interested beam; and Kate was glad that she had been wearing her new plaid aniline dress, for the somewhat garish colours became her sallow skin; not everyone could wear them.

Meantime, life at the manse was turned completely upside down by no other than Lissy; Alicia, the quiet, apologetic, frightened and very plain younger sister of Kate herself, and second daughter of the dead Marie. Lissy had never caused anyone a day's trouble, nor was expected to; lamentably ugly, with a long yellow face, an expression of permanent melancholy—for what had she to be glad about?—and a strange pointed tongue that sometimes flicked in and out like a snake's, she was at once the butt and prop of her stepmother when Georgy or Kate were unavailable. If anyone had to run a disagreeable errand, it would be Lissy Heatherton; if there were parcels of discarded clothes to be distributed to the poor in their, at times, terrible and insanitary dwellings, it was oftener Lissy than Kate who went, though Kate herself was never lazy. It was accountable, therefore, that when a prosy old China missionary, a widower with four children, visited Savill's, it was Lissy who went oftenest to hear him, Lissy who took his youngest child, who was feeling sick, on her knee, and later physicked the boy till he was better. The accounts of the China station enraptured the younger Miss Heatherton; time after time she would come home from Mr. Cowell's meetings with shining eyes, and for the first time Kate, who was not unobservant, noticed that these were grey, clear and beautiful. Katc quelled her customary acid tongue, and did not mock at Lissy's elderly beau. It was a different matter when he proposed, correctly, to Lissy's father for his younger daughter's hand; Margaret was informed of this event by Georgy, and there were tears and scenes.

"Mama will never permit it," said Georgy placidly. It had not been allowed for herself; why should William Heatherton's daughters fare differently? The spectacle of poor Lissy's equine nose, made red with weeping, mollified Georgina; she went and looked at herself in the mirror, and thought of herself, as she sometimes did, as the permanent and unchanging shrine of the rejected love of a baronet. It was certain that one could not disobey Mama; but comforting to learn, as Georgy had not failed to do, that Sir James to date had married no one else. She returned to her tasks, smiling a little. What a contented family they all were here, with Mama! "No one of us should wish to change our state," thought Georgy. "We have everything we want." She smoothed Wilhelmine's curls where the child sat dreaming over her dolls. "Is it not time to dust the chairs in the little drawing-room, darling?" she said. "The visitors will spoil their gowns, if you do not." The visitors were all dolls, dressed by Wilhelmine and Georgy together; daily they had tea-parties, dinner-parties, conversation-pieces in the drawing-room and dining-room of the doll's house, and were put to bed at night. It was an occupation that left no prospect of boredom even into old age; why did other people want what they had not got and could perhaps never have? She and Wilhelmine would be happy to their lives' end, playing with the dolls. Even if Mama died ... but one must not think of that.

Lissy came silently to her own and Kate's room late one night, they shared a bed, and as she undressed Lissy emitted sibilant, joyful hissings; no one must know, but Papa had permitted that she and Eustace be married, only it mustn't be in the church, still less the house. "It is to be in——" and Lissy named a little-known mission church hall, in a quarter which could not by any means be spoken of as select, or suitable for Dr. Heatherton's daughter. Kate frowned a little, secure in her curl-papers and cap.

"Why do it in such a hidden way?" she asked. "It is as though Papa is openly admitted to be afraid of that woman." She herself, if Richard asked her, she knew, would—But Lissy was beside herself with mingled terror, excitement, and joy.

"You will be there, will you not, as my bride-attendant?" she asked. "Eustace understands the situation, and dearest Papa has given me money to buy a wedding gown, and a bonnet."

"What has Eustace to say to it?" enquired Kate drily; but in face of Lissy's childlike pleasure and continued fear she could deny her nothing. They were, or had been, she was thinking, all their lives, each of them, the only close company one another had had, ever since Jenny ran away that time, to be brought up at Imrie. They went to visit Jenny sometimes, but she was changed, a quiet discreet stranger in somebody else's gowns. Papa might well purchase a wedding gown for poor Lissy.

"I will come with you to choose the gown, if you like," Kate said, and to her surprise Lissy said she had already chosen it; the exhibition of independence was rare in the second sister.

When Kate saw the gown, she was uncertain whether to laugh or cry; Lissy had chosen a confection of creamy-white lace, caught at each abundant frill with tiny rosebuds; a gown fit for a blonde young bride at a great gathering of guests, not this hole-and-corner ceremony at a mission. But all of Lissy's poor parishioners to whom she had taken parcels and soup-jelly were there; and William took the plain bride on his arm with great dignity to where the old bridegroom waited, beaming a little uncertainly on this manifestation of extravagance in his bride. "It will be her only one, as he will certainly find," thought Kate, following. She hoped Lissy would be happy.

Afterwards, she returned home with William to the storm which she knew was brewing. How strange that yielding Lissy should have been the steel which first breached the wall! As for herself——

Richard Urquhart proposed some weeks later, after Lissy and her missionary had returned to the China station. It happened on a rainy day when Kate was returning from the greengrocer's, and had a cabbage among other items in her basket. Afterwards she was to reflect wryly that romance took strange aspects; a cabbage, and the rain dripping down on her shoulder-cape, so that Richard in his tall hat held an umbrella over her. The drips fell about them still; but screwing his monocle further into his eye—she never knew, till afterwards, whether he wore it to enhance his appearance, or because his sight was short—gave her his arm, took the basket firmly, and said, "Miss Heatherton, I know that circumstances do not permit that I should easily approach your father, as I should like to do. But were I to do so—Miss Heatherton—Kate—could you, might I hope that you—might I hope that some day, perhaps, we...?"

And seeing him in difficulties, which aroused in her a great tenderness—he had always seemed so assured!—Kate looked at him with her dark eyes and said steadily, which remark was to be passed to her children,

"I will be married in my father's church in decency, or not at all." And she then began to cry, romantically enough, but it might have been the rain; in any case, Richard comforted her.

The marriage of Catherine and Richard Urquhart took place after such storms as had never been known even in the time of Lissy or Jenny; Kate had, her stepmother assured her, been a disappointment. In fact, Margaret had relied on the practical, pithy girl's company more than she knew; Kate was less yielding than Lissy, less adoring than Georgy; in fact, as Margaret knew very well, her eldest stepdaughter did not adore her at all. But they had liked one another's company, in a way; and Kate had absorbed all Margaret and, also, Sarah could teach her of the craft of housekeeping, cookery, and the making of preserves; she would, no doubt, be an excellent wife to Richard Urquhart, and the prospect of their happiness together made Margaret rail like a madwoman. "What are you thinking of?" she cried. "You know very well that when you were sixteen years old the physician prescribed a mouth-mask for you when you went out in the cold, and quilted petticoats. How can you hope to endure the stresses of matrimony if your lungs are weak? You are saddling this Urquhart"—Margaret almost spat out the words—"with an invalid for his pains, and it will be the wrath of the Almighty fixed upon you both for flouting His Will."

"Richard is an excellent churchman, Mrs. Heatherton," Kate replied, keeping a calm outward exterior although her slight bosom seethed with rage, and addressing her stepmother with the title she had always used to her: if the old woman told Richard any such thing, she'd— But it was true about the mask; and Kate made up her mind on one thing. She would never trouble Richard with complaints of her health; she would bear his children gladly—Kate was ignorant, as were most gently brought up young women of her day, but she was not a fool—and if the Almighty wanted a hand in it, He could see that during the foggy winters she kept herself well wrapped up, and didn't catch cold, and perhaps would perform a latter-day miracle, and ensure that she became all that Richard, the handsomest man and finest tenor in the city, wanted. For her own good fortune in atracting his attention still left Kate somewhat dazed; so many other young ladies, of greater fortune and much greater beauty, had tried to attract Richard, and had failed.

If Kate had known, it was her common sense and kindness that Richard Urquhart loved most. They were married in Savill's, and on the wedding day Margaret Heatherton, who had at last been prevailed upon to appear at such a ceremony, did so for the first and last time, veiled from head to foot in black crape, a widow's weeds. Yet had she known, there was still one other occasion on which she would want to wear them; this concerned her son John, and little Jenny Heatherton.

William himself was more firmly rooted in unhappiness as the years went by; a second terrible thing had helped to alienate him from Margaret.

Was it her fault or his? He often asked himself, going over and over the matter in his own mind, abovestairs in the haunted study where by now, except on Sundays, he spent most of his waking hours. It had happened up here, the episode with the housemaid. He hadn't meant it to happen; but Margaret would never understand or forgive that, or care when she knew. Sarah Court had told her, of course. Sarah's eyes were everywhere, and she had had the evidence from the police.

The housemaid had been new at Savill's manse, little more than an ignorant Highland girl, with the hazel eyes of Miss Flora Urquhart who by then was dead long ago. Otherwise there had been nothing notable about her, a little plump thing she'd been, with cheeks like red apples, perhaps sixteen years old. William had felt a sudden lust rise, as it would do in the night in his unslaked body, and had forced the girl into a corner and had taken her, and forbidden her to cry out or unlock the door. At the end, he recalled, he'd given her a coin. That had perhaps been a mistake; they would wonder, Sarah and the others, where the child had got hold of half a crown, and would perhaps suspect him. But he'd wrestled night after night with the uncontrolled demands of his own flesh, and could endure no longer.

It had been two months later that the girl had flung herself over one of the river bridges. The police had come to William as her employer, and told him the little maid had been found to be pregnant. He'd shown shocked surprise, demurred, gone through the usual processes, horribly like the days following Chantal's disappearance, of informing relatives, dealing with enquiries, and, this time, paying for the funeral.

He had known almost at once that Sarah knew ... and his wife, or the woman who had once been so, had turned one narrow contemptuous glance at him from where she sat by the fire, and said, "The Lord will punish the evildoer."

That was all they had spoken of concerning it; but William remembered. Since then he had struggled to impose on his own flesh, by constant prayer and self-discipline, a rigorous denial. By now he was a man of cold inward fire and outward formality, and his parishioners spoke of him as formal.

He was glad that Catherine and Alicia were married suitably. It had given him pain to disobey Margaret on this point—was a man to admit inwardly to obeying his wife, who was a wife no longer?—but he was glad for his daughters. Jenny he felt no longer to be his responsibility; he had tried to assume parentage for her, but it had all been so long ago . . .

The news regarding Jenny and John came two years after Kate's marriage, when William and Marie's first grandchild had been born, and named Catherine for her mother. Kate was happy and had had her portrait painted, full-length in a turquoise silk crinoline, with a Richelieu lace shawl Richard had bought her from abroad, and a gold bracelet set with amethysts which her stepmother, relenting, sent her at last as a marriage-gift. Lissy had had her baby at the China station and it had died, but she also was happy and at times sent home strange, luxurious things; books bound in silk and painted on rice-paper, of strange warriors and ladies in jewel-bright gowns and masks; and a pen-drawing of herself, by a Chinese artist, framed in crimson silk. She was fond of her stepchildren and, as it was said she could never have another child, this was fortunate.

But Jenny, Jenny! John Howie and Jenny! If anything else had been calculated to drive William Heatherton's wife mad, it was the news about her only son.

XI

William Heatherton's affection for his brother James had remained unchanged since the episode of Jenny's flight, and he knew that, correspondingly, James would remain the same loyal, taciturn ally that he had always been, towards himself, ever since the days when their mother would not permit Willie to help his brother blow the bellows at the forge. Old Jean was dead now, and the family gathering at Hogmanay would no longer take place at the riverside cottage; in the nature of things it had transferred itself to Imrie, where most years William, his two elder daughters, and his youngest were reunited in the blaze of the great chandeliers James had had installed in the gallery where he housed the ever-increasing models of his ships. Select, almost royal company met there now; it was no longer so much of a family gathering since the death of old Nathan, who had surprisingly survived Jean herself by two years and had been looked after, with devotion, by his daughter-in-law Alicia at Imrie. Before he died the old man had managed to speak again.

"Jean wasna for the marriage," he told her, and she knew that he meant her own, long ago, to her cousin James. "She didna think ye wad mak' a right wife, being overmuch of a fine lady. But she was wrong, ay, poor Jean," and then his eyes filled with tears, for he had loved his difficult consort and knew well enough she was dead. He himself made a peaceful end, in his sleep; he was buried in the new mausoleum James had had made for himself and his family at Imrie.

Imrie itself was like a palace now. It might have been thought that Margaret Heatherton, with her love of fine things and show, would have rejoiced in the winter-garden, the opulent rose-beds set out with rare species from England and abroad, the clipped maze and gilded clock-tower, which critical folk said was a trifle top-heavy for the house. But the tick of the great clock, which James had had installed by a maker from Birmingham, sounded night and day like Imrie's very heart; it chimed at the hours and the quarters. Once only Margaret came down with her husband, by invitation to dinner, but it was not at Hogmanay or Christmas, which she preferred to keep with her own family as a festival. That time Margaret came, Jenny Heatherton, consumed with horror and fear of her stepmother still, begged Alicia with tears to permit her to be absent, and to have her dinner separately in the schoolroom. Her aunt allowed it, and William went up by himself to see Jenny afterwards; James sadly watched him go.

"It is not a right situation between them," he said afterwards to his wife. Margaret Heatherton had been affable, but it had been a little like entertaining a Grand Duchess, which James Heatherton and his wife had in fact already done, not long before, at Imrie. Their fame and hospitality was known now in foreign lands, and Alicia Heatherton kept a notable table. But William's second wife seemed no closer to his first family, or to William, than she had been now for many years.

"Jenny gives no trouble, and the girls love her," said Alicia with truth, for Jenny, somewhat to everyone's surprise, had settled down at Imrie to become a small colourless thing, a kind of cross between a poor relation and governess, though she lacked accomplishments to fill the latter task. Nor had she—and for this Alicia was thankful, having her own mild ambition for them—shown any signs of falling in love with her staid cousins, Jonathan and David, who took after their father and were both now employed by him creditably in the foundries and the yards. Nor did Jenny, of course, rival Maudie and Evangeline who were both of them beauties as their mother had long ago been and, many said, was still. Maudie had recently attracted a proposal from a suitable young man of good local family, and the double occasion of her betrothal, and of Eva's coming-out, was to be celebrated by a ball, with coloured lamps shining out over the great water that lapped for ever below Imrie, and an orchestra to play till past midnight.

All was therefore preparation, excitement and some subterfuge; Alicia had to hide her own private grief, which concerned her elder brother David, for whom her second son had been named. Some years before, one of his numerous inventions, perhaps the same he had discussed with Flora Urquhart that far-off night over dinner, had ended in disaster for forty workmen, who had been killed in the explosion of a new steam-boiler. David had never recovered from this tragedy, and had sold out his holding to James and other shareholders, himself retiring to the south where he was still living, a recluse. Alicia received word that week that he showed signs of going out of his mind, eccentric as he had always been; this news she kept to herself. How thin a line there was between sanity and madness, particularly in the case of genius, as it was found in her brother and her husband! She watched James going quietly about his daily life, and thanked God for her husband as he was, not as he might have become. There were those who, she was aware, poked sly fun at James and his social ambitions, and his entertainment to dinner of a Grand Duke, royalty, and the rest. Even his ambition in building Imrie had been criticised, as too grandiose even for the millionaire he had long ago become; such a fantasy translated into stone would not last, they prophesied, more than a hundred years. "But we shall neither of us be here then, and for the present, save for the news of poor Davie, we are happy as always," James's wife thought.

She herself had chosen a gown of emerald satin for the ball, of a shade calculated to set off her blonde, fading beauty and also to give her standing as the mother of the new fiancée and of the débutante. Maude's gown was to be blue, Evangeline's moiré rose; that she had not considered the question of Jenny till the last minute was an occasion of some self-reproach to Alicia. But Jenny was brusque nowadays, sulking because her stepmother and the rest had been invited (but how could one do less?) and had sworn she would not appear at the ball at all; and her aunt, who seldom lost patience with her, had replied somewhat tartly that in that case she need not, and there were plenty of other things to see to without heeding the demands of a spoilt young miss.

Jenny had been contrite at once. "Of course I will come, and will wear one of Eva's old dresses, if you would like it, aunt," she said. "I know I'm a trial to you; but, truth to tell, I've not set eyes on Georgy or Johnny since—you know—and I am uncertain what to say, or how to behave when we shall meet."

Alicia promised that there should be no difficulty, and that Jenny should have Eva's last year's dove-grey gown. "As for the Howie family, why, behave as if nothing had happened amiss, and no doubt they will be glad enough to do the same," she told the girl. "Is it not all of it a very long time ago, and best forgotten?"

Jenny tossed her dark curls back out of her eyes. Aunt couldn't understand—could not be expected to, for gentle people, who'd never lived close to horrifying things, had no notion of what went on in half the world, the young girl decided somewhat arrogantly—couldn't ever understand what her own feelings had been, and had remained, that time of John Howie's betrayal long ago. It was as though God had come down out of the sky and had ceased to be; as if the world stopped turning on its axis. How she would hate Johnny all her life now, whether or not she ever saw him again! He'd be a man by this, still thinking he knew everything, but weak as water when it came to the test, and afraid of his mama.

Jenny could have consoled herself on one point; Margaret Heatherton declined the invitation for herself and her eldest daughter Georgina, who she said was growing past the age of frivolity; Eva breathed sighs of relief also on hearing this, for Georgy's fabled beauty, albeit by now becoming a trifle like that of a waxen figure in a glass case, had once, it was still admitted, ensnared the baronet; and Evangeline wanted to be the central figure tonight apart from her sister, who was safely betrothed. The appearance of Jenny at the ball, in her own last year's gown, did not trouble Eva; poor little Jenny was quite plain, although an engaging enough little creature, and one had to be sorry for her with no home, or rather only a queer one inhabited by a mad stepmother and her earlier brood. Poor Uncle William! He, being of too sober a habit, would not attend the ball either; but John Howie and his younger sisters, Molly and Ann and Eliza, would come.

When the four young Howies arrived, the orchestra had already taken up their places on the great dais, and dancing was about to begin. John Howie, who was voted by the various young ladies to be excessively handsome, with his dark-gold hair and sleek side-chops, dark eyes, broad shoulders and a narrow waist above long elegant legs, led Evangeline out to dance. They made polite conversation, rendered the more innocuous by the rumour, which Maudie had told Eva of and swore it was true, that old Mrs. Heatherton would never, never permit John Howie to marry.

"It is too bad, when he is as handsome as that, and with all the money; but of course with the way it's been left, she can cut him off with sixpence if she chooses," had stated Maudie, whose betrothed status gave her the right to keep a somewhat worldly ear to the ground. "So don't worry about *him*, my dear; look about you for young Mackenzie, who'd like Papa to take him into the yard-shops, and has money as well; only he's something of a bore, it's true, and with no great looks."

Eva had replied with spirit that she could very well look out for herself; and at that moment saw John Howie's lambent glance wander across the top of her own head to the stairs, above which, as Eva knew, was a marble balustrade between whose urns one could see the ballroom. Twirled about in the waltz, she found her own indignant gaze fixed on Jenny's abovestairs pointed chin. Little minx, sitting up there slyly watching the dancing!

"I will return you to your mama," said John politely, and then, as Eva had perhaps foreseen, he was off—up the marble staircase, intent on his own concerns, and not even so much as an offer to bring her an ice, or fan her cool! James Heatherton's spoilt beauty of a younger daughter pouted, and failed to enjoy the first part, at any rate, of her own triumphal evening; it was annoying to have so handsome, and ineligible, a bachelor taken from one's side by that plain chit.

"Why will you not dance with me? Why are you not downstairs dancing with anyone ... sitting up here by yourself, I might never have set eyes on you again ... Jenny!"

His voice lingered deeply over the syllables of her name. John Howie was a practised charmer; he regarded his own unmarriageable status rather as a prize bull might regard his agricultural show rosettes; all was grist that came to his mill, and he had captivated many women, some older than himself, none unattractive or poor. But Mama had been a match for them all, and when they found out that there would be no money in the bargain, they'd cried off. But this elfin, elusive girl, with her pointed chin and tangle of dark unruly curls, was different from anyone he'd ever met or flirted with. Jenny. Jenny Heatherton. She had, he recalled, made a little nuisance of herself, hanging on to his coat-tails when she was a child, following him. If only she'd do so now!

"It wouldn't have mattered," said Jenny sullenly to his remark. "Why should I want to meet you again, John Howie? You told a lie that time, long ago." She stared down at the dancers, seen twirling like many-coloured petals of flowers, a floor below them. How silly it all was, how unreal! As silly and unreal as the portrait, painted some years ago now, of Aunt Alicia, shown at a spinning-wheel with the thread running through her white, slender fingers. Aunt never spun, wouldn't have known what to do with a wheel, though the sunlight painted filtering through the Gothic window of Imrie shone, suitably gold, on her hair. "I couldn't lead that kind of life, pretending all the time," thought Jenny. The remembrance of how Johnny had betrayed her long ago came back, increasing her misery. They were all dressed up to the eyes down there and waltzing, but she, in Eva's last year's dress——

"Do you not like the waltz?" said John. He had decided to ignore the taunt about the lie. He eyed Jenny covertly and wondered what it was about her that attracted him so sharply. She wasn't beautiful, like her cousins; rather plain, though still more appealingly so than her sisters, that horse-faced pair, he thought again ungallantly. Jenny's features were rounded and immature, her mouth a button of obstinacy he'd like to kiss; her plump breasts strained at Eva's grey gown. Desire rose in John's throat; he almost made to rise and go, aware that one must not behave, in Uncle James's house, as might be the case in a tap-room, or an inn-parlour. Not that one would class little Jenny with the wenches found in those, any more than she belonged to the waltzing, artificial set downstairs! John lost interest in Cousin Eva's ball. Beyond the steady beat of the fiddles and 'cellos came another sound, insistent, regular and clear, if one listened; the great Imrie clock.

"Show me the clock, in its tower; come on." He pulled her to her feet, only half willing; as if to evade him she turned and fled upstairs, and John followed, laughing and out of breath; what a girl she was! He felt free, for the first time in his pampered life, to do as he chose; the tick of the clock sounded louder and ever louder, till it hammered against his ear-drums. He had caught up with Jenny; her grey skirts mounted ahead of him. A faint scent, Eva's scent, of lavender-flowers drifted back to John; it titillated his physical need, making the red blood of George Howie pulsate together with the blue, somewhat adulterated by now, of the Reverend Alfred. She'd come up with him, after all, as no properly brought up young lady would have done; he'd see, maybe. What a din the clock made! As they came out on to its containing platform, breathing in the coolness of the night, a whirring started; the great quarter chime rang, with echo and clamour. Jenny stuck her fingers in her ears, and began to sob. He could hear nothing for the din, and reached out, clutching her to him. They stayed close in one another's arms.

What happened then was swift enough to be inexplicable to John as well as Jenny. Neither had any notion of vice; it would have given John Howie thought had he known, as he told himself later he should have done, that what happened was going to happen. It was as though a fire, long kindled in them both, fanned itself suddenly into flame; a high and searing flame, burning upwards into the sky, consuming him and her together. At the end, he was sated. He heard her murmur, still held fast in his arms. "John. Ah, dear, dear John." He felt the hot tears wet on her cheeks. He kissed her, and knew that he'd kissed her before; her little button of a mouth had dropped open to receive his tongue in it, when it had all happened; now it was over, and neither of them would ever be the same again, and he——

"It was true about the boot, wasn't it?" he heard her say; and squeezed her the harder in his sudden laughter. To trouble, at such a moment, about—about that; and there were other things.

"We must forget it," he said to her, and held her upper arms firmly; they were plump little arms, she was like a partridge, he thought; full-breasted, trapped, frightened and shivering. He dared say it mattered more to a girl if——

"Come downstairs with me at once, Cousin Jenny, if you please. John, my father will deal with you presently."

It was young Jonathan Heatherton: relentless, shocked, no longer young. He must have followed them upstairs. How long had it taken, all of it? All their lives, caught in a breathless moment; and yet, all the time Jonathan had been following. John drew away, shamed, and then heard his own voice speaking.

"I have something to say on my own account; and Jenny shall do as she pleases; she's not your chattel." As he spoke, he felt a mixture of pride and shame rise. Mama, who talked to him of business sometimes, had indicated that it might be a good thing if he were to make a friend out of young Jonathan Heatherton, get him perhaps to offer shares in the parent company, with a view to partnership later. "You can't be a playboy all of your life, my son." But now——

James himself was called; Alicia was somehow altered. The ball swept on, unheeding; Jenny was sent upstairs to her room. "I don't want to see her again," Alicia cried, "she cannot stay on here." It was a shame too great, too heinous to be mentioned; and that it should have taken place in their very house——

Then John Howie heard himself speaking, for the second time that evening, like a man; but this speech had taken the more resolution.

"You are not to punish Jenny, aunt." Was she his aunt? "The fault was mine. I shall atone for it. I want to marry Jenny; I shall ask her father's permission to do so tomorrow."

Then he turned away, aware of their shocked silence; nothing he could say or do now would fail to shock them. As for Mama, she must be dealt with above all . . . But he'd do it. He'd do it for Jenny. The suddenness of his own feelings did not astonish John Howie, nor did his obstinacy in this matter; though he had no means of assessing the full measure of his own heredity.

The storm of all storms broke on the return, the following day, of John and his sisters; the two girls went straight to their Mama, and by the time John himself emerged, having been closeted with William for over an hour, the whole house brooded angrily.

James himself was to call, by arrangement, in the afternoon; he had persuaded Alicia to keep Jenny, and be tolerant of her, meantime. But it was a worried, anxious man who let his long legs down from the carriage in due course: if young John had had the courage to broach the subject with William, there'd be trouble to meet; and if he hadn't, the trouble was still to come, James thought. What had possessed the boy to forget himself, and behave so? "And yet, he's a likeable boy," the shipbuilder told himself, and resolved to help young Howie, if his mother proved adamant, by offering him a place in the yards. "Mind, he'll need to work." James himself, who knew every part of a ship from boiler to keel, and had wrought at all of them, was no advocate of softness as far as his youngsters were concerned; his own sons had had to work as hard as he himself had done, from the beginning. By the end, they would be knowledgeable shipmasters.

But ships and all else fled from James's thoughts when he was confronted with the situation in Savill's manse. The widow—since poor Kate's wedding James and Alicia had always referred to William's second wife as such—sat at the centre of the storm, surrounded by her red-eyed daughters. It had been made known to them that John had somehow disgraced himself; more was unsuitable for their ears, nor would the name of Jenny pass the lips of any present, until William at last spoke it.

"John was tempted," said the grey-faced, haggard woman James Heatherton remembered as handsome. "He was tempted by the devil which comes to us all. He will not sin again. I refuse to hear further mention of the matter; you will not discuss it among yourselves, Georgina."

She rose, and being about to sweep from the room would have ended the business, no doubt, in such a way; but William, for once rising to his full dignity, barred her exit. John Howie stood by his side; but for the present it was not poor Johnny his sisters looked at, but William himself: Dr. Heatherton, the man who had married Mama, but who had always seemed like a visitor in the house, until now.

"I have something to say," said William. "I have talked of the matter with John; what I have to say concerns both him and yourselves, and my daughter." The emphasis on the last two words was certain; William's myopic eyes focused themselves on his wife's face, as if daring her to speak and deny it. She did not, but stayed where she was, staring at the door through which he would not let her go out. Her face was blank and set, a mask. She might have understood nothing, until he spoke again; and when she heard of the impending marriage of John, she gave a great cry, and Georgy moved to go to her; William stayed the young woman with a raised finger.

"The marriage will take place here," said William, "in the drawing-room. All of you, all of the family, will be present. I myself will conduct the ceremony."

"If he marries her," said Margaret Heatherton, "I shall never speak to him in my life again. Do you hear me, my son?"

John inclined his head. "Then which are you to choose, her or myself?" screamed his mother. "I who bore you, and have given all in this world you can ever want, every refinement of living, every interest; or that, that——"

But John and William would hear no word against the absent Jenny. "Then if she is your choice, so be it," said Margaret. "You may earn your bread; you're nothing more to me."

"Ah, mother——"

"Let me pass," she said, and this time William and John stood aside, and let her go; followed by her daughters, Wilhelmine clutching her dolls with blue eyes vague, Margaret Heatherton went; out of their lives, out of the everyday world of sanity, into a place peopled only by her imaginings, and what she had seen; afterwards, William remembered, she could have endeavoured to blackmail him, but had not. Possibly her mind was too much impaired by now to plan succinctly.

The marriage of John Howie and Jenny Heatherton took place on the morning of the day arranged, and James brought the bride, in her plaid dress and trimmed straw bonnet, over in his carriage. Alicia did not accompany them. When they entered the manse William came out to greet his daughter, and she was moved by the sight of his pale, set face; what a trial she must have been to poor Papa! With her lips pursed, to still their trembling, and her head held high in its newly-trimmed bonnet, she went to meet her bridegroom, handsome John; he smiled and the sight of him cheered Jenny despite all that had happened, and the scoldings and shame. They loved one another, and they'd be happy, somehow, without any money; Uncle James had offered dear John a place, which he'd accepted, in the yards.

Afterwards the carriage drove off. One of the servants, noting the lack of rejoicing despite the formal handing round of wine and cake, pelted the departing couple with old slippers. They fell in the dust the departing wheels made in the ghostly street.

It was said by those who observed her through the years that Margaret Heatherton began to die the day she lost her son. He, more even than Georgina, had been the light of her very life; but Margaret was adamant. Not only did she refuse him any money, in her lifetime or after her death, but she was as good as her word; she never spoke to John again. Each Sunday he, who was grateful to his new father-in-law and desired to support him, would walk with his wife from their rented lodging nearby to Savill's church. There they would occupy one half of the manse pew, the Howie family the other; never once did Margaret turn her head or, before or after the service, greet or acknowledge her son. The sad travesty went on until John died some years later. It might have been argued that he and his wife might have sat in another pew, both for their convenience and Jenny's comfort; she found the occasions trying. But that, perhaps, would have been too much in the way of capitulation, even before John contracted an inflammation of his delicate lungs after a chill caught following a day's work in atrocious heat, among James Heatherton's boilers.

When he was dying, the mother did not go to visit him. When he was dead, she did not attend the funeral. There was a son born to the couple, at the last, whom she never saw. She had no further communication with Jenny.

IV

I

THE OLD MAN STOOD BY THE WINDOW AND DREW BACK THE green felt curtains, furtively. Now that the funeral was over and they had taken away the body of the strange woman who had been his wife, William might with propriety let the daylight in. Yet he hesitated, as if some remnant stayed with him of the artificial, external nature of mourning; the sable plumes nodding on the hired horses' heads as they drew away the hearse, and the lugubrious faces of the hired mourners, with crape and weepers, behind. Genuine mourners there had been a few; not from the congregation, who had not, in her latter days, known Margaret Heatherton at all, so withdrawn was she in her inner madness. They had come out of a sense—William's mind registered a great weariness—of what was proper, what was due to the aged minister of Savill's who had preached, Sunday after Sunday, over them now for almost fifty years. Many of them had filed past afterwards to condole with him, the widower, and shake him by the hand. That had been in the Necropolis, where women did not attend burials. The red-eyed family, Georgy and the other daughters in black veils, had withdrawn by then, perhaps to begin, that very night, packing their goods to go.

Georgy had informed William after the funeral that she would be leaving, with her younger sisters and Wilhelmine. William's permission had not been asked and he had long since ceased to regard his youngest child as in any way his property. Georgy's by adoption Wilhelmine had become, and had remained; her weak wits had been inherited from her mother's blood. William did not regret her loss, merely wondering, with his hand still on the curtain, what had set them all so firmly against him during these many years. *That* could never have been spoken of; perhaps it was the later affair of the maidservant and her suicide. Whatever it was had never been breathed outside the wall of his house ... his house, for long years now two houses in one.

The house next door had been abandoned to dust and neglect since he himself grew too old to visit it often. He would not be persuaded either to sell or let it, and nobody but himself held the key. Some day, soon perhaps, he would unlock the great door and walk through the echoing empty house, and see that all was right, no unbarred windows, no theft of any unimportant matters which had been stored in there for years, in packing-cases. They took it as a sign of his own dotage, William knew, that he would neither occupy the house himself nor allow others to do so. He must be failing, they said; when he was dead, they might walk in and do as they chose. They might think what they would, when they found ... what? A heap of bones?

He had faced it, that hidden memory from the furthermost recesses of his mind, that token of a lifetime's payment for a moment of swift anger; no more, it had been.

"I did not mean to kill him," the old man told himself. As he had done before, he looked down at his hands. They were still strong enough to wrench a bolt, to tear down an erected barrier.

Would not it be better to face the truth?

Vestiges of his early Biblical training recurred to him, now when his mind was in chaos. The truth shall make you free ... what a man has sown, that shall he reap ... a house built on sand ...

Would Jenny come herself in reply to his letter? He had sent it early today, by a servant, not to be seen in person on the streets the day of the funeral. She would have the letter by now. Soon, if she came, and the boy with her, there would be no more opportunity to be alone, to do entirely as he would, without eyes watching, for the first time in years. When the Howie women left the house, she would enter it ... if she came. Perhaps she would refuse. What had he ever done for her to earn her care and love in his old age, as her father?

"Her father," he thought. That other had always come between himself and his thoughts of Jenny. Perhaps that was why he had acquiesced so readily in James and Alicia's offer to bring the girl up; had contrived to forget her, then at last, after the episode with John Howie, had commanded that she be brought home for her marriage, despite them all. How Margaret's narrow eyes had glittered at that! Yet he had won the victory, that time, over Margaret.

"Perhaps she will not come," he thought, and a great weakness pervaded him at the thought of renewed enmity and strife, of never seeing his grandson. To have a child running about his house again would give him pleasure; Wilhelmine in her childhood had crept about mostly in her half-sister's shadow, a little secret withdrawn thing. Was the doll's house packed yet? he thought wryly.

A sudden disgust with all things pertaining to pretence took him, and picking out the key from among others in his desk drawer he went out, and downstairs to where his tall hat and cane waited in the hall. A door shut somewhere in the house; they had heard him come, the women, and would be murmuring now among themselves as to his callousness in going out, the day of their mother's funeral. "Let the dead bury their dead," thought William Heatherton.

He closed the outer door of the manse behind him and with firm slow steps, feeling for the pavement with his cane, betook himself next door to the house which had once been Miss Hyslop's. On the opposite side of the street, they would often have seen him go thus, and enter, slowly turning the key in the lock; though not of late years. A smell of unaired empty rooms, dust and damp stone met William; the hall was uncarpeted, and at its far end a twisting flight of stairs led down to the cellar. William had never been there. He ignored the downward flight now, and lifted his head in the pallid daylight and regarded the bare upper staircase, ascending to the first floor; down these stairs and those above, Paul Chantal had once come and gone on his daily concerns. There would be small company now for his ghost to keep. William felt no awareness of Paul, now, as he mounted the stairs. Wherever that young man's spirit had fled, it had not remained here. His own footsteps made the only sound in the house, his shadow on the wall the only moving shape. He was alone here, for as long as he chose; alone.

To know the truth! That was what he should have forced himself to do years since, when Margaret first manifested her strange moods towards him. He should have asked her, as a man unafraid, what she knew, and what she had seen and learned, if anything. "It might have been nothing," William thought sadly. He should have established mastery over her. How easy it was to think of all one might have done, when it was too late!

Here now, beyond the door, was Chantal's room; nothing in it had been changed, except that at the time he himself had come up here, with Miss Hyslop's grateful connivance, and had destroyed all traces of Chantal's recent whereabouts, any sign of the visits of Marie.

Marie! Her worn slipper, seen that time below the bed-frill, had goaded him to madness; it had been that, rather than the sight of the letter in Chantal's hand, that had made him do it. What man but would have acted similarly?

"How could she judge me?" he thought, remembering Margaret. How could she have had any notion of the feeling that drove a man to act thus? It was not for any human being to judge another and find him wanting, as Margaret had done to him, William, her husband; he had been judged and sentence passed on him without a chance to defend himself, explain: a loving wife would have wanted to hear his story, begged him, perhaps with tears, to let her know why he had acted so. But Margaret! "She can never have loved me," he thought. "She can never have known what love is." Did he himself know?

To know the truth. The certainty had come to William that he would find neither rest nor peace till he had come face to face with Chantal's bones. What were they, after all, a handful of bones? The man had been small enough, and the quicklime, all those years ago, would have eaten away those parts that rotted. There would be nothing for him to face today, in the nature of time, but ... bones. Yet he must look on them again. It occurred to him now how strange it was that all this time he had been afraid of facing them, afraid of the sight of what would bring home to him what he, as a man, had been. Yet if a man might not know himself, who except God could know him?

"When I face God, He will know that I did not have intent to kill. He will understand all things. I need not be afraid."

The farther door, past the cobwebbed bed and disturbed

dust-particles in sunlight, was roughly hammered shut with a bar of wood; he himself had done that, he remembered, years ago. He pulled at the bar now with all his strength, feeling the powerful muscles of the blacksmith's son again come to his aid; one didn't lose it, that garnered inherited strength. James, who had been older than he was now, could still bend a bar of iron in the year he died. James, in his palace full of ships' models, statues and paintings, lonely and broken at last by his wife's death! But why mock at James? Why mock at anyone?

"I have done my best in the way of life to which God called me," William told himself. As the bar rent away from its door with a wrenching sound which disturbed the thick layers of dust, William bent his head in an instant's prayer. Then he pulled open the door and went in. The truth, forty years old now, awaited him. He turned his head to where the trunk had lain; and gave a great cry.

Nothing was there but dust. The tomb was empty.

It was the following day before they found William's body: the neighbour opposite, from behind her curtains, had watched him go into the house, but had not seen him come out. With so old a man, she said, one had to keep watch. That day had seen the departure of Margaret's daughters, with the old man lying dead upstairs in the adjoining house. "After a while I came over; and then the servants went up, and found him."

They had had to break down the outer door. Afterwards arrangements were, almost to the letter, as they had been for the late Mrs. Heatherton's funeral; the sable-plumed horses, hired mourners, weepers, the rest. But on this occasion the street itself was lined with folk anxious to pay their last respects to the aged minister of Savill's. A difficult man they said he'd been, not one whom folk knew well; always courteous, a gentleman, but formal, very! It was the manners of the old school, no doubt, which now, with the coming of education for everyone, were less often met with than formerly; folk were more on an equal par with one another than in the days when Dr. Heatherton was young. But he'd been a good old man, and had done his duty, and still preached a fine sermon. As for what they said about his differences with his wife, there!

didn't it show they must have been devoted, with the old man dying on the very day of her funeral? "As though she sent him a message from the Beyond," said a narrow-skirted devotee of the new teachings of Mrs. Eddy from America, which were not yet accepted by orthodox persons. The devotee beamed. Everyone else looked grave as the long coffin passed; some of the older folk present remembered the first wife's funeral, and recalled that he'd had his difficulties and his sorrows, that old gentleman. There wouldn't be anyone like him again, that was certain; and whoever came to preach at Savill's would move into the new manse they'd bought elsewhere years back, and these old houses, the two of them, would doubtless go up for sale ... who was Dr. Heatherton's heir? No doubt his eldest daughter and her children.

Kate and Richard had attended the funeral-service together, and then, as she was expecting another child shortly, the wife went home, while Richard himself followed the coffin to the graveside. On the return of the carriages he went, as promised, to convey Mrs. Jenny Howie and her boy to the old manse, as desired in Dr. Heatherton's last letter to her. Jenny's eyes were red. "To think that he needed me at the last, poor Papa, and that I did not go to him in time! But I thought that as it was so late, and Johnny in bed, I'd wait till the next day and perhaps take Johnny with me; poor Papa for the first time expressed a wish to see him, and have his company." It was too late for everything now, Jenny knew; that day she had been touched also to receive word from the lawyers that William Heatherton had named her boy chief inheritor in his will, made afresh after his wife's death only a few days ago. "It makes me feel guilty to have done so little for him, but *she* would not have let me come in," Jenny reflected. "Poor Papa!"

The carriage stopped at the manse door, out of which, earlier that day, all of Margaret's daughters, taking Sarah Court with them, had departed; they had not even attended William's funeral service. They had purchased a house in another part of town, in which they would live out their lives as they always had. Jenny and little John cared nothing for this. They would sell the two houses soon, Jenny thought; they were too large, and gloomy. A pleasant little flat, where she could keep her few belongings including a photograph of the full-length portrait, painted when he had been a boy, of her dear husband John . . .

Young Johnny, assessing the situation with the self-same eyes and enquiring features of Paul Chantal, ran unafraid into the house. It was full of promise, and contained mysterious passages; the shadows swallowed him.

THE MALVIE INHERITANCE

PAMELA HILL

For Morven Doon, disinherited and driven from his home, only one thing mattered in life. At all costs he must make himself master of the house on the cliffs that should have been his by right.

Fragile golden-haired Annabel Doon, heiress to Malvie, was no more than a means of procuring the son who would inherit the house. But then there was Livia, beautiful and headstrong, the only woman whose fierce passions matched his own . . .

Once again Pamela Hill has written a towering historical novel in the great tradition of WUTHERING HEIGHTS and PENMARRIC.

CORONET BOOKS

THE WILD HUNT

JILL TATTERSALL

'Why they are witches, Miss Fabian—witches! And you must never, never forget it.'

The chilling words of young Sir Hugo Perowne were a discouraging welcome for his new governess. Orphaned and penniless, Chantal Fabian had been whisked from the security of her exclusive boarding school to live in this strangely unhappy household. A household fiercely dominated by its dark forbidding master, the Earl of Mortmain.

Some memory from Chantal's unsettled past, so terrible that she had erased it completely from her mind, concerned this man. But what was it? And who were these witches? Where in the twisting passages and hidden rooms of Holy Mote were they hiding, secretly using her charge against her? Why had Chantal at once became the object of their terrifying attention?

CORONET BOOKS